Lecture Notes in Computer Science   8458

Commenced Publication in 1973
Founding and Former Series Editors:
Gerhard Goos, Juris Hartmanis, and Jan van Leeuwen

Abdelhamid Mellouk   Scott Fowler
Saïd Hoceini   Boubaker Daachi (Eds.)

Wired/Wireless Internet Communications

12th International Conference, WWIC 2014
Paris, France, May 26-28, 2014
Proceedings

 Springer

Volume Editors

Abdelhamid Mellouk
Saïd Hoceini
Boubaker Daachi
University of Paris Est
Image, Signal and Intelligent Systems Laboratory
Créteil - Val de Marne, 122 rue Paul Armangot
94400 Vitry sur Seine, France
E-mail: {mellouk, hoceini, daachi}@u-pec.fr

Scott Fowler
Linköping University
Department of Science and Technology
ITN Bredgatan 34, 601 74 Norrköping, Sweden
E-mail: scott.fowler@liu.se

ISSN 0302-9743   e-ISSN 1611-3349
ISBN 978-3-319-13173-3   e-ISBN 978-3-319-13174-0
DOI 10.1007/978-3-319-13174-0
Springer Cham Heidelberg New York Dordrecht London

Library of Congress Control Number: 2014953847

LNCS Sublibrary: SL 5 – Computer Communication Networks
and Telecommunications

Typesetting: Camera-ready by author, data conversion by Scientific Publishing Services, Chennai, India

Printed on acid-free paper

Springer is part of Springer Science+Business Media (www.springer.com)

Preface

On behalf of all WWIC committee members, we welcome you to the proceedings of the 12th International Conference on Wired and Wireless Internet Communications(WWIC 2014), which was held in Paris, France, during May 27-28, 2014.

The WWIC conference is now a well-established conference in all Internet communications aspects. This 12th edition focused on new trends in the Internet and extension beyond traditional boundaries (i.e., areas with network infrastructure) through gradually incorporating a wide range of challenging networks and autonomous devices. From traditional wireless networks to opportunistic networks of mobile devices in urban environments and deep-space communications, the new approaches require an efficient integration with the traditional wired infrastructure. The need for novel all-weather protocols, clean-slate or evolutionary architectures, merging and assembling of different network technologies, unified operation and management of the heterogeneous components, and support for new multimedia services are only a few examples of the wide range of technologies building up this new global network. WWIC addresses research topics such as the design and evaluation of protocols, the dynamics of the integration, the performance trade-offs, the need for new performance metrics, and cross-layer interactions. The goal of the conference is to present high-quality results in the field, and to provide a framework for research collaboration through focused discussions that will initiate future research efforts and directions.

A major outcome of this conference is to provide researchers and designers with a better understanding of real-world challenges for wired and wireless technologies and enable them to develop innovative solutions to address such challenges. We also hope to be able to identify critical issues that will require further investigations and analysis in the future. The conference attracted many high-quality submissions from around the world. Each paper went through a rigorous peer-review process that was made possible by members of the international Technical Program Committee as well as additional reviewers. Based on the detailed comments from the reviews, we accepted 22 papers for presentation and publication. These papers cover a range of topics that include: wireless and wired networks; resource management; next-generation services; network architecture and applications.

We thank all authors who submitted their papers for consideration for this conference. We would also like to thank the members of the Technical Program Committee and additional reviewers for their feedback and review support that helped us to prepare a high-quality technical program.

Finally, we wish to thank many people who contributed to the local organization. We are particularly grateful to José Diaz, Sami Souihi, Mohamed Souidi, all and the PhD students (Oussama Soualah, Abdelkrim Senouci, Boutheina

Dab, Benaouda Farida, and Sajid Mushtaq) for their dedication and hard work throughout the preparation of this conference.

We believe the 12th WWIC conference provided an interesting and up-to-date scientific program. We hope that all participants enjoyed the technical and social conference program, the French hospitality, and the beautiful city of Paris.

May 2014

Abdelhamid Mellouk
Scott Fowler
Said Hoceini
Boubaker Daachi
Sami Souihi
José Diaz

Organization

General Chair

Abdelhamid Mellouk, France

General Co-chairs

Prosper Chemouil, France
Mari Carmen A. Torres, Spain

TPC Co-chairs

Scott Fowler, Sweden
Said Hoceini, France

Proceedings Chair

Boubaker Daachi, France

Conference Operation Co-chairs

Sami Souihi, France
José Diaz, France

Asia/Pacific Liaison Co-chairs

Nadeem Javaid, Pakistan
Lei Shu, China

America Liaison Chair

Eduardo Cerqueira, Brazil

Europe Liaison Chair

Periklis Chatzimisios, Greece

Middle East/Africa Liaison Co-chairs

Samira Moussaoui, Algeria
Nidal Nasser, KSA
Salim Bitam, Algeria

Workshop Chair

Ioannis Anagnostopoulos, Greece

Web Chair

Eric Deléchelle, France

Technical Program Committee

Sachin Agrawal, India
Khalid Al-Begain, UK
Vangelis Angelakis, Sweden
Andreas Aurelius, Sweden
Bigomokero Bagula, South Africa
Paolo Bellavista, Italy
Fernando Boavida, Portugal
Malika Bourenane, Algeria
Wojciech Burakowski, Poland
Scott Burleigh, USA
Maria Calderon, Spain
Paulo Carvalho, Portugal
Ana Cavalli, France
Eduardo Cerqueira, Brazil
Periklis Chatzimisios, Greece
Abdellah Chehri, Canada
Ken Chen, France
Dalila Chiadmi, Morocco
Feng-Tsun Chien, Taiwan
Arsenia Chorti, UK
Marilia Curado, Portugal
Boubaker Daachi, France
Stylianos Dimitriou, Greece
Aïssani Djamil, Algeria
Ognjen Dobrijevic, Croatia
Ilhem Fajjari, France
Scott Fowler, Sweden

Paul Gendron, USA
Yassine Hadjadj-Aoul, France
Haffaf Hafid, Algeria
Jarmo Harju, Finland
Qing He, Sweden
Sonia Heemstra de Groot,
    The Netherlands
Said Hoceini, France
Muhammad Imran, Saudi Arabia
Malika Ioualalen, Algeria
Bouabdellah Kechar, Algeria
Adlen Ksentini, France
Peter Langendoerfer, Germany
Sekhri Larbi, Algeria
D. Larrabeiti, Spain
Jukka-Pekka Laulajainen, Finland
Lei Lei, Sweden
Pascal Lorenz, France
Pavel Loskot, UK
Chung-Horng Lung, Canada
Christian Maihöfer, Germany
Christian Makaya, USA
Eva Marín-Tordera, Spain
Abdelhamid Mellouk, France
Paulo Mendes, Portugal
Lynda Mokdad, France
Edmundo Monteiro, Portugal

Table of Contents

Wireless and Wired Networks

Resource Management

Resource Management and Next Generation Services

Next Generation Services, Network Architecture and Applications

An Automated Application-Independent Approach to Anomaly Detection in Wireless Sensor Networks

André Rodrigues[1,2], Jorge Sá Silva[1], and Fernando Boavida[1]

[1] Centre of Informatics and Systems of the University of Coimbra, Coimbra, Portugal
[2] Polytechnic Institute of Coimbra, ISCAC, Coimbra, Portugal
{arod,sasilva,boavida}@dei.uc.pt

Abstract. As Wireless Sensor Networks (WSN) gain momentum in what concerns applications and deployment, monitoring is becoming crucial in order to guarantee that anomalies are promptly detected. Unfortunately, current WSN monitoring solutions have several limitations, such as being tailored for specific applications, requiring dedicated or specific hardware, consuming precious energy and/or processing resources, or relying on manual or offline intervention. In this paper we propose an approach to anomaly detection in WSNs that addresses these limitations. The approach is based on two very simple metrics, a logging tool, and a data-mining algorithm, thus leading to the following key characteristics: very low resource consumption, application independency, very good potential for multi-WSN monitoring, and automation and simplification of the detection process. The proposed approach was validated by implementation, which showed that it is quite effective in detecting several typical anomalies.

Keywords: wireless sensor networks; anomaly detection; monitoring, testing and debugging.

1 Introduction

Detecting and diagnosing problems in Wireless Sensor Networks (WSNs) is now considered essential, due to the fact that the installed basis of this type of networks is growing at a fast pace. Numerous deployments exist, either of experimental or of commercial nature.

One such example, pertaining to the research area, is a recent deployment by Intel, which equipped a few hundred homes with devices that enabled the collection of a set of parameter values (environmental, physiological and behavioral), with the objective of assessing the potential of the WSN technology in the study of aging and chronic diseases [1]. One of the conclusions of the study was the need for tools for managing research infrastructures characterized by a large number of geographically dispersed facilities, where their direct users (in this case the elderly) do not have enough technological expertise to assist in diagnosing and solving problems that inevitably occur in the installed systems.

In what concerns commercial deployments, it is expected that WSN technology will be extensively used for supporting real time monitoring of multiple installations

A. Mellouk et al. (Eds.): WWIC 2014, LNCS 8458, pp. 1–14, 2014.

belonging to the same or different entities. For instance, one can easily foresee its use in farms to support animal health condition monitoring. As an example, a WSN-based system could support the collection of several parameters (e.g. environmental, physiological and behavioral parameters) and, based on their values and on a set of rules, generate alarms if something abnormal happened. Such a system could easily be deployed at several facilities and, naturally, would require adequate monitoring in order to ensure its proper functioning. This is clearly an example of a scenario in which the entity that commercializes / supports the system must also have the capability to real-time monitor the installations in operation at the various customers.

Although the scenarios for the monitoring of multiple and/or large scale WSN installations are rapidly emerging, existing tools have not yet met the requirements of simple, effective, automated, distributed, and general anomaly detection. Typically, monitoring tools are application-specific, resource-consuming, complex to configure and/or use, or restricted to a single WSN.

The work presented in the current paper is an attempt to prove that it is possible to explore anomaly detection approaches that meet the above-mentioned requirements by using two simple metrics, an existing logging tool, and a data-mining algorithm. Note that the main contribution of this paper is not the presentation of a monitoring tool but, rather, the demonstration that it is possible to develop general, application-independent, lightweight WSN monitoring tools that use simple metrics.

The paper is organized as follows. Section 2 identifies the set of requirements that should be met by WSN monitoring tools. Section 3 is dedicated to the detailed presentation of the developed approach, namely in what concerns its hardware and software platforms, used metrics, logs collection and parsing, data transformation, and detection and diagnosis. The proof-of-concept implementation was subject to evaluation in two simple scenarios comprising several anomalous conditions. Evaluation results are discussed in section 4. Section 5 identifies related work, by briefly presenting and discussing a representative set of WSN monitoring tools. Section 6 provides the conclusions and guidelines for further work.

2   Requirements

This section briefly presents and discusses the requirements that a WSN monitoring tool should address. These requirements were divided into two categories: scenario-related requirements, and performance/usage requirements.

2.1   Scenario-Related Requirements

- **Scalability** – the tool should be able to scale, both in terms of the number of nodes per WSN and the number of supported WSNs. As mentioned before, scenarios comprising the monitoring of several WSNs are likely to appear.
- **Support for inter-WSN homogeneity and intra-WSN heterogeneity** – in any given WSN there is often some heterogeneity at hardware and firmware levels; nevertheless, when looking at multiple WSNs run or supported by a given

organization, one can see that they mostly run the same applications on the same platforms. Thus, monitoring tools should enable to take advantage of this inter-WSN homogeneity, and also support intra-WSN heterogeneity.

- **Support geographically dispersed WSNs** – the existence of WSNs located at several locations is a factor that must be taken into consideration in the design of a monitoring tool, as suitable communication mechanisms must be in place.
- **Support for mobile nodes** – in WSNs it is quite common to have mobile nodes; this type of nodes has no negligible impact on data collection strategies and on communications; monitoring tools should be able to cope with these nodes.

2.2   Performance/Usage Requirements

- **Support all application paradigms** – in order to not be limited by the application paradigm (i.e., schedule-driven, query-driven, event-driven) the tool must not rely on the existence of specific operation patterns.
- **Support diverse hardware platforms and operating systems (OSs)** – WSN technology is fast changing, so it is important to ensure that a tool can be used with multiple OSs and platforms in order to cope with current and future needs.
- **Minimize the use of WSN resources** – typically, WSN nodes are resource constrained; thus, monitoring tools should minimize WSN resource consumption, such as energy, processing, and memory.
- **Easy to install and to use** – the effort required for integrating a monitoring tool in a WSN or a set of WSNs should be minimized. The same applies to the effort required to use the tool.
- **Flexibility and extensibility** – it is important to support mechanisms that allow the manager to tailor the tool to its needs (at deployment and at runtime) in order to enable wider applicability.

3   Proposed Approach

Having in mind the requirements identified in the previous section, we set out to demonstrate that it is possible to construct a simple, effective, automated, and application-independent anomaly detection tool.

To this effect, we developed a proof-of-concept implementation. This section provides details on this implementation, namely, on the used hardware and software platforms and on the overall design, including metrics calculation, logs collection, logs parsing, data transformation, anomalous events detection, and anomalous events diagnosis.

3.1   Selected Platform and Operating System

The tool prototype was implemented using TinyOS [2] on a new hardware platform called Hermes [3]. This platform includes a recent MSP430, an 868 MHz band radio, an SD card reader, an accelerometer, a gyroscope, a thermometer, an heartbeat receiver, and a power management system.

Having used an event-based operation system, the metrics that will be used as the basis for anomaly detection will be collected during event procedure instances. An event procedure instance [4] is the sequence that begins with a hardware interrupt and ends with the execution of the last code associated with the initial event.

It should also be noted that, although they are essential, the collected metrics must be complemented with additional information in order to effectively pinpoint the reasons for anomalous behavior. In the case of this proof-of-concept implementation, we decided to additionally collect call traces for the application code, and also log the executed tasks.

As a final remark, it should be noted that despite the specific choice of hardware platform, operating system, and implementation, the principles that guided the tool's construction (i.e., simple metrics, application-independence, logging, and data-mining) are general and can easily be implemented using other OSs and platforms.

3.2   Metrics Calculation

When considering the issue of what metrics to use for characterizing behavior as normal or abnormal, one should take into account aspects such as impact on node resources, applicability to diverse application paradigms, descriptive power, and hardware platforms and OSs specificity. Metrics with the following characteristics should thus be avoided:

- Application dependent (e.g., using statists on specific application events);
- Requiring detailed logs (e.g., complete call traces, or vectors of instruction counters as in [4]);
- Application paradigm dependent (e.g., counters on traffic);
- Requiring dedicated hardware or OS support (e.g., dedicated energy measurement devices, OS-integrated logging mechanisms).

From the above, one can conclude that elapsed time, processing, and energy are good candidates to characterize what happens between two consecutive application level events. These metrics are general, light to compute, and do not require sophisticated support mechanisms.

In the case of the proof-of-concept implementation, the selected metrics were processing and energy. The main reason for excluding the elapsed time was that, for typical WSN applications, it does not provide much information about the used processing resources, as the majority of time between two application level events is sleep time. This also means that, for instance, an anomaly leading to an increase in active time could easily be "concealed" by a slight variation in sleep time without much impact on the elapsed time metric value.

Each metric is calculated in the following way. At boot time the metric counter is reset. When the next application event happens the metric counter value is logged and associated to the previous application event. Finally, the metric counter is reset.

Processing Metric. The first approach to calculate a processing metric was to count the microcontroller (MCU) instructions (or the MCU cycles) executed between two consecutive application level events. Unfortunately, the Hermes platform does not directly support this.

The followed approach was to count the MCU (i.e. MSP430F2618) sub-main clock (SMCLK) cycles between consecutive application level events. The SMCLK in Hermes is defined to be based on the master clock (MCLK) divided by 4. The MCU TimerA was configured to be sourced by the SMCLK, resulting that when the MCU is not sleeping the SMCLK is running and TimerA is incremented.

This is an extremely light metric as the only processing required is to read or update the counter-associated variable. For simplicity reasons, from this point onward this metric will be called MCU cycles.

Energy Metric. In iCount [5] the authors explained how a carefully selected switching regulator used to provide regulated power to a sensor node can be used to provide energy consumption measurements, almost for free. Because the regulator they selected uses pulse frequency modulation, the switching frequency is almost directly related to the load current. Their idea was to connect the output of the regulator inductor to the MCU input clock (INCLK) line that can be used to source the TimerA. In this way, each time the voltage at the inductor crosses zero in the ascending direction, TimerA is incremented as a new switching cycle was detected.

Hermes uses a Power Management System (PMS) that includes two switching regulators based in the Pulse Wide Modulation (PWM) technique. Those regulators also support pulse skipping at light loads.

Being a PWM-based part, it does not enable to directly use the iCount approach. However, at light loads, the PMS supports a burst mode where energy is provided in a burst of pulses to minimize switching losses. During this operation mode it is possible to count the pulses (using an approach similar to iCount) to obtain an estimation of the consumed energy. From now on, for simplicity reasons, this metric is called energy consumption.

3.3 Logs Collection and Parsing

Logging mechanisms are required to collect the metrics and the information on the executed application events calls and tasks from the sensor nodes, and to forward it to the management system in order to support the detection and diagnostics functionality.

The logging mechanism should be flexible and expandable, avoid application source code modifications, be easy to install and use, take advantage of main application communication capabilities, introduce small latency, be light in terms of resources usage, be easily portable to other OSs / platforms, and support node heterogeneity.

Having to decide between developing a logging system according to the previous requirements or using an already available one, the decision was to use LIS [6], as it supports most of the requirements.

In LIS, a developer has to produce a LIS script using a declarative language, describing the logging mechanisms to be deployed and their location in the WSN application source code. Then, a PC-based instrumentation engine modifies the WSN application source code, according to the LIS script, in order to include logging statements. Also added to the sensor node code are a runtime library that supports the node logging function calls, and a code module supporting log data storage and retrieving functionality.

During runtime, execution traces and state are saved on local memory and can be sent to the sink node using either wired communication (i.e., SerialActiveMessages), or wireless communication (i.e., TinyOS CTP for multi-hop, or ActiveMessages for single-hop). When the packets arrive at the sink node they are parsed using a generic LIS parser and the LIS script information to produce meaningful information.

The LIS language can be used directly or as an intermediate language supporting reusable high-level task definitions. One of these high-level tasks is Region Of Interest (ROI) call trace monitoring, where the developer specifies a ROI (e.g. one TinyOS subsystem) and the system generates the corresponding LIS script that will enable to create a log of the function calls inside that subsystem. This functionality is very useful because it enables to avoid the need for manually creating a LIS script.

In the case of the current proof-of-concept implementation, it was necessary to modify the Python scripts associated with the ROI analysis functionality, in order to enable LIS to automatically instrument the application source code with the objective of generating call traces and metrics logs.

Finally, collecting the logs is done via the "timestampedlisten" console command, provided by TinyOS, which collects the packets sent by the sensor nodes where the logging mechanism is running. The collected packets are submitted to the LIS parser, which makes use of the LIS script information to output an easy-to-read listing of the logged call traces and collected metrics.

3.4   Data Transformation

The data file produced by the LIS parser is filtered to remove incomplete application event level details that resulted from packet losses. This is necessary because if some packets are lost they can compromise the parsing of the next log entries. LIS supports a mechanism to discard incomplete log entries. However, it was necessary to enhance this mechanism, as incorrect application event information was found in the parsed logs.

After this phase, the logs are parsed in order to generate an application-level event list file with the intended data format. This new file also contains additional information required to support further diagnosis of the anomalous events. To support all these transformations, a set of Python-based scripts was developed.

Each line in the generated file has the following format:

```
<class> <m1>:<v1> <m2>:<v2> # <event> <begin> <end>
```

In this format, <class> designates the class the event belongs to, <m1>:<v1> designates a metric/value pair, <event> is the name of the application-level event, and <begin> and <end> identify, respectively, the line of the LIS parsed file where log entries related to this event begin, and the line where they end.

The data before the "#" is used by the classification algorithm used to identify anomalous events. The data after the "#" is ignored by the classification algorithm, but is used to locate, in the LIS parsed file, the log information related to the detected anomalous events.

3.5 Anomalous Events Detection and Diagnosis

The selected classification algorithm is based on a machine learning technique, called Support Vector Machines (SVM) [7], which generates a model that can be used to predict the class of an instance. In this case, an instance is an application level event instance that has metrics values as attributes, and can be classified as normal or anomalous.

In the present scenario there are, nevertheless, two issues. First, a labeled training set is not available. Second, it is expected that the anomalous application level events represent a small fraction of all application level events (as the goal is to detect sporadic problems).

Considering this scenario, the selected approach (also followed by [4]) was to use an SVM variant called one-class SVM, and to assume that the training set only contains normal events, knowing that a small percentage of them may have been misclassified as such. By defining the percentage of misclassified events in the training set, one-class SVM will create a model that places the majority of the events in normal class side of the hyper-plane, while the remaining are placed on the anomalous class side. This learned model is then used to predict the class of future received application level events. The learned model can be periodically updated, in case it is required that the anomalous event detection mechanism has some flexibility to adapt to environment / system changes.

The reasons to select this technique were the following: it does not require previously labeled data, it can work with unbalanced data sets (i.e. sets with classes not equality represented), and the existence of a well documented and easy to use code library (LIBSVM [8]). This library includes Python scripts for simplifying its use, namely scaling data sets, selecting optimized kernel function parameters, training the model, and testing the data.

The output of LIBSVM is a classification for each application level event. An analysis script was developed that uses this information to locate, in the LIS parsed file, the logged information related to the application level events classified as anomalous. This enables the responsible person to analyze them in order to identify possible reasons for their classification.

Fig. 1 summarizes the activities involved in the anomalous events detection and diagnosis functionality detailed in this section.

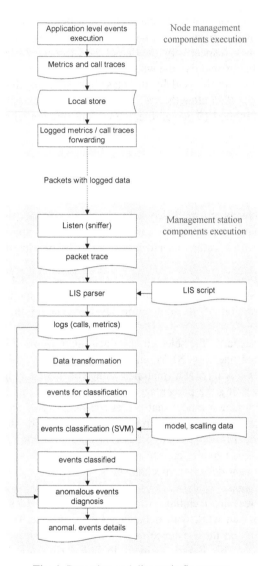

Fig. 1. Detection and diagnosis fluxogram

4   Evaluation

The presented proof-of-concept implementation was subject to several tests, in order to assess the effectiveness and efficiency of the underlying concepts. This section begins by describing and presenting the results of a set of experiments carried on for evaluating the tool's detection and diagnosis capabilities. Subsequently, the tool is evaluated under the light of the initial requirements.

4.1   Experimental Results

Two sets of tests were carried out. In the first group of experiments the goal was to assess the MCU cycles metric for detecting anomalous behaviors.

The selected application was RadioCountToLeds (a standard TinyOS application where two nodes periodically broadcast packets containing a counter, and each time a node receives a packet it displays the counter's last 3 bits on the LEDs). This application was selected because it has a simple behavior and is publicly available, enabling the community to validate the paper results. The application code includes the events MilliTimer.fired, Receive.receive, and AMSend.sendDone. These are regularly triggered during normal application execution.

In the scenario used for the experiments two nodes executed RadioCountToLeds, and another one just collected the packets with the logs and send them, via USB, to the management station (Fig. 2).

The application source code was automatically transformed to include the logging mechanisms required to generate the call traces and the MCU cycles metric for the application level events, and to generate the call traces for the executed tasks.

For obtaining the training set, the RadioCountToLeds application was executed during 15 minutes under normal conditions, then the collected packet trace was parsed by LIS, transformed to remove incomplete application level events and to provide the event list in the LIBSVM format, and finally submitted to the LIBSVM script. This script scaled the data, selected the kernel function parameters (by using a grid-search approach and cross-validation), and finally outputted the learned model and the used scale data. The percentage of misclassified events in the training set was set at 1%. The events set used to train the classifier included 1486 events instances.

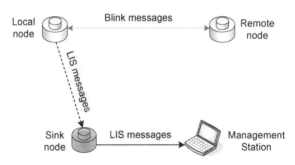

Fig. 2. Evaluation scenario

All the experiments had 5 minutes duration and the results are presented in Table 1. Before proceeding to analyse the results, two aspects should be highlighted. Firstly, it should be noted that, in the absence of problems, the percentage of events classified as normal should be around 99% (as the defined threshold for misclassified events in the training phase was 1%). Secondly, in Table 1, the 'Remarks' column presents the details found in anomalous events logs that provided clues for events classification.

Experiment #1 was designed to evaluate how the anomaly detection functionality reacted to a permanent failure, such as the remote node stopping to broadcast its counter messages. The low percentage of normal events, with more than 40% of the events being classified as anomalous, clearly points to some kind of error. This was easily diagnosed by observing the absence of Receive.receive events in the logs.

The goal of experiments #2 and #3 was to determine if a logic error (that resulted in additional execution of code) could be detected. The MilliTimer.fired event code was changed to contain a cycle that incremented a counter from 1 to 100 (or to 1000 in the case of experiment #3). This cycle was executed in 10% of the MilliTimer.fired event executions. In both cases, the anomalous events (an excess of MilliTimer.fired events with a high MCU cycles value) were detected, as indicated by a percentage of normal events below 99%.

The goal of experiment #4 was slightly more ambitious, namely to determine if another type of logic error (specifically, in this case, the counter for the broadcast message being incorrectly increment twice in 10% of the cases) could be detected. This was done by modifying the MilliTimer.fired event code. The impact on the application executing in the local node was minimal and, thus, was not detected.

Another set of experiments aimed at evaluating the efficacy of the energy consumption metric in the detection of anomalous behaviors. In these experiments the timer used to send the counter messages was increased from 1.9 s to 5 s. and the experiments duration was 10 minutes. Table 2 presents the experiments' results.

Table 1. Classification summary (MCU cycles metric)

#	Condition	Normal events %	Events (norm/total)	Remarks
1	remote node off	58.21%	163/280	no Receive.receive events
2	100 i++	98.66%	443/449	MilliTimer.fired > 21750
3	1000 i++	95.53%	406/425	MilliTimer.fired > 23600
4	extra op	99.04%	416/420	not detected

Table 2. Classification summary (energy metric)

#	Condition	Normal events %	Events (norm/total)	Remarks
5	5 remote reboots	98.77%	322/326	AMSend = 6.213.697
6	1 local reboot	96.93%	347/358	Boot.booted
7	up 1 floor	91.97%	229/249	AMSend > 6.000.000
8	gyro ON	75.36%	260/345	AMSend ~ 3.200.000

In experiment #5, one node was rebooted 5 times. By analysing the logs from the other node, it was possible to detect the existence of anomalous behaviour (as indicated by a percentage of normal events below 99%), and subsequently identify AMSend.sendDone anomalous events with high-energy values. This seemed to indicate that some messages were not sent by the rebooted node or that they got lost.

In experiment #6 the significantly lower percentage of normal events gives a hint on some anomaly. After inspecting the logs for the anomalous events, a local node reboot was detected (specifically, one of the anomalous events was a Boot.booted).

In experiment #7, one node was moved away from the other one floor up. The relatively low percentage of normal events, in conjunction with fewer events in the data set for the node that did not move, was a hint for problems. By inspecting the anomalous events logs it was possible to identify several AMSend.sendDone anomalous events with high-energy values. This suggested that packet losses had occurred, but required an analysis of the other node logs.

Experiment #8 was designed to determine if a wrong power state in a device would be detectable. Specifically, the gyroscope was not turned off at boot time in order to create an anomaly. The considerably low percentage of normal events clearly indicated that something was wrong. Also, the existence in the logs of several AMSend.sendDone anomalous events with energy values higher than 3.000.000 confirmed it. Nevertheless, because this type of problem does not impact program execution, there was no information in the logs that helped diagnosing it.

In light of the achieved results, it is clear that the simple metrics approach combined with logging analysis and data mining allowed the detection of most anomalous conditions. It should be noted that the objectives of this proof-of-concept implementation and the associated experiments were the assessment of the efficacy of the automatic anomaly detection, not the diagnosis itself.

4.2   Requirements Analysis

The goal of developing and evaluating the presented prototype implementation was, on one side, to validate the concepts on which it was based – namely, the use of simple metrics, light logging tool, and data-mining – and, on the other hand, to assess its ability to meet the identified requirements. In the previous sub-section, the tool was assessed with respect to the former. In the current sub-section, an analysis pertaining to the latter is presented.

- **Scalability** – in the current implementation, the parsing, data transformation, and classification tasks required to process a 10 min log took less than 1.5 s (1.295 s, 0.172 s, and 0.023 s, respectively) per sensor node, in an Intel Core 2 Duo 2.4 GHz computer with 3 MB of RAM. This is a low processing time. To maintain low parsing times with a high number of nodes and with more components having their function calls logged, an optimised implementation should only send the metrics at detection time, locally saving the call trace logs, for on-request later inspection.
- **Support sensor node heterogeneity** – the tool can support WSN devices with diverse hardware and software. This could be done by grouping logs, at the management system, according to their software and hardware configuration. In this way, each group of log information contains events data from sensor nodes with the same hardware / software. Each group is then analyzed individually according to the fluxogram presented in Fig. 1.
- **Support geographically dispersed WSNs** – tools implemented according to the presented principles can transparently work with monitoring data originating from multiple WSNs, provided each WSN is connected to the Internet via a gateway device that communicates with the management system.

- **Support mobile nodes** – LIS communications can use TinyOS Active Messages or CTP. For WSN applications using these protocols, the tool will support the same mobility pattern as the application.

- **Support all application paradigms** – the detection functionality is based on the occurrence of application level events on the monitored sensor nodes and uses general metrics. In this way, it supports all type of application paradigms. Nevertheless, for WSNs applications where sensor nodes sleep for long periods of time and only wakeup on rare events, this approach alone will not work. This is a common problem, not specific to the presented approach, and the usual solution is to support mechanisms, either initiated by sensor nodes or by the sink, that enable to know if a sensor node is alive.

- **Support diverse hardware platforms and OSs** – most of the detection functionality at sensor nodes is based on LIS, the exception being the metrics calculation. Currently, LIS is directly supported by Mica2/Z, TelosB, and Hermes. Using it with other OSs, like Contiki, should not be too difficult, given that LIS operates by modifying C language based applications.

- **Minimize the use of WSN resources** – MCU, RAM, and ROM consumption are minimized because LIS is a very efficient log tool and because the metrics calculation is very light. The impact in energy and bandwidth is mostly related to the number of components having its function calls logged. Only sending call traces on demand will enable further savings.

- **Be easy to install and to use** – in the case of this proof-of-concept implementation, deploying the tool on a sensor node just requires compiling the WSN application with an option stating which components should have their activity logged (in the presented evaluation experiments, these were the application and the scheduler components). Usability can only be evaluated with an integrated platform and not with a proof-of-concept prototype implementation. However the experiments did not require much analysis work.

- **Be flexible and extensible** – post deployment configuration of the logging functionality at sensor nodes was not supported in the current implementation. The implemented functionality was based on an enhanced version of the ROI mechanism provided by LIS. This work can be easily extended by using the LIS script language, more metrics, and additional classification algorithms. Most of the work would be in enhancing the parser to support the new metrics, and on developing Python scripts to support the data formats required by the new classification algorithms.

5   Related Work

Several pieces of work have addressed the problem of WSN monitoring. They are briefly mentioned in this section, with a focus on the ones that had a higher impact on the presented proof-of-concept design and implementation.

MANNA [9] was one of the first management frameworks for WSNs. In spite of being a very flexible and general architecture, it did not target the support of automatic detection and diagnosis mechanisms for the joint management of WSNs.

SWARMS [10] target the management of wide area WSNs in diverse geographic locations, providing diagnostic and programming functionalities. It was designed to be scalable, flexible, and extensible. The major concern with this architecture is the fact that it requires each sensor node to be directly connected to a computer that executes a node mate process. Moreover, there are no provisions for supporting automatic detection and diagnosis.

MARWIS [11] targets the management of a heterogeneous WSN by dividing it into homogeneous WSNs connected by a mesh network. It was designed to be scalable, flexible, and extensible. The major problem with this architecture is that supporting sensor node heterogeneity by dividing a WSN in a set of homogenous WSNs does not fit well when there is a need to manage several heterogeneous WSNs belonging to diverse organizations. Moreover, MARWIS assumes sensor nodes are executing Contiki-based applications and there are no provisions for supporting automatic detection and diagnosis.

Sentomist [4] is a tool for identifying potential transient bugs in WSN applications, which also uses SVM to identify anomalous events. Nevertheless, by using a metric based on information from the specific processor instructions executed in each event, it requires the use of the Avrora emulator, which restricts it to lab use.

Finally, there are several tools developed to help diagnose WSNs operating in the field. We have realized an extensive survey [12] that describes, analyses, and compares a representative set of them. This work guided us in the development of the current approach to WSN anomaly detection, and in identifying LIS as a good candidate to be used.

6   Conclusion

This paper proposed a simple approach to anomaly detection in wireless sensor networks, based on the use of two general metrics, a light logging strategy, and a machine learning technique. The thesis was that these underlying concepts would be enough to develop an automated, application-independent, light tool, capable of monitoring multiple WSNs. In order to assess this, a proof-of-concept implementation was developed and subject to testing. The results have shown that the proposed approach has very good potential and characteristics, being able to detect hardware and software anomalies in a very effective way, and without compromising the identified requirements, such as scalability, heterogeneity, applicability, generality and ease of use.

The presented work opens many lines for further work. First and foremost, a more extensive and broader scope evaluation should be done. In addition, other general metrics should be identified and explored. The development of a full implementation for use in existing, deployed WSNs would also very interesting, as well as the support for IPv6 (6LoWPAN) in order to increase the tool's applicability.

Acknowledgment. We would like to thank Roy Shea (from UCLA) for clarifying several aspects of the LIS operation. This work was partially financed by the iCIS project (CENTRO-07-ST24-FEDER-002003).

References

1. Hayes, T., Pavel, M., Kaye, J.: Gathering the Evidence: Supporting Large-Scale Research Deployments. Intel Technology Journal 13(3) (2009)
2. Levis, P., Madden, S., Polastre, J., Szewczyk, R., Whitehouse, K., Woo, A., Gay, D., Hill, J., Welsh, M., Brewer, E., Culler, D.: Tinyos: An operating system for wireless sensor networks. In: Weber, W., Rabaey, J., Aarts, E. (eds.) Ambient Intelligence. Springer (2004)
3. Rodrigues, A., Silva, M., Camilo, T., Blanco, N., Pedro, J., Martins, J., Silva, J.S., Boavida, F.: Hermes: A versatile platform for wireless embedded systems. In: Proceedings of the IEEE WoWMoM 2012. IEEE, San Francisco (2012)
4. Zhou, Y., Chen, X., Lyu, M., Liu, J.: Sentomist: Unveiling Transient Sensor Network Bugs via Symptom Mining. In: Proceedings of the IEEE ICDCS, pp. 784–794 (2010)
5. Dutta, P., Feldmeier, M., Paradiso, J., Culler, D.: Energy Metering for Free: Augmenting Switching Regulators for Real-Time Monitoring. In: Proceedings of the IPSN 2008, pp. 283–294. IEEE (2008)
6. Shea, R., Cho, Y., Srivastava, M.: LIS is More: Improved Diagnostic Logging in Sensor Networks with Log Instrumentation Specifications. TR-UCLA-NESL-200906-01 (2009)
7. Hsu, C.-W., Chang, C.-C., Lin, C.-J.: A Practical Guide to Support Vector Classification. Technical Report, Department of Computer Science, National Taiwan University (2010), http://www.csie.ntu.edu.tw/~cjlin/papers/guide/guide.pdf
8. Chang, C.-C., Lin, C.-J.: LIBSVM: A library for support vector machines. ACM Transactions on Intelligent Systems and Technology 2(3), article no. 27 (2011)
9. Ruiz, B., Nogueira, J., Loureiro, A.: MANNA: A management architecture for wireless sensor networks. IEEE Communications Magazine 41(2), 116–125 (2003)
10. Gruenwald, C., Hustvedt, A., Beach, A., Han, R.: SWARMS: A sensornet wide area remote management system. In: Proceedings of the TridentCom (2007)
11. Wagenknecht, G., Anwander, M., Braun, T., Staub, T., Matheka, J., Morgenthaler, S.: MARWIS: A management architecture for heterogeneous wireless sensor networks. In: Harju, J., Heijenk, G., Langendörfer, P., Siris, V.A. (eds.) WWIC 2008. LNCS, vol. 5031, pp. 177–188. Springer, Heidelberg (2008)
12. Rodrigues, A., Camilo, T., Silva, J.S., Boavida, F.: Diagnostic Tools for Wireless Sensor Networks: A Comparative Survey. Journal of Network and Systems Management 21(3), 408–452 (2013), doi:10.1007/s10922-012-9240-6

A Novel Handover Self-Optimization Algorithm for 4G and Beyond Networks

Maissa Boujelben, Sonia Ben Rejeb, and Sami Tabbane

MEDIATRON Laboratory, Higher School of Communications (Sup'Com), Ariana - Tunisia
maissa.boujelben@supcom.tn,
benrejeb.sonia@voila.fr,
sami.tabbane@supcom.rnu.tn

Abstract. The recently emerging fourth generation networks, notably LTE-Advanced, are expected to meet the requirements of higher bit rates with excellent quality of service. The expansion and the heterogeneity of these networks have made their operational cost higher. Therefore, automatic engineering has been recently addressed as a feature for remote network managing while minimizing human intervention. Our paper is part of this context. We propose a novel framework based on Statistical Learning, Fuzzy Logic and Reinforcement Learning for Handover parameter self-tuning followed by Handover self-optimization based on Load Balancing in LTE-Advanced networks. We aim at optimizing some Key Performance Indicators (KPIs) such as cells load, Call Drop Rate and Call Blocking Rate.

Keywords: Statistical Learning; Fuzzy Logic; Reinforcement Learning; Handover; self-optimization; KPIs.

1 Introduction

Fourth generation networks are still the object of several research and standardization works aiming at enhancing capacity and reaching high data rates with satisfying Quality of Service (QoS). The operators' first concern is to meet these requirements while maintaining their costs at the minimum possible level. One relevant idea is to perform the heavy tasks in an automated way. Self-Organizing Networks (SON) offer the possibility to remotely control the network. Although SON functions are explicitly defined by standardization bodies, their implementation is left vendor specific.

There are multiple possible tools for each SON function. Statistical learning (SL) is a framework for machine learning [1] that deals with the problem of finding a predictive function based on data. Assuming the existence of a database of Key Performance Indicators (KPIs) and the corresponding RRM parameters, the use of a simple SL technique such as regression, can approximate the functional relations between KPIs and the RRM parameters. Fuzzy logic (FL) is another recent and largely used mathematical tool. Compared to traditional binary sets (where variables may take on true or false values), FL variables may have a truth value that ranges in degree between 0 and 1. Furthermore, when linguistic variables are used, these degrees may be managed by specific functions.

A. Mellouk et al. (Eds.): WWIC 2014, LNCS 8458, pp. 15–28, 2014.
© Springer International Publishing Switzerland 2014

Another powerful tool is Reinforcement Learning (RL) which is an area of machine learning that aims to learn, from experiences, the best decision to make in different situations in order to maximize a numerical reward over the time. RL is a kind of semi-supervised learning where the learner is assisted indirectly by a teacher via the reward received for each couple of input output. Q-learning, the most well-known example of RL is a model-free technique. Specifically, Q-learning can be used to find an optimal action-selection policy for any given (finite) Markov decision process (MDP).

Our work is related to this context. Since users are moving all the time with often important speeds, a specific attention should be paid for Handover (HO) issues. In fact, a bad configuration of HO parameters could lead to several problems such as the increase of blocked or dropped calls. Besides, the HO policy must be controlled to insure a certain balance of cell loads in the network so that the available resources could be used efficiently. Finally, all these tasks should be performed in an automatic way to act rapidly in failure cases and also to reduce costs. In this paper, we propose a solution for these issues. The approach that we present consists of developing a new procedure for HO self-optimization composed of two main parts: the first aims at tuning a HO parameter and is composed of four interacting blocks: a SL block, a FL controller working jointly with a Q-learning block to choose the optimal corrections, and a Q-storage Data Base. The obtained correction will be used as an input for a new HO optimization algorithm based on Load Balancing (LB).

The remainder of this paper is outlined as follows. In the next section, previous works related respectively to SL, FL and RL are discussed. Then, the proposed approach is introduced. Finally, the performance of our approach will be evaluated and analyzed, followed by the conclusions and perspectives of this work.

2   State of the Art

A set of existent works concerning the different listed tools used for dynamic configuration and automated optimization of mobile networks are studied.

The author in [1] has been interested to the automated healing of Radio Access part of the wireless networks using statistical learning. The author focus concerns the faults related to Radio Resource Management (RRM) parameters. This is achieved by modeling the functional relationships between the RRM parameters and KPIs. The used Statistical Learning technique is regression. The automated healing methodology has been applied to 3G Long Term Evolution (LTE) use cases for healing the mobility and interference mitigation parameter settings. Simulation results have shown the effectiveness of this healing method. Nevertheless, this method's major limitation is that some assumptions and approximations made in the simulation may be different from an actual operating network.

In [2], the author H.D had been interested to optimization methods of Fuzzy Logic controllers for UMTS mobile networks auto-tuning. The inputs and outputs of this model are respectively the network KPIs and the corrections to be applied for RRM parameters. This method allowed the test and implementation of elementary concepts of automatic tuning of admission control and macro diversity algorithms. For the optimization of Fuzzy Logic Controllers, the author used two methods: optimization by swarm of particles and optimization by RL. The RL chosen technique is the Q-learning. Finally, the obtained results show that Q-learning optimization method produced much important gains especially in terms of call blocking rate in the network.

The author in [3] deals with dynamic tuning and automatic optimization of 3G and 3G+ mobile networks. The FL Controller concept was introduced and explained. To provide more explications, an example of auto-tuning UMTS admission control threshold parameter according to the observed blocking and dropping rates was treated. Then, the mathematical framework of RL was detailed. Q-learning was chosen as a RL method. Thus, Q-learning was adapted to Fuzzy Inference. This controller was tested on Self optimization of mobility algorithm in LTE networks .Simulation results show that the optimization of HO margin in a LTE network can improve basic KPIs, namely blocking rates and system throughput by a few percent.

In [4], the author investigates the problem of re-distributing traffic demand between Long-Term Evolution (LTE) Femto cells in an enterprise scenario. Several traffic sharing algorithms based on automatic tuning of Femto cell parameters are considered. The proposed algorithms are implemented by fuzzy logic controllers. Performance assessment is carried out in a dynamic system-level simulator. Results show that tuning HO margins and transmit power can be an effective means to solve localized congestion problems in these scenarios.

In our work, we propose a new framework for the self-tuning of an RRM parameter which is HO Hysteresis followed by HO optimization based on LB technique. The first part is composed of a combination of three techniques: Statistical Learning, Fuzzy Logic and Reinforcement Learning in order to optimize some related KPIs and so enhance QoS for the user.

In [1], the approximation of linear functions of KPIs and RRM parameter always generates an error which could falsify the obtained results. In our work, we will correct the errors generated by statistical learning with the utilization of fuzzy logic controllers coupled with Q-learning algorithm.

In both articles [2] and [3], the authors have used engineers experience in the inference system to determine the needed modification of RRM parameter in each state of input KPIs. Despite its importance, this method is not sophisticated enough. To bypass this major limitation, we will use statistical learning tools to calculate the correction in each input state.

3   Proposed Approach

As mentioned above, our approach deals with one function of SON networks which is HO self-optimization. Our new method is divided into two parts: HO parameter self-tuning and HO optimization based on LB.

3.1   System Model for Hysteresis Self-tuning

In this section, we will discuss the architecture of the first part of our proposed model called: LTE advanced Statistical Learning based Fuzzy Q-learning Controller (LTE-A SL-FQLC).

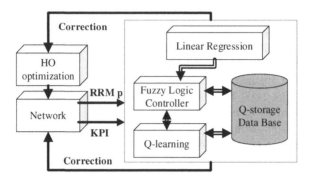

Fig. 1. Proposed scheme for SL-FQLC

Our approach consists of combining three different methods in order to optimize some essential KPIs such as cell load, Call Dropping Rate (CDR) and Call Blocking Rate (CBR) by the appropriate self-tuning of one HO parameter which is Hysteresis (Hyst). This part is composed of four blocks and the output correction of the RRM parameter will be an entry for the HO optimization block (see Fig. 1).

Statistical Learning Block. From experimental observations, the relationship between Hysteresis and the selected KPIs is almost linear. Therefore, the selected statistical learning method is the Linear Regression. This block gets as input the combination of the RRM parameter and the related KPIs (Hysteresis, Load, CDR, and CBR) from the LTE-A network or the simulator. The role of this part is to elaborate functional relationship between RRM parameter and the KPIs using linear regression. In forward regression, the KPIs are tried to be estimated as a function of the RRM parameter:

$$KPI_i = f_i(Hyst) \tag{1}$$

Where i =1, 2, 3 and KPI is in the set {load, CDR, CBR}.

Note that here, there are three regressions and each regression has just one explanatory variable. To obtain precise coefficients, many samples should be considered. Since we consider linear functions (f_i 's are linear), the above equation can be re-written using the vector-matrix notation:

$$Y = X\beta + \epsilon \tag{2}$$

Where Y contains the different obtained results for $KPIi \, ; i = 1..l$, X contains the different sample values of Hysteresis parameter $Hyst_i$, β is the weighting factors vector that we are looking for, and ϵ represents the error term.

The criterion used to find the best fitting coefficients β and ϵ is generally the least squares criterion where the sum of the squares of the Euclidean distance between each sample and its estimate $KPI'_i = \beta_0 + \beta_1 Hyst_i$ is minimized:

$$\beta^* = arg \, min_\beta \sum_{j=1}^{l}(KPIi_j - KPIi'_j)^2 \qquad (3)$$

The least squares estimates are given as:

$$\beta^* = (X'X)^{-1}X'Y \qquad (4)$$

Forward regression helps us to see how a change in a certain RRM parameter influences several different KPIs. In this way, we can determine the effect of modifying the RRM parameter on different KPIs. Backward regression tries to estimate the Hyst value as a function of the KPIs:

$$Hyst = \beta_0 + \beta_1 KPI_1 + \beta_2 KPI_2 + \beta_3 KPI_3 \qquad (5)$$

Backward regression helps us to determine which RRM parameter yields a given KPI vector. In this way, we can determine the exact value of the RRM parameter for a desired KPI performance. This step will contribute to the construction of the rule data base in the Fuzzy Logic Controller instead of the experts' knowledge.

Fuzzy Logic Controller. Fuzzy logic theory inventors split the fuzzy control process into three phases as illustrated in Fig. 2. The first phase is the fuzzification step and consists of converting the crisp input data to fuzzy data sets. This mapping process involves finding the degree of membership of the crisp input in predefined fuzzy sets. The second phase is the inference process and consists of making decision from the "if then" rules by combining all fuzzy input sets. The last phase is the defuzzification which maps the fuzzy outputs to the final controlled crisp parameters.

In the first phase of FLC, each crisp input variable x_i (i=1, 2...n) is mapped into mi fuzzy variables (or sets), denoted $E_{ij_i}(j_i =1, 2...m_i)$. This procedure allows mapping a continuous state space into a discrete space. In our case, we will divide each variable to exactly m fuzzy sets; in this case, $m_i = m, \forall \, i$.

The mapping between the crisp and the fuzzy variables is made by a membership function $\mu_{ij}(x_i)$ which defines the membership degree of the crisp input x_i with the fuzzy variable E_{ij}. In our work we use the triangular membership function:

$$\mu_{ij}(x_i) = \begin{cases} 1 - (E_{ij} - x_i)/(E_{ij} - E_{ij-1}), if \; E_{ij-1} \le x_i \le E_{ij} \\ 1 + (E_{ij} - x_i)/(E_{ij+1} - E_{ij}), if \; E_{ij} \le x_i \le E_{ij+1} \\ 0 \, , else \end{cases} \qquad (6)$$

Where $i \in \{1,2,...n\} \; and \; j \in \{1,2,...m\}$.

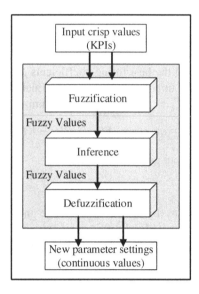

Fig. 2. Fuzzy Control process

The inference phase is constituted by a set of rules having the following form:

$$if \ x \ is \ s \ then \ a = \ o_s \tag{7}$$

$$where \ (x \ is \ s) \sim \left[\left(x_1 \ is \ E_{1j} \right) and \ \left(x_i \ is \ E_{ij} \right) and.. \left(x_n \ is \ E_{nj} \right) \right]$$

Rules form a space set denoted S and each rule is denoted by s∈ S. The cardinal of S is equal to $K = m^n$. a is the crisp FLC output variable and o_s is its fuzzy realization in the rule s. The rule s has a membership function deduced from those of E_{ij} :

$$\alpha_s(x) = \prod_{i=1}^{n} \mu_{ij}(x_i) \tag{8}$$

In the defuzzification phase, the FLC output a corresponding to the input $x = (x_1, x_2, ..., x_n)$ is given by the gravity center of conclusions o_s in each rule weighted by the membership function $\alpha_s(x)$. If the member functions α_s are chosen to satisfy the normalized condition. i.e. $\sum_{s \in S} \alpha_s(x) = 1$, the output action a is:

$$a = \sum_{s \in S} \alpha_s(x). o_s \tag{9}$$

Q-learning Block. As mentioned above, this method is the most spread RL technique. The fundamental purpose of RL is to improve a current agent policy after each interaction with the environment. In fact, RL algorithms do not use directly the policy but evaluate the performances of the strategy via a set of value functions resulting from the theory of Markovian Decision Process (MDP) [5]. A MDP is a controlled stochastic process similar to Markov chain, except that the transition probability depends on the action taken by the decision maker (agent or controller) at each time step. The MDP is formulated by the quintuple (S, A, T, p, r); where: S is a state space that contains a finite number of states; A is a finite set of actions. We denote by A(s) ⊂ A those actions that are available at state s; T is the time. T is a sub-set of positive real number; p are the transition probabilities between states; r is the reinforcement function or reward depending on states and actions. At each time t of T, the agent observes the current state s ∈ S and performs an action a∈ A that shifts the system to another state s'∈ S with a probability $p_t(s'/s, a)$. One step later, the agent receives a reward $r_t(s, a) \in \mathbb{R}$.

The agent policy implements a mapping from state space and action space. RL methods specify how the agent changes its policy as a result of its experience. The set of all policies forms a space, denoted Π = {π: s∈ S →a =π (s) ∈ A}. For each policy π, we denote $q_\pi(a, h_t)$ the probability that in a given history h_t the action a is triggered. The agent's goal is to maximize the total amount of reward it receives, called goal or return function. This means maximizing not just immediate reward, but cumulative reward in the long run. The use of a reward signal to formalize the idea of a goal is one of the most distinctive features of RL [6]. The most commonly used return function, and the one that will be used throughout this paper, is the discounted cumulative future reward, expressed as:

$$R = \sum_{t=0}^{\infty} \gamma^t r_t \tag{10}$$

Where γ is a parameter in [0, 1] called discount factor.

Almost all RL algorithms are based on estimating some value functions, functions of states (or of state-action pairs), that estimate how good it is for the agent to be in a given state (or how good it is to perform a given action in a given state). Accordingly, value functions are defined with respect to particular policies. So for each policy π, the value function V^π is expressed by the expected return function:

$$\forall \pi, \forall s \in S, V^\pi(s) = E^\pi[R/s_0 = s] \tag{11}$$

There is always at least one policy that is better than or equal to all other policies. This is an optimal policy. Although there may be more than one, we denote all the optimal policies by π*. They share the same value function, called the optimal value function, denoted V*, and defined as:

$$V^*(s) = max_{\pi \in \Pi} V^\pi(s) , \forall s \in S \tag{12}$$

The objective of RL is then to find a policy π* that corresponds to the optimal value function. V* is the unique solution of the Bellman equation:

$$\forall s \in S, V(s) = max_{a \in A}(r(s, a) + \gamma \sum_{s' \in S} p(s'/s, a)V(s')) \tag{13}$$

Q-learning is a stochastic approximation-based solution approach to solving Bellman equation. Instead of using only one value function, Q-learning algorithm employs another value function depending on both state and action, called quality function or Q-function:

$$Q^\pi(s, a) = r(s, a) + \gamma \sum_{s' \in S} p(s'/s, a)V(s') \tag{14}$$

The convergence of the Q-learning algorithm requires that the state space S should be finite. Since KPIs are continuous variables (infinite space), instead of applying the learning directly to the input indictor, the agent learns on the rules and fuzzy actions. To do this, a fuzzy quality-value q is assigned to each rule and each action. Unlike simple fuzzy inference system, in fuzzy Q-learning, each rule s has A(s) possible competing discrete actions $\{o_k\}$.

$$if\ x\ is\ s = R_{j_1 j_2 \dots j_n}\quad then\ \begin{cases} a = o_1\ with\ quality\ q(s, o_1) \\ \dots \dots \\ or\ a = o_{A(s)}\ with\ quality\ q(s, o_{A(s)}) \end{cases} \tag{15}$$

The agent stores the parameter vector q(s,ok) associated with each of these state-action couples in the Q-storage table. These q-values are updated whenever the agent performs an action and the system visits a new crisp state. The value functions of crisp input x and crisp action a, at time t, is calculated as a linear interpolation of the q-values:

$$Q_t(x, a) = \sum_{s \in S} \alpha_s(x) q_t(s, o_s) \tag{16}$$

$$V_t(x) = \sum_{s \in S} \alpha_s(x) \max_{o \in A(s)} q_t(s, o) \tag{17}$$

The update of the q-value is similar to the update of Q-function in simple Q-learning algorithm. So, for fuzzy Q-learning:

$$q_{t+1}(s, o) = q_t(s, o) + \alpha_s(x_t) K_t (r_t + \gamma V_t(x_{t+1}) - Q_t(x_t, a)) \tag{18}$$

Q-storage Data Base. This data base is used to store the q values for all (state /action) couples during the different iterations of the algorithm.

Self-Optimization Algorithm. Finally, the fuzzy Q-learning algorithm is below:

1. Perform a list of KPIs and RRM measurements for linear regression
2. Deduce the decision rules for fuzzy logic controller
3. Initialize Q-storage table: q(s,o)=0 for all s ∈ S, o ∈ A
4. Time t=0; Repeat
5. Receive the crisp system input Xt=(CDR, CBR, Load) from the system
6. Fuzzification: mapping from Xt to fuzzy states s
7. For each rule s, select an action Os with maximum q value
8. Calculate the inferred action (Eq 9) and its quality (Eq 15)
9. Execute the action at that leads the system to the state Xt+1. The controller receives the reinforcement rt
10. Calculate the membership functions for s (Eq 8) and the new state (Eq 16)
11. Update the elementary quality q(s,o) of each rule s and action o∈A(s) (Eq 17)
12. Save the elementary quality q(s,o) in the Q-storage table.
13. If convergence is obtained then stop the(n) learning process ($max|q_{t+1}(s, o) = q_t(s, o)| \le \theta_c$)
14. t=t+1

3.2   Handover Optimization Based on Load Balancing

In the previous part, we dealt with the self-tuning of Hyst parameter. This parameter update will be done at each observation time. Then, if the A3 condition is met, the HO optimization block based on LB will be triggered (see Fig.3).

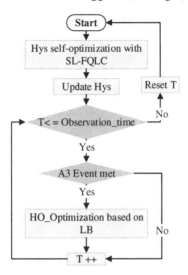

Fig. 3. Global procedure scheme

The HO optimization module aims at minimizing the RLF_number and balancing the load between the different cells. The HO decision criterion is based on RSRP level. Each User Equipment (UE) performs measurements with the serving cell as well as all the cells in neighbor list. When the UE received RSRP from the serving cell is decreasing (UE at the cell edge), the cells satisfying the A3 event condition are identified by a Candidate_List and the target cell is chosen on a load base. To reach the load balance between all cells in the network, the cell from the Candidate_List with the lowest Cell_load is selected as target cell (see fig. 4).

Before HO is executed, the target cell should satisfy the Admission Control condition:

$$C' + C_{req} \leq Th_{HO} * C \tag{19}$$

Where C is the total capacity of the cell, C' is the actual capacity needed for active users, and C_{req} is the requested capacity by HO call. If this condition is met, the HO is triggered from source to target cell. If no RLF occurs, a HO command is sent from source to target cell. Therefore, AC condition should be verified. If this condition is met, HO command is normally executed. Otherwise, the concerned cell is removed from Candidate_List and the same process is repeated for the next cell. If all the cells in the list do not satisfy the AC condition, the call is dropped.

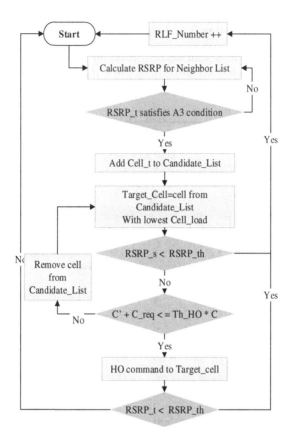

Fig. 4. HO optimization based on LB

4   Performance Evaluation

To evaluate our proposed approach, we consider an LTE-Advanced network with 7 Macro cells. 620 mobile users are initially randomly distributed. The simulation parameters are as follows [7]:

Table 1. Simulation parameters

Parameter	Value
UE speed	5 Km/h
Frequency	2,6 GHz
Bandwidth	20 MHz
Th_HO	0.7

As discussed before, we aim at optimizing some KPIs (load, CDR and CBR) by automatic adjustment of an RRM parameter which is HO Hyst followed by LB technique.

The first step is the construction of a base of samples of RRM parameter and KPIs. In fact, for a certain number of simulations, we modify each time the Hysteresis parameter and record the obtained KPIs values. The precision of the calculated regression functions highly depends on the number of samples: the biggest is the number of simulations, the more accurate our functions are. The table below summarizes the format of desired results:

Table 2. Samples of RRM parameter and KPIs

Hysteresis value	Load	CDR	CBR
0	L1	D1	B1
0.5	L2	D2	B2
...	...	...	...
12	L25	D25	B25

The optimal solution for our regression problem given by equation 4 is:

$$Load = \alpha_{01} + \alpha_{11} * \text{Hyst}$$
$$CDR = \alpha_{02} + \alpha_{12} * \text{Hyst}$$
$$CBR = \alpha_{03} + \alpha_{13} * \text{Hyst}$$
$$Hyst = \beta_0 + \beta_1 * Load + \beta_2 * CDR + \beta_3 * CBR$$

For the fuzzy logic controller, we define three fuzzy states for the input KPIs: {Low (L), Medium (M), and High (H)}. As mentioned before, the triangular membership function is used (see Fig. 5). For example, a value of CDR equal to 0.4 corresponds to the fuzzy value: 0.4= 0.5 * M + 0.5 * H.

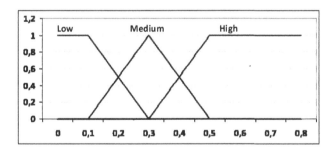

Fig. 5. Membership function

Based on the functional relationship between Hysteresis and KPIs, we define the following data base of decision rules for fuzzy logic controller inference part shown by Fig. 6. The output action or correction obtained from defuzzification step is calculated by equation 9. For example if the set of input KPIs {Load, CDR, CBR} is equal to {0.6; 0.4; 0.15}, then the correction of Hysteresis is equal to:

$$\Delta \text{Hyst} = (0.6 * 0.5 * 0.75) * 13 + (0.6 * 0.5 * 0.25) * C223 + (0.6 * 0.5 * 0.75) * C113 + (0.6 * 0.5 * 0.25) * C123 \quad (20)$$

The aim of this work is to find an optimal strategy that maximizes the sum of received reward over the time. The instantaneous reward is set as a linear sum of the differences between target and current KPIs:

$$r_t = \sum_{i=1}^{3} KPI_{i_{target}} - KPI_{i_t} \tag{21}$$

The choice of the discount factor in equation 10 depends on the strategy of the operator which could be to give more importance to old or recent rewards.

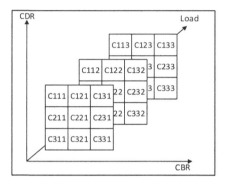

Fig. 6. Inference decision rules

The Q-algorithm is then run until convergence is obtained which results on an optimal correction of the Hyst value. Once the adjustment of Hyst parameter is injected into the network, the HO optimization algorithm based on LB technique is executed.

Fig. 7 shows the initial big difference of load of all macro cells which varies from 10% to 97%.

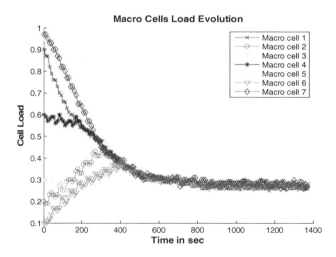

Fig. 7. Macro Cells load evolution

Thanks to our proposed algorithm, high loaded cells are gradually offloaded by shifting edge users to neighbor low loaded macro cells. As a result, the users are fairly redistributed over the entire region and all macro cells have almost the same load.

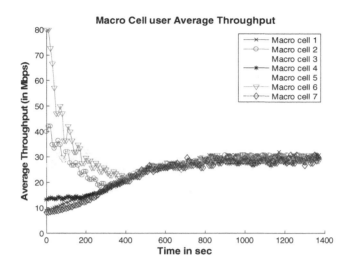

Fig. 8. Macro Cell user Average Throughput

Another expected result is the alignment of average throughput per user which is a direct consequence of HO optimization based on LB. Fig. 8 shows the balanced average throughput for Macro cell users. Therefore, all users will benefit from almost the same service quality independently of their location in the network.

5   Conclusion and Perspectives

In this paper, we give the detailed analytic study of a new combined method in order to optimize some relevant KPIs by the means of automated adjustment of an RRM parameter which is HO Hysteresis followed by HO optimization based on LB technique. The obtained results show the efficiency of our novel approach to balance the load between the different cells. Furthermore, our new algorithm allows all users profit from nearly the same throughput regardless of their position in the network.

In future work, we aim at evaluating other KPIs such as CDR, CBR and the number of radio link failures. Furthermore, we will take into account both slow and very rapid UEs and update our HO algorithm to minimize call drops.

A potential evolution of this work would be to test a parallel use of our proposed approach for simultaneous self-optimization of more KPIs with the optimized adjustment of different RRM parameters.

Finally, we will focus on the compatibility of our work with heterogeneous deployment (small cells) and advanced networks beyond 4G.

References

1. Tiwana, M.I.: Automated RRM Optimization of LTE networks using Statistical Learning. Thesis Report (2011)
2. Dubreil, H.: Méthodes d'optimisation de contrôleurs de logique floue pour le paramétrage automatique des réseaux mobiles UMTS. Thesis Report (2005)
3. Nasri, R.: Paramétrage Dynamique et Optimisation Automatique des Réseaux Mobiles 3G et 3G+. Thesis Report (2010)
4. Ruiz-Aviles, Luna-Ramírez, S., Toril, M., Ruiz, F.: Fuzzy Logic Controllers for Traffic Sharing in Enterprise LTE Femtocells. In: IEEE 75th Vehicular Technology Conference, VTC Spring (2012)
5. Chang, H.S., Fu, M.C., Hu, J., Marcus, S.I.: Simulation-based algorithms for Markov decision processes. Springer (2007)
6. Sutton, S.R., Barto, A.G.: Reinforcement Learning: An Introduction. MIT Press, Cambridge (1998)
7. Technical Specification Group RAN: E-UTRA; LTE RF system scenarios. 3rd Generation Partnership Project (3GPP), Tech. Rep. TS 36.942 (2008-2009)

Design of Wireless Sensor Network
for Intra-vehicular Communications

Md. Arafatur Rahman[1,2]

[1] Department of Electrical Engineering and Information Technologies (DIETI)
University of Naples Federico II, Naples, Italy
[2] Laboratorio Nazionale di Comunicazioni Multimediali (CNIT), Naples, Italy
arafatur.rahman@unina.it

Abstract. The number of sensor nodes in the vehicle has increased significantly due to the increasing of different vehicular applications. Since, the wired architecture is not scalable and flexible because of the internal structure of the vehicle, therefore, there is an increasing level of appeal to design a system in which the wired connections to the sensor nodes are replaced with wireless links. Design a wireless sensor network inside the vehicle is more challenging to other networks, e.g., wireless, sensor and computer networks, because of the complex environment inside the vehicle. In this paper, we design a wireless sensor network for intra-vehicular communications. Firstly, we discuss about the link design between a base station and a sensor node and then we design a network scenario inside the vehicle for reliable communication. Finally, the performance is evaluated in terms of network reliability. The simulation results assist to design a robust system for intra-vehicular communications.

Keywords: Controller Area Network, ZigBee, Intra-vehicular Communications.

1 Introduction

The Controller Area Network (CAN) is a serial communication protocol capable of managing high efficiency distributed realtime control with a high level of security. A CAN network is composed of a linear bus made with a twisted pair of wires and number of nodes connected to each other via the transmission medium. It is the most widespread system of communication between Sensor Nodes (SNs) inside a vehicle with wired connections. Fig. 1 is the example of a controller area networks and Fig. 2 depicts the frame format of CAN. For more information about CAN, we refer to [1,2].

The number of sensors in the vehicle has increased significantly due to the various safety and convenience applications. Since, the wired architecture is not scalable and flexible because of the internal structure of the vehicle [3]. Therefore, there is an increasing level of appeal to design a system in which the wired connections to the SNs are replaced with wireless links. To this end, several technologies, such as Radio Frequency IDentification (RFID) and Zigbee, have been investigated in literature [4,5,6].

A. Mellouk et al. (Eds.): WWIC 2014, LNCS 8458, pp. 29–40, 2014.

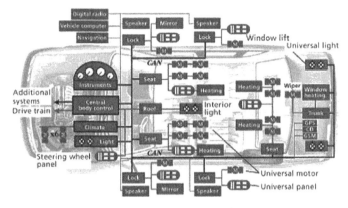

Fig. 1. Example of a Controller Area Network

S O F	11-bit Identifier	R T R	I D E	r0	DLC	0...8 Bytes Data	CRC	ACK	E O F	I F S

Fig. 2. CAN Frame Format

Wireless channels are by nature extremely complex and unpredictable systems. Several models and parameters are used to characterize wireless channel [7,8], whereas many of them are backed up by intuition and physical theory [9,10]. However, no single concrete method for determining the characteristics of a wireless channel has been established. Therefore, the most accurate method of characterizing a particular wireless channel is experimental measurements, particularly for practical purposes.

The design of an Intra-Vehicle Wireless Sensor Networks (IVWSNs) can not be separated from the study on the link between the different sensor nodes distributed in the vehicle. Therefore, link designing between Base Station (BS) an SN is an important issue in IVWSNs. The level of network performance varies with different communication parameters such as distance between BS and SN, transmission power and channel fading. From Fig. 3, we can see that the transmission power of the BS is set P_{t1} if the distance between BS and SN is d_1. When the distance is increased from d_1 to d_2 then the transmit power needs to be increased from P_{t1} to P_{t2} for receiving the same level of received signal by the SN. We also notice that due to the increasing of distance between BS and SN, the obstacles may come in the propagation path that changes the line-of-sight (LOS) to non LOS (NLOS). As a result, the fading distribution of a channel will be changed. For achieving the better performance in IVWSNs, the above parameters need to be adjusted. In fact, design a wireless sensor network inside the vehicle is more challenging to other networks, e.g., wireless, sensor and computer networks, because of the complex environment created by a large number of parts inside the vehicle. Therefore, it is an active research area to design a network for intra-vehicle communications.

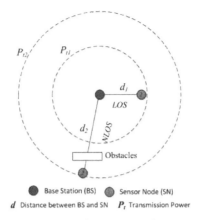

Fig. 3. Scenario is changed with the varying of communication parameters

In this paper, we design a wireless sensor network for intra-vehicular communications and evaluate its performance in terms of network reliability. More in details, firstly, we study about the link analysis between BS and SN, then based on that we design an IVWSNs by utilizing ZigBee standard instead of the traditional CAN technology. Finally, we define network reliability in terms of end-to-end delay to measure the performance of the networks. The simulation results assist to design a robust system for intra vehicular communications.

The rest of the paper is organized as follows. In Section 2, we provide the related works, while in Section 3, we describe the design of IVWSNs. In Section 4, we discuss about the network reliability, while in Section 5, we present the simulation results. Finally, in Section. 6, we conclude the paper.

2   Related Works

There have been active researches on the design of wireless and sensor networks [12,14,15,16]. For example, In [12], the authors present an empirical study based reliability estimation in wireless networks. However, there are less numbers of work have addressed particularly the design of network for intra-vehicular communications [3,11,17,18,19,20]. In [19], the authors present the viability of the optical wireless channel for use in intra-vehicular communications applications. In [20], the authors investigate the coverage area performance of multi band orthogonal frequency division multiplex ultra wide band intra-vehicular communication in the presence of plural mobile terminals.

The ZigBee is a key technology to design a wireless sensor network for various purposes. In [21,22], the authors design a monitoring and control system based on ZigBee wireless sensor network. In addition, it plays an important role in the intra-vehicle networks. However, few works have addressed this technology for intra-vehicular communications. In [3], the authors report the statistical characteristics of 4 representative intra-vehicle wireless channels on the basis of the results of received power measurements and verify the level of reliability of the channels. In [11], the authors propose another work to characterize the wireless channel for intra-vehicle wireless communication. In [17], the authors design and analysis a robust broad-cast scheme for the safety related services of the vehicular networks. In [18], the authors study the performance of ZigBee sensor networks for intra-vehicle communications, in the presence of blue-tooth interference.

Unlike all the aforementioned works, in this paper we design a ZigBee based wireless sensor network for intra-vehicular communications and evaluate its performance in terms of network reliability.

3   Design of IVWSNs

The main design of the intra-vehicle wireless sensor networks including two parts: link design between BS and SN and network scenario design. The link design presents the suitability of the communication parameters for single link in IVWSNs, such as transmit power and the distance between BS and SN. The network scenario design part presents the detailed description about IVWSNs. We are explaining them in the following.

3.1   Link Design between BS and SN

In this sub-section, we study about the analysis of single link between BS and SN, since the design of a IVWSNs can not be separated from the study on the link between the different sensor nodes distributed in the vehicle. In order to do that, we have carried out a simulation through a discrete event simulation software, OPNET, with the relative packages for the ZigBee module. A pair of transmitter (i.e., SN) and receiver (i.e., BS) communicates each other within a vehicle. The BS collects the packets that are transmitting periodically by the SN. The BS and the SN are placed at a distance d. The Transmit Power set: {-10, -15, -20, -25} dBm, which is suitable for ZigBee, such as the Crossbow MICAz MPR2400 [24]. The Carrier frequency is 2.4 GHz (ISM band). There are two channels 1 (a, b), which are for NLOS paths with Rayleigh fading. The path loss exponent γ for channel 1(a) 3 and for channel 1(b) is 4. The values of shadowing deviation $\sigma[dB]$ is 8. The suitability of the considered parameters has been discussed elaborately in our previous work [23].

Fig. 4 shows the behavior of the average throughput with the variation of distance between BS and SN for Channel 1 (a, b). The figure clearly shows a decreasing trend of the average throughput with increasing distance. The cause of this trend is due to the low power level of the packets arriving to the antenna of BS. We know that the path loss increases with distance and the effect of the log-normal shadowing involves a fluctuation in time of the received power, which can further degrade the performance of the communication. These fluctuations may lead the level of received power below the receiver sensitivity (-95 dBm). Then, the BS evaluates the received packet as noise and consequently, the packet is lost. From this analysis, we can see that the transmit power -15 dBm (both

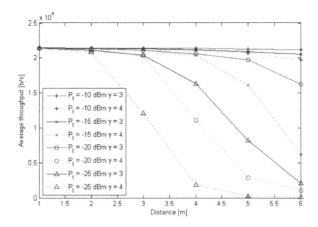

Fig. 4. Average throughput versus Distance between BS and SN with the varying of Transmit power

$\gamma = 3$ and 4) is suitable for IVWSNs. We also notice that when the distance between BS and SN is less than 4 the performance is very good, consequently, we can say the BS should be placed in the center of the car for getting good performance. The detailed analysis for single BS and SN is found in [23].

3.2   Network Scenario Design

There is only on BS that is placed in the center of the vehicle and several number of SNs are placed around it, as shown in Fig. 5. In this way, the distance between SN and BS will be less than any other scenarios where BS is set at any palace in the vehicle, as a result the BS can receive packets from the SNs with better signal strength. Two different SNs are considered: one is Green (G) and other is Yellow (Y), whose transmission period is 120 ms and 60 ms, respectively. We also consider four different cases according to traffic load in the networks. These considerations will help to measure the performance of the network while the traffic load is high. In case I, 100% Green, in case II, 70% Green and 30% Yellow, in case III, 50% Green and 50% Yellow and in case IV, 30% Green and 70% Yellow SNs will be from the total sensor nodes, see Table 1. The more number of Yellow SNs means the more traffic in the network because of its less transmission period. The number of sensor node set is {10, 30, 50, 70, 90, 110}. The communication parameters of the networks are as follows:

- Transmit Power: -15 dBM, as discussed in the previous subsections;
- Carrier frequency: 2.4 GHz (ISM band), which is used on ZigBee sensor node [24]
- Receiver sensitivity: The reception threshold of the BS is set equal to -95 dBm, typical for ZigBee [24];
- Transmission Period: 120 ms and 60 ms for Green and Yellow SN, respectively ;

Table 1. Considered Cases

Number	Case I		Case II		Case III		Case IV	
of NS	G	Y	G	Y	G	Y	G	Y
10	10	0	7	3	5	5	3	7
30	30	0	21	9	15	15	9	21
50	50	0	35	15	25	25	15	35
70	70	0	49	21	35	35	21	49
90	90	0	63	27	45	45	27	63
110	110	0	77	33	55	55	33	77

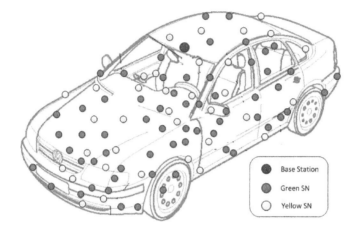

Fig. 5. Example of SNs distribution inside the vehicle

- Channel: The channel is for NLOS paths with Rayleigh fading. The path loss exponent γ is 4. The values of shadowing deviation $\sigma[dB]$ is 8. These values are suitable for intra-vehicle communication [3,11].
- Packet size: 210 bits (ZigBee packet header 120 bits + data 90 bits);

Remark 1. 90 bits for data is selected with the reference of CAN message used in [13].

- Parameters MAC:
  - ACK Mechanism:
    * ACK Wait Duration: 0.05 second;
    * Number of retransmissions: 5.
  - CSMA-CA Parameters:
    * Minimum Backoff Exponent: 3;
    * Maximum Number of Backoffs: 4;
    * Channel Sensig Duration: 0.1 second.

4   Network Reliability

In this section, we define the network reliability, which will be utilized for measuring the performance of the network. The definition is in the following:

Definition 1 (Network Reliability R). *Network reliability is defined as the ability to deliver the packets to the destination (BS) within a certain time limit (called Deadline). The expression of the reliability can be written:*

$$R = P_r(D_{ete} \leq D) \tag{1}$$

were R is the network reliability, D_{ete} is the end to end delay (i.e., the overall delay between the time instant when it creates a package from the application layer and the time instant when it is received) and D is the deadline (i.e., the limits on the chosen end-to-end delay of the packet).

Remark 2. In this paper, we consider two deadlines: one is called restrictive deadline denoted as D_1 and other is called less restrictive deadline denoted as D_2. Note that D_1 and D_2 represent 25% and 50% of the maximum SN transmission period, i.e., 120 ms. This consideration is reasonable because less end to end delay of the packet increases the reliability of the network due to its less packet retransmission.

5   Simulation Results

In this section, we analyse the reliability of the network, varying of traffic load, by taking account of Definition 1. Due to the increasing of traffic load, the intra-vehicle network becomes congested. The effect of congestion on the network is also investigated. In order to assess the level of reliability, we have carried out a series of simulations through a discrete event simulation software, OPNET, with the relative packages for the ZigBee module. The performance of the network is measured based on this network reliability.

In Fig. 6, we report the CDF of the end-to-end delay versus the number of nodes for analyzing the reliability in the case I. From the figure, we notice that as the number of SN increases in IVWSN, the CDF shift to the right. The cause of this performance is due to the collisions among the packets, which increases with the increasing number of SN in the network. In fact, after the collision SN waits for a certain period of time (Backoff + sensing period) and then if the channel is free, it retransmits the packet that already caused collision previously. The new re-transmissions can be subjected to other collision. The repetition of the procedures is explained under the CSMA-CA protocol. It is easy to understand at this point that the increasing number of collisions results the increasing end-to-end delay experienced by the packets.

As in the first case there is only Green SN and the considered deadlines are $D_1 = 30ms$ and $D_2 = 60ms$. As it can be seen in Fig. 6, the condition on less restrictive deadline, D_2, is fully satisfied, as shown in Table 2. On the other

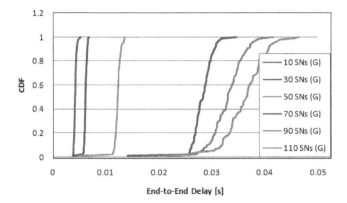

Fig. 6. CDF of end-to-end delays Vs the number of nodes in the case I

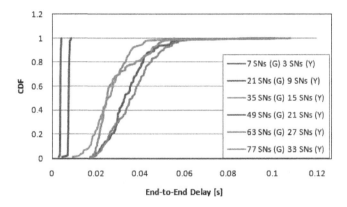

Fig. 7. CDF of end-to-end delays Vs the number of nodes in the case II

hand, the restrictive condition, $D_1 = 30ms$, it is satisfied in the case of 10, 30, 50 and 70 SNs, while in other cases (90, 110 SNs) are satisfied with a probability not adequate (about 16% in best case) in terms of reliability.

We also report the CDF of the end-to-end delay versus the number of nodes for analyzing the reliability in other cases, as shown in Fig. 7 - 9. The above figures show that the introducing of more Yellow SNs in the network, the end-to-end delay is increasing i.e., the reliability of the network decreases. In fact, in the case I with 70 NS, the reliability is 100% for less restrictive deadline. D_2, whereas in case II, this falls to about 96% and continuously falling while increasing in the number of Yellow SNs in the network.

In addition, the increasing number of SN, in particular when it increases the number of Yellow SN, in the intra-vehicle WSN is subjected to the phenomenon of congestion. In fact, increasing the traffic up to a certain point where the network is no longer able to handle the traffic then it enters into congestion. As a result a number of transmitted packets (including retransmitted packets) by SN

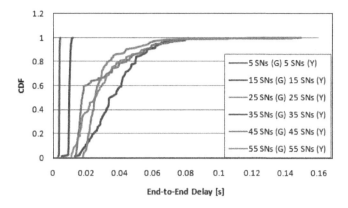

Fig. 8. CDF of end-to-end delays Vs the number of nodes in the case III

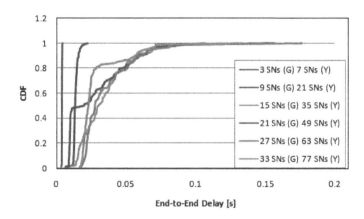

Fig. 9. CDF of end-to-end delays Vs the number of nodes in the case IV

never reaches its destination. Higher the degree of congestion of the network, the greater will be the number of packets that never arrives at the destination. The Table 2 summarizes the results obtained in four cases, the results highlighted in bold are "distorted" due to congestion of the network. The phenomenon of congestion decreases the end-to-end delay that causes the distortion of the results, since in OPNET the end-to-end delay is calculated on the basis of packets that reach to their destination.

To mitigate the problem of congestion, we introduce two BSs in the network. Each BS is consisting of 50% SNs from the total SNs. In Fig. 10, there is 90 SNs with half Green and half Yellow SNs in case of both single and double BS. We note, in case of single BS, initially the result is distorted due to the large number of packets that do not reach to the destination because of the congestion in the network. In case of double BS, there is no congestion effects because of the proper traffic load distribution. However, introducing additional BS increases

Table 2. Reliability in Different Cases

Number of NS	R in case I		R in case II		R in case III		R in case IV	
	D_1	D_2	D_1	D_2	D_1	D_2	D_1	D_2
10	100%	100%	100%	100%	100%	100%	100%	100%
30	100%	100%	100%	100%	100%	100%	100%	100%
50	100%	100%	72%	97%	52%	90%	45%	87%
70	92%	100%	40%	96%	25%	88%	**66%**	86%
90	16%	100%	30%	95%	**62%**	89%	**63%**	**87%**
110	6%	100%	**65%**	75%	**77%**	**92%**	**82%**	**89%**

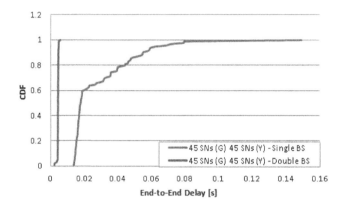

Fig. 10. Comparison between CDF in the case of single BS and double BSs

the design complexity of the networks. Therefore, a new MAC strategy can be designed for congestion network that will be the future direction of this work. We will also investigate the performance by introducing the concept of cognitive radio in intra-vehicle wireless sensor networks [25]-[30].

6   Conclusion

In this paper, we design a wireless sensor network for intra-vehicular communication. We define the network reliability in terms of end-to-end delay to measure the performance of the networks. After the analysis, we note that, the phenomenon of congestion plays an important role in the network while the traffic load is high. To mitigate the congestion problem, we could increase the number of BS in the network. In fact, introducing additional BS increases the design complexity of the networks. Therefore, a new MAC strategy can be designed for congestion network that will be the future direction of this work. The simulation results assist to design a robust system for intra vehicular communications.

Acknowledgments. This work is partially supported by the project "Mobile Continuos Connected Comprehensive Care (MC3CARE), "DRIVEr monitoring: technologies, methodologies, and IN-vehicle INnovative systems for a safe and ecocompatible driving (DRIVE IN^2)" founded by the Italian national program Piano Operativo Nazionale Ricerca e Competitivit 2007-2013 and the project, "Sviluppo di Tecniche di Comunicazione di Sistemi Embedded Distribuiti" founded by POR Campania FSE 2007/2013.

References

1. Tindell, K.W., Hansson, H., Wellings, A.J.: Analysing real-time communications: Controller Area Network (CAN). In: Proc. of 15th Real-Time Systems Symposium, pp. 259–263. IEEE Computer Society Press (1994)
2. Tindell, K., Burns, A.: Guaranteeing Message Latencies on Controller Area Network (CAN). In: Proc. of 1st International CAN Conference, pp. 1–11 (1994)
3. Tsai, H.M., Viriyasitavat, W., Tonguz, O.K., Saraydar, C., Talty, T., Macdonald, A.: Feasibility of In-car Wireless Sensor Networks: A Statistical Evaluation. In: Proc. IEEE SECON, pp. 101–111 (2007)
4. Tonguz, O.K., Tsai, H.M., Saraydar, C., Talty, T., Macdonald, A.: Intra-car wireless sensor networks using RFID: Opportunities and challenges. In: Proc. INFOCOM MOVE Workshop, pp. 43–48 (2007)
5. Tsai, H.M., Tonguz, O.K., Saraydar, C., Talty, T., Ames, M., Macdonald, A.: Zigbee-based intra-car wireless sensor networks: A case study. IEEE Wireless Commun. 14, 67–77 (2007)
6. Niu, W., Li, J., Liu, S., Talty, T.: Intra-vehicle ultra-wideband communication testbed. In: Proc. MILCOM, pp. 1–6 (2007)
7. Cacciapuoti, A.S., Calabrese, F., Caleffi, M., Di Lorenzo, G., Paura, L.: Human-mobility enabled wireless networks for emergency communications during special events. Elsevier Pervasive and Mobile Computing 9, 472–483 (2013)
8. Cacciapuoti, A.S., Calabrese, F., Caleffi, M., Di Lorenzo, G., Paura, L.: Human-mobility enabled networks in urban environments: Is there any (mobile wireless) small world out there? Elsevier Ad Hoc Networks 10, 1520–1531 (2012)
9. Hashemi, H.: Impulse response modeling of indoor radio propagation channels. IEEE J. Sel. Areas Commun. 11, 967–978 (1993)
10. Saleh, A., Valenzuela, R.: A statistical model for indoor multipath propagation. IEEE J. Sel. Areas Commun., SAC-5, 128–137 (1987)
11. Moghimi, A.R., Tsai, H.M., Saraydar, C.U., Tonguz, O.K.: Characterizing IntraCar Wireless Channels. IEEE Transactions on Vehicular Technology 58, 5299–5305 (2009)
12. Woo, S., Kim, H.: Estimating Link Reliability in Wireless Networks: An Empirical Study and Interference Modeling. In: Proc. INFOCOM, pp. 1–5 (2010)
13. Ellims, M., Parker, S., Zurlo, J.: Design and Analysis of a Robust Real-Time Engine. IEEE Micro 22, 20–27 (2002)
14. Xing, B., Mehrotra, S., Venkatasubramanian, N.: RADcast: Enabling reliability guarantees for content dissemination in ad hoc networks. In: Proc. IEEE INFOCOM, pp. 1998–2006 (2009)
15. Cacciapuoti, A.S., Caleffi, M., Paura, L.: A theoretical model for opportunistic routing in ad hoc networks. In: Proc. of International Conference on Ultra Modern Telecommunications Workshops (ICUMT 2009), pp. 1–7 (2009)
16. Cacciapuoti, A.S., Caleffi, M., Paura, L.: Optimal Constrained Candidate Selection for Opportunistic Routing. In: Proc. of IEEE Global Telecommunications Conference (GLOBECOM 2010), pp. 1–5 (2010)

17. Ma, X., Zhang, J., Yin, X., Trivedi, K.S.: Design and Analysis of a Robust Broadcast Scheme for VANET Safety-Related Services. IEEE Transactions on Vehicular Technology 61, 46–61 (2012)

18. Francisco, R.D., Huang, L., Dolmans, G., Groot, H.D.: Coexistence of ZigBee wireless sensor networks and Bluetooth inside a vehicle. In: IEEE 20th International Symposium on Personal, Indoor and Mobile Radio Communications, pp. 2700–2704 (2009)

19. Higgins, M.D., Green, R.J., Leeson, M.S.: Channel viability of intra-vehicle optical wireless communications. In: Proc. IEEE GLOBECOM Workshops, pp. 813–817 (2011)

20. Arai, T., Shirai, T., Watanabe, Y., Maehara, F.: Coverage performance of UWB in-car wireless communication in the presence of multiple terminals. In: IEEE Radio and Wireless Symposium (RWS), pp. 111–114 (2012)

21. Yiming, Z., Xianglong, Y., Xishan, G., Mingang, Z., Liren, W.: A Design of Greenhouse Monitoring and Control System Based on ZigBee Wireless Sensor Network. In: Proc of International Conference on Wireless Communications, Networking and Mobile Computing, pp. 2563–2567 (2007)

22. Chen, L., Yang, S., Xi, Y.: Based on ZigBee wireless sensor network the monitoring system design for chemical production process toxic and harmful gas. In: Proc. of International Conference on Computer, Mechatronics, Control and Electronic Engineering, pp. 425–428 (2010)

23. Rahman, M.A.: Reliability Analysis of ZigBee based Intra-vehicle Wireless Sensor Networks. In: Proc of Nets4Cars 6th International Workshop on Communication Technologies for Vehicles, pp. 101-112 (2014)

24. MPR/MIB mote hardware users manual, http://www.xbow.com

25. Cacciapuoti, A.S., Caleffi, M., Paura, L., Savoia, R.: Decision Maker Approaches for Cooperative Spectrum Sensing: Participate or Not Participate in Sensing? IEEE Transactions on Wireless Communications 12, 2445–2457 (2013)

26. Cacciapuoti, A.S., Caleffi, M., Paura, L.: Reactive routing for mobile cognitive radio ad hoc networks. Elsevier Ad Hoc Networks 10, 803–805 (2012)

27. Rahman, M.A., Caleffi, M., Paura, L.: Joint path and spectrum diversity in cognitive radio ad-hoc networks. EURASIP Journal on Wireless Communications and Networking 2012(1), 1–9 (2012)

28. Cacciapuoti, A.S., Calcagno, C., Caleffi, M., Paura, L.: CAODV: Routing in Mobile Ad-hoc Cognitive Radio Networks. In: Proc. of IEEE IFIP Wireless Days 2010, pp. 1–5 (2010)

29. Cacciapuoti, A.S., Caleffi, M., Paura, L.: Widely Linear Cooperative Spectrum Sensing for Cognitive Radio Networks. In: Proc. of IEEE Global Telecommunications Conference (GLOBECOM 2010), pp. 1–5 (2010)

30. Cacciapuoti, A.S., Caleffi, M., Izzo, D., Paura, L.: Cooperative Spectrum Sensing Techniques with Temporal Dispersive Reporting Channels. IEEE Transactions on Wireless Communications 10, 3392–3402 (2011)

Financing and Pricing Small Cells in Next-Generation Mobile Networks

Christos Bouras[1,2], Vasileios Kokkinos[2], and Andreas Papazois[2]

[1] Computer Technology Institute & Press "Diophantus"
N. Kazantzaki, Rio, 26504 Greece
[2] University of Patras
Building B, University campus, Rio, 26504 Greece
{bouras,kokkinos}@cti.gr, papazois@ceid.upatras.gr
http://ru6.cti.gr/bouras/

Abstract. Small cells technology has also strong potentials for enhancing cell coverage and network capacity of next-generation cellular networks including 5G. From mobile network operators' perspective, small cell deployment will additionally achieve large reduction to the network costs in both fields of capital expenditure and operational expenditure. In this study, we analyze the benefits of small cells' deployment for operators and we list the subscriber incentives for choosing small cells instead of other access types, such as WiFi, for indoor deployment. Furthermore, we provide a financial analysis of the small cell costs for deployment and operation against the corresponding macrocellular costs. We also examine pricing models that could be used to incentivize subscribers and to expedite the small cells' penetration into the market so as to become an economically viable solution. Finally, we present our experimental results demonstrating possible use cases of our cost and pricing models.

Keywords: Small cells, next-generation mobile, 5G, financing, pricing.

1 Introduction

Next-generation mobile technologies, such as 5G, will achieve impressive system's peak data rates and round-trip delays. Nevertheless, the problem of poor connectivity of indoor users is still not expected to be adequately addressed by the existing macrocellular network infrastructure. The solution of condensing the existing mobile network through the deployment of additional macrocells results in high operational and capital expenditures. Thus, the extended use of small cells is the most prominent solution for increasing efficiency in indoor coverage, expanding network capacity without the need of more spectrum resources, and exploiting the capabilities of future mobile networks.

Small cells are short-range, low-cost, low-power base stations connected back to the core network through a broadband Internet connection, such as DSL, cable or a wireless connection. They are based on femtocell (or home base station) technology which has been expanded to include more types of larger cells like

A. Mellouk et al. (Eds.): WWIC 2014, LNCS 8458, pp. 41–54, 2014.

picocell, metrocell, and microcell [1]. Compared to other techniques for increasing system capacity, such as distributed antenna systems, the key advantage of small cells is that there is very low upfront cost for the mobile network operator. Due to the short transmission and reception ranges of the small cell, this technology improves reception experience and higher capacity for indoor users compared to other deployments and simultaneously the power consumption can be kept in low levels [2].

A significant scientific work on small cell technology has been conducted in the recent years. It initially started from femtocells and later expanding to the more generic concept of small cells. The vast majority of the related scientific literature studies technological issues related with several different areas, such as the spectrum usage, the self-organization, cross-tier and intra-tier interference mitigation, as well as backhauling issues, thus contributing to the expediting evolution of small cell technology. Nevertheless, research on small cells' financing and pricing was triggered from their early appearance, not always in the form of small cells but alternatively over home-deployed femtocells or picocells [3].

The economics of small cells is a field of major importance in this area, since it affects strongly their adoption by both operators and subscribers and therefore has a critical impact on the total success of this technology in terms of commercialization [4]. In the past, operators provided conventional mobile voice and data services through the establishment of a wide area access that was based mainly on macrocellular network infrastructure. However, the introduction of small cell technology poses a new set of challenges to mobile network operators. They certainly should not rely only on the conventional wide area infrastructure to achieve profitable future business, instead they should exploit the business potentials of small cells. Small cells can be a viable service and, furthermore, they can produce high financial benefits for the mobile network operators [5].

In this paper, we present and analyze the benefits of small cells' deployment and we present the mobile network operator's incentives for including small cells in their service offerings as well as the subscriber's incentives for choosing small cells instead of other access types, such as WiFi, for indoor deployment. Furthermore, we address financing and pricing issues of small cells in next-generation mobile networks. The analytical models that we present estimate capital and operational expenditures for the macrocellular and small cell cases. We also provide an analysis for pricing of small cells as an additional mobile service. The proposed pricing models take into consideration the mobile network's utility as well as its valuation from subscriber's point of view. The interesting evaluation results provided by our models can be further utilized in order to incentivize subscribers and to expedite their penetration to the market so as to make small cells a economically viable solution.

The remaining part of this paper is structured as follows: Section 2 presents the key arguments for adopting the small cell technology from both subscriber's and operator's perspective. Section 3 explores the cost issues of small cell technology and describes how the mobile network operator revenues will be generated. Section 4 presents pricing models of small cell service provision that could further used to make it economically viable and profitable for the operators. In Section 5 we make use of our analytical models to obtain numerical results on small cells' financing and pricing under various conditions. Finally, in Section 6 we present our concluding remarks as well as some ideas for future research work in this field.

2   Opting for Small Cells

Small cell technology has several significant benefits for both subscribers and mobile network operators that make it an appealing service and a solution that can compete successfully against the conventional macrocellular coverage as well as solutions based on other standards such as 802.11 series. Table 1 summarizes the most important benefits for both interested parties.

Table 1. Benefits of Small Cells for Subscribers and Operators

Subscribers	Operators
1) Increased data rates	1) Lower capital expenditure
2) Lower end-to-end latency	2) Lower operational expenditure
3) Seamless connectivity from indoors to outdoors and vice-versa	3) Offloading traffic in macrocellular infrastructure
4) Increased security	4) Efficient spectrum reuse
5) Ability for closed access	5) Increased network capacity
6) Ability to behave as relay node	6) Lower power consumption
7) Improved indoor coverage and quality	7) Avoidance of macrocell tower installations

From subscriber's point of view, small cell technology brings the base station closer to the mobile terminal and therefore it achieves increased data rates and lower end-to-end latency compared to conventional macrocellular networks. This is a very important feature especially in locations where macrocellular signal strength is poor and mobile connectivity is limited and it can improve not only data services but also mobile voice services. Seamless connectivity from outdoor macrocellular access to indoor small cell is a significant benefit which exploits the mobile flawless handover capabilities. The small cell's ability to behave as a relay node is another important feature that permits the subscriber to expand the macrocellular coverage by using his own equipment. Small cells also offer increased security along with the ability to define a selected group with access permissions. This is an interesting aspect especially when comparing small cells with the conventional WiFi access networks where security and access control is a controversial issue.

From mobile network operator's perspective, small cells permit the expansion of the mobile network in terms of coverage and capacity without any need for investments in new equipment and infrastructures, such as acquisition of new sites, installations of new towers or expansion of the backhaul. At the same time the need for additional operational activities is kept low and other important operational expenses, such as the energy consumption at the access network, are limited. Macrocellular infrastructure is offloaded from a portion of the traffic originating from indoor users, thus increasing the system's capacity. System's capacity is also increased in terms of spectrum, since that the available spectral resources are reused much more frequently.

3   Cost Analysis

In this section we analyze the trade-off between macrocells and small cells in the terms of cost. To this direction we propose two financial models that can be used for the cost estimation, one for the macrocellular case and one for small cells, which are presented below.

3.1   Macrocellular Cost

The macrocellular cost for the mobile network operator is split in two main categories, namely the capital expenditure and the operational expenditure. Typically, both of these cost categories are borne by the operator.

Capital Expenditure. The capital expenditure is the budget that the network operator invests to acquire and deploy new assets that are non-consumable and to deploy them. Typical examples of such types of non-consumable assets are various types of equipment, new sites, such as buildings, and installation of new links. The capital expenditure also includes the budget invested to upgrade existing assets.

Before estimating the capital expenditure for the macrocellular coverage we will estimate the cost for a single evolved Node-B (eNB), which is the macrocellular base station. The estimation of this cost is straight-forward since it consists by the network equipment cost and thus it can be given by the following expression: $C_{eNB} + C_{EPC}$. The amounts C_{eNB} and C_{EPC} are the costs for eNB and Evolved Packet Core (EPC), which is the term used for LTE-A's core network, respectively. At this point, it should be clarified that the C_{eNB} apart from the costs related to the eNB equipment and deployment, it also includes any potential additional costs for the site acquisition and construction as well as any costs related with eNB's backhaul. The amount C_{EPC} includes all the costs related to the core network such as the costs of core packet routers.

In order to have a common reference, the estimation of the capital expenditure for the macrocellular coverage should be done on an annual basis by taking the annual installment payments of the investment into consideration. Therefore we assume a total investment of capital expenditure for N eNBs that is expressed by: $N(C_{eNB}+C_{EPC})$ and that is repaid annually. Generally, the annual installment A for an principal amount P is expressed by:

$$A = \frac{i}{1-(1+i)^{-n}}C \tag{1}$$

where i represents the interest rate and n represents the length of the installment plan in years.

Assuming that all the capital expenditure is made in advance, then the principal amount C equals to the capital expenditure. Thus, the capital expenditure estimation on an annual basis is expressed by the following equation:

$$c_{macro}^{capex} = \frac{i}{1-(1+i)^{-n}}N(C_{eNB}+C_{EPC}) \tag{2}$$

where c_{macro}^{capex} denotes the annual total cost of capital expenditure and N is the number of eNBs.

Operational Expenditure. The operational expenditure is the day-to-day ongoing costs for running the system, for the network's maintenance, as well as for any additional supporting activities. In case the site is leased, then the leasing costs are also included in the operational expenditure. Thus, the annual operational expenditure c_{macro}^{opex} is expressed by the following equation:

$$c_{macro}^{opex} = N(c_{running}+c_{backhaul})$$

where $c_{running}$ denotes the annual total cost for running a single site including the power consumption, in-site and off-site support, as well as in-site and off-site maintenance. For simplicity, maintenance costs are generally considered as linearly proportional to the capital expenditure with a coefficient f_{site}, and all the rest site costs are expressed by the amount c_{site}. Thus, the total running cost can be further expressed as: $Nc_{running} = f_{site}c_{macro}^{capex} + Nc_{site}$. On the other hand, the amount $c_{backhaul}$ expresses the backhaul costs which are generally linearly proportional to the used bandwidth BW with a coefficient f_{BW}.

To summarize, the total operational expenditure per annum can be expressed as follows:

$$\begin{aligned} c_{macro}^{opex} &= f_{site}c_{macro}^{capex} + Nc_{site} + f_{BW}BW \\ &= f_{site}\frac{i}{1-(1+i)^{-n}}N(C_{eNB}+C_{EPC})+ \\ & \quad Nc_{site} + f_{BW}BW \end{aligned} \tag{3}$$

Based on (2) and (3) the total macrocellular cost for the mobile network operator on an annual basis is expressed by the following equation:

$$c_{macro} = \frac{i}{1-(1+i)^{-n}}N(C_{eNB}+C_{EPC})+$$
$$f_{site}\frac{i}{1-(1+i)^{-n}}N(C_{eNB}+C_{EPC})+$$
$$Nc_{site} + f_{BW}BW \tag{4}$$

where i is the interest rate and n is the duration of the installment plan in years.

3.2   Cost for Small Cells

The cost in case of the small cells is split in the same two categories. However, the cost model applied is totally different from that of the macrocellular case.

Capital Expenditure. Before estimating the capital expenditure for the case of small cells, we should clarify that several assumptions can take place prior to the installation of the Home eNB (HeNB). First, the existence of a home broadband connection is a prerequisite since it provides connectivity to the small cell as backhaul. Second, an arrangement should be made on which side (either the operator or the subscriber) will bear the cost of the HeNB equipment and installation. In this study we assume that a broadband connection preexists, so the first cost for backhaul is ignored, whereas the cost for the equipment and the HeNB installation is paid by the subscriber himself. It is obvious that, due to the non-layered network architecture for the small cell case and the absence of intermediate radio access and core network nodes, costs for EPC nodes is also not included. Therefore the only capital expenditure that we consider in this case is the cost for network equipment for interfacing and routing the traffic to/from operator's core network. This cost is denoted by $C_{i/f}$ and represents the total capital expenditure in the case of small cells. Similarly to the macrocellular case, the annual installment for the capital expenditure for this case is expressed as follows:

$$c_{small}^{capex} = \frac{i}{1-(1+i)^{-n}}NC_{i/f} \tag{5}$$

where c_{small}^{capex} denotes the annual total cost of capital expenditure and N is the number of HeNBs.

Operational Expenditure. Similarly to the capital expenditure, the estimation of the operational expenditure for small cells is radically different from the macrocellular case since: (a) site leasing cost does not exist given that the HeNB is installed by the subscriber in his premise, (b) power consumption bears only the subscriber, (c) support and maintenance costs, apart from the networking equipment for interfacing, are not considered since they are negligible and given that the broadband connection is provided by the subscriber himself and all issues address mainly to the subscriber and/or the broadband service provider.

Therefore, similarly to the macrocellular case the operational expenditure is expressed by the following:

$$c_{small}^{opex} = f_{site} \frac{i}{1 - (1 + i)^{-n}} NC_{i/f} \tag{6}$$

Subsequently, the following equation:

$$c_{small} = (1 + f_{site}) \frac{i}{1 - (1 + i)^{-n}} NC_{i/f} \tag{7}$$

expresses the total cost for small cell deployment that bears the mobile network operator's side on an annual basis. This expression is based on (5) and (6) and it should be reminded that i is the interest rate and n is the duration of the installment plan in years.

4   Pricing Models

In this section we present the pricing models for small cell service provision, which can be used towards making it an economically viable and profitable solution for the operators. According to [6] two main pricing schemes apply. Both of these schemes follow a fixed rate policy for the service provision since other policies, e.g., separate volume-based charges for the small cell data traffic, would be rather complex to be implemented.

The first main pricing scheme is the one preferred by most operators as reported in [7] and defines a fixed service fee for accessing small cells. This scheme can be applied in various forms, such as monthly service fee for accessing small cells, monthly service fee for hosting small cell equipment, or at once charging, i.e., when the small cell is initially acquired and deployed. There is also the case, although rather rare, that some operators provide free of charge small cell services to all subscribers or to subscribers having a monthly mobile contract above a certain threshold, e.g., the case of Vodafone in Greece and SoftBank in Japan.

In the second pricing scheme, again a fixed service fee is charged to grant access to small cells. Its difference from the previous scheme is that in this case the amount is defined proportionally to the monthly mobile contract that the subscribers have for their conventional macrocell access. Based on the pricing of current commercial deployments described in [6] this pricing scheme is not at all popular among the mobile operators.

Assuming that p_j is the price paid by subscriber j for his selected service plan, then for a population of users U the price vector $p = (p_j : j \in U)$ includes all the charging data for all subscribers. Therefore, the total revenue R of the operator is given by:

$$R = \sum_{j \in U} p_j \tag{8}$$

and is the amount, which the operator wishes to maximize through the applied pricing policy. Since the goal of this paper is to study the financial and pricing aspects of small cells against macrocells we consider two prices, and therefore:

$$p_j \in \{p_m, p_s\}, \forall j \in U$$

where p_m is the price for the basic macrocellular service subscription and p_s is the price that additionally to the macrocellular access, it offers access through a small cell owned by the subscriber. If N_m and N_s is the number of subscriptions of macrocellular and small cell access respectively then the revenue from (8) that the operator wishes to maximize, can also be expressed as:

$$R = N_m p_m + N_s p_s \tag{9}$$

where $N_m + N_s = j$.

In order to decide whether a specific subscriber j selects macrocellular subscription plan only or a subscription plan that combines macrocellular with small cell access, we suppose that the subscribers act in a selfish manner. Therefore the subscribers try to maximize their benefit given the achieved indoor and outdoor throughput as well as the corresponding subscription charges. Other QoS parameters such as delay, delay jitter and loss are ignored for the sake of simplicity. To this direction we define a function that quantifies utility [8] by associating the utility with throughput and price as follows:

$$u_j = \gamma f(T_j) - p_j \tag{10}$$

where the coefficient γ is a subjective measure of user type that expresses how willing to pay the subscriber is for a given throughput T_j. Function f expresses the relation between the level of throughput T_j and an objective measure of throughput's valuation. It is obvious that f should be a concave function, since, for higher throughput levels, changes in the throughput value tend to have lower impact on its valuation. Therefore although the derivative of f is positive, its second derivative should output always negative numbers. On the other hand, throughput T_j depends on various parameters, e.g., user location, user speed, and network conditions.

A user selects a plan including small cell service when $u_s > u_m$ which from (10) means that the necessary condition is that the following expression should be positive:

$$\gamma(f(T_s) - f(T_m)) - p_s + p_m \tag{11}$$

As previously explained function f is concave, but for simplicity's sake we will assume that its output is linear with throughput. The corresponding constant of proportionality is κ and therefore the expression described in (11) gives:

$$\gamma\kappa(T_s - T_m) - p_s + p_m = \gamma\kappa T_{eNB} - p_s + p_m \tag{12}$$

where T_{eNB} is the throughput obtained by the user inside their home using their HeNB. A user that adopts the small cell service obtains T_{eNB} throughput when locating at his home, whereas when locating outside his home it receives the same throughput T_m as a typical user subscribed to the basic macrocellular service. It is important to note that the throughput T_{eNB} can be easily quantified since it depends essentially on the user's broadband connection and any throughput variations due to the user location inside his home are considered negligible.

The value of amount $\gamma\kappa$ depends on the user valuation of the throughput and it is important to specify the threshold value of $\gamma\kappa$ that makes (15) being a positive number.

5   Experimentation

In this section, we make use of the previous analysis in order to investigate the behavior of the financing and pricing models under various conditions. We first explain the methodology followed and then we present the derived results.

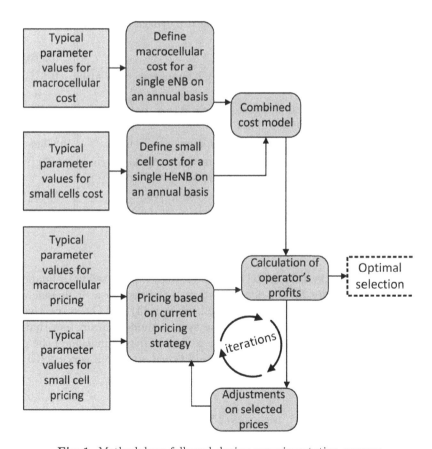

Fig. 1. Methodology followed during experimentation process

5.1   Methodology

Figure 1 illustrates a methodology that is recommended to be followed during the experimentation process. In brief, first we determine the typical values for the parameters used by our analytical models, based on literature review. The next step of the process the application of the models derived from the previous analysis presented in Section 3 and Section 4. The pricing parameters are adjusted through an iterative process in order to eventually lead to the optimal solution.

In order to obtain significant and meaningful results we determined the parameter values based on a review the latest bibliography in the field. The parameters and system variables used, their recommended values as well as a reference to the corresponding study are listed in Table 2 and Table 3.

Table 2. Cost Parameters and System Variables

Parameter	Description	Value
C_{eNB}	Capital cost for eNB	1000 € [9]
C_{EPC}	Core network's capital cost for the deployment of a single eNB	* [9]
i	Annual interest rate	6% [10]
f_{site}	Linear coefficient correlating site maintenance costs with capital expenditure	0.8 [11]
c_{site}	Site costs apart from maintenance cost, e.g., power, in-site and off-site support	3100 € [12]
BW	Backhaul bandwidth for a site's interconnection	10 Gbps [13]
f_{BW}	Linear coefficient correlating site annual backhaul costs with provided bandwidth – expressed in €/Gbps	1170 [14]
n	Duration of installment plan of a site in years	10 yrs [15]
$C_{i/f}$	Capital cost for interfacing a single small cell	110 € [16]

*: Included in the above cost.

Table 2 lists all the system model parameters that are related with financing. These values can be used for the determination of the cost for a single macrocell base station as well as for a single small cell through (4) and (7), respectively.

On the other hand, Table 3 lists all the system model parameters that are related with pricing. These values will be used for the determination of the price that a subscriber is willing to pay for an additional small cell service. To this end, the calculations are based on (15).

$$c_{macro} = 15045 \; € \qquad (13)$$

Table 3. Pricing Parameters and System Variables

Parameter	Description	Value
T_{eNB}	Indoor throughput provided by HeNB	15 Mbps [17]
γ	Coefficient correlating throughput with customer's willingness to pay – expressed in €/Mbps	2.8 [18]
κ	Coefficient correlating throughput with its valuation	** [18]
p_m	Price for the basic macrocellular service	295 € [19]
p_s	Price for private small cell access on top of macrocellular one	60 € [20]

**: Included in the above coefficient.

Similarly, deriving from (7) the final annual cost for a single small cell is the following:

$$c_{small} = 27 \ € \tag{14}$$

5.2   Results

The experimental results present indicative usages of the previously presented models. From financing perspective, based on the values presented in Table 2, (4) provides the following cost for a single macrocellular cost for a single base station.

Fig. 2. Maximal price based against offered additional throughput

Based on the values presented in Table 3, (15) provides the following condition that should be true in order for a customer to select small cell service in its subscription plan:

$$p_s < 2.8 * T_{eNB} \tag{15}$$

Figure 2 derives from the above expression and provides an overview of the maximal price against the offered additional throughput. Apart from this relation, for comparison purposes, it illustrates the line from (14) that corresponds to the annual cost for the provision of a single small cell service. It is obvious that the provision of a small cell starts becoming profitable for the operator's side.

Figure 3 visualizes the annual cost for the deployment of a given number of small cells that is listed in the horizontal axis. It also compares this cost with the corresponding total cost for a single macrocellular base station. It is shown that the cost for a single macrocell corresponds to the total annual cost needed from the operator's side for 550 small cells. Additionally, the total profit for the operator is presented. For the calculation of profit the typical value of p_s listed in 3 is used. Please note that this typical value of 60 €implies an average of at least 20 Mbps of additional throughput supported via each one of deployed small cells.

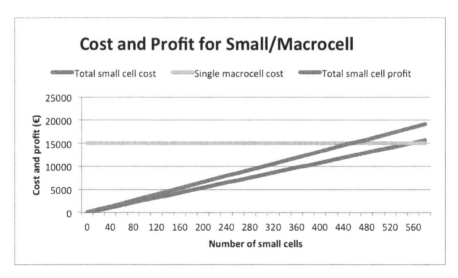

Fig. 3. Small cell cost and profit against macrocellular cost and small cells that are deployed

6   Conclusions and Future Work

In this paper, we analyzed the benefits of small cells' deployment and we presented the mobile network operator's incentives for including small cells in their service offerings as well as the subscriber's incentives for choosing small cells instead of other access types, such as WiFi, for indoor deployment. Furthermore, we addressed financing and pricing issues of small cells in next-generation mobile networks. The analytical models that we presented estimate capital and operational expenditures for the macrocellular and small cell cases. We also provided an analysis for pricing of small cells as an additional mobile service. The proposed pricing models take into consideration the mobile network's utility as well as its valuation from subscriber's point of view. The interesting evaluation results provided by our models can be further utilized in order to incentivize subscribers and to expedite the penetration into the market so as to make small cells a economically viable solution.

Possible future steps following the presented work could extend current analytical models in order to include various access types to small cells. Indicative example is the distinction of open access type and closed access types for HeNB. Another possible future direction could be the organization of the implemented software as a framework that will provide solutions that can be easily utilized, modified or extended by researchers and analysts interested in the topic in order to experiment on similar issues.

References

1. 3GPP TR 36.922 V11.0.0: Evolved Universal Terrestrial Radio Access (E-UTRA); TDD Home eNode B (HeNB) Radio Frequency (RF) requirements analysis (Release 11). Technical report, 3rd Generation Partnership Project (2012)
2. Guvenc, I., Quek, T., Kountouris, M., Lopez-Perez, D.: Heterogeneous and small cell networks: part 1 [guest editorial]. IEEE Communications Magazine 51(5), 34–35 (2013)
3. Shetty, N., Parekh, S., Walrand, J.: Economics of femtocells. In: IEEE Global Telecommunications Conference, GLOBECOM 2009, pp. 1–6 (December 2009)
4. Duan, L., Huang, J.: Economic viability of femtocell service provision. In: Jain, R., Kannan, R. (eds.) Gamenets 2011. LNICST, vol. 75, pp. 413–428. Springer, Heidelberg (2012)
5. Wang, C.Y., Wei, H.Y.: Profit maximization in femtocell service with contract design. IEEE Transactions on Wireless Communications 12(5), 1978–1988 (2013)
6. Yun, S.Y., Yi, Y., Cho, D.H., Mo, J.: The economic effects of sharing femtocells. IEEE Journal on Selected Areas in Communications 30(3), 595–606 (2012)
7. Informa Telecoms & Media: Small cell market status. Technical report, Small Cell Forum (February 2013), http://www.smallcellforum.org/resources-reports
8. Fiedler, M., Tutschku, K., Chevul, S., Isaksson, L., Binzenhöfer, A.: The throughput utility function: Assessing network impact on mobile services. In: Cesana, M., Fratta, L. (eds.) Euro-NGI 2005. LNCS, vol. 3883, pp. 242–254. Springer, Heidelberg (2006)
9. Markendahl, J., Mkitalo, O.: A comparative study of deployment options, capacity and cost structure for macrocellular and femtocell networks. In: 2010 IEEE 21st International Symposium on Personal, Indoor and Mobile Radio Communications Workshops (PIMRC Workshops), pp. 145–150 (2010)
10. Hu, B., Leopold, A., Pickl, S.: Transition towards renewable energy supplya system dynamics approach. In: Crespo Cuaresma, J., Palokangas, T., Tarasyev, A. (eds.) Green Growth and Sustainable Development. Dynamic Modeling and Econometrics in Economics and Finance, vol. 14, pp. 217–226. Springer, Heidelberg (2013)

11. Johansson, K., Furuskar, A.: Cost efficient capacity expansion strategies using multi-access networks. In: 2005 IEEE 61st Vehicular Technology Conference, VTC 2005-Spring, vol. 5, pp. 2989–2993 (2005)
12. Correia, L., Zeller, D., Blume, O., Ferling, D., Jading, Y., Gdor, I., Auer, G., Van der Perre, L.: Challenges and enabling technologies for energy aware mobile radio networks. IEEE Communications Magazine 48(11), 66–72 (2010)
13. Bock, C., Figuerola, S., Parker, M., Walker, S., Mendes, T., Marques, V., Jungnickel, V., Habel, K., Levi, D.: Convergent radio and fibre architectures for high-speed access. In: 2013 15th International Conference on Transparent Optical Networks (ICTON), pp. 1–4 (2013)
14. Glass, V., Stefanova, S.: Economies of scale for broadband in rural united states. Journal of Regulatory Economics 41(1), 100–119 (2012)
15. Johansson, K., Zander, J., Furuskar, A.: Modelling the cost of heterogeneous wireless access networks. Int. J. Mob. Netw. Des. Innov. 2(1), 58–66 (2007)
16. Chambers, D.: Femtocell versus macrocell voice coverage cost calculator. ThinkSmallCell (February 2009)
17. Babkin, A., Pylenok, A., Ryzhkov, A., Trofimov, A.: Lte network throughput estimation. In: INternet of THings and ITs ENablers (INTHITEN 2013), pp. 95–104 (June 2013)
18. Yamori, K., Ito, H., Tanaka, Y.: Optimum pricing methods for multiple guaranteed bandwidth service. In: Proc. of the 2005, Networking and Electronic Commerce Research Conference, Riva Del Garda, Italy, pp. 349–355 (2005)
19. Canada, C.: The price of staying connected. CBCNews (2013)
20. Vezin, J.B., Giupponi, L., Tyrrell, A., Mino, E., Miroslaw, B.: A femtocell business model: The befemto view. In: Future Network Mobile Summit (FutureNetw), pp. 1–8 (2011)

A Directional Geocast Warning Dissemination Protocol for Vehicular Ad Hoc NETworks (VANETs)

Zouina Doukha[1], Sherali Zeadally[2], and Samira Moussaoui[1]

[1] Department of computer science, University of science and Technology
Houari Boumedienne, Algiers, Algeria
{zdoukha,smoussaoui}@usthb.dz
[2] College of Communication and Information, University of Kentucky, Lexington,
KY 40506-0224, USA
szeadally@uky.edu

Abstract. Multi-hop broadcasting is commonly used by safety applications in Vehicular Ad Hoc Networks (VANETs). By using a multi-hop technique and relay nodes, a sender in VANET can reach all other nodes outside of its communication range. A major problem with this well-known flooding approach is the congestion it causes on the network. Recently proposed protocols aim to reduce congestion by decreasing the number of relaying nodes. However, performing broadcast at each hop causes the same message to be received multiple times at the nodes located between two relays (intermediate nodes). To deal with this problem, we propose a Directional Geocast (DGcast) dissemination protocol aimed at distributing warning messages in VANET. The proposed protocol filters data according to the region it is addressed. We evaluated the performance of DGcast and compared the results with those obtained with previous protocols. DGcast outperforms its peers in term of latency and redundancy.

Keywords: Cross-layer, Geocast, Vehicular, Multi-hop, Network, Protocol, Performance, Safety.

1   Introduction

The design, implementation, and deployment issues of Vehicular Ad hoc NETworks (VANETS) have been reviewed in several papers [1][4]. There is a growing need to make vehicular safety applications reliable and efficient. Thus, it is important for a VANET Media Access Control (MAC) protocol to reduce the medium access delay and packet loss. Currently, safety applications in the VANET environment are mainly based on multi-hop broadcast which is known to be unreliable because the Request To Send/Clear To Send (RTS/CTS) handshaking method [27] is not used. In this work, we focus on safety applications that rely on the dissemination of pertinent information about traffic status to enable drivers to become aware of any hazard or danger in advance. Current warning dissemination protocols for VANETS can be classified into three main categories namely, topology-based, time-based, and cluster-based. In the case of topology-based protocols, nodes maintain a local table about their neighborhood that is updated by periodic beacons. So, the relay node can be designated by the

A. Mellouk et al. (Eds.): WWIC 2014, LNCS 8458, pp. 55–67, 2014.
© Springer International Publishing Switzerland 2014

sender because it knows the nodes in its vicinity. With time-based protocols, the sender has no knowledge about its environment; it simply broadcasts its warning messages. When receiving the warning message, all the nodes wait for some duration of time which can be based on a random value or can be calculated by using functions making use of parameters such as latency and the distance separating the sender and the receiver. The node that waits for the shortest duration sends the message first. All other nodes, while they are in their waiting time, can receive the message again which means that there is a node that relays the communication; they stop waiting consequently and abstain from sending the message. In the case of cluster-based protocols, the network is structured into clusters where the cluster head acts as the relay node. The above strategies still suffer from the redundancy problem because the broadcast transmission is performed at every hop so that the nodes located in the common region covered by two relays therefore receive the message at least twice; multiple receipts of the same message can increase when there is a communication failure during which a retransmission of the message occurs. In fact, existing protocols process messages at the application level and use an acknowledgment as a way to increase the broadcast reliability which is an important contribution but performance of these protocols depends on the MAC level functionalities; yet, as contention, redundancy and collision are problems intrinsically linked to the broadcast communication mode, more effort is needed to address these aforementioned problems. In this work we propose a directional geocast dissemination protocol called DGcast which delivers messages in VANETs by avoiding congestion. This is achieved by filtering data according to the region under consideration. The filter module is added as a sub-layer above the MAC layer. Similar to the other geocast protocols [9][10], in DGcast the message is forwarded in a muli-hop manner to a predefined geographical location known as the geocast region. In addition DGcast affects one-hop neighbors in the surrounding area with the forward and backward areas identified differently. The identifier of the addressed area is enclosed in the forwarded packet to limit the destinations of the packet only to the vehicles located in this area. The remainder of the paper is structured as follows. Existing safety message dissemination protocols for VANET are briefly reviewed in section 2. We present our proposed Directional Geocast (DGcast) dissemination protocol in Section 3. Performance evaluation results are presented in section 4. Section 5 concludes the paper.

2   Related Works and Contributions of This Work

2.1   Related Works

Safety applications are an important component of VANETs and they require efficient strategies that can reduce the probability and the severity of accidents on the roads. There are essentially two principal approaches to address these issues: the first approach makes use of proactive applications that use sensor technologies. In these applications, vehicles can sense the surrounding traffic situation in order to communicate and coordinate their behaviors [5][7]. The second approach makes use of reactive applications that take decision to disseminate warnings when an accident or a risky incident has occurred. In this work we focus on the second approach.

A warning message is characterized by its location, its zone of relevance and its validity duration. So, any warning message dissemination protocol has to ensure these spatial and temporal constraints. Indeed, all vehicles close to the location of the incident have to be advised on time so that they can take the appropriate actions in a timely manner. In this context, various research efforts have investigated various issues related to Vehicle to Infrastructure (V2I) and Vehicle-to-Vehicle (V2V) communications. In V2I applications, proposed solutions [8] take advantage of existing road infrastructures such as traffic sign panels to install equipment called Road Side Units (RSUs) to enable the communication with On Board Units (OBUs) that are embedded inside the vehicles. These approaches are suitable particularly in applications that require connection to a backbone network (traffic management, Internet services, etc.) or for use in environments with low density where the connectivity between vehicles is weak such as highways. However, in emergency situations, the use of infrastructure-based services is problematic because when an accident (or a catastrophe) occurs the installed infrastructure can be easily damaged resulting in communication failures.

In V2V communications, the multi hop broadcast mode is the most often used. Flooding is the simplest technique which is used to perform the dissemination: when a node receives a broadcast message for the first time, it rebroadcasts it immediately. This naïve strategy causes collisions, contention and redundancy problems well known as the "Broadcast storm problem" [15]. One of the main issues investigated by many multi hop broadcast mode protocols is how to decrease the number of nodes (relay nodes) that are responsible of re-broadcasting. As we mentioned previously, warning dissemination protocols can be classified into three classes based on the way that relays are selected as shown in fig.1. In the topology-based class [14][22][25], the use of periodic beacon messages allows the sender to know about its neighborhood, so it selects among its neighbors the farthest one in the opposite direction of the road traffic and designates it as a relay node. The topology-based approach suffers from the drawback that the beacon messages increase the broadcast storm problem.

Some other solutions [12][13] take advantage of the existence of beacons by piggybacking the dissemination packets on beacons frames.

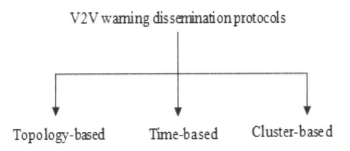

Fig. 1. Warning dissemination protocols

We cannot avoid using the beacon messages because, on one hand, the information (e.g., position, direction, speed, status of neighboring nodes) carried by these messages is very important and on the other hand several protocols such as routing protocols are topology-based. We argue that further solutions need to be developed to keep this mode of communication while eliminating drawbacks such as redundancy, collisions, and contention. In [3], the authors addressed the issue of neighborhood discovery for safety applications, and consider the neighborhood service separately from the application. Several other similar efforts [16][17] attempt to minimize the effect of beacons on safety applications.

Many recently proposed warning protocols belong to the time-based class [11][18][19][20][24][30]. In this class, the receivers of the warning messages wait for a duration of time called the Waiting Time (WT) to decide whether they have to re-broadcast the message. In the best case scenario, the node that has the lowest waiting time re-broadcasts the message. Other nodes when receiving the message again stop their waiting time and abstain from forwarding the message considering they are informed and do not take the role of relay because there is one node that has done. In [18][19], the value of "WT" is inversely proportional to the distance between the sender and the receiver. So, the farthest node located in the transmission range of the sender is always the relay node. In [24] the dissemination message contains a stamp that gives a location 'DP' on the road behind the sender where the signal is stable. A receiver calculates a waiting time commensurately with its distance to the 'DP' point. So, the nearest node to the 'DP' point is the next relay. This means that the farthest node from the sender is not necessarily the relay node. This strategy heightens message receptions which can improve the dissemination reliability, but causes message redundancies. The authors in [20][24] proposed probabilistic solutions to minimize redundancies by integrating parameters such as distance, density and velocity. In [24] the authors argued that the spatial storm problem is due to multiple forwarding by nodes at the boundary. This is because their waiting times are close to each other when the network density increases. They propose p-IVG protocol which is based on decreasing the number of nodes that start their timers when the density increases. This strategy suffers from the drawback that no node relays the transmission. In [30] the authors propose to elect the relay in the border area based on the traffic density. When receiving the message, nodes located in this area wait for a random duration of time. The node that waits the shortest time forwards the message. In this strategy, several nodes can wait for the same duration of time which can cause contention when accessing the communication channel.

Other protocols use directional antennas to decrease the effect of the broadcast storm problem [11]. Directional antennas physically point to a certain direction with a small beam-width that can achieve longer transmission range and better Signal-to-Noise Ratio (SNR). Moreover, in warning applications the message only needs to be sent backward to reach vehicles that are moving in the direction of the danger. So, when a directional antenna is used for broadcasting, it can alleviate the redundant transmission by forwarding the message only in the direction of the dissemination. However, it is shown in [26] that with directional carrier sensing, there are more possible scenarios where a parallel signal transmission may not be detected which can cause collisions so the dissemination application needs to use explicit acknowledgment (ACK) to notify the success of the transmission which is unnecessary with omni-directional antennas. The concept of clusters is largely investigated with both infrastructure-based applications and V2V applications [2][6][21]. The main difficulty with cluster-based solutions is cluster formation and its maintenance in a distributed manner. In cluster-based protocols the network is divided into several clusters; a head is selected among nodes (known as members) within a cluster and it has the responsibility of forwarding the warning message. In [21], the authors proposed a Directional Propagation Protocol (DPP) where the data is propagated in multiple hops within a cluster; but they do not make a reference to the cluster formation. In [6], a cluster is considered as a group of vehicles with multi hop radio connectivity. In Both [6] and [21] the dissemination protocol uses the opposite direction to relay messages between clusters which cannot communicate directly. The use of clusters can be suitable when the topology of the network does not change fast.

2.2 Contributions of This Work

Displayed Emergency dissemination protocol requirements are very strict. Indeed, such protocols have to ensure a high delivery ratio of warning messages with low latency which is difficult to obtain because of the congestion problem caused by broadcast. Many past efforts have previously explored how to avoid unnecessary forwarding at the application layer. However, since the MAC layer approach has a direct impact on upper layers, we need to take MAC layer factors also into consideration to achieve fast, reliable warning message delivery. In this context we propose a cross layer solution that can disseminate warning messages and avoids congestion by filtering unnecessary data using a filter module residing above the MAC layer. This filter module discards unnecessary messages (redundant messages) from being processed by the application layer. So, the region where a vehicle is located can be considered as a dynamic multicast address that allows the vehicle to know early at the MAC level whether it is a destination of a message.

3 DGcast: Our Proposed Warning Dissemination Protocol

3.1 Assumptions

We assume that vehicles use wireless communication through omni-directional radio antennas with a transmission range R. Each vehicle is equipped with a device (such as a Global Positioning System (GPS) device) enabling it to obtain its geographical location at any time and a preloaded digital map, which provides general information about roads. The MAC layer provides information about the neighborhood by making use of periodic beacon transmissions. A beacon packet contains information such as physical location, velocity and direction of the vehicle. The neighborhood service allows vehicles to construct tables containing neighbors' status making it more reliable [3]. Emergency messages are transmitted in the opposite direction of vehicle's motions. We consider only a section of road.

3.2 System Overview

An emergency message can be generated by a vehicle (called initiator) in a dangerous situation. For example, in case of an accident, a vehicle can recognize by itself that it is in a dangerous situation through sensors that are able to detect internal events like airbag ignition; it can also sense a danger around it by using sensors and cameras. Omni-directional antennas used in wireless transmissions allow a mobile node to transmit its signal all around it within a transmission range R. Most of the recently proposed dissemination protocols have improved their performances by decreasing the effects of the broadcast storm problem [15]. However, the fact that the message is broadcasted at every one hop causes unavoidable redundancy in the zone between two relay vehicles. As we mentioned previously, redundant messages can cause congestion in internal queues of the nodes. Other protocols which use directional antennas to focus the signal's energy in one direction can increase the communication range of nodes, and can yield better signal quality by covering only the relevant zones. However, the longer the communication range the higher is the risk of collisions. In addition, the sender of the warning message needs an explicit acknowledgment to ensure that its packet has been received. Our proposed strategy is topology-based because it takes advantage of the neighborhood information such as neighbors' positions provided by the periodic beacons so that the relay node is selected in advance by the sender; and use multi-hop broadcast to achieve the dissemination through all the nodes in a section of the road. We propose a cross layer approach that operates above the MAC layer to filter data so that only pertinent information is communicated to the application layer which processes it. All redundant messages are destroyed at the cross layer. In this section we introduce our proposed DGcast protocol design.

3.3   DGast Protocol Design

When a node holding a warning message has to forward it as an initiator or a relay node, it considers its surrounding area as two geographical regions: the region it is moving toward (region 0) and the region behind it (region 1) as shown in fig.2. It selects among its neighbors located in region 1 the furthest one and elects it as the next relay, and then the packet is broadcasted. When receiving the warning message, each node determines whether it is located in region 1 or not based on the locations of vehicles and the digital map. The major benefit in determining the node's region is to avoid processing the message if the node is located in region 0. So, we use a common reference point such as the next intersection which is considered as a specific point on the road. The receiver of the message calculates 'ds' and 'dr' values, where 'ds' is the Euclidean distance between the sender and the next intersection and 'dr' is the Euclidean distance between the receiver and the next intersection. In fig.2., 'dr' belongs to the current relay; all the nodes that are in the sender vicinity calculate their local 'dr'. If 'dr' is greater than 'ds', a node concludes that it is located in the addressed region (region 1) otherwise it is not. In the first case, it compares its identifier with the identifier of the next relay vehicle enclosed in the packet and if it is the same the node recognizes itself as the relay. It then updates the packet with information such as next relay, previous relay, etc. and rebroadcasts the message. If the receiver node is not designated as the relay by the sender, it keeps itself informed. In the second case, the receiver is located in region 0 ('dr' less than 'ds').

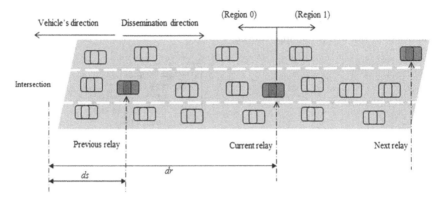

Fig. 2. Proposed Dissemination Strategy

The receiver checks whether it is the previous relay; it then considers the packet as an acknowledgment, otherwise it simply ignores the packet. If the previous relay does not receive the packet after a short time it considers the packet as lost and repeats its transmission until it receives the acknowledgement. If a relay node senses no neighbors, it first broadcasts the message that serves as an acknowledgement to the previous relay and keeps it until a vehicle enters its vicinity. It then executes the same algorithm as a relay node.

Our proposed DGcast dissemination protocol makes use of two modules: a filter module above the MAC layer and an application module as shown in fig.3. The filter module determines whether the node is located in the addressed region by comparing the two values 'ds' and 'dr'. If it is in the region, it passes the message to the application module which processes it.

The application module has to determine one of the two cases:

- If the current node is a relay node,
- If the message is a warning or an acknowledgment: the only case where the message reaches the application layer in (region 0) is when the receiver is the previous relay vehicular node.

The DGcast protocol has four characteristics which can be summarized as follows:

- There is no need to incur the *'waiting time'* because the application makes use of the neighborhood table which stores information such as the identifiers of the neighbors, their positions, speed etc.

- There is no need to have multiple antenna systems which need be properly oriented (positioned) and synchronized between the sender and the receiver and do not need explicit acknowledgement.

- The filter module does not process the message in the sense of making decisions such as forwarding or selecting the next relay. The module only decides if a vehicle is a relevant target for the warning message according to its location.

Since the filter module resides above the MAC layer, only relevant packets are processed by the application, so the receipt of multiple copies of the same message by the nodes does not affect the application.

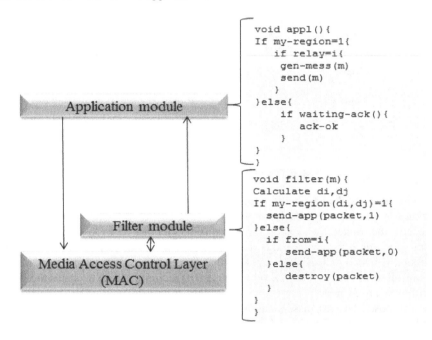

Fig. 3. Proposed Architecture

3.4   Message Format

The format of an emergency message is described in Table 1. When a warning message "*m*" is received by a node "i" from a node "j", the filter module is executed to decide whether the message has to be passed to the application layer. To achieve this, the filter uses local information that gives the vehicle location, the field 'Origin' that is used to get the location of the sender and the location of the next intersection to determine if the vehicle is located in region 0 or region 1. There are three cases: in the first case, the node can be in region 0 but its identifier matches the '*from*' field of the packet, thus the message is an acknowledgment and it is passed to the application module. In the second case, the node is located in region 1 and is therefore one of the multiple destinations of the message. The node's application module has to determine if it is selected as a relay; if so, it rebroadcasts the message otherwise, it just keeps it. In the third case the node is located in region 0 and its identifier does not match the 'from' field of the packet; the packet is discarded (ignored).

Table 1. Messsage format

Field	Description
Id_mess	Sequence number
Type_mess	Emergency
R	The region; 0=before the vehicle, 1=behind the vehicle
Data	Message content
From	The identifier of the previous relay
Origin	The identifier of the sender
Nxt_relay	The identifier of the next relay

4 Performance Evaluation of Proposed DGcast Dissemination Protocol

4.1 Measurement Procedure

We used the Network Simulator NS2 [28] in all simulation tests. In our experiments, we simulated a road of 4 lanes and 10 km. Vehicles moved with a mean velocity of 30 m/s. We studied the behavior of our proposed protocol under various mobility scenarios generated with the MOVE generator [29] by varying the vehicles densities (respectively 2, 4, 6 and 8 vehicles per lane per kilometer). To evaluate the performance of our proposed DGcast protocol, we compared it to three previously proposed approaches namely, the topology-based, time-based and cluster-based approaches. For the topology-based approach, the one that is closest to our approach for comparison is [14]. For the time-based approach, we used the formula in [19] to calculate the waiting time. For the cluster-based strategy we used the approach in [21] with one hop forwarding to make it close to our proposed DGcast approach and to enable the communication between clusters, two successive clusters are considered as a non-disjoint sets of nodes. At the MAC layer we used the IEEE 802.11p standard and a transmission range of 250 m. The radio propagation model is set to the Two Ray Ground model. We used the following performance metrics in our performance evaluation tests:

- *Dissemination delivery ratio*: The number of the informed nodes out of the number of the nodes in the network.

- *Number of generated messages*: the number dissemination messages transmitted by relays along the road.

- *Number of redundant messages*: where a redundancy occurs when an informed node receives the same message again.

- *Number of redundant messages eliminated*: The number of redundant message that had been discarded at the filter module.

- *Dissemination delay*: The dissemination delay is the time interval between the first generated message and the first message received by the last informed vehicle in the network.

4.2   Analysis of Performance Results

The simulation results show that the delivery ratio reaches 100% for all mobility scenarios. Indeed, all vehicles used in the simulation tests received the emergency message. Our simulation results demonstrate that DGcast is reliable. This result will be a requirement for future dissemination protocols because several protocols reached the same delivery ratio [9] [10][19] as we obtained for those we simulated. Fig.4. shows the simulation results.

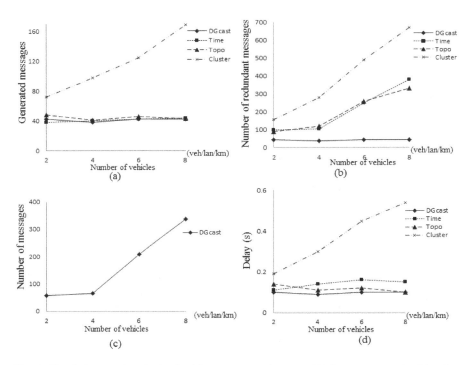

Fig. 4. Simulation results obtained with our proposed protocol DGcast compared with other approaches

In terms of the number of generated messages, we note from the results in fig.4.a, that the cluster approach generates the highest number of messages. This is because the cluster heads which are the relay nodes are located in the front of each cluster and have the responsibility of forwarding even there is a farther node from the previous cluster head in the common area between clusters. Other solutions yield fairly similar results regardless of the vehicle density.

In terms of the number of redundant messages, our proposed protocol (DGcast) does not generate redundant messages because the filter module eliminates all unnecessary messages. In contrast, other (topology-based, time-based and cluster-based) protocols suffer from a large number of redundant messages especially when the vehicle density increases (as shown in fig.4.b). fig.4.c confirms this result by giving the number of redundant messages that have been eliminated by the filter module. In terms of the dissemination delay, small delays are obtained with all protocols except the cluster-based protocol due to the high number of hops. Fig.4.d shows that DGcast gives lower dissemination delays compared to the time-based protocol. This is due to the fact that a relay node is chosen by the sender in the case of DGcast while with the time-based protocol a relay node has to wait for duration of time before retransmitting the message.

5   Conclusion

In this paper we showed that our proposed protocol DGcast gives better performances in terms of delivery ratio, redundancies and dissemination delay over other approaches. Moreover, the use of a filter as a sublayer above the MAC layer helps to avoid the handling of unnecessary (redundant) messages by the application layer. Our study can provide a guideline for improving the design of protocols that suffer from redundant messages at the application level.

References

1. Zeadally, S., Hunt, R., Chen, Y.S., Irwin, A., Hassan, A.: Vehicular ad hoc networks (VANETS): Status, Results, and Challenges. Telecommunication Systems 50(4) (2012)
2. Zaydoun, Y., SyedMasud, M.: A novel algorithm to form stable clusters in vehicular ad hoc networks on highways. EURASIP Journal on Wireless Communications and Networking (2012)
3. Schmidt, R.K., Leinmüller, T., Schoch, E., Kargl, F., Schäfer, G.: Exploration of Adaptive Beaconing for Efficient Intervehicle Safety Communication. IEEE Network 24(1), 14–19 (2010)
4. Theodore, L., Tientrakool, W., Nicholas, F.: A Survey of Inter-Vehicle Communication Protocols and their Applications. IEEE Comm. Surveys and Tutorials 11(2) (2009)
5. Eigner, R., Lutz, G.: Collision Avoidance in VANETs: An Application for ontological context models. In: Proceedings of Sixth Annual IEEE International Conference on Pervasive Computing and Communications (2008)
6. Schwartz, R., Barbosa, R., Meratnia, N., Heinjek, G., Scholten, H.: A Simple and Robust Dissemination Protocol for VANETs. In: Proceedings of the 16th European Wireless Conference, Italy, pp. 214–222 (2010)
7. Taleb, T., Benslimane, A., Letaief, K.: Toward an Effective Risk-Conscious and Collaborative Vehicular Collision Avoidance System. IEEE Transactions on Veficular Technology 59(3) (2010)
8. Nisha, K.W., Dorle, S.S.: Implementation of Protocol for Efficient Data Storage and Data Dissemination in VANET. International Journal of Advanced Research in Computer Science and Electronics Engineering 1(2) (2012)
9. Yu, Q., Heijenk, G.: Abiding geocast for warning message dissemination in vehicular ad hoc networks. In: Proceedings of the IEEE Vehicular Networks and Applications Workshop, Beijing, pp. 400–404 (May 2008)
10. Kheawchaoom, P., Kittipiyakul, S., Ayutaya, K.S.N.: iDTSG time-stable geocast for post crash notification in vehicular highway networks. In: Proceedings of the 9th International Conference on Electrical Engineering/Electronics. Computer, Telecommunications and Information Technology (ECTI-CON), Phetchaburi, pp. 1–4 (May 2012)

11. Da, L., Hongyu, H., Xu, L., Minglu, L., Feilong, T.: A Distance-based Directional Broadcast Protocol for Urban Vehicular Ad Hoc Network. In: Proceedings of International Conference on Wireless Communications, Networking and Mobile Computing (WiCom), pp. 1520–1523 (2007)
12. Wolterink, K., Heijenk, G.J., Karagiannis, G.: Information Dissemination in VANETS by Piggybacking on Beacons – An Analysis of the impact of Network Parameters. In: Proceedings of IEEE Vehicular Networking Conference (VNC), Amsterdam, pp. 94–101 (2011)
13. Yousefi, S., Fathy, M., Benslimane, A.: Performance of beacon safety message dissemination in Vehicular Ad hoc Networks (VANETs). Journal of Zhejiang University Science (JZUS) 8(12) (2007)
14. Sun, M.T., Feng, W.C., Lai, T.H., Yamada, K., Okada, H.: Gps-based message broadcast for adaptive inter-vehicle communications. In: Proceedings of the 52nd IEEE Vehicular Technology Conference (VTC), Boston, vol. (6), pp. 2685–2692 (September 2000)
15. Ni, S.Y., Tseng, Y.C., Chen, Y.S., Sheu, J.P.: The Broadcast Storm Problem in a Mobile Ad Hoc Network. Wireless Networks 8(2-3), 153–167 (2002)
16. Ghafoor, K.Z., Bakar, K.A., Eenennaam, E.M., Khokhar, R.H., Gonzalez, A.J.: A Fuzzy Logic Approach to Beaconing for Vehicular Ad hoc Networks. Telecommunication Systems 52(1), 139–149 (2013)
17. Alvin, S., Maolin, T., Yanming, F., Looi, M.: Context-aware rate-adaptive beaconing for efficient and scalable vehicular safety communication. International Journal of Communications, Network and System Sciences 5(9), 534–547 (2012)
18. Briesemeister, L., Schafers, L., Hommel, G.: Dissemination Messages among Highly Mobile Hosts Based on Inter Vehicle Communication. In: Proceedings of IEEE Intelligent Vehicles Symposium, USA, pp. 522–527 (2000)
19. Benslimane, A.: Optimized Dissemination of Alarm messages in Vehicular Ad Hoc Networks. In: Proceedings of the 7th IEEE International Conference (HSNMC), France, pp. 655–666 (2004)
20. Ihn-Han, B.: Design and Evaluation of a Hybrid Intelligent Broadcast Algorithm for Alert Message Dissemination in VANETs. International Journal of Grid and Distributed Computing 4(4) (2011)
21. Little, T., Agarwal, A.: An Information Propagation Scheme for VANETs. In: Proceedings of the 8th IEEE Conference on Intelligent Transportation Systems, Austria, pp. 155–160 (September 2005)
22. Samara, S.R.G., Alsalihy, W.A.H.A., Ramadass, S.: Increase emergency message reception in vanet. Journal of Applied Sciences 11(14), 2606–2612 (2011)
23. Yu, S., Cho, G.H.: An effective message flooding method for vehicle safety communication. In: Ma, J., Jin, H., Yang, L.T., Tsai, J.J.-P. (eds.) UIC 2006. LNCS, vol. 4159, pp. 219–228. Springer, Heidelberg (2006)
24. Khaled, I., Weigle, M., Abuelela, M.: p-IVG: Probabilistic Inter-Vehicle Geocast for Dense Vehicular Networks. In: Proceedings of 69th IEEE Conference on Vehicular Technology, VTC (2009)
25. Doukha, Z., Moussaoui, S., Haouari, N., Delhoum, M.E.A.: An efficient emergency message dissemination protocol in a vehicular ad hoc network. In: Benlamri, R. (ed.) NDT 2012, Part I. CCIS, vol. 293, pp. 459–469. Springer, Heidelberg (2012)
26. Vilzmann, R., Bettstetter, C.: A Survey on MAC Protocols for Ad Hoc Networks with Directional Antennas. In: Proceedings of (EUNICE) Open European Summer School, Colmenarejo, Spain, pp. 268–274 (July 2005)

27. IEEE, 'IEEE 802.11 Standard for Information Technology– Telecommunications and Information Exchange Between Systems– Local and Metropolitan Area Networks–Specific Requirements Part11: Wireless LAN Medium Access Control and Physical Layer'. IEEE P802.11p/D10.0 (2007)
28. The Network Simulator NS2
29. Karnadi, F., Mo, Z., Lan, K.: Rapid Generation of Realistic Mobility Models for VANET. In: Proceedings of IEEE Wireless Communication and Networking Conference (WCNC), pp. 2506–2511 (2007)
30. Rezaei, F., Naik, K., Nayak, A., Yousefi, S.: Effective Warning Data Dissemination Scheme in Vehicular Networks for Intelligent Transportation System Applications. In: Proceedings of 16th IEEE International Conference on Intelligent Transportation Systems, The Hague, Netherland, pp. 1071–1076 (October 2013)

Cost Modeling of Advanced Heterogeneous Wireless Networks under Excessive User Demand

Vladimir Nikolikj[1] and Toni Janevski[2]

[1] Vip operator - Member of Telekom Austria Group, Skopje, Macedonia
v.nikolikj@vipoperator.mk
[2] Ss. Cyril and Methodius University, Faculty of Electrical Engineering and Information Technologies, Skopje, Macedonia
tonij@feit.ukim.edu.mk

Abstract. In this article we aim to determine the most cost-effective deployment strategies for heterogeneous wireless networks through up-to-date comparative cost analysis. For that purpose we develop a cost model using as input base station class specific parameters related to unit cost, coverage and capacity. The network dimensioning is done for different volumes of data served with advanced radio access technologies like: LTE-Advanced and IEEE 802.11n. For the evaluation of moderate area capacity, outdoor pico cell deployment appears to be most cost-effective solution for the assessed dense urban area. Additionally, through case study we compare the cost-capacity performance of the macro and femto cell networks under the high to excessive demand of up to 80 GB/user/month. Femto cell solution is more cost efficient when new macro base station sites need to be deployed, unless the macro cell network is strengthened with more spectrum or the LTE-Advanced carrier aggregation functionality is introduced.

Keywords: Cost modeling, Heterogonous Wireless Networks, LTE-Advanced, IEEE 802.11n.

1 Introduction

The future wireless network architectures are heterogeneous, with hierarchically ranged macro (MaBS), micro (MiBS), pico (PBS) and femto (FBS) base stations sites/cells complemented with particular wireless local area network (WLAN/Wi-Fi). While the MaBS and MiBS cover a larger outdoor area, PBS could be deployed indoor and outdoor (like metro cell). FBS is exclusively deployed indoor. FBS, PBS and MiBS cells are referred as "small cells" [1]. In case when user's capacity demand increase by 100% annually according to [2], operators are forced to increase their cost efficiency especially due to severe decoupling of the incomes from the traffic. A number of papers have been published on modeling the cost-efficiency by comparison of the MaBS cell deployment with the small-cell deployment and suggesting utilization of joint or heterogeneous and even cooperative networks. Analysis of MaBS, MiBS and PBS HSPA cells capacity-cost comparisons including IEEE 802.11a, are provided within [3], [4] and [5]. Cost comparisons of LTE with HSPA deployed

A. Mellouk et al. (Eds.): WWIC 2014, LNCS 8458, pp. 68–81, 2014.

MaBS networks and FBS solutions are extensively covered within [5] and [6]. Additionally the evaluation of the economic gain provided by various deployments of FBS and MaBS for LTE mobile broadband services is outlined in [7].

In this article we originally introduce the techno-economics evaluation and comparative cost modeling of MaBS, MiBS, PBS and FBS utilizing LTE Releases 10 and 11 or LTE-Advanced (LTE-A) RAT ([8] and [9]), alongside with Wi-Fi standard IEEE 802.11n [10]. We propose model for evaluating the setup costs of heterogeneous wireless systems through providing estimates for CAPEX/OPEX per cost unit of various wireless network deployments. Furthermore the model provides estimates for the total discounted deployment cost as a function of user demand for different BS classes. Consequently, the ultimate contribution of this article comes with the extensive and "up to date" comparative analysis needed to properly model advanced heterogonous wireless networks from cost perspective and under heavy traffic load.

Additionally, the special focus is set on the comparison between MaBS and FBS deployment taking into account the current developments in spectral efficiency coming with the LTE-A, and the use of up to 30 MHz aggregated spectrum for the MaBS scenarios. As according to [11], more than 80% of the mobile traffic is generated in indoors, we create long-term investment case study related to indoor office users. In order to determine more realistically the cost-capacity performance, besides already discussed wall attenuation and indoor coverage strategies into [5] and [6], additionally we consider the use of the carrier aggregation functionality of LTE-A RAT. For all deployment scenarios we analyze: deploying new sites and reusing the existing sites.

The article is structured as follows. The next section provides estimates for the coverage and base station classes specific parameters. In the section 3 we outline capacity related inputs. Next section provides user demand analysis for RAT used. In section 5 a general cost model for heterogeneous wireless networks is introduced by showing average cost inputs per unit. Further, we turn to cost-effectiveness determination of different network configurations. Prior the last section we develop case study for MaBS and FBS. The article concludes with a summary of key findings.

2   Coverage of the Heterogeneous Base Stations

We model the coverage of particular cell area of the BS site A_{cell}, as follows:

$$A_{cell} = \pi \times r_{cell}^2 \qquad (1)$$

where r_{cell} is the cell range which primarily gives the number of the BS sites required to cover the targeted geographical coverage area over which the users can be served. The signal strength depends on the distance from the base station and for indoor users on the amount of attenuation in walls and floors [12]. According to [13], the maximum allowed signal attenuation or path loss, between the mobile and base station antenna is estimated by the "link budget" calculations. The maximum path loss allows the maximum cell range to be estimated with a suitable propagation model [14]. Within [13], the LTE link budgets and the cell ranges are calculated using the Okumura–Hata propagation model. The calculation shows that urban cell range varies from 0.6 km at 2.6 GHz to 1.4 km at 900 MHz. Thus, when evaluating the cell range, we use the smallest cell range of 0.6 km (in the band 2.6 GHz) as reference to ensure 1 Mbps even at the cell borders [13]. This means that all average user data rates lower than 1 Mbps will be met even at the cell borders for the cell ranges equal or lower than 0.6 km. Based on the elaborations in [3] and [4] we assume 0.57 km for MaBS, 0.27 km for MiBS and 0.15 km range for the outdoor PBS. FBS cell range in [5] is assumed to be 0.050 km and 0.01 – 0.030 km in [15]. In this article we put accent on the IEEE 802.11n Wi-Fi standard, operating at the 5GHz carrier frequency. According to [3], we assume approximately 50% shorter cell range compared to PBS. Within Table 1, we summarize BS site specific parameters related to coverage.

3   Capacity of the Radio Access Technology

Based on [6] the peak, the average and cell edge spectral efficiency are identified. According to [12], we model the capacity of certain BS site as follows:

$$C_{site} = W \times N_{cell} \times S_{eff} \tag{2}$$

where W is allocated bandwidth in MHz, N_{cell} is the number of cells within the site and S_{eff} is the cell spectral efficiency in bps/Hz. Based on [8] and [9] the average spectral efficiency for LTE-A varies from 6.6, 4.2 and 3.8 bit/s/Hz/cell for the indoor, microcellular and base coverage urban environments, respectively (environment definitions are according to [16]). According to [17], an interference problem occurs to non-FBS cell with the creation of the so called "Closed User Group" deployment FBS model (access granted to only small group of users). As proposed by [18], in adjacent-channel deployments (the FBS is deployed on a dedicated carrier), the coverage holes are considerably easier to minimize and control than when the FBS is deployed on the same carrier as the macro layer (co-channel deployment - sharing the channel) with the MaBS network). Hence, in this article we consider FBS deployment in a different frequency band than MaBS. Currently, the LTE FBS are developed with 5, 10 and 15 MHz bandwidth (achieving up to 37, 75 and 112 Mbps in downlink, respectively) and available from 8 to 16 users simultaneously [19]. Author in [15], indicates that 4G FBS will utilize the bandwidth of 20 MHz per carrier. We use the indoor average spectral efficiency of 6.6 bps/Hz and 20 MHz of spectrum for FBS.

Table 1. Base station class - coverage specific parameters

BS Parameter	Macro	Micro	Pico	Femto	IEEE 802.11n
Range (km)	0.57	0.27	0.15	0.030	0.050
Coverage (km²)	1.020	0.229	0.071	0.003	0.008
Sectors per BS	3	1	1	1	1
Carriers per Sector	1 – 3	1 – 2	1	1	1
Cells per BS	3 – 9	1 – 2	1	1	1

Table 2. Radio access technology – bandwidth and capacity specfic parameters

Cell Type/RAT	Bandwidth (MHz)	Sectors x Carriers	Av. Cell Spectr. Ef. (bps/Hz/cell)	Av. BS Cell Capacity (Mbps)	Av. BS Site Capacity (Mbps)
Macro LTE	20	3 x 1	1.67	33.4	100.2
Macro LTE-A	20	3 x 1	3.80	76.0	228.0
Micro LTE-A	20	1 x 1	4.20	84.0	84.0
Pico LTE-A	20	1 x 1	4.20	84.0	84.0
Femto LTE-A	20	1 x 1	6.60	132.0	132.0
IEEE 802.11n	40	1 x 2	6.00	240.0	240.0

According to [20], it is very difficult to exceed 50-60% of the nominal bit rate of the underlying physical layer of Wi-Fi. Frame aggregations techniques are used to improve the MAC efficiency [21]. Authors in [22] by using IEEE 802.11n yield MAC channel efficiency of 61.5%. Authors in [23] pointed that 802.11n performs less efficiently in higher speeds or 40% for 648Mbps. According to [10], IEEE 802.11n expands the bandwidth to 40 MHz channel and data rate increase up to a 600 Mbps with up to 4 streams of the Wi-Fi AP. Hence, in this article we use 40% MAC efficiency level. Table 2 summarizes the RAT specific parameters.

4   Cost Modeling of Different Base Station Classes

For the cost analysis in this paper we limit the infrastructure cost model to the radio access network (RAN), including only capital expenditures (CAPEX) and operational expenditures (OPEX) for the BS equipment, site and transmission. We base our cost structure modelling to the methodology developed in [3]. For a given BS i, the sum of the annual expenditures are discounted as follows [4]:

$$\xi_i = \sum_{k=0}^{K-1} \frac{\alpha_{k,i}}{(1+\beta)^k} \tag{3}$$

where $\alpha_{k,i}$ is the sum of expenditures occurred within year k of a BS of class i and β is the discount rate. In all analyzed scenarios in this paper we assume K = 5 years, and β = 10 %. Also, according to [24], [25], we consider the price erosion of 10% letting $\alpha_{k,i}$ to reduce from CAPEX perspective. Authors in [5] for 2010 year estimate that cost for deploying a new MaBS site in the urban area is 110 k€ including transmission and that the cost for radio equipment supporting three sectors and 5–20 MHz to 10 k€, yielding to total CAPEX of 120 k€. According to [3] for the reference year 2007 the price of a single-carrier MaBS equals 20 k€, and the price of additional transceivers is e 5 k€ per sector per carrier frequency. This gives that cost for 2-carrier and 3-carrier MaBS site equipment is 35 k€ and 50 k€, respectively. Radio network controller cost in 2007 is estimated at 1.3 k€ per cell, upfront cost for transmission 5 k€ and 30 k€ is the price for the installation & deployment of the site. This results with the total CAPEX of 97 k€ for the 3-carrier MaBS, and 20% to 40% cheaper investment for

2-carrier and single carrier MaBS deployment, respectively. According to [3], we also consider that the price of a MiBS and PBS station equals 50% and 15%, respectively, of a single-carrier MaBS equipment, with a note that PBS needs 2 k€ for transmission, and MiBS and PBS requires 10 k€ and 2 k€ for the site deployment, respectively. Furthermore, a carrier grade Wi-Fi access point costs is 1 k€, plus additional cost of e 2 k€ per supporting equipment.

Regarding the OPEX, authors in [5] assumes 30 k€ annual cost for the new MaBS sites deployment with 10% annual OPEX growth and author of [3] considers 13.4 k€ for the single carrier MaBS. In this paper we assume 20 k€ OPEX for the 3-carrier MaBS site. According to [6], on average the deployment of one FBS is around 1 k€. Regarding FBS, authors in [5] estimated the annual OPEX to be 0.5 k€ per access point. Table 3 summarizes the cost assumptions on CAPEX, annual OPEX and total discounted cost for each BS class of the greenfield deployment.

5   User Demand and Traffic Densities

The mobile broadband penetration of all active users has reached 54% in EU countries and the volume of mobile data traffic is expected to grow more than tenfold in the period from 2010 to 2015, reaching almost 8.000 million GB of data in Europe [26]. According to [27], in 2013 the total monthly smartphone traffic reached 1.0 Exabyte. Accordingly, in the modeling analysis we assume three levels of demand: moderate 9.0 GB, high 27.0 GB and rather excessive usage of 80 GB per user and month (31 days). We consider that the usage will be spread out over 8 hours per day, translating into a busy hour rate of 12.5%, in line with the industry standard as assumed in [28]. Also, we consider only uniform spatial traffic density within the simulated test area [29]. Conversion of the load/user/month to the user data rates (Mbps) and capacity per area unit for 10.000 users (Gbps/km²) is given in Table 4. The presumed demand levels corresponds to average user data rates from approximately 100, 300 and up to 900 kbit/s, respectively during the 8 busy working hours. Also, we can see that the total data demand for the 10000 users in 1 km² area, moves from 1.0 to 9.0 Gbps. Additionally we assume radio resources utilization rate of 80%, meaning there is considerate spare capacity of 25% left on top of the demanded capacity for the burst traffic (see e.g. [30] for analysis of LTE-A with bursty traffic model).

Table 3. Estimates of the initial, operational and total discounted cost in present value for new base stations deployment, using LTE-A and IEEE 802.11n

Cell Type/RAT	CAPEX	OPEX	*Total discounted cost for 5 years*
Macro (1 carrier)	60.7	15.5	100.4
Macro (2 carriers)	80.2	17.8	127.9
Macro (3 carriers)	100.0	20.0	151.2
Micro LTE-A	29.8	10.4	61.9
Pico LTE-A	11.2	3.4	21.2
Femto LTE-A	1.0	0.5	2.7
IEEE 802.11n	3.1	1.6	8.5

Table 4. Conversion of load/user/month to the user data rates (Mbps) and capacity per area unit (Gbps/km²)

Load	GB/user/month	Mbit/s/user	Mbit/s/user (80% utilization)	Gbit/s/km²
Moderate	9.0	0.081	0.101	1.0
High	27.0	0.242	0.302	3.0
Excessive	80.0	0.717	0.896	9.0

6   Deployment Cost Comparisons with Moderate Demand

In this section the costs for different network configurations are evaluated to respond to the moderate user demand within the considered office center area. We compare the total discounted cost, coverage and capacity estimates for each of the BS technologies as elaborated within the previous sections. Fig. 1 depicts the total cost as a function of area capacity or its throughput. At traffic load of 1 000 Mbit/s/km², 5 x LTE-A 3-sector MaBS equipped with 3 carriers are required per km². LTE-A MaBS deployment has the lowest cost for the capacities below 0.5 Gbps, regardless that owns highest cost per unit. The total cost of MaBS is lower due to the more limited coverage area of MiBS and PBS deployments. Nevertheless, for capacity above 400 Mbit/s/km², the deployment cost with MiBS almost follows the deployment cost with MaBS, what could be explained with almost perfect balance of the ranges and the ratio of the cost per unit of these two solutions. Thus, PBS and MiBS are with almost the same total cost of around 400 k€ up to the 400 Mbit/s. PBS continuous to be the most cost effective deployment scenario above the 400 Mbit/s.

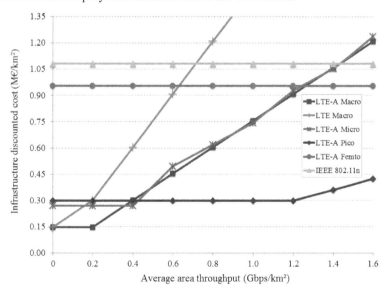

Fig. 1. Total discounted infrastructure cost in Million € as function of capacity per km² for different cellular LTE/LTE-A base station classes and IEEE 802.11n Wi-Fi deployment

Thus, the outdoor PBS (or metro BS) cellular network deployed with LTE-A RAT should be the most cost effective greenfield deployment for metro services requiring low area coverage, having in mind that within the densely populated urban area the BS ranges are from the lower importance compared to the goal the capacity to be achieved with lower cost. From other side the MaBS network for greenfield deployments could be the most cost effective system for services primarily requiring wide area coverage. Still, FBS are less expensive than MaBS and MiBS for traffic densities above 1.2 Gbps/km² and Wi-Fi above 1.4 Gbps/km². The most ineffective cost solution is the MaBS deployment with LTE RAT, becoming more expensive than FBS and Wi-Fi solution for above 600 and 700 Mbps/km², respectively. In Fig. 1, it can be noticed exactly for what traffic loads the particular base station class becomes range limited (coverage area with single BS is below 1 km²) and capacity limited (capacity with single BS is below the targeted capacity of 1000 Mbit/s/km² in this observation). The corresponding breakeven points are given in Table 5. It can be noticed that the PBS will provide most adequate balance between the cost effectiveness and coverage limitation. Furthermore, with the cost estimates we elaborated above, the MaBS and MiBS deployment very likely will be capacity limited for the higher capacity demands than 1.0 Gbps/km².   Consequently within the next section we analyze the case study where for one of the deployment options with MaBS we include additional carrier, in order to assess the impact of the second carrier towards making the MaBS less capacity limited. Finally, despite that it is obvious that Wi-Fi and FBS are strictly range limited, it can be noticed that these deployment options are almost unlimited from the capacity point of view. Even more, the FBS solution is more cost effective than Wi-Fi deployment. Consequently, we will develop one of the deployment scenarios with FBS in the case study outlined in the next section.

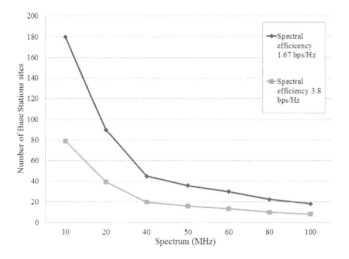

Fig. 2. Number of macro base station sites as function of spectral efficiency (LTE (1.67 bps/Hz) and LTE-Advanced (3.8 bps/Hz)) and bandwidth (MHz)

Table 5. Breakeven points when the particular BS class becomes capacity limited

BS Class (sectors x carriers)	LTE Macro (3x1)	LTE-A Macro (3x1)	LTE-A Micro (1x1)	LTE-A Pico (1x1)	LTE-A Femto (1x1)	IEEE 802.11n
BS per km²	0.980	0.980	4.37	14.2	353.9	127.4
Area capacity Mbps/km²	98	223	367	1189	46709	30573

7   Long-Term Investment Case Study

7.1   Case Study Inputs Modeling

In this section trough the case study we will compare from primarily CAPEX perspective various deployment strategies using LTE-A RAT at 3-sector MaBS or FBS and taking into account the demand, coverage, capacity and cost modeling as presented into the previous sections. In particular, we consider construction of a new office center for 10000 office workers, consisted of 10 five floor buildings within 1 km² urban area (for comparison purposes inputs are identical as in [6]). We evaluate the network dimensioning options with high (3.0 Gbit/s/km²) and with excessive (9.0 Gbit/s/km²) capacity demand, in accordance with Table 5. For the dimensioning of the MaBS network we consider three different scenarios. First within the initial scenario, we perform the cost analysis using for the 20 MHz for macro-layer in the 2.6 GHz band together with the average spectral efficiency of LTE-A RAT. Within the second scenario we consider two strategies to compensate for wall penetration losses: leveraging the coverage layer and/or increasing the capacity layer. The third scenario covers the MaBS deployment with use of carrier aggregation as capacity improvement option. We consider two separated cases for each of the three deployment strategies: first presuming that all MaBS sites need to be deployed from start and second that there are sites that can be re-used. Since a cell area of 1 km² corresponds to a cell radius of 0.57 km, our requirements on average user data rates during busy hours would be met even at the cell borders with the excessive broadband demand (~ 0.9 Mbps compared to 1 Mbps as defined in [13]). Table 6 summarizes the capacity per MaBS site for various chunks of available bandwidth in MHz, for LTE and LTE-A RATs deployments in urban environment. With these capacity figures we can estimate the number of MaBS sites required to satisfy the user demand with different amounts of bandwidth and RAT in place. Accordingly, Fig. 2 depicts the comparison of the needed BS sites for various amounts of used bandwidth for the demand of 80 GB per user per month. As example, the use of the technology with lower spectral efficiency and 10 – 20 MHz of bandwidth will result in a high number of BSs sites,

Table 6. Capacity for a three-sector base station site for different bandwidth amount

RAT (Capacity)	5 MHz	10 MHz	20 MHz	30 MHz
LTE (Mbps)	25.05	50.1	100.4	150.3
LTE-A (Mbps)	57.0	114.0	228.0	342.0

45 – 100, in order to satisfy the demand in the 1 km² office area. In accordance with
[5], for the dimensioning of the FBS we consider the following two methods: 1) the
user oriented method - in line with Section 3, we allocate 4, 8, 16 or 32 users to each
FBS (regardless of the demand); and 2) coverage oriented method - a number of FBSs
(7 or 11) we allocate per each floor. Based on Table 5, around 7 FBS per floor is the
optimal FBS density. We consider 50% higher density, too. According to Table 3, the
LTE-A deployed FBS capacity equals to 132.0 Mbps. For the cost modeling we will
use the inputs from the Table 4, or: total CAPEX for the new MaBS site 100 k€, and
20 k€ for existing site (cost for upgrading an existing site is estimated to 10 k€ and the
cost for radio equipment supporting three sectors and 5–20 MHz to 10 k€); total
OPEX: 20 k€ for the new site, and 10 k€ for existing site. Regarding the FBS, we
estimate 1.0 k€ and 0.5 k€ for OPEX. In this case study we assume that the whole
network is deployed during the first year.

7.2   Initial Scenario

Assuming the carrier frequency in the 2.6 GHz band and 20 MHz of bandwidth for the
MaBS deployment and both user and coverage approach for the FBS sites, here we
create the initial deployment scenario of the business center to be built. Together with
the CAPEX estimates per single MaBS and FBS as elaborated above, Tables 7 and 8
summarize the total cost needed for the network deployment to fulfill high and excessive demand levels. As anticipated, the cost to satisfy the excessive demand with the
implementation of the existing MaBS is comparable to the cost needed to ensure almost 3 times less capacity by constructing the new sites.   Regarding the FBS deployment, it is noticeable that even high level demand is satisfied with the sparsest deployment (approximately 5 time higher capacity) and that the capacity will not be the limit-
ing factor. The coverage is key main cost driver for the FBS scenario and we can see
that the high density indicates high network costs. Nevertheless, FBS are more cost
effective solution comparing to MaBS deployment with the new sites. This is especially valid for the excessive demand. For the high demand level, the CAPEX for FBS and
re-used MaBS networks is equal. Even more, for the excessive demand using the user
oriented approach (4 or 8 users per FBS) the FBS network is more expensive than re-
used MaBS deployment. Nevertheless, it is important to notice that MaBS network
deployment is based on path loss assumption of 20 dB, what is not sufficient to consider the wall penetration losses that exceed this level. Hence, within the next section we
do a comparison analysis for the wall penetration losses above the assumed 20 dB.

Table 7. Investments and capacity (macro sites initial deployment - Case 1)

Macro Case 1: Initial Scenario (2.6 GHz)	Number of sites	Total CAPEX (Mil. €)	Capacity achieved (Gbps)
New sites - High demand	14	1.4	3.2
New sites - Excessive demand	40	4.0	9.1
Sites reuse - High demand	14	0.28	3.2
Sites reuse - Excessive demand	40	0.8	9.1

Table 8. Investments and capacity (femto sites initial deployment)

Femto BS Deployment	Number of sites	Total CAPEX (Mil. €)	Capacity achieved (Gbps)
7 FBS per floor	350	0.35	46.2
11 FBS per floor	550	0.55	72.6
4 users per FBS	2500	2.50	330.0
8 users per FBS	1250	1.25	165.0
16 users per FBS	625	0.63	82.5
32 users per FBS	313	0.31	41.3

7.3   Compensation of Wall Penetration Losses

When trying to compensate for the wall penetration losses, according [5] and [6], to two compensation options are possible: building a denser 2.6 GHz network and deployment using 10 MHz within the 800 MHz band, i.e. better indoor coverage. As based on the Okumura–Hata propagation model, the difference in path loss between operation in the 800 MHz and the 2.6 GHz band is around 12 dB, we assume that we need to compensate for another 12 dB of attenuation. Authors in [5] calculated that in order to compensate the additional 12 dB of attenuation, 5 times denser network should build at 2.6 GHz band. Nevertheless, when using only 10 MHz spectrum in the 800 MHz band, for the capacity limitation reasons, the number of sites needs to be doubled comparing to the initial case scenario which considers 20 MHz of spectrum (see Table 6). The respective, cost-capacity outcomes are summarized within the Table 9. We can see that the deployment of a large number of new sites is very costly (e.g. 7.9 - 20.0 M€ for the excessive demand). Again, the re-use of existing sites leads to less costly deployment even when many sites need to be equipped with new radio transceivers (4.0 M€). Still, due to the high coverage performance, the most cost-efficient option is reuse of the existing sites for 800 MHz frequency carrier and 10 MHz (only 1.58 M€ to satisfy the excessive demand). Even more, use of the 800 MHz for the new MaBS sites is comparable to FBS most user oriented deployment cost (4 users per FBS) for the high demand level (2.7 vs. 2.5 M€), but much higher for the excessive demand level (7.9 vs. 2.5 M€). Though, the re-use of existing sites in the 800 MHz band is very cost-efficient compared to the most user oriented FBS deployment (for almost 1.0 M€).

7.4   Carrier Aggregation with LTE-Advanced

According to [31], carrier aggregation as characteristic of LTE-A RAT, allows combining lower and higher bands — leveraging better coverage of the former with higher availability of the latter (up to 5 carriers and up to 100 MHz supported in standards). Accordingly, in order to fully assess the cost-efficiency possibilities we create one more deployment scenario assuming the aggregation of the both frequency carriers at 800 MHz and 2.6 GHz bands. By this, the available bandwidth will be increased to 30 MHz, and with that the capacity will be increased according to Table 6. Exactly this is going to be the solution how to increase the capacity (even for 3 times) compared to the use of only 10 MHz bandwidth in 800 MHz band, but without increase the number of sites due to coverage reasons. From the cost perspective, this will mean that we need to install two type of different radio equipment per BS. Consequently, the CAPEX will increase for additional 10 k€, and the total CAPEX per site will be 110 k€ for the new sites and 30 k€ for the existing sites. The Table 10 summarizes the number of needed BS sites using the carrier aggregation functionality and the relevant costs-capacity outcomes. Findings indicate that for only around 0.8 M€ upgrade of the existing sites, the excessive user demands will be ensured. Even more, with 1.0 M€ of investment and construction of new sites the high demands can be satisfied as well. For comparison under the Case 2, around 1.0 M€ is sufficient only to satisfy high demands with the reusing sites for 800 MHz or barely to satisfy the high demands with the reuse of the 5 time denser deployed network in the 2.6 GHz band. The comparison of the Case 3 with FBS options shows that implementing the carrier aggregation on the existing sites will be less costly solution than the moderate to high user approach (8 users per FBS). This is also valid for the high demand when deploying new sites with LTE-A carrier aggregation. In such case, deployment of the new sites with carrier aggregation for excessive demands has "bearable" higher cost of around 0.5 M€) than the moderate to high user oriented FBS deployment (8 users FBS).

7.5   Cost-Capacity Discussions

Investment costs for different strategies of MaBS and FBS network deployments are depicted in Fig. 3 as function of user demand (Gbps). For the MaBS solutions, there is linear increase with demand. In the second deployment strategy and using LTE-A RAT, we determine relatively low to moderate figures of base station densities, 27 – 70 per km², when satisfying low to high demand, as well as large figures, 79 – 200 per km², in order to satisfy excessive demand together with denser deployment to compensate for additional wall penetration losses. The most cost-efficient option out of second case is the reuse of the existing sites by installation of additional radio equipment operating at 800 MHz carrier frequency. From other side out of Fig. 3 we can see that if deploying 5 time denser new sites with LTA-A RAT in the 2.6 GHz band it will be only sufficient to ensure around 3.0 Gbps/km². Yet, the solution to deploy the denser network at 2.6 GHz band with re-use of the existing sites is more than twice cost-efficient than the solution to construct new sites with 800 MHz carrier, what shows the importance of the available spectrum, too.

Table 9. Investments and capacity (macro sites wall losses compensation deployment - Case 2)

Macro Case 2: *Wall Losses Compensation*	Number of sites	Total CAPEX (Mil. €)	Capacity (Gbps)
New 800 MHz sites - High demand	27	2.7	3.1
New 800 MHz sites – Excess. demand	79	7.9	9.1
800 MHz sites reuse - High demand	27	0.54	3.1
800 MHz sites reuse – Excess. demand	79	1.58	9.1
New 5 x 2.6 GHz sites - High demand	70	7.0	15.9
New 5 x 2.6 GHz MHz sites – Excess. demand	200	20.0	45.6
5 x 2.6 GHz MHz sites reuse - High demand	70	1.4	15.9
5 x 2.6 GHz MHz sites reuse – Excess. demand	200	4.0	45.6

Table 10. Investments and capacity (macro sites with carrier aggregation - Case 3)

Macro Case 3: LTE-A and carrier aggregation (800 & 2600 MHz)	Number of sites	Total CAPEX (Mil. €)	Capacity Achieved (Gbps)
New sites - High demand	9	0.99	3.1
New sites - Excessive demand	27	2.97	9.2
Sites reuse - High demand	9	0.27	3.1
Sites reuse - Excessive demand	27	0.81	9.2

The key finding of the different MaBS deployment comparisons is that the utilization of carrier aggregation functionality of the LTE-A RAT is by far the most cost-efficient scenario. With this strategy high to excessive demands can be ensured with rather small number of base station densities, 9 – 27 per km². Even more, the option of deploying new sites with carrier aggregation is more cost-efficient strategy comparing to all deployment strategies from the second case, with exception to the re-use of the existing sites in the 800 MHz band. Still, the difference even between these two possibilities is rather acceptable and below 1.4 M€. Regarding the FBS network, the key obstacle is its limitation coming from coverage perspective. As shown in Figure 3, deployment of dense network e.g. supporting of 4 users per FBS as most user oriented approach is not economical except for the over excessive demand (above the 9.0 Gbps/km² as excessive area demand considered within this paper). Nevertheless, the FBS deployment becomes significantly cost efficient in case when FBS deployment can support large number of up to 32 users (or 7-11 FBS per floor). Anyhow, in such case the trade should be done with the user satisfaction, too.

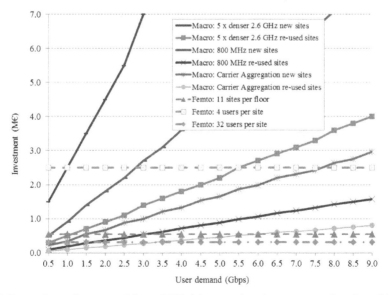

Fig. 3. Comparison of macro and femto LTE-A base stations investment as function of the user demand

8   Conclusions and Future Work

In this article we propose a model for appraising the setup and operational costs of heterogeneous wireless systems. Providing estimates for CAPEX/OPEX per base station class of various cellular deployments enabled with LTE-A and IEEE 802.11n RATs, with the model we analyze the total discounted deployment cost as a function of user demand. Findings show that the picocellular deployment provides the lowest cost for the moderate user demand. This indicates that coverage (cell range) is an essential constraint to "balance with" when dimensioning wireless access systems.

We have compared the cost-capacity performance for macro and femto cell networks through the case study assuming high to excessive user demands within the densely populated and rather small indoor area. For deployment of mobile broadband with high capacity demand we highlighted that the re-use of sites have a large impact also when a "denser" macro network is deployed in order to compensate for wall attenuation. However, in areas without any existing infrastructure the situation is different, unless the carrier aggregation functionality of the LTE-A RAT is used. Hence, it could be concluded that new market entrant would have no particular issues to compete with existing operators if introduces LTE-A supporting carrier aggregation. All in all we can draw a conclusion that with LTE-A RAT, the lack of macrocelluar networks recognized as capacity limited networks, become insignificant. Also we prove that a dense deployment of femtocells is less cost efficient, but compared to the macrocellular case there is no need to deploy additional capacity in order to compensate for propagation loss. Hence, the key challenge of femtocells for the future is to become less coverage limited networks.

Further studies in this field could introduce dimensioning methods for assessing cost effectiveness of wide deployment of outdoor pico base stations, or other classes of small cells under the umbrella of the heterogeneous wireless networks. Other option is to investigate the cooperative layouts of macro with femto cells or Wi-Fi by consideration of the beyond 2020 mobile and wireless system targets.

References

1. The Small Cell Forum: What is a small cell?, http://www.smallcellforum.org
2. Zander, J.: Challenge 2020: 1000 times more capacity at todays cost & energy. KTH – The Royal Institute of Technology, Stockholm, Sweden (2012)
3. Johansson, K.: Cost Effective Deployment Strategies for Heterogeneous Wireless Networks", PhD Dissertation. The Royal Institute of Technology, Stockholm (2007)
4. Johansson, K., Furuskar, A., Karlsson, P., Zander, J.: Relation between base station characteristics and cost structure in cellular systems. In: Proceedings of IEEE International Symposium on Personal, Indoor and Mobile Radio Communications (2004)
5. Markendahl, J., Mäkitalo, Ö.: A comparative study of deployment options, capacity and cost structure for macrocellular and femtocell networks. IOFC (2010)
6. Markendahl, J.: Mobile Network Operators and Cooperation. PhD Dissertation. The Royal Institute of Technology, Stockholm (2011)

7. Frias, Z., Pérez, J.: Techno-economic analysis of femtocell deployment in long-term evolution networks. EURASIP 2012, 288 (2012)
8. ETSI TR 136 913 V10.0.0 (2011-04) LTE: ETSI (2011)
9. ETSI TR 136 912 V11.0.0 (2012-10): ETSI (2012)
10. Wi-Fi Alliance.: Wi-Fi CERTIFIED^{TM} n: Longer-Range, Faster-Throughput, Multi-media-Grade. Wi-Fi® Networks (2009)
11. AnalysisMason.: Wireless network traffic 2010–2015: Forecast and analysis (2010)
12. Mölleryd, B.G., Markendahl, J., Mäkitalo, Ö.: Spectrum valuation derived from network deployment and strategic positioning with different levels of spectrum in 800 MHz. In: Bi-Annual Conference, Tokyo (June 2010)
13. Holma, H., Toskala, A.: LTE for UMTS – OFDMA and SC-FDMA Based Radio Access. John Wiley & Sons (2009)
14. Johansson, K., Furuskär, A.: Cost efficient capacity expansion strategies using multi-access networks. In: Proc. IEEE VTC-Spring (2005)
15. Choi, S.: Femtocell vs. WiFi. In: The 22nd High-Speed Network Workshop. Multimedia & Wireless Networking Lab (2012)
16. REPORT ITU-R M.2134.: Requirements related to technical performance for IMT-Advanced radio interface(s) (2008)
17. R4-071231.: Open and Closed Access for Home NodeBs. "Nortel, Vodafone", 3GPP TSG RAN Working Group 4 (Radio) meeting #44 (2007)
18. Femto Forum.: Interference Management in UMTS Femtocells (2010)
19. Fujitsu: Network BroadOne LTE Femtocell Product Lineup, http://www.fujitsu.com; Gast, M.: 802.11 Wireless Networks – The Definitive Guide, 2nd edn. O'Reilly (2005)
20. Xiao, Y.: IEEE 802.11n: Enhancements for higher throughput in wireless LANs. IEEE WirelCommun. 12(6), 82–91 (2005)
21. Wang, C., Wei, H.: IEEE 802.11n MAC Enhancement and Performance Evaluation. Mobile Networks and Applications 14(6), 760–771 (2009)
22. Mohammad, R., et al.: Evaluating Effectiveness of DSDV Routing Protocol on IEEE 802.11n Wireless LANs. IJENS 10(4), 41 (2010)
23. Carson, S.: Total cost of ownership – creating value for operators. Presentation Ericsson Capital Markets Day (2007)
24. Stanley, M.: Hopes of growth fade away: A proprietary approach. Financial analyst report (2004)
25. European Commission. Digital Agenda Scoreboard 2013, Commission Staff Working Document SWD (2013) 217 final. Brussels (December 6, 2013)
26. Ericsson.:Telebriefing: Ericsson Mobility Report - On the pulse of the networked society. Ericsson (November 11, 2013)
27. Mölleryd, B.G., Markendahl, J., Werding, J., Mäkitalo, Ö.: Decoupling of revenues and traffic - Is there a revenue gap for mobile broadband (CTTE 2010)
28. Furuskär, A., Almgren, M.: An Infrastructure Cost Evaluation of Single- and Multi-Access Networks with Heterogeneous Traffic Density. IEEE VTC (2005)
29. Ghosh, A., Ratasuk, R., Mondal, B., Mangalvedhe, N., Thomas, T.: LTE-Advanced: Next-Generation Wireless Broadband Technology. IEEE WC (2010)
30. Hata, M.: Empirical Formula for Propagation Loss in Land Mobile Radio Services. IEEE Transactions on Vehicular Technology VT-29(3) (1980)
31. Qualcomm.: LTE Advanced—Leading in chipsets and evolution (2013)

Fairness Enhancement Based on Virtual PRB Allocation in MIMO-OFDMA Systems

Wafa Ben Hassen, Mériem Afif, and Sami Tabbane

Mediatron Lab, Sup'Com, Carthage University, Tunis-Tunisia
{benhassen.wafa,mariem.afif,sami.tabbane}@supcom.rnu.tn

Abstract. This paper presents a new resource allocation problem in Long Term Evolution (LTE) down-link transmission. It aims at maximizing the total system capacity with fairness consideration. The optimization problem is divided into sub-optimal ones for complexity mitigation. Firstly, a recursive Physical Resource Block (PRB) allocation scheme is introduced. After PRB allocation, the Evolved Node B (eNodeB) aggregates the unused sub-carriers by each User Equipment (UE) to construct a virtual PRB which is allocated to the UE with the highest current throughput to the past average throughput ratio for fairness improvement. Secondly, a power allocation procedure is performed. Finally, a more appropriate Modulation and Coding Scheme (MCS) is selected. Simulation results show that the proposed algorithm provides better performance than other existing ones such as Min-MCS, Max-SINR and PF.

Keywords: LTE, MIMO, OFDMA, AMC, fairness, virtual PRB.

1 Introduction

Nowadays, LTE [1] is commonly considered as a suitable candidate for beyond fourth generation networks thanks to its radio link flexibility using Adaptive Modulation and Coding (AMC), Multiple Input Multiple Output (MIMO) and Orthogonal Frequency Division Multiple Access (OFDMA) technologies. In LTE down-link scheduling, the smallest radio resource unit that may be allocated to the UE is named a PRB [2]. It contains 7 consecutive Orthogonal Frequency Division Multiplexing (OFDM) symbols in the time domain and 12 adjacent sub-carriers per OFDM symbol in the frequency domain. According to LTE specification, all PRBs assigned to the same UE must use the same MCS. However, the UE connected to the same eNodeB may have different MCSs based on the corresponding Channel Quality Indicator (CQI). This constraint reduces the resource allocation complexity [3]. In this paper, a new adaptive resource allocation scheme, aiming at maximizing the total system capacity with fairness consideration, is proposed. Here, the optimization problem is divided into two sub-optimal ones. Firstly, a PRB allocation scheme based on a recursive function is developed where the Effective Signal-plus-Interference-to-Noise Ratio (ESINR) [4] metric is used to properly characterize the CQI. After PRB allocation, the eNodeB aggregates the unused sub-carriers by each UE to construct

A. Mellouk et al. (Eds.): WWIC 2014, LNCS 8458, pp. 82–95, 2014.

virtual PRBs which are allocated to the UE with the highest current through-put to the past average throughput ratio for fairness improvement. Secondly, a power allocation scheme is performed. Motivated by results obtained in [5], the power optimization sub-problem includes several stages: Power Allocation among PRBs (PAaPRB), Power Allocation among Antennas (PAaA) and Power Allocation among User equipment (PAaU). Finally, a more appropriate MCS is selected according to the obtained power optimization solution to maximize the total system capacity. The remaining of this paper is described as follows. In Section 2, related works are discussed. The system model is presented in section 3. Then, the studied optimization problem is formulated. After that, the proposed resource allocation method is introduced in section 5. Finally, simulation results and performance analysis are presented in section 6.

2   Related Works

We focus on well-known schemes such as Max-SINR [5], Min-MCS [6] and Proportional Fairness (PF) [19]. In Max-SINR, a two-step resource allocation scheme is proposed. In PRB allocation phase, each PRB is allocated to the user with the highest ESINR to achieve the highest throughput. Moreover, if several users have the same ESINR at a PRB, then this PRB is assigned to the user with minimum average throughput for fairness. In power allocation phase, the optimization problem includes two stages which are power allocation among PRBs and users. Even the Max-SINR algorithm is interesting, it seems a quite conservative as it prioritizes the user with minimum average throughput if two users or more have the same ESINR at a PRB. This solution prevents the system capacity maximization.

   In Min-MCS, authors propose to select the MCS based on the worst Channel Sate Information (CSI) in order to guarantee a lower BLock Error Rate (BLER) of a poor PRB. Firstly, the number of PRBs to be allocated for each user is de-termined based on the ratio of user's minimum data rate requirement to user's average channel gain. Secondly, the PRBs are allocated to users where the MCS must be chosen based on the worst CSI. Here, the power is equally distributed over PRBs for complexity mitigation. Min-MCS is unsuitable for the capacity maximization, since it tolerates a throughput loss for the PRB with a good CSI. Designed to maximize the data rate sum, user scheduling schemes suffer from the monopolization of resources by users with a good channel, thus making those with bad channel are seldom served [7]. The PF scheme [8] can solve this problem efficiently since it introduces the fairness criteria based on the ratio of instantaneous channel quality and average throughput. Although, PF provides a fairer behavior, it decreases the total system capacity.

   As a remedy, we propose a new PRB, power and MCS allocation scheme for the system capacity maximization. The unused sub-carriers are gathered into virtual PRBs and then, allocated to users with the highest ratio of the current throughput to the past average throughput. The proposed scheme achieves a good trade-off between the system capacity and the fairness.

3   System Model

In LTE systems, the bandwidth B is divided into N PRBs where each PRB contains M data sub-carriers for Q OFDM symbols per Time Slot (TS). Here, a single eNodeB with N_t antennas and K UEs equipped with N_r antennas are considered. The eNodeB antenna elements are separated by $\lambda/2$ where λ is the radio wavelength, then the radio channels between the eNodeB and the UE are considered uncorrelated [9]. Each sub-carrier is allocated to only one UE for interference and complexity mitigation [10]. The gain matrix of the channel between the UE k and the eNodeB on the sub-carrier m is $G_{k,m} = \left[g_{i,j}^{k,m} \right]$ where $i \in \{1, ...N_t\}$ and $j \in \{1, ...N_r\}$. $\left[g_{i,j}^{k,m} \right]$ is the channel gain between the transmit antenna i and the receive one j when the UE k is connected to the eNodeB on sub-carrier m. $G_{k,m}$ is decomposed by Singular Value Decomposition (SVD) as:

$$G_{k,m} = U_{k,m} \Lambda_{k,m} V_{k,m}^{\dagger} = \sum_{i=1}^{r} u_{k,m}^{i} \lambda_{k,m}^{i} v_{k,m}^{i\dagger}. \tag{1}$$

where $\dagger$ is the conjugate transpose and r is obtained by $r = min\,(N_r, N_t)$. Here, $U_{k,m}$ and $V_{k,m}$ are unitary matrices. $\Lambda_{k,m}$ is a diagonal matrix with the diagonal elements $\lambda_{k,m}^{i}$ denoting the ordered eigenvalues of $G_{k,m}$. The vectors $u_{k,m}^{i}$ and $v_{k,m}^{i}$ represent the left and right eigen-vectors of $G_{k,m}$, respectively. The SINR experienced by UE k on sub-carrier m, using antenna i, is expressed as follows:

$$\delta_{k,m}^{i} = \frac{p_{k,m}^{i} \left(\lambda_{k,m}^{i} \right)^2}{\sigma^2 + \sum_{e' \neq e}^{E} \Upsilon_{e,e'} \chi_{e'} \sum_{j=1}^{r} p_{k',m}^{j} \left(\lambda_{k',m}^{j} \right)^2}. \tag{2}$$

where $p_{k',m}^{i}$ is the transmit power on sub-carrier m using antenna i, for UE $k' \in e'$, while E is the set of neighbor cells in the network. e is the serving cell. $\chi_{e'}$ is the probability that the same sub-carrier used by the UE k is used at the same time by another UE served by the eNodeB $e' \in E$. $\Upsilon_{e,e'}$ denotes the interference matrix, where the coefficient $\Upsilon_{e,e'}$ is equal to 1 if cells e and e' use the same band and zero otherwise. σ^2 is the noise variance. As PRB is the smallest resource unit, the ESINR on each one is calculated as follows [4,11]:

$$\gamma_{k,n}^{i} = -\beta \ln \left(\frac{1}{M} \sum_{m=1}^{M} e^{-\frac{\delta_{k,m}^{i}}{\beta}} \right). \tag{3}$$

where β is a parameter that must be optimized from link level simulation results for each MCS. The use of AMC allows the system to adjust the channel MCS with the ESINR of the available radio link [12]. Since 3GPP LTE specification requires that the PRBs of the same UE use the same MCS [5], it is considered that all sub-carriers in the same PRB employ the same MCS index. Then, the throughput for PRB n of UE k using antenna i in a sub-frame is given as:

$$Th_{PRB_{k,n}^{i}} = \frac{M \cdot N_{sym/SF} \cdot R_{sbc_{k,n}^{i}}}{T_{SF}} \left(1 - BLER_{k,n}^{i} \right). \tag{4}$$

where $N_{sym/SF}$ is the number of symbols per sub-frame and T_{SF} is the sub-frame duration. $R_{sbc_{k,n}^i}$ is the transmitted information quantity for UE k on PRB n using antenna i. From [13], the BLER for a PRB with a given MCS can be accurately predicted from its ESINR by:

$$BLER_{k,n}^i = \frac{1}{2} erfc \left(\frac{\gamma_{k,n}^i - b_m}{\sqrt{2} c_m} \right). \tag{5}$$

where $erfc()$ is the complementary error function. b_m and c_m are the corresponding fitting parameters for a given MCS with m index [14]. The transmitted information quantity $R_{sbc_{k,n}}$ for UE k on PRB n using antenna i, depends of the radio link quality using AMC and is expressed as $R_{sbc_{k,n}^i} = N_{AMC} \cdot N_{FEC}$. N_{AMC} and N_{FEC} denote, respectively, the number of bits per sub-carrier and Forward Error Coding (FEC) rate [15]. Considering the simulation time T is a multiple of the sub-frame delay T_{SF}, the system capacity is obtained as follows:

$$C_{sys} = \frac{B}{N} \sum_{t=1}^{T} \sum_{k=1}^{K} \sum_{n=1}^{N_k} \sum_{i=1}^{r} Th_{PRB_{k,n}^i} \left(m_{k,n}^i, \gamma_{k,n}^i \right). \tag{6}$$

where $m_{k,n}^i$ is the MCS index corresponding to the PRB of UE k and $\gamma_{k,n}^i$ is the ESINR on PRB n (3). N_k is the number of PRBs to be allocated to UE k while $N_k = \lceil \phi N \rceil$, $\phi \in]0,1[$. Based on $\gamma_{k,n}^i$ value, the maximum data rate $N_{sym/SF}$ is selected using AMC scheme [3,16].

4   Optimization Problem Formulation

The system capacity (6) implies that, a combination of MIMO, AMC and flexible PRB allocation is needed for the radio link performance maximization. We suppose that all users require the same service. Each UE has a perfect CSI feedback. In order to enhance the system performance, the power allocation scheme is performed, which will result in a new ESINR called $\zeta_{k,n}^i$ based on $\rho_{k,n}^i$. $\zeta_{k,n}^i$ is the power allocation scale and is given as [5]:

$$\zeta_{k,n}^i = \rho_{k,n}^i \gamma_{k,n}^i. \tag{7}$$

Having the goal to maximize the system capacity on each sub-frame, the optimization problem is formulated as follows:

$$\arg\max \frac{B}{N} \sum_{k=1}^{K} \sum_{n=1}^{N_k} \sum_{i=1}^{r} Th_{PRB_{k,n}^i} \left(m_{k,n}^i, \zeta_{k,n}^i \right).$$

$$\text{subject to} \begin{cases} \sum_{k=1}^{K} N_k = N. \\ \sum_{k=1}^{K} \sum_{n=1}^{N_k} \rho_{k,n}^i = N : \text{the total power budget.} \\ \rho_{k,n}^i \geq 0, \forall k, n, i. \end{cases} \tag{8}$$

5   Proposed Resource Allocation Scheme

5.1   PRB Allocation Based on a Recursive Function

In this section, the power allocation constraints are relaxed for the complexity mitigation. Therefore, the power is equally distributed, where $\rho_{k,n}^i = 1$. Consequently, the PRB assignment problem can be formulated as:

$$\arg\max \frac{B}{N} \sum_{k=1}^{K} \sum_{n=1}^{N_k} \sum_{i=1}^{r} Th_{PRB_{k,n}^i} \left(m_{k,n}^i \gamma_{k,n}^i \right).$$
$$\text{subject to } \sum_{k=1}^{K} N_k = N. \tag{9}$$

Each PRB should be allocated to the UE with the highest ESINR for capacity maximization [18]. Algorithm 1 describes the proposed PRB allocation scheme. After parameters initialization, dominant eigen-channels are used to sort the PRBs based on their highest ESINR. Then, a recursive PRB allocation function is applied until all UEs requirements are satisfied as shown in algorithm 2. Here, UEs are scheduled in decreasing order based on their best PRB. Then, each UE is assigned its best PRB with the highest ESINR. If the PRB is yet allocated to a more prior UE, the second best PRB is allocated to that UE. Then, the throughput of each user k (4) and the other parameters are updated. In order to improve fairness, a further PRB allocation step is introduced. The eNodeB aggregates the unused sub-carriers by each UE to build virtual PRBs as shown in Fig.1. This step is applied until the set of virtual PRBs $\Gamma_{vir} = 0$. Then, UEs are scheduled in decreasing order based on their highest PF_k. It represents the current throughput achievable to the past average throughput received ratio.

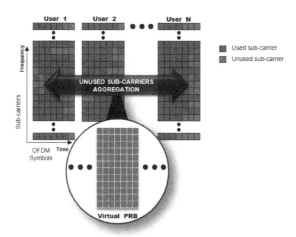

Fig. 1. Unused Sub-carriers Aggregation for Virtual PRBs Construction

Algorithm 1. PRB Allocation Algorithm

1. **BEGIN**
2. **(I) Initialization**
3. $\Lambda = \{1, 2, \cdots, K\}$; $\Gamma = \{1, 2, \cdots, N\}$;
4. $Th_{PRB_k} = 0$; $\Omega_k = \phi$; $N_k = \phi N$;
5. **(II) Dominant Eigen-Channels Determination**
6. **for** $k = 1 \rightarrow K$ **do**
7.   **for** $n = 1 \rightarrow N$ **do**
8. $\lambda_{k,n}^{\wedge} \leftarrow$ Find dominant eigen-channel.
9.   **end for**
10. **end for**
11. **(III) PRB Sorting in Decreasing Order**
12. **for** $k = 1 \rightarrow K$ **do**
13. $H_{k,n}' \leftarrow$ Sort PRB according to $\lambda_{k,n}^{\wedge}$.
14. **end for**
15. **(IV)** $H_{k,n}' = $ **Recursive PRB Allocation Fn** $(H_{k,n}')$
16. **(V) Virtual PRB Allocation**
17. **for** $n = 1 \rightarrow N$ **do**
18. $\hat{m}_n \leftarrow$ Determine the set of unused sub-carriers.
19. **end for**
20. $\Gamma_{vir} \leftarrow \Gamma_{vir} + \{\hat{m}_n\}$.
21. Construct N_v virtual PRBs according to Γ_{vir}.
22. **for** $k = 1 \rightarrow K$ **do**
23. $H_{k,n_v}' \leftarrow$ Sort PRB according to the highest PF_k.
24. **end for**
25. **(VI)** $H_{k,n_v}' = $ **Recursive PRB Allocation Fn**(H_{k,n_v}')
26. **END**

Algorithm 2. $H_{k,n}' = $ Recursive PRB Allocation Fn $(H_{k,n}')$

1. **while** $(\Gamma \neq \phi)$ **or** $(N_{1 \rightarrow K} \neq 0)$ **do**
2. $n = 1$
3. $H_{k,n}'' \longleftarrow$ Schedule users according to $H_{k,n}'$
4.   **for** $k = 1 \rightarrow K$ where $order(k) < order(k+1)$ **do**
5.   **if** $N_k = 0$ **then**
6.   k=k+1 and jump to line 5
7.   **else**
8.   **if** PRB n is allocated **then**
9.   n=n+1 and jump to line 8
10.   **else**
11.   Allocate PRB n to user k
12.   Update Th_{PRB_k} ; $N_k = N_k - 1$; $\Omega_k = \Omega_k + \{n\}$; $\Gamma = \Gamma - \{n\}$.
13. $H_{k,n}' \longleftarrow$ Truncate the first column from $H_{k,n}''$.
14. $H_{k,n}' = $ Recursive PRB Allocation Fn$(H_{k,n}')$
15.   **end if**
16.   **end if**
17.   **end for**
18. **end while**

5.2   Sub-optimal Power Allocation Scheme

Once PRB allocation is performed, the optimization problem is rewritten as:

$$\arg\max \frac{B}{N} \sum_{k=1}^{K} \sum_{n=1}^{N_k} \sum_{i=1}^{r} Th_{PRB_{k,n}^i}\left(m_{k,n}^i, \zeta_{k,n}^i\right).$$
$$\text{subject to} \begin{cases} \sum_{k=1}^{K} \sum_{n=1}^{N_k} \rho_{k,n}^i = N. \\ \rho_{k,n}^i \geq 0, \forall k, n, i. \end{cases} \tag{10}$$

To simplify the optimization process, the power allocation problem is separated into three ones: Power Allocation among PRBs (PAaPRB), Power Allocation among Antennas (PAaA) and Power Allocation among User equipment (PAaU). To perform the power allocation among PRBs, antennas and UEs separately, a new variable is introduced: $\rho_{k,n}^i = \sigma_k^i \mu_{k,n}^i$. $\mu_{k,n}^i$ and σ_k^i represent, respectively, the power at PRB n of UE k and the power for UE k on antenna i.

Power Allocation among PRBs (PAaPRB): Here, power allocation among PRBs for a single UE k is discussed where $\sigma_k^i = 1$. Then, we obtain:

$$\arg\max \sum_{n=1}^{N_k} Th_{PRB_{k,n}^i}\left(m_{k,n}^i, \mu_{k,n}^i \gamma_{k,n}^i\right).$$
$$\text{subject to} \sum_{n=1}^{N_k} \mu_{k,n}^i = N_k. \tag{11}$$

Based on the LTE specification, PRBs of the same UE should use the same MCS. In this case, the power is allocated to improve the minimum ESINR and thereby the data transmission rate for each UE. Therefore, the power should be allocated whereby all PRBs of the same UE have the same ESINR, $\mu_{k,n}^i \gamma_{k,n}^i = c$, where c is a constant variable. It can, also, be written as follows:

$$\sum_{n=1}^{N_k} \mu_{k,n}^i = \sum_{j=1}^{N_k} \frac{c}{\gamma_{k,j}^i} = N_k. \tag{12}$$

From equation (12), it is obtained:

$$\mu_{k,n}^i = \frac{N_k}{\gamma_{k,n}^i \sum_{j=1}^{N_k} \frac{1}{\gamma_{k,j}^i}}, \forall n \in \Gamma. \tag{13}$$

After that, the ESINR for each UE k on antenna i is given by:

$$\gamma_k^i = \frac{N_k}{\sum_{j=1}^{N_k} \frac{1}{\gamma_{k,j}^i}}. \tag{14}$$

Power Allocation among Antennas (PAaA): Once PAaPRB is performed, the optimization problem is given by:

$$\arg\max \frac{B}{N} \sum_{k=1}^{K} \sum_{i=1}^{r} N_k Th_{PRB_k^i}\left(m_k^i, \sigma_k^i \gamma_k^i\right).$$
$$\text{subject to} \sum_{k=1}^{K} \sum_{i=1}^{r} N_k \sigma_k^i = N. \tag{15}$$

In MIMO systems, dominant eigen-channels are used for the complexity mitigation. Then, the ESINR for each UE k on antenna i can be rewritten as:

$$\gamma_k^i = \gamma_k^\wedge = \frac{N_k}{\sum_{n=1}^{N_k} \frac{1}{\gamma_{k,n}^\wedge}}.$$
(16)

Power Allocation among User Equipment (PAaU): The system throughput can be further improved by power allocation among UEs based on the waterfilling algorithm [5]. The optimization problem is:

$$\arg\max \frac{B}{N} \sum_{k=1}^K N_k Th_{PRB_k^\wedge} \left(m_k^\wedge, \sigma_k^\wedge \gamma_k^\wedge \right).$$
$$\text{subject to } \sum_{k=1}^K N_k \sigma_k^\wedge = N.$$
(17)

In order to reduce the optimization complexity, a differentiable continuous function is used, $\log_2(1 + \frac{\sigma_k^\wedge \gamma_k^\wedge}{\varepsilon})$ [17]. ε is the SNR gap between the Shannon channel capacity and a practical MCS. The optimization problem is:

$$\arg\max \frac{B}{N} \sum_{k=1}^K N_k \log_2 \left(1 + \frac{\sigma_k^\wedge \gamma_k^\wedge}{\varepsilon} \right).$$
$$\text{subject to } \sum_{k=1}^K N_k \sigma_k^\wedge = N.$$
(18)

The power allocation is found by the Lagrange multiplier method as follows:

$$L\left(\sigma_k^\wedge\right) = \sum_{k=1}^K N_k \log_2 \left(1 + \frac{\sigma_k^\wedge \gamma_k^\wedge}{\varepsilon} \right) - \varrho \sum_{k=1}^K \left(N_k \sigma_k^\wedge - N \right).$$
(19)

where ϱ is a Lagrange multiplier, so the water-filling power scale is obtained as:

$$\sigma_k^\wedge = \left(\frac{1}{\varrho} - \frac{\varepsilon}{\gamma_k^\wedge} \right)^+.$$
(20)

where $(x)^+ \triangleq \max\{x, 0\}$ and ϱ is a water-filling level threshold and is given as:

$$\varrho = \frac{1}{\left(1 + \frac{\varepsilon}{N} \sum_{k=1}^K \sum_{n=1}^{N_k} \frac{1}{\gamma_{k,n}^\wedge} \right)}.$$
(21)

After power allocation, the ESINR for each UE k is given by:

$$\zeta_k^\wedge = \sigma_k^\wedge N_k \left(\sum_{n=1}^{N_k} \frac{1}{\gamma_{k,n}^\wedge} \right)^{-1}.$$
(22)

5.3   Computational Complexity Analysis

In this section, the computational complexity of our scheme is studied. In our PRB allocation algorithm, step (III) sorts available PRBs for each user which requires $KN \log_2(N)$. Then, in step (IV), users are putted in order N times needing $NK \log_2(K)$ operations. In step (V), N_v virtual PRBs are constructed based on the unused sub-carriers aggregation and then sorted according to the highest current throughput to the past average throughput ratio (PF_k) for each user k which requires $KN_v \log_2(N_v)$. Then, the recursive allocation function is called where $N_v K \log_2(K)$ operations are needed. Thus, the asymptotic complexity of the proposed PRB assignment is $O\left(K(N + N_v) \log_2(K(N + N_v))\right)$. In power allocation phase, the PAaPRB scheme requires (N_k) operations where N_k is the number of PRB to be allocated to each user k. Then, the PAaA scheme, dominant eigen-channels are used to reduce the complexity. Finally, water-filling is performed to compute the ESINR of each user k, requiring KN_k operations to define the water-filling level ϱ. After that, $\zeta_k^\wedge$ is computed, needing $N_k(KN_k)$ operations. As $N \gg N_v$, the resource allocation complexity is $O\left(N^2 K\right)$. In Max-SINR [5], PRB assignment scheme needs to compare the ESINRs of all users to allocate to each user the PRB with the highest ESINR. Here, if two users have the same ESINR, the user with the minimum average throughput is selected. This step requires $KN(K-1)$. The power allocation step requires $N(KN)$ operations. The overall resource allocation algorithm complexity is $O\left(N^2 K + K^2 N - KN\right)$. In Min-MCS [6], a sub-optimal radio resource allocation algorithm is proposed which comprises two steps: (1) Estimate the number of PRBs for each user based on the ratio of users' minimum rate requirements to its average channel gain. Here, ($K\alpha_k$) operations are required to calculate users' average channel gain where $\alpha_k \leq N$ is the number of PRBs with CSI fed backed. (2) Allocate PRBs to users according to users' priorities. The users priority computation needs $K(K - 1)$ operations and sorting users in descending order requires ($N_k K (\log_2(N_k K))$. The power is equally distributed for the complexity mitigation. Then, the resource allocation algorithm complexity is $O(K\alpha_k + K^2 - K + N_k K(\log_2(N_k K))$. Therefore, we can note that the complexity of our proposed scheme $O\left(N^2 K\right)$ is less than the complexity of the Min-MCS $(O(K\alpha_k + K^2 - K + N_k K(\log_2(N_k K)))$ and Max-SINR $O\left(N^2 K + K^2 N - KN\right)$. In PF [8], a radio resource allocation algorithm is proposed. Firstly, the number of PRBs which can be allocated for users is calculated. This needs KN operation times. Secondly, K operation times are needed for initialization of resource allocation for all users. After that, the "argmax" operation needs $K(N - i + 1)$ times operations at i^{th} PRBs allocation event. Then, $\sum_{i=1}^{N} Ki = K(N(N + 1))/2$. Since, the power is equally distributed, the total computational complexity is obtained as: $K(N + 1) + K(N(N + 1))/2 = KN^2$.

By comparing the complexity of our proposed resource scheme and other existing ones, we can recognize that the suggested algorithm achieved interesting performance without increasing the complexity level.

6   Performance Evaluation

Simulation results for the proposed resource allocation algorithm are provided. The bandwidth is 10 MHz. The number of occupied sub-carriers is 601.

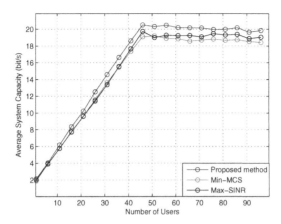

Fig. 2. Average system capacity versus number of users

Table 1. Variation intervals in terms of system capacity

Number of users	[1, 25[	[25, 50[	[50, 75[	[75, 100[
C_{PMax} (bit/s)	0.4576	1.0585	1.0819	1.0983
C_{PMin} (bit/s)	0.5186	1.1612	1.3822	1.3921

The number of available PRBs is 50. The SNR gap between the Shannon channel capacity and a practical MCS ε is set to be 2 [17]. The channel is modeled as a Rayleigh Channel with four multi-paths. To consider the channel state variation, the channel state matrix changes every sub-frame duration. A $(4{\times}4)$ MIMO system is considered. In Fig.2, we compare our proposed PRB allocation scheme performance with well-known methods such as Max-SINR [5] and Min-MCS [6]. Table 1 shows variation intervals in terms of average system capacity. Let C_{PMax} and C_{PMin} denote, respectively, the average system capacity difference between the proposed algorithm and Max-SINR and Min-MCS for various users' intervals. Our method provides greater capacity as $C_{PMax}{>}0$ and $C_{PMin}{>}0$. Min-MCS introduces a throughput loss for the PRB with a good CSI to decrease the BLER. While Max-SINR prioritizes the user with the minimum average throughput if two users have the same ESINR at a PRB, our proposed scheme prioritizes the one with the less ESINR on the second best PRB to avoid the capacity decrease. Moreover, we include a users scheduling ensuring that each PRB is assigned to its best user. In Fig.3, we study the rule of the virtual PRB allocation in the improvement of the system capacity. Table 2 shows variation intervals in terms of average system capacity. C_{vNv} represents the average system capacity difference between the performance of our proposed algorithm with virtual PRB allocation and without virtual PRB allocation phase.

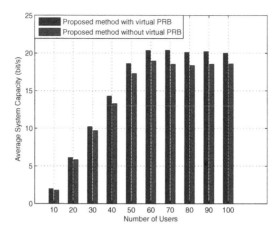

Fig. 3. Average system capacity with and without virtual PRB allocation

Table 2. Virtual PBR allocation performance in terms system capacity

Number of users	$[1, 25[$	$[25, 50[$	$[50, 75[$	$[75, 100[$
C_{vNv}(**bit/s**)	0.4607	1.0165	1.0793	1.0831

As $C_{vNv} > 0$, we show that the virtual PRB allocation phase enhances the system capacity since the unused sub-carriers of each user are reallocated to other ones which are seldom served due to their bad channel gains.

The Jain Fairness Index is used to characterize the fairness behaviour of the proposed algorithm and expressed as follows:

$$J_{FairIndex} = \frac{\left(\sum_{k=1}^{K} Th_{PRB_{k,mean}}\right)^2}{K \cdot \sum_{k=1}^{K} \left(Th_{PRB_{k,mean}}\right)^2} \tag{23}$$

where $Th_{PRB_{k,mean}}$ is the mean throughput of user k during a simulation window. Fig.4 compares the proposed algorithm with oher existing ones such as Max-SINR, Min-MCS and PF. Designed to ensure the fairness criteria, the PF scheme [8] schedules users based on the ratio of instantaneous channel quality and average throughput. Table 3 shows variation intervals in terms of Jain Fairness Index. Let F_{PMax}, F_{PMin} and F_{PPF} denote, respectively, the fairness difference between the proposed algorithm and Max-SINR, Min-MCS and PF for various users' intervals. As $F_{PPF} > 0$, we show that the proposed scheme provides better performance in terms of fairness compared to PF thanks to the proposed virtual PRB allocation phase. Here, the unused sub-carriers of each user are reallocated to other seldom served ones based on the achieved average throughput. In Fig.5, we compare our proposed PRB allocation scheme performance with Min-MCS and MaX-SINR in terms of BLER defined in (5). Table 4 shows variation intervals in terms of BLER. Let B_{PMax} and B_{PMin}

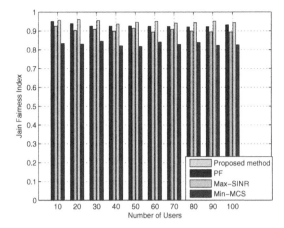

Fig. 4. Jain Fairness Index versus number of users

Table 3. Variation intervals in terms of Jain Fairness Index

Number of users	$[1, 25[$	$[25, 50[$	$[50, 75[$	$[75, 100[$
F_{PMax}	0.0447	0.0422	0.0405	0.0504
F_{PMin}	0.1169	0.1124	0.1172	0.1173
F_{PPF}	0.0141	0.0208	0.0213	0.0214

denote, respectively, the BLER difference between the proposed algorithm and MAX-SINR and Min-MCS. As $B_{PMax} > 0$, for all users number, the proposed method provides better performance than MAX-SINR. Designed to reduce the BLER, Min-MCS provides better performance in the case of unloaded networks ($B_{PMin} > 0$) as it proposes to choose the PRB based on the worst channel quality for each user. However, in the case of loaded networks, the proposed scheme and Min-MCS converge to the same values as $B_{PMin} \simeq 0$ for $k \geq 100$.

Simulation results demonstrate that our proposed resource allocation permits to achieve better performance compared to other existing methods in terms of system capacity and fairness. Since it allocates to each user its best PRB with the highest ESINR, the proposed PRB allocation phase permits to enhance the system capacity as shown in Fig.2. If two users or more have the same order at a PRB, this latter is allocated to the user with the less ESINR on the second best PRB to avoid the decrease of the system capacity. Moreover, the virtual PRB allocation phase gathers the unused sub-carriers to reallocate them to other users with poor channel gains. This permits not only to improve the fairness criteria as shown in Fig.4, but also to improve the system capacity as described in Fig.3. Although Min-MCS is designed to reduce the BLER, our proposed scheme provides similar values in loaded systems as shown in Fig.5.

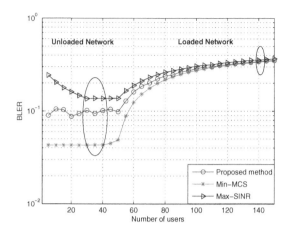

Fig. 5. The BLER versus the number of users

Table 4. Variation intervals in terms of BLER

	$[1, 50[$	$[50, 75[$	$[75, 100[$	$[100, 125[$	$[125, 150]$
B_{PMax}	-0.0531	-0.0272	-0.0159	-0.0143	-0.0141
B_{PMin}	0.0447	0.0367	0.0214	0.006	0

7   Conclusion

A new efficient method for resource allocation in context of MIMO-OFDMA systems has been introduced. It is well suited for system capacity maximization with fairness improvement. Firstly, a PRB allocation algorithm based on a recursive function has been developed. Here, the ESINR metric has been used to properly characterize the CSI. A virtual PRB allocation procedure has been introduced where unused sub-carriers are gathered into virtual PRBs and then reallocated to users with bad average throughput. This procedure enhances the fairness criteria. Secondly, a power allocation procedure, including three steps, has been performed. Finally, a more appropriate MCS has been selected. By comparing the complexity of our proposed resource scheme and other existing ones such as Max-SINR, Min-MCS and PF, we can recognize that the suggested algorithm has achieved interesting performance in terms of system capacity and fairness without increasing the computational complexity level.

References

1. Evolved Universal Terrestrial Radio Access (E-UTRA): Physical Layer Procedures (Release 11), Tech. Rep. 3GPP TS 36.213 V11.5.0 (January 2014), http://www.3gpp.org
2. Tran, S.V., Eltawil, A.M.: Optimized Scheduling Algorithm for LTE Downlink System. In: IEEE WCNC, Princeton, USA, pp. 1462–1466 (April 2012)

3. Perez, D.L., Ladanyi, A., Juttner, A., Rivano, H., Zhang, J.: Optimization Method for the Joint Allocation of Modulation Schemes, Coding Rates, Resource Blocks and Power in Self-Organizing LTE Networks. In: IEEE INFOCOM, pp. 111–115 (2011)
4. Lei, H., Yu, M., Zhao, A., Chang, Y., Yang, D.: Adaptive Connection Admission Control Algorithm for LTE Systems. IEEE VTC Spring, 2336–2340 (2008)
5. Jiancun, F., Qinye, Y., Li, G., Bingguang, P., Xiaolong, Z.: Adaptive Block-Level Resource Allocation in OFDMA Networks. IEEE Transactions on Wireless Communications 10(11), 3966–3972 (2011)
6. Guan, N., Zhou, Y., Tian, L., Sun, G., Shi, J.: QoS Quaranteed Resource Block Allocation Algorithm for LTE Systems. In: IEEE WiMob, pp. 307–312 (2011)
7. Wang, W.M.H., Nguyen, T.: User Fairness Scheme with Proportional Fair Scheduling in Multi-User MIMO Limited Feedback System. Communications and Network 5(3B), 113–118 (2013)
8. Tuan, L.T., Yoo, D., Kim, H., Jin, G., Jang, B., Ro, S.H.: The Modified Proportional Fair Packet Scheduling Algorithm for Multimedia Traffic in LTE System. In: ICHIT, August 23-25, pp. 122–129 (2012)
9. Karachontzitis, S., Dagiuklas, T.: A Chunk-based Resource Allocation Scheme for Downlink MIMO-OFDMA Channel using Linear Precoding. In: IEEE ISCC, pp. 931–936 (2011)
10. Lo, E., Chan, P., Lau, V., Cheng, R., Letaief, K., Murch, R.D., Mow, W.H.: Adaptive Resource Allocation and Capacity Comparison of Downlink Multi-user MIMO-MC-CDMA and MIMO-OFDMA. IEEE Transactions on Wireless Communications 6(3), 1083–1093 (2007)
11. Oborina, A., Henttonen, T., Koivunen, V., Moisio, M.: Efficient Computation of Effective SINR. In: CISS, Princeton, USA (March 2012)
12. Bian, Y., Nix, A., Sun, Y., Strauch, P.: Performance Evaluation of Mobile WiMAX with MIMO and Relay Extensions. In: IEEE WCNC, pp. 1814–1819 (2007)
13. Ikuno, J., Wrulich, M., Rupp, M.: System Level Simulation of LTE Networks. In: IEEE VTC Spring, pp. 1–5 (2010)
14. Sayana, K., Zhang, J., Stewart, K.: Link Performance Abstraction based on Mean Mutual Information per Bit (MMIB) of the LLR Channel, IEEE 802.16 Broadband Wireless Access Working Group., Tech. Rep. (2007)
15. Hassen, W.B., Afif, M.: A Gain-Computation Enhancements Resource Allocation for Heterogeneous Service Flows in IEEE 802. 16m Mobile Networks, International Journal of Digital Multimedia Broadcasting 2012, 1–13 (2012)
16. Olmos, J., Serra, A., Ruiz, S., Garcia-Lozano, M., Gonzalez, D.: Exponential Effective SIR metric for LTE downlink. In: IEEE PIMRC, pp. 900–904 (2009)
17. Yeh, S.P., Talwar, S., Lee, S., Kim, H.: Wimax femtocells: A perspective on network architecture, capacity, and coverage. IEEE Communications Magazine 46(10), 58–65 (2008)
18. Hassen, W.B., Afif, M., Tabbane, S.: An Adaptive PRB, Power and MCS Allocation Using AMC for MIMO-OFDMA Systems. Wireless Personal Communications 75(4), 2549–2567 (2014)
19. Kwan, R., Leung, C., Zhang, J.: Proportional Fair Multiuser Scheduling in LTE. IEEE Signal Processing Letters, 461–464 (June 2009)

Radio Resource Management in Integrated Wired/Wireless LTE Femtocell Networks

Elias Yaacoub

Qatar Mobility Innovations Center
Qatar Science and Technology Park, Doha, Qatar
eliasy@qmic.com

Abstract. In this paper, radio resource management (RRM) in LTE femtocell networks is investigated in an integrated wired/wireless environment. In such a scenario, femtocell access points (FAPs) are assumed connected via wired links to a central controller within a certain vicinity (e.g. building, compound, hotel, campus, etc.). Consequently, it becomes possible to perform RRM in a centralized and controlled way in order to enhance the quality of service (QoS) performance for the users in the network. A utility maximization framework is presented, and an RRM algorithm that can be used to maximize various utility functions is proposed. The performance tradeoffs between various utility functions are studied and assessed. Furthermore, the joint wired/wireless RRM approach is compared to the distributed RRM case, where each FAP acts as an independent wireless network without central control. Simulation results show that the integrated wired/wireless approach leads to significant gains compared to the wireless only case.

Keywords: Radio resource management, femtocell, LTE, proportional fair, wired/wireless networks.

1 Introduction

The proliferation of small cells, notably femtocells, is expected to increase in the coming years [1]. Since most of the wireless traffic is initiated indoors, Femtocell Access Points (FAPs) are designed to handle this traffic and reduce the load on macrocell base stations (BSs). They are small, low power, plug and play devices providing indoor wireless coverage to meet the quality of service (QoS) requirements for indoor data users [2]. FAPs are generally installed inside the home or office of a given subscriber. They are connected to the mobile operator's core network via wired links, e.g. digital subscriber line (DSL) [3]. However, they are not under the direct control of the mobile operator since they are not connected to neighboring macrocell BSs through the standardized interfaces, e.g., the X2 interface for the long term evolution (LTE) cellular system.

Therefore, a main challenge is that the overall interference levels in the network depend on the density of small cells and their operation, which affects the configuration of macrocell sites [4]. In [5], this problem was addressed by proposing macrocell-femtocell cooperation, where a femtocell user may act as a relay for macrocell users, and in return each cooperative macrocell user grants the femtocell user a fraction of its

A. Mellouk et al. (Eds.): WWIC 2014, LNCS 8458, pp. 96–108, 2014.
© Springer International Publishing Switzerland 2014

superframe. In [6], it was assumed that both macrocells and small cells are controlled by the same operator, and it was shown that in this case the operator can control the system loads by tuning the pricing and the bandwidth allocation policy between macrocells and small cells.

On the other hand, other works investigated radio resource management (RRM) in femtocell networks by avoiding interference to/from macrocells. Most of these works focused on using cognitive radio (CR) channel sensing techniques to determine channel availability. In [7], the femtocell uses cognitive radio to sense the spectrum and detect macrocell transmissions to avoid interference. It then performs radio resource management on the free channels. However, there is a time dedicated for sensing the channel that cannot overlap with transmission/RRM time. A channel sensing approach for improving the capacity of femtocell users in macro-femto overlay networks is proposed in [8]. It is based on spatial radio resource reuse based on the channel sensing outcomes. In [9], enhanced spectrum sensing algorithms are proposed for femtocell networks in order to ensure better detection accuracy of channels occupied by macrocell traffic.

In this paper, LTE femtocell networks are investigated. FAPs are not assumed to be controlled by the mobile operator. However, in certain scenarios, FAPs at a given location can be controlled by a single entity. This can happen, for example, in a university campus, hotel, housing complex, or office building. In such scenarios, in addition to the wireless connection between FAPs and mobile terminals (MTs), FAPs can be connected via a wired high-speed network to a central controller within the building or campus. This can allow more efficient RRM decisions leading to significant QoS enhancements for mobile users. Hence, this scenario is studied in this paper, and a utility maximizing RRM algorithm is proposed to perform joint resource allocation over the FAPs controlled by the same entity. Significant gains are shown to be achieved under this integrated wired/wireless scenario compared to the case where each FAP acts independently.

The paper is organized as follows. The system model is presented in Section 2. The utility metrics leading to different QoS and performance targets are described in Section 3. The joint RRM algorithm implemented at the central controller is presented in Section 4. Simulation results are presented and analyzed in Section 5. Finally, in Section 6, conclusions are drawn and indications for future research directions are described.

2 System Model

The system model is shown in Fig. 1. A building with three apartments per floor is considered. One FAP is available in each apartment, and it serves only the users (MTs) available in that apartment. In other words, closed access FAPs are assumed. The FAPs are connected wirelessly to the MTs, but they are connected via a wired network (dashed lines in Fig. 1) to a central controller located within the building (for example, in a room hosting telecom/networking equipment in the basement). Interference is caused by the transmissions of a FAP to the users served by the other FAPs in other apartments. Centralized RRM in an integrated wired/wireless scenario, as shown in Fig. 1, can be used to mitigate the impact of interference and enhance QoS performance. In the absence of

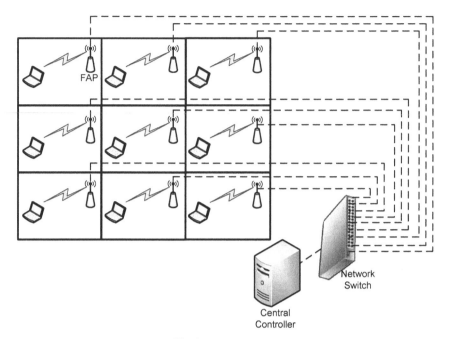

Fig. 1. System model

the central controller and wired connections between FAPs, each FAP would act inde-pendently, without being aware of the network conditions within the coverage areas of other FAPs. This case is referred to as the distributed RRM scenario (as opposed to the centralized case in the presence of the controller). The building of Fig. 1 is considered to be located within the coverage area of a macrocell BS, positioned at a distance d_{BS} from the building. The interference from the macro BS to the FAPs is taken into account in the analysis: it is assumed in this paper that the macro BS is fully loaded, i.e. all its resource blocks (RBs) are occupied, which causes macro interference to all the FAPs in the building, in both the centralized and distributed RRM cases. No coordination is assumed between the mobile operator of the macro BS and the central controller of the building FAPs.

LTE RRM is considered in this paper. The downlink direction (DL) from the FAPs to the MTs is studied, although the presented approach can be easily adapted to the uplink (UL) case, i.e. the direction from the MTs to the FAPs. In LTE, orthogonal frequency division multiple access (OFDMA) is the access scheme used for DL com-munications. The spectrum is divided into RBs, with each RB consisting of 12 adjacent subcarriers. The assignment of an RB takes place every 1 ms, which is the duration of one transmission time interval (TTI), or, equivalently, the duration of two 0.5 ms slots [10,11]. LTE allows bandwidth scalability, where a bandwidth of 1.4, 3, 5, 10, 15, and 20 MHz corresponds to 6, 15, 25, 50, 75, and 100 RBs, respectively [11,12]. In this paper, scenarios where the macro BS and the FAPs are using the same bandwidth are assumed (i.e. a frequency reuse of one where bandwidth chunks in different cells are not orthogonal). Scenarios where the available bandwidth can be either 1.4, 3, or 5 MHz, thus corresponding to 6, 15, or 25 RBs available for resource allocation in each FAP, are considered.

2.1 Channel Model

The pathloss between user k_l (connected to FAP l) and FAP j is given by [13]:

$$PL_{k_l,j,\text{dB}} = 38.46 + 20\log_{10} d_{k_l,j} + 0.3 d_{k_l,j} + 18.3 n^{((n+2)/(n+1)-0.46)} + qL_{\text{iw}} \quad (1)$$

where $d_{k_l,j}$ is the indoor distance between user k_l and FAP j, n is the number of floors separating user k_l and FAP j, q is the number of walls between apartments, and L_{iw} is a per wall penetration loss. In (1), the first term $38.46 + 20\log_{10} d_{k_l,j}$ is the distance dependent free space path loss, the term $0.3 d_{k_l,j}$ models indoor distance dependent attenuation, the term $18.3 n^{((n+2)/(n+1)-0.46)}$ indicates losses due to propagation across floors, and qL_{iw} corresponds to losses across apartment walls in the same floor. In this paper, $L_{\text{iw}} = 5$ dB is used as recommended in [13]. The pathloss between user k_l and its serving FAP l is a special case of (1), with $j = l$, $n = 0$, and $q = 0$.

The FAPs in this paper are assumed to be numbered from $j = 1$ to $j = L$, and the outdoor macro BS is represented by $j = 0$. The pathloss between user k_l connected to FAP l and the macro BS $j = 0$ is given by [13]:

$$PL_{k_l,j,\text{dB}} = 15.3 + 37.6\log_{10} d_{\text{out},k_l,j} + 0.3 d_{\text{in},k_l,j} + qL_{\text{iw}} + L_{\text{ow}} \quad (2)$$

where $d_{\text{out},k_l,j}$ is the distance traveled outdoor between the macro BS and the building external wall, $d_{\text{in},k_l,j}$ is the indoor traveled distance between the building wall and user k_l, and L_{ow} is an outdoor-indoor penetration loss (loss incurred by the outdoor signal to penetrate the building). It is set to $L_{\text{ow}} = 20$ dB [13]. In this paper, the macro BS is considered to be located at a distance d_{BS} from the building. Thus, the indoor distance can be considered negligible compared to the outdoor distance. Furthermore, the macro BS is assumed to be facing the building of Fig. 1, such that $q = 0$ can be used. Thus, the outdoor-indoor propagation model of (2) becomes:

$$PL_{k_l,j,\text{dB}} = 15.3 + 37.6\log_{10} d_{k_l,j} + L_{\text{ow}} \quad (3)$$

Taking into account fading fluctuations in addition to pathloss, the channel gain between user k_l and FAP/BS j can be expressed as:

$$H_{k_l,i,j,\text{dB}} = -PL_{k_l,j,\text{dB}} + \xi_{k_l,j} + 10\log_{10} F_{k_l,i,j} \quad (4)$$

where the first factor captures propagation loss, according to (1) or (2)-(3). The second factor, $\xi_{k_l,j}$, captures log-normal shadowing with zero-mean and a standard deviation σ_ξ (set to $\sigma_\xi = 8$ dB in this paper), whereas the last factor, $F_{k_l,i,j}$, corresponds to Rayleigh fading power between user k_l and FAP or BS j over RB i, with a Rayleigh parameter b such that $E\{|b|^2\} = 1$. It should be noted that fast Rayleigh fading is assumed to be approximately constant over the subcarriers of a given RB, and independent identically distributed (iid) over RBs.

2.2   Calculation of the Data Rates

Letting $\mathcal{I}_{\mathrm{sub},k_l}$ and $\mathcal{I}_{\mathrm{RB},k_l}$ be the sets of subcarriers and RBs, respectively, allocated to user k_l in femtocell l, N_{RB} the total number of RBs, L the number of FAPs, K_l the number of users connected to FAP l, $P_{i,l}^{(\mathrm{DL})}$ the power transmitted over subcarrier i by FAP l, $P_{l,\mathrm{max}}$ the maximum transmission power of FAP l, and R_{k_l} the achievable data rate of user k_l in cell l, then the OFDMA throughput of user k_l in cell l is given by:

$$R_{k_l}(\mathbf{P}_1, \mathcal{I}_{\mathrm{sub},k_l}) = \sum_{i \in \mathcal{I}_{\mathrm{sub},k_l}} B_{\mathrm{sub}} \cdot \log_2\left(1 + \beta \gamma_{k_l,i,l}\right) \tag{5}$$

where B_{sub} is the subcarrier bandwidth. It is expressed as:

$$B_{\mathrm{sub}} = \frac{B}{N_{\mathrm{sub}}} \tag{6}$$

with B the total usable bandwidth, and N_{sub} the total number of subcarriers. In (5), β refers to the so-called signal to noise ratio (SNR) gap. It indicates the difference between the SNR needed to achieve a certain data transmission rate for a practical M-QAM (quadrature amplitude modulation) system and the theoretical limit (Shannon capacity) [14]. It is given by:

$$\beta = \frac{-1.5}{\ln(5P_b)} \tag{7}$$

where P_b denotes the target bit error rate (BER), set to $P_b = 10^{-6}$ in this paper.

In addition, in (5), $\mathbf{P}_1$ represents a vector of the transmitted power on each subcarrier by FAP/BS l, $P_{i,l}$. In this paper, the transmit power is considered to be equally allocated over the subcarriers. Hence, for all i:

$$P_{i,l} = \frac{P_{l,\mathrm{max}}}{N_{\mathrm{sub}}} \tag{8}$$

The signal to interference plus noise ratio (SINR) of user k_l over subcarrier i in cell l in the DL, $\gamma_{k_l,i,l}$, is expressed as:

$$\gamma_{k_l,i,l} = \frac{P_{i,l} H_{k_l,i,l}}{I_{i,k_l} + \sigma_{i,k_l}^2} \tag{9}$$

where σ_{i,k_l}^2 is the noise power over subcarrier i in the receiver of user k_l, and I_{i,k_l} is the interference on subcarrier i measured at the receiver of user k_l. The expression of the interference is given by:

$$I_{i,k_l} = \sum_{j \neq l, j=0}^{L} \left(\sum_{k_j=1}^{K_j} \alpha_{k_j,i,j} \right) \cdot P_{i,j} H_{k_l,i,j} \tag{10}$$

In (10), $\alpha_{k_j,i,j}$ is a binary variable representing the exclusivity of subcarrier allocation: $\alpha_{k_j,i,j} = 1$ if subcarrier i is allocated to user k_j in cell j, i.e., $i \in \mathcal{I}_{\mathrm{sub},k_j}$, and $\alpha_{k_j,i,j} = 0$ otherwise. In fact, in each cell, an LTE RB, along with the subcarriers constituting that RB, can be allocated to a single user at a given TTI. Consequently, the following is verified in each cell j:

$$\sum_{k_j=1}^{K_j} \alpha_{k_j,i,j} \leq 1 \tag{11}$$

The term corresponding to $j = 0$ in (10) represents the interference from the macro BS, whereas the terms corresponding to $j = 1$ to $j = L$ represent the interference from the other FAPs in the building.

3   Network Utility Maximization

In this section, the problem formulation for maximizing the network utility is presented. In addition, different utility metrics leading to different QoS objectives are presented and discussed.

3.1   Problem Formulation

With $U^{(l)}$ and U_{k_l} denoting the utility of FAP l and user k_l, respectively, such that $U^{(l)} = \sum_{k_l=1}^{K_l} U_{k_l}$, then the objective is to maximize the total utility in the network of Fig. 1, $\sum_{l=1}^{L} U^{(l)}$:

$$\max_{\alpha_{k_l,i,l},P_{i,l}} U_{\text{tot}} = \sum_{l=1}^{L} U^{(l)} \tag{12}$$

Subject to:

$$\sum_{i=1}^{N_{\text{sub}}} P_{i,l} \leq P_{l,\max}; \forall l = 1, ..., L \tag{13}$$

$$\sum_{k_l=1}^{K_l} \alpha_{k_l,i,l} \leq 1; \forall i = 1, ..., N_{\text{sub}}; \forall l = 1, ..., L \tag{14}$$

The constraint in (13) indicates that the transmit power cannot exceed the maximum FAP transmit power, whereas he constraint in (14) corresponds to the exclusivity of subcarrier allocation in each femtocell, since in each LTE cell, a subcarrier can be allocated at most to a unique user at a given scheduling instant. Different utility functions depending on the users' data rates are described next.

3.2   Utility Selection

The utility metrics investigated include Max C/I, proportional fair (PF), and Max-Min utilities. The impact of their implementation on the sum-rate, geometric mean, maximum and minimum data rates in the network is studied in Section 5 using the Algorithm of Section 4.

Max C/I Utility: Letting the utility equal to the data rate $U_k = R_k$, the formulation in (12) becomes a greedy maximization of the sum-rate in the network. This approach is known in the literature as Max C/I. However, in this case, users with favorable channel and interference conditions will be allocated most of the resources and will achieve very high data rates, whereas users suffering from higher propagation losses and/or interference levels will be deprived from RBs and will have very low data rates.

Min-Max Utility: Due to the unfairness of Max C/I resource allocation, the need for more fair utility metrics arises. Max-Min utilities are a family of utility functions attempting to maximize the minimum data rate in the network, e.g., [15,16]. A vector $\mathbf{R}$ of user data rates is Max-Min fair if and only if, for each k, an increase in R_k leads to a decrease in R_j for some j with $R_j < R_k$ [15]. By increasing the priority of users having lower rates, Max-Min utilities lead to more fairness in the network. It was shown that Max-Min fairness can be achieved by utilities of the form [16]:

$$U_k(R_k) = -\frac{R_k^{-a}}{a}, a > 0 \tag{15}$$

where the parameter a determines the degree of fairness. Max-Min fairness is attained when $a \to \infty$ [16]. we use $a = 10$ in this paper. However, enhancing the worst case performance could come at the expense of users with good channel conditions (and who could achieve high data rates) that will be unfavored by the RRM algorithms in order to increase the rates of worst case users. A tradeoff between max C/I and Max-Min RRM can be achieved through proportional fair (PF) utilities, described next.

Proportional Fair Utility: A tradeoff between the maximization of the sum rate and the maximization of the minimum rate could be the maximization of the geometric mean data rate. The geometric mean data rate for K users is given by:

$$R^{(\mathrm{gm})} = \left(\prod_{k=1}^{K} R_k\right)^{1/K} \tag{16}$$

The metric (16) is fair, since a user with a data rate close to zero will make the whole product in $R^{(\mathrm{gm})}$ go to zero. Hence, any RRM algorithm maximizing $R^{(\mathrm{gm})}$ would avoid having any user with very low data rate. In addition, the metric (16) will reasonably favor users with good wireless channels (capable of achieving high data rate), since a high data rate will contribute in increasing the product in (16).

To be able to write the geometric mean in a sum-utility form as in (12), it can be noted that maximizing the geometric mean in (16) is equivalent to maximizing the product, which is equivalent to maximizing the sum of logarithms:

$$\max \prod_{k=1}^{K} R_k \iff \max \ln\left(\prod_{k=1}^{K} R_k\right)$$

$$= \max \sum_{k=1}^{K} \ln(R_k) \tag{17}$$

Consequently, the algorithmic implementation of (17) can be handled by the algorithm of Section 4, by using, in that algorithm, $U_k = \ln(R_k)$ as the utility of user k, where $\ln$ represents the natural logarithm. Maximizing the sum of logarithms in (17) is equivalent to maximizing the product and is easier to implement numerically. Hence, letting $U = \ln(R)$ provides proportional fairness [16,17].

Algorithm 1. Utility Maximization Algorithm

1: **for all** FAP l and user k_l **do**
2:      **for all** RB j **do**
3:          $\alpha_{k_l,j}^{\text{old}} = 0$
4:          $U_{k_l}^{\text{old}}(\alpha^{\text{old}}) = 0$
5:      **end for**
6: **end for**
7: $U_{\text{tot}}^{\text{old}} = \sum_{l=1}^{L} \sum_{k_l=1}^{K_l} U_{k_l}^{\text{old}}(\alpha^{\text{old}})$
8: $I_{\text{Improvement}} = 1$
9: **while** $I_{\text{Improvement}} = 1$ **do**
10:      **for all** FAP l and user k_l **do**
11:          **for all** RB j **do**
12:              $\alpha^{\text{new}} = \alpha^{\text{old}}$
13:              $\alpha_{k_l,j}^{\text{new}} = 1$
14:              **for all** FAP m and user k_m **do**
15:                  Calculate the interference and achievable data rates in the network
16:                  Calculate $U_{k_m}^{\text{new}}(\alpha^{\text{new}})$
17:              **end for**
18:              $U_{\text{tot}}^{\text{new}} = \sum_{l=1}^{L} \sum_{k_l=1}^{K_l} U_{k_l}^{\text{new}}(\alpha^{\text{new}})$
19:              $\delta_{k_l,j} = U_{\text{tot}}^{\text{new}} - U_{\text{tot}}^{\text{old}}$
20:          **end for**
21:      **end for**
22:      Find $(k^*, l^*, j^*) = \arg\max_{k,l,j} \delta_{k_l,j}$
23:      **if** $\delta_{k_{l*}^*,j^*} > 0$ **then**
24:          $\alpha_{k_{l*}^*,j^*}^{\text{old}} = 1$
25:          **for all** FAP m and user k_m **do**
26:              Calculate the interference and achievable data rates in the network
27:              Calculate $U_{k_m}^{\text{old}}(\alpha^{\text{old}})$
28:          **end for**
29:          $U_{\text{tot}}^{\text{old}} = \sum_{l=1}^{L} \sum_{k_l=1}^{K_l} U_{k_l}^{\text{old}}(\alpha^{\text{old}})$
30:          $I_{\text{Improvement}} = 1$
31:      **else**
32:          $I_{\text{Improvement}} = 0$
33:      **end if**
34: **end while**

---

4   Centralized RRM Algorithm

To perform the maximization of (12), we use the utility maximization algorithm, Algorithm 1, described in this section. The proposed algorithm can be applied with a wide range of utility functions, thus being able to achieve various objectives, with each objective represented by a certain utility function. Hence, it can be used for max C/I, PF, and Max-Min RRM, with the utilities derived in Section 3.2.

Lines 1-8 in Algorithm 1 are used for initialization. The loop in lines 10-21 determines the network utility enhancement that can be achieved by each (user, RB) allocation. The allocation leading to maximum enhancement (Line 22) is performed if it leads to an increase in network utility (Lines 23-30). After each allocation, the interference levels in the network vary. Hence, interference and data rates are updated and the novel utilities are computed. The process is repeated until no additional improvement can be obtained (Lines 9-34), with $I_{\mathrm{Improvement}}$ being an indicator variable tracking if an improvement in network utility has been achieved ($I_{\mathrm{Improvement}} = 1$) or not ($I_{\mathrm{Improvement}} = 0$).

Algorithm 1 is implemented by the central controller in the scenario described in Section 2. In this paper, one user is considered to be active per femtocell, without loss of generality. In the case where each FAP performs RRM in a distributed way (without wired connections to a central controller), then the maximization of the three utility types in each femtocell is achieved by allocating all the RBs of a given FAP to the active user. In fact, in this case, there would be no information about the channel gains and interference levels in the other femtocells. Thus, it makes sense for each FAP to try to maximize the QoS of its served user by allocating all available resources to that user. For a given FAP l, this corresponds, simultaneously, to maximizing the sum rate, maximizing the logarithm of the rate, and maximizing the minimum rate (In fact, with one user k_l present, R_{k_l} is the only rate and thus would correspond to the sum rate, the minimum rate, and the geometric mean data rate in cell l). This uncoordinated allocation will lead to an increase in interference levels, and to an overall degradation of performance in the network, as shown by the results of Section 5.

5   Results and Discussion

This section presents the Matlab simulation results obtained by implementing the proposed approach under the system model of Section 2. We consider a building as shown in Fig. 1. Three apartments per floor are assumed, with one active user per apartment using the FAP to access the network (assuming one FAP per apartment). Scenarios with one floor only (three apartments on ground floor), two floors (six apartments), and three floors (nine apartments) are investigated, with the results shown in Figs. 2, 3, and 4, respectively. The maximum FAP transmit power is set to 1 Watt, whereas the transmit power of the macro BS is set to 10 Watts.

The figures show that max C/I scheduling leads to the highest sum-rate in the network. However, this comes at the expense of fairness, as it can be seen from the geometric mean results of max C/I. In fact, the bottom subfigures of Figs. 2 to 4 show that max C/I enhances the maximum rate in the network, by allocating most of the resources

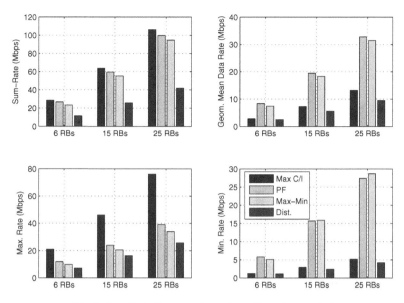

Fig. 2. Results in the case of one floor (three femtocells)

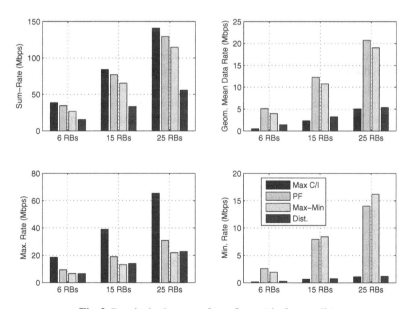

Fig. 3. Results in the case of two floors (six femtocells)

to the user having the best channel and interference conditions, while depriving other users from sufficient resources, thus leading to unfairness, as shown by the minimum rate plots. On the other hand, PF scheduling maximizes the geometric mean for all the investigated scenarios. Clearly, the minimum rates achieved with PF indicate that a PF

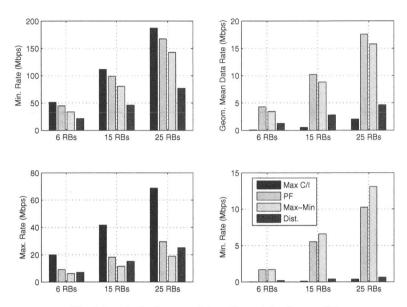

Fig. 4. Results in the case of three floors (nine femtocells)

utility is significantly more fair than max C/I. The results of Max-Min scheduling also show a fair performance. In fact, Max-Min resource allocation leads to maximizing the minimum rate in the network for almost all the studied scenarios, except in the case of one and two floors with six RBs, where it is slightly outperformed by PF. This is due to the approximation performed by taking, in (15), $a = 10$ instead of $a = \infty$. When the number of resources increases to 15 and 25 RBs, the algorithm has additional flexibility to implement RRM with Max-Min such that the minimum rate is maximized compared to the other methods. It can also be noted that Max-Min scheduling leads to a geometric mean performance that is reasonably close to that of PF scheduling, indicating that it also enhances overall fairness in the network. Figs. 2 to 4 also show that, as expected, the data rates increase for all the studied metrics when the number of RBs increases.

Comparing the joint wired/wireless case to the distributed scenario where each FAP performs RRM independently without centralized control, it can be seen that the distributed scenario is outperformed by the integrated wired/wireless approach for all the investigated metrics: Max C/I leads to a higher sum-rate, PF leads to a higher geometric mean, and Max-Min leads to a higher minimum rate. This is due to the fact that with distributed RRM, a FAP is not aware of the interference conditions to/from other FAPs and users. This leads to a severe performance degradation, as can be seen in Figs. 2 to 4, although all the RBs of a given FAP are allocated to the user served by that FAP.

6   Conclusions and Future Work

In this paper, radio resource management in LTE femtocell networks was investigated. The studied scenario consisted of an integrated wired/wireless environment, where the femtocell access points are controlled by a single entity. This permits performing joint radio resource management in a centralized and controlled way in order to enhance the quality of service performance for all users in the networks. A utility maximizing radio resource management algorithm was presented, and it was used to maximize different utility functions leading to different target objectives in terms of network sum-rate, fairness, and enhancing the worst-case performance in the network. The joint wired/wireless resource management approach was compared to the distributed resource management case, where each femtocell acts as an independent wireless network unaware of the channel and interference conditions with the other cells. The integrated wired/wireless approach led to significant gains compared to the wireless only case, and the performance tradeoffs between the various utility functions were analyzed and assessed.

Although centralized control was considered, it was assumed in this paper that each user is served by a single FAP. An interesting topic for future investigation consists of allowing users to use the resources of other FAPs in the joint wired/wireless case, in order to enhance the performance even more. This requires that the users accept that their FAPs be open access. Furthermore, instead of considering the maximization of utility functions, different services categorized by different QoS requirements (e.g. different data rate thresholds) can be considered. Another interesting research direction is to investigate distributed measures for intercell interference mitigation in the absence of centralized control, with or without resorting to cognitive radio channel sensing techniques.

Acknowledgment. This work was made possible by NPRP grant # 4-347-2-127 from the Qatar National Research Fund (a member of The Qatar Foundation). The statements made herein are solely the responsibility of the author.

References

1. Andrews, J.G., Claussen, H., Dohler, M., Rangan, S., Reed, M.C.: Femtocells: Past, Present, and Future. IEEE Journal on Selected Areas in Communications 30(3), 497–508 (2012)
2. Chandrasekkhar, V., Andrews, J., Gatherer, A.: Femtocell Networks: A Survey. IEEE Communications Magazine 46(9), 59–67 (2008)
3. Knisely, D., Yoshizawa, T., Favichia, F.: Standardization of Femtocells in 3GPP. IEEE Communications Magazine 47(9), 68–75 (2009)
4. Chandrasekhar, V., Kountouris, M., Andrews, J.G.: Coverage in Multi-Antenna Two-Tier Networks. IEEE Transactions on Wireless Communications 8(10), 5314–5327 (2009)
5. Pantisano, F., Bennis, M., Saad, W., Debbah, M.: Spectrum Leasing as an Incentive towards Uplink Macrocell and Femtocell Cooperation. IEEE Journal on Selected Areas in Communications 30(3), 617–630 (2012)
6. Gussen, C., Belmega, V., Debbah, M.: Pricing and Bandwidth Allocation Problems in Wireless Multi-Tier Networks. In: Proceedings of Asilomar Conference on Signals Systems and Computers, pp. 1633–1637 (2011)
7. Lien, S.-Y., Tseng, C.-C., Chen, K.-C., Su, C.-W.: Cognitive Radio Resource Management for QoS Guarantees in Autonomous Femtocell Networks. In: Proceedings of the IEEE International Conference on Communications (ICC 2010), pp. 1–6 (2010)

8. Hong, S., Oh, C.-Y., Lee, T.-J.: Resource Allocation Method Using Channel Sensing and Resource Reuse for Cognitive Femtocells. International Journal of Information and Electronics Engineering 3(3), 309–312 (2013)

9. Abdelmonem, M.A., Nafie, M., Ismail, M.H., El-Soudani, M.S.: Optimized Spectrum Sensing Algorithms for Cognitive LTE Femtocells. EURASIP Journal on Wireless Communications and Networking 2012(6), 19 p. (Open Access) (2012)

10. 3rd Generation Partnership Project (3GPP). 3GPP TS 36.211 3GPP TSG RAN Evolved Universal Terrestrial Radio Access (E-UTRA) Physical Channels and Modulation, version 11.4.0, Release 11 (2013)

11. 3rd Generation Partnership Project (3GPP). 3GPP TS 36.213 3GPP TSG RAN Evolved Universal Terrestrial Radio Access (E-UTRA) Physical layer procedures, version 11.4.0, Release 11 (2013)

12. Myung, H.G., Goodman, D.J.: Single Carrier FDMA: A New Air Interface for Long Term Evolution. John Wiley and Sons, Chichester (2008)

13. Qualcomm Inc., 3GPP TSG-RAN WG1 #72 R1-130598, Agenda item: 7.3.7. Channel Models for D2D Deployments. St. Julian's, Malta (2013)

14. Qiu, X., Chawla, K.: On the Performance of Adaptive Modulation in Cellular Systems. IEEE Transactions on Communications 47(6), 884–895 (1999)

15. Le Boudec, J.-Y.: Rate adaptation, Congestion Control and Fairness: A Tutorial. Tech. Report, Ecole Polytechnique Federale de Lausanne (EPFL), Lausanne, Switzerland (2008)

16. Song, G., Li, Y.: Cross-Layer Optimization for OFDM Wireless Networks-Part I: Theoretical Framework. IEEE Transactions on Wireless Communications 4(2), 614–624 (2005)

17. Yaacoub, E., Dawy, Z.: Resource Allocation in Uplink OFDMA Wireless Systems: Optimal Solutions and Practical Implementations. John Wiley and Sons / IEEE Press, NY (2012) ISBN: 978-1-1180-7450-3

Peer-to-Peer Adaptive Forward Error Correction in Live Video Streaming over Wireless Mesh Network

Hamid Reza Ghaeini[1] and Behzad Akbari[2]

[1]Multimedia and Networking Lab, Department of Electrical and Computer Engineering,
Tarbiat Modares University, Tehran, Iran
Ghaeini.Hamid.R@IEEE.org
[2] Department of Electrical and Computer Engineering,
Tarbiat Modares University, Tehran, Iran
B.Akbari@Modares.ac.ir

Abstract. Recently, Peer-to-Peer (P2P) video streaming over multi-hop wireless networks such as Wireless Mesh Networks (WMNs) has been of great interest among users. Although low implementation/maintenance cost, high network throughput, easy implementation, self-configuration and self-healing make WMNs as a suitable infrastructure for multimedia streaming, providing high level of Quality-of-Service (QoS) remains as an open issue. QoS improvement is an important and fundamental problem in P2P live video streaming over WMNs. In order to address this issue, this study proposes an efficient adaptive hybrid Forward Error Correction (FEC) P2P video loss recovery method with low overhead. We formulate the problem as a residual loss probability and show that an adaptive distributed method can significantly reduce video distortion and end-to-end delay while it reduces the imposed overhead due to data protection. Also the comprehensive simulation results show that the proposed method provides high video quality in comparison with other analyzed methods.

Keywords: Quality-of-Service; Video Streaming; Peer-to-Peer; Wireless Mesh Network.

1 Introduction

Wireless mesh network (WMN) is an emerging communication network for seamlessly Internet access over the Internet, which will be the key infrastructure of future wireless communications. In recent years, multimedia networking over disruptive networks such as WMNs has been of great interest among users and researchers. Low implementation and maintenance costs, high network throughout, easy implementation, self-configuration and self-healing are the most important advantages of this type of networks. Moreover, WMNs provide access to large bandwidth over wireless networks while supporting mobility of users under the network coverage. Video streaming can efficiently exploit the advantages of enough bandwidth over WMNs.

A. Mellouk et al. (Eds.): WWIC 2014, LNCS 8458, pp. 109–121, 2014.
© Springer International Publishing Switzerland 2014

In WMN, each packet from the source node can arrive at the destination node in a multi-hop manner according to the employed path selection routing protocol [1]. Most of the handheld wireless mesh devices such as laptop, tablet and mobile phones cannot transmit the radio signal in a long distance. Moreover, they may have mobility inside or often get outside the network coverage. Each node, according to the employed path selection algorithm, may use nearby wireless mesh node or wireless mesh router for communicating to other nodes. Node to node communication in WMN lets the network provide wide coverage area and robust against peer departure [2]. A wireless mesh network is a special type of mobile ad-hoc networks (MANET) which uses modified MANET routing protocols. However, an important difference between MANET and WMN is that wireless mesh networks consist of stable backbone with mixed Wire and Wireless structure, large coverage area and high power nodes i.e. wireless mesh routers. There are three types of routing protocols in WMNs including reactive, proactive and hybrid routing protocols. New advances in hybrid routing protocols made these routing protocols suitable for video streaming over WMN [3].

Peer-to-Peer (P2P) video streaming is also interesting for service providers, because of low implementation and maintenance cost. A P2P system is a distributed system so that clients directly communicate to each other without specific need to an infrastructure or a central server. Clients can simultaneously act as a server or a client. P2P networks can be setup over LAN, WAN or the Internet. Each peer needs specific or compatible software for participating in the P2P overlay.

To provide high Quality-of-Service (QoS) is the main goal of such a video streaming system over WMNs. Therefore, the necessity of introducing enhanced and new techniques for providing high QoS on nodes is inevitable. Two main important parameters, which can measure video streaming quality, are video distortion and end-to-end delay [4]. This study introduces such an efficient method and measures its performance based on these two metrics.

The rest of the paper is organized as follows. In section 2, we discuss some newly introduced adaptive packet loss recovery methods as related work to our proposed method. The details of the proposed method are explained in section 3. In section 4, the simulation results are presented and discussed. Finally, the paper is concluded in section 5.

2   Related Works

2.1   P2P Video Streaming over WMNs

Multimedia networking is one of the most interesting applications of P2P networking. Nowadays, P2P video and audio conferencing can be adopted by P2P platforms so that recent conferencing applications such as Skype use P2P communication for providing better performance. There are many P2P structures for P2P content sharing applications [5]. P2P architecture can be divided into three categories including structured, unstructured and hybrid systems [6].

Efficient architecture for video streaming applications in P2P system is mesh-root architecture [7]. The root architecture is good for live video streaming [8]. In contrast to simple mesh or tree architecture, the mesh-tree architecture performs better in disruptive networks like WMN [9,10]. Figure 1 shows simple mesh-tree architecture for video streaming over WMN.

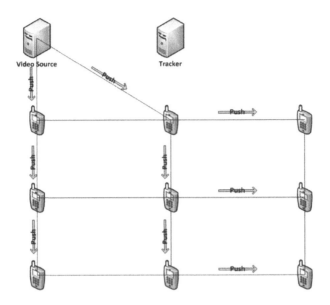

Fig. 1. Simple Mesh-Tree architecture for P2P video streaming over WMN

2.2   Packet Loss Recovery

Packet loss recovery methods can improve the quality of video streaming services and reduce video distortion. Packet loss recovery methods improve overall video streaming quality in P2P video streaming over WMNs. Hybrid packet loss recovery methods consider the overall loss probability of a node to other nodes and compute the FEC overhead based on this loss probability. However, in P2P networks, there are specific neighbors that communicate to that node and it is better to consider the loss probability between two specific nodes for computing. In disruptive networks, because of high loss probability, packet loss recovery is a fundamental method for recovering errors and is one the important parts of video streaming applications over disruptive networks. There are three types of packet loss recovery methods in video streaming over WMNs:

- Backward Error Correction (BEC): In this method every packet loss will be recovered after packet transmission and ask the sender for retransmission.
- Forward Error Correction (FEC): Using this method, some overhead will be added to the original packets before packet transmission and this overhead can be used for recovering the corrupted packet.

- Hybrid Error Correction: In this method, some packets may be protected by FEC and after receiving corrupted packet, if FEC method can't recover the lost packets, BEC will be used for recovering the loss.

Recent studies such as [11] compare different packet loss recovery schemes in P2P video streaming over WMNs. The obtained results show that unequal importance packet loss recovery schemes provide better performance than that of other packet loss recovery schemes. The performed study in [12] proposes an adaptive packet loss recovery method for P2P video streaming over WMNs. As a common hybrid packet loss recovery method, authors of [12] used local residual loss probability estimation and did not consider loss probability between the sender and the receiver in P2P video streaming over WMNs. In WMNs, loss probability between neighbors of a peer is highly different. So, distributed residual loss probability estimation can provide better performance than that of local residual loss probability estimation method.

3   Proposed Method

In this paper, a distributed residual loss probability estimation method for Adaptive FEC in P2P video streaming over WMNs is proposed. Our proposed method focuses on protecting high importance frames same as performed study in [12]. In this architecture, a central server, named Tracker, keeps the statuses of all peers and their neighbors. If one peer wants to join the mesh, it first asks the tracker for neighbor's lists and then, randomly sends joining messages to some of them. After mesh overlay construction, pull-based video streaming will start. Loss probability among a node and its neighbors will be estimated during video streaming session. In single layer MPEG4 video coding, that is a common video coding structure for P2P video streaming applications, a group of pictures (GOP) consists of specific number of frames and each GOP consist of three types of frames [13] as follows:

- Intra coded picture (I-frame): This frame is a reference frame for other frames P and B in decoding. In fact, it can be used as a reference point in video recovery process. In this regard, frame I is larger in size than other frames. The whole of GOP will be lost if frame I cannot be decoded.
- Predictive coded picture (P-frame): Successfully decoding of Predictive frames depend on the preceding I or P-frame.
- Bidirectional predictive coded picture (B-frame): Successfully decoding of Bidirectional predictive coded frames depend on the preceding and following I- or P-frame within a GOP.

Figure 2 shows sample Group of picture structure with three P-frames between I-frames and two B-frames between I- or P-frames and an example of corresponding frames in the silence of the lamb video.

Fig. 2. Group of picture structure with three P-frames between I-frames and two B-frames between I- or P-frames (GOP12)

After a time period of loss probability estimation, each node starts to protect high importance video frames like I-frames according to the employed adaptive loss recovery scheme. In WMNs, packet error rate is high and FEC protection must be considered in all multimedia applications over WMNs. In these networks, each wireless mesh node has a limitation in retransmission of sending NAK in the physical layer. Hence, the retransmission approach is very conventional in these networks. In the application layer and in the loss situations, the system will try up to N_{max} retransmissions so that receive the parity packets or original packet regarding to architecture of loss recovery method. In FEC method, based on the packet error rate of channel, packet redundancy can be increased.

We call packet loss probability in node i as p_i. In adaptive FEC based R packets will be added to the D original packets. If there are more than R packet losses within the same FEC protected video packet, the entire of video packets will not be decodable. Video packets will be decodable unless video packets will not be decodable if there are packet losses between 0 to R. Hence, the upper bound of residual loss probability will be [14]:

$$\varepsilon_i = \sum_{k=R+1}^{D+R} \binom{D+R}{k} p_i^k (1-p_i)^{R+D-k} \qquad (1)$$

However if there are some original video packets that do not affected by error during communication, these video packets can be used and the remaining lost video packets need to be retransmitted. Let there be k lost packets, the probability that v of them are original video packets and others are redundant packets can be given by Equation 2:

$$Pr\{v \mid k \; packet \; loss\} = \frac{\binom{D}{v}\binom{R}{k-v}}{\binom{D+R}{k}} \qquad (2)$$

So, the average number of original video packet losses in k packet losses of protected video packets is:

$$\sum_{v=1}^{v=\min(D,k)} vPr\{v|k \; packet \; loss\} = \frac{kD}{D+R} \qquad (3)$$

By conditioning k, residual loss probability is given by:

$$\varepsilon_i = \sum_{k=R+1}^{D+R} \binom{D+R}{k} p_i^k (1-p_i)^{R+D-k} \frac{k}{D+R} \tag{4}$$

For protecting original video packets by FEC redundant packets that maintain a residual loss probability no more than p_{max}, redundant FEC packets must be at least:

$$R_{FEC(i)} = min\{R|\varepsilon_i \leq p_{max}\} \tag{5}$$

In contrast to simple video streaming, in P2P video streaming over WMNs each node has specific neighbors that transmit video stream. Also because of multi-hop manner of communication in WMN loss probability between WMN nodes is highly different. Proposed distributed residual loss probability estimation method considers loss probability between two specific WMN nodes. Let p_{ij} be the packet loss probability of video streaming between node i and node j. So the residual loss probability between nodes i and j is given by ε_{ij}.

$$\varepsilon_{ij} = \sum_{k=R+1}^{D+R} \binom{D+R}{k} p_{ij}^k (1-p_{ij})^{R+D-k} \frac{k}{D+R} \tag{6}$$

And redundant FEC packets must be at least as depicted in (7):

$$R_{FEC(j,i)} = min\{R|\varepsilon_{ij} \leq p_{max}\} \tag{7}$$

Hence the overhead of sending the same video packet to specific n neighbors of node i can be given by (8):

$$R_{FEC} = \sum_{j=1}^{n} min\{R|\varepsilon_{ij} \leq p_{max}\} \tag{8}$$

4   Simulation and Results

In this section, the proposed method is comprehensively evaluated by analytical and network simulations. First, the imposed overhead by the proposed method is analytically evaluated with different parameter in a P2P network using MATLAB based on Equations (5) and (8). Then, a comprehensive evaluation of P2P video streaming over WMNs between local and distributed residual loss probability estimation in adaptive hybrid FEC is presented.

4.1   Overhead Analysis

In this test, we evaluate what the impact of distributed residual loss probability estimation is on the overhead of communication of different P2P video streaming scenarios.

First, local and distributed residual loss probability estimation has been implemented in MATLAB [15] and this code generates 600 video frames that each frame divided from 10 to 30 video packets and protected by FEC redundant packets based on the p_{max} value. Table I shows the conditions of this typical experiment.

Table 1. Conditions of Typical Experiment

Variable	Value
Number of video frames	600 frames (20 sec. video:30 frame/sec.)
Number of packets per frame	Uniform(10,30)
Pmax	0.001,0.0005,0.0001
Loss probability	Uniform(0.1,0.3)

Figures 3 to 5 show the results of typical experiment between number of redundant video packets for maintaining local and distributed residual loss probability less than P_{max} values. Also these picture show analytical comparison between distributed and local FEC methods when P_{max}=0.0001, 0.0005 and 0.001. What can be inferred from these figures is that, by increasing in the number of neighbors, the rate of the overhead packets in distributed method are decreased in comparison with those related to local method. Actually, more number of overhead packets is imposed on the network when P_{max}=0.0001.

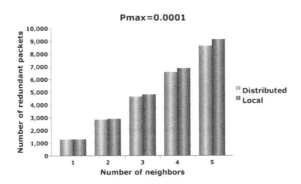

Fig. 3. Experimental overhead analysis between Distributed and Local residual loss probability estimation with P_{max}=0.0001

Figure 3 shows the number of overhead packets with the highest amount of FEC loss tolerance when P_{max}=0.00001. In this case, more number of overhead packets are imposed in comparison with other cases. As can be seen, in the most resilience case, the difference in the number of introduced overhead packets by distributed method is lower than that of introduced by local method.

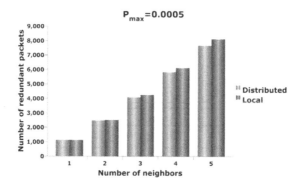

Fig. 4. Experimental overhead analysis between Distributed and Local residual loss probability estimation with P_{max}=0.0005

Figure 4 shows the number of introduced overhead packets with medium FEC loss tolerance when P_{max}=0.0005. In this case, more and less number of overhead packets are imposed in comparison with the cases of P_{max}=0.001 and P_{max}=0.0001, respectively. As can be seen in this figure, the difference in the number of overhead packets due to using distributed method is smaller than that of local method when medium FEC loss tolerance is considered.

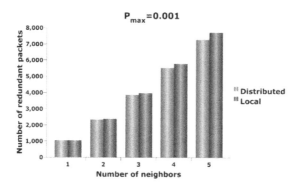

Fig. 5. Experimental overhead analysis between Distributed and Local residual loss probability estimation with P_{max}=0.001

Figure 5 shows the number of generated overhead packets with the least amount of FEC loss tolerance when P_{max}=0.001. In this case, less number of overhead packets is generated in comparison with other two cases. As can be seen in this figure, the difference in the number of overhead packets due to using distributed method is smaller than that of local method when low FEC loss tolerance is considered. As can be seen, the distributed residual loss probability estimation method imposes lower overhead than that of the local residual loss probability estimation method in a P2P network with different amount of FEC loss tolerance.

4.2   Network Simulation

OMNeT++ [16], an open source scientific network tool, is a discrete event simulator for computer networks. There are several different simulation frameworks in OM-NeT++. In this research, the OverSim 2.0 [17] and the INETMANET 2.0 [18] frameworks are employed. INETMANET 2.0 is a leading wireless communication simulation framework which can be efficiently used for simulation of WMNs. OverSim 2.0 is a P2P simulator that builds a P2P overlay on the top of INETMANET 2.0 networks like WMN. Table 2 describes simulation conditions considering by this study.

Video distortion and end-to-end delay are the most important QoS parameters in video streaming systems. Video distortion is the capacity of not decodable frames to the total amount of capacity of all frames in percent. End-to-end delay is the average of delay that a frame sent from source to the destination. Video distortion and end-to-end delay are the most important parameters in video QoS measurement [8].

Table 2. OMNeT++ Simulation Conditions

Variable	Value
Simulation time	600s
Video Trace File	The Silence of the Lambs
Standard codec	MPEG4
Packet size	100 Kb
Wireless propagation model	Path Loss Reception
Number of P-frames in a GOP	3
Number of B-frames between two I- or P-frames	2
Peer Video Buffer	100s
Average Chunk Length	130 Kb
MTU	7891
P_{max}	0.001,0.0005,0.0001
Neighbors	Uniform (3,5)
Node mobility	Random Walk
Wireless node mobility speed	Uniform(2mps,6mps)

Figures 6 to 8 shows the amount of video distortion in P2P live video streaming over WMNs using the CoolStreaming [19], distributed and local residual loss probability estimation in adaptive FEC method.

Figure 6 shows that in the highest level of FEC loss tolerance, our method provides the least amount of the video distortion for various network sizes from 20 to 100 peers.

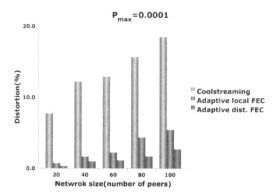

Fig. 6. Video distortion comparison between simple Coolstreaming, Adaptive FEC with Distributed and Local residual loss probability estimation with P_{max}=0.0001

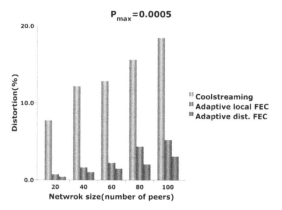

Fig. 7. Video distortion comparison between simple Coolstreaming, Adaptive FEC with Distributed and Local residual loss probability estimation with P_{max}=0.005

According to Figure 7, this is the same for medium FEC loss tolerance.

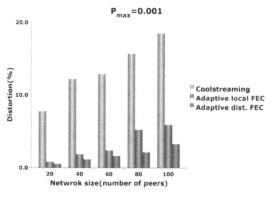

Fig. 8. Video distortion comparison between simple Coolstreaming, Adaptive FEC with Distributed and Local residual loss probability estimation with P_{max}=0.001

Finally, Figure 8 shows that the same trends can be seen with the lowest amount of FEC loss tolerance for different network sizes from 20 to 100 peers. Figures 9 to 11 compares the amounts of end-to-end delays in P2P live video streaming over WMNs using CoolStreaming, distributed and local residual loss probability estimation in adaptive FEC method, respectively.

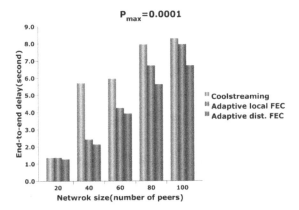

Fig. 9. End-to-end delay comparison between simple Coolstreaming, Adaptive FEC with Distributed and Local residual loss probability estimation with P_{max}=0.0001

Figure 9 shows that distributed method introduces less amount of end-to-end delay in the highest level of FEC loss tolerance and for different network sizes.

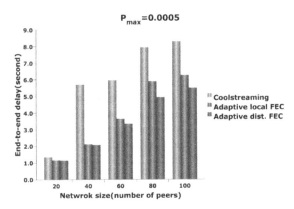

Fig. 10. End-to-end delay comparison between simple Coolstreaming, Adaptive FEC with Distributed and Local residual loss probability estimation with P_{max}=0.0005

According to Figures 10 and 11, this trend is also the same for medium and low FEC loss tolerances, respectively. According to the obtained results, the proposed method considerably decreases the number of imposed overhead packets on the network. The simulation results also confirm this fact that video distortion and End-to-end delay are noticeably decreased in a P2P live video streaming system over WMNs.

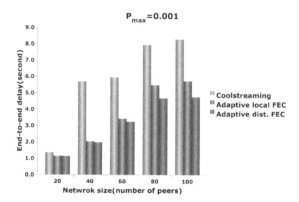

Fig. 11. End-to-end delay comparison between simple Coolstreaming, Adaptive FEC with Distributed and Local residual loss probability estimation with $P_{max}=0.001$

Based on the employed multi-hopping approach in WMNs, less number of overhead packets has considerable effect on the live streaming metrics such as video distortion and end-to-end delay. This is while residual loss probability remains no more than P_{max} and video frames significantly protected by redundant FEC packets. In fact, distributed residual loss probability estimation method provides better video QoS while the amount of protection packets are also decreased using the proposed method.

5   Conclusion

In this paper, we proposed an adaptive hybrid FEC method with distributed residual loss probability estimation for reducing overhead of FEC packet protection and consequently improve the overall QoS of P2P video streaming over WMNs. Existing works only estimate average loss probability of the source node and do not consider loss probability between source and destination. In the proposed method, by considering the loss probability in P2P video streaming between source and destination, the overall overhead of FEC protection significantly reduced while residual packet loss probability maintained less than p_{max}. We evaluated distributed residual loss probability estimation with analytical and extensive simulation, and comprehensive results show the efficiency of the proposed method. The results show that the proposed method not only provides high video quality in terms of the video distortion, but it also decreases the amount of experienced end-to-end delay, which is important in live video applications.

Acknowledgment. The authors are indebted to Dr. Behrang Barekatain, Prof. Mohammad Ghanbari, Prof. Alfonso Ariza Quintana and Dr. Alicia Cabrera Trivino for many clarifying discussions and their support. The authors would also like to thank Mr. Yasser Seyyedi and Mr. Adel Ghanbari of the DenaCast group at Sharif University of Technology for their assistance.

References

1. Akyildiz, I., Wang, X., Wang, W.: Wireless mesh networks: A survey. Computer Networks 47(4), 445–487 (2005)
2. IEEE 802.11 Standard in IEEE Standard for Information technology–Telecommunications and information exchange between systems Local and metropolitan area networks–Specific requirements Part 11: Wireless LAN Medium Access Control (MAC) and Physical. IEEE
3. Barekatain, B., Maarof, M.A., Quintana, A.A., Ghaeini, H.R.: Performance Evaluation of Routing Protocols in Live Video Streaming over Wireless Mesh Networks. Jurnal Teknologi 62(1), 85–94 (2013)
4. Moltchanov, D.: Service quality in P2P streaming systems. Computer Science Review 5(4), 319–340 (2011)
5. Lindeberg, M., Plagemann, T., Kristiansen, S., Goebel, V.: Challenges and techniques for video streaming over mobile ad hoc networks. Multimedia Systems 17, 51–82 (2011)
6. Buford, J.F., Yu, H., Lua, E.K.: P2P Networking and Applications, pp. 183–202. Morgan Kaufmann, Boston (2009)
7. Liu, Y., Guo, Y., Liang, C.: A survey on peer-to-peer video streaming systems. Peer-to-Peer Networking and Applications I, 18–28 (2008)
8. Ghanbari, A., Rabiee, H., Khansari, M., Salehi, M.: PPM - A Hybrid Push-Pull Mesh-Based Peer-to-Peer Live Video Streaming Protocol. In: 21st International Conference on Computer Communications and Networks (ICCCN), Munich, Germany (2012)
9. Liotta, A., Altaf, M., Fleury, M., Ghanbari, M.: Effective Video Streaming using Mesh P2P with MDC over MANETs. Journal on Mobile Multimedia 5, 301–316 (2009)
10. Kuo, J.-L., Shih, C.-H., Ho, C.-Y., Chen, Y.-C.: A cross-layer approach for real-time multimedia streaming on wireless peer-to-peer ad hoc network. Ad Hoc Networks 11(1), 339–354 (2013)
11. Ghaeini, H.R., Akbari, B., Barekatain, B.: A Comprehensive Evaluation of Different Loss Recovery Schemes in Peer-to-Peer Live Video Streaming over WMNs. In: ACM/IEEE/IFAC/TRB International Conference on Connected Vehicles & Expo, Beijing, China (2012)
12. Ghaeini, H.R., Akbari, B., Barekatain, B.: An Adaptive Packet Loss Recovery Method for Peer-to-Peer Video Streaming Over Wireless Mesh Network. In: Wong, W.E., Ma, T. (eds.) Emerging Technologies for Information Systems, Computing, and Management. LNEE, vol. 236, pp. 713–721. Springer, Heidelberg (2012)
13. Ghanbari, M.: Standard Codecs, Image compression to advanced video coding, 3rd edn. The Institution of Engineering and Technology, pp. 372–385 (2011)
14. Luo, F.-L.: Mobile Multimedia Broadcasting Standards. Springer (2009)
15. (2013), http://www.mathworks.com/
16. OMNeT++ (2013), http://www.OMNETPP.org/
17. (2013), http://www.oversim.org/
18. (2013), https://github.com/aarizaq/inetmanet-2.0
19. Zhang, X., Liu, J., Li, B., Yum, T.-S.: DONet/CoolStreaming: A data-driven overlay network for live media streaming. In: Proceedings of IEEE INFOCOM (2005)

Cooperative Localization Algorithm Based on Reference Selection of Selective Weighting ILS Technique

Leïla Gazzah and Leïla Najjar

Lab. COSIM, Higher School of Communication of Tunis,
Carthage University Tunisia
{gazzah.leila,leila.najjar}@supcom.rnu.tn

Abstract. The choice of the reference node in the Least Squares (LS) approach based on received signal strength (RSS) is an important aspect that can have a significant impact on localization accuracy. Recently, a LS selective and weighting approach was proposed in the non cooperative frame for localization in NLOS environments. In this paper, we rather consider the cooperative scenario and we optimize the reference node choice. By analyzing the objective function of LS algorithm, a new cooperative method for selecting the reference node is proposed, which selects the reference node based on two existing algorithms for reference selection (RS) minimum residual and residual weighting for reference selection (RS) to form a new algorithm which we denote Cooperative-Rwgh-RS. Using numerical results, we demonstrate the impact of the proposed cooperative method and the node selection procedure on the localization accuracy.

Keywords: Cooperative localization, Reference selection, Iterative Least-squares, selective, weighting, Radio Signal Strength.

1 Introduction

Wireless localization has gained considerable attention over the past decade [1]. The capability of accurately positioning a mobile station in cellular networks enables many innovative applications. In addition, wireless localization is an indispensable component of wireless sensor networks since the readings from a large number of sensor nodes are meaningful only when the geolocation of these readings are known. In this paper, we will refer to the base stations in cellular networks and the anchor nodes in wireless sensor networks with known locations as reference nodes (RNs) and the mobile stations and sensor nodes with unknown locations as blind nodes (BNs).

A variety of wireless location techniques including angle of arrival (AOA), radio signal strength (RSS), time of arrival (TOA) and time difference of arrival (TDOA) are conventionally used in estimating the BNs locations. Determining the location of a BN given the measurements of one or several aforementioned parameters can be formulated as an estimation problem. The commonly used

A. Mellouk et al. (Eds.): WWIC 2014, LNCS 8458, pp. 122–133, 2014.
© Springer International Publishing Switzerland 2014

estimators fall into the following two main categories : the maximum likelihood (ML) estimator [2] and the linearized least squares (LLS) estimator [3]. LLS estimation is a low complexity but suboptimum method for estimating the location of a BN from some measured distances. It requires selecting one of the known RNs as a reference RN for obtaining a linear set of expressions. In [4], a noncooperative system is used and the effect of the reference RN choice is investigated. By analyzing the objective function of LLS algorithm, a new method for selecting the reference RN is proposed, which selects the reference RN based on the minimum residual (denoted as MR-RS) rather than the smallest measured distance. The MR-RS is found to improve the localization accuracy significantly in Line of sight (LOS) environment. In Non-line of sight (NLOS) environment, we combine MR-RS algorithm with an existing algorithm (residual weighting (Rwgh-RS) algorithm) to form a new algorithm.

The possibility of performing range measurements between any pair of nodes enables the use of cooperation, where the BN uses range information not only from the RNs but also from other BNs. It is expected that cooperative positioning achieves better accuracy and coverage than positioning relying solely on the RNs [5]. Several approaches have been proposed in the literature to obtain low-complexity cooperative positioning schemes; a survey can be found in [5]. Among them is a suboptimal hierarchical algorithm for cooperative ML which is proposed in [6] and applied to a scenario where range measurements are estimated from received power measurements. An iterative version of the LS technique that accounts for cooperation among targets is proposed in [7].

In this paper, we propose an RSS-based selective weighting iterative LS algorithm to estimate BN location when the best RNs and virtual RNs (BNs with known location), in terms of higher RSS measurements, are available and NLOS are not identified from Line-of-Sight LOS measurements. Also, this paper proposes reference selection technique in the selective weighting iterative LS estimator which is an important aspect that can have a significant impact on localization accuracy for cooperative systems. Therefore, applying the cooperative system, we combine the Rwgh algorithm [8] with MR-RS [4] to form a new reference selection method (noted as Cooperative-Rwgh-RS).

The rest of the paper is organized as follows. Section 2 introduces the system model. Section 3 introduces the proposed algorithm. Section 4 provides the simulation results and section 5 concludes the paper.

2   System Model

Let us now suppose that $M \geq 2$ BNs are present in a network. In the absence of cooperation, each node interacts only with the RNs and estimates its position using, for example, the LS approach. It is expected that if the BNs are able to make range measurements not only from the RNs but also from each other, thus cooperating, then they can potentially improve their position estimation accuracy.

We define $U = M + N$ as the total number of radio devices (M BNs plus N RNs) present in the system. Denote the coordinates of the ith BN (unknown) as $\theta_i = [x_i, y_i]^T$ $(i = 1, ..., M)$ and the coordinates of the jth RN (known) as $\Phi_j = [X_j, Y_j]^T$ $(j = 1, ..., N)$. The distance between the jth RN and the ith BN, denoted by R_{ij}, is given by

$$R_{ij} = \sqrt{(x_i - X_j)^2 + (y_i - Y_j)^2}, i = 1, ..., M, j = 1, ..., N.$$

The distance between the ith BN and the kth BN, denoted by r_{ik}, is given by

$$r_{ik} = \sqrt{(x_i - x_k)^2 + (y_i - y_k)^2}, i = 1, ..., M, k = 1, ..., M.$$

The RSS (from the ith BN and received by the jth RN (respectively the kth BN) or vice versa), which is denoted as RSS_{ij} (respectively RSS_{ik}), can be related to the distance between the ith BN and the jth RN (respectively the kth BN) through the path loss model for cooperative localization is

$$RSS_{ij} = PL(d_0) - 10\gamma \log_{10}(\frac{R_{ij}}{d_0}) + X_{\sigma RSS_{ij}}, \tag{1}$$

$$RSS_{ik} = PL(d_0) - 10\gamma \log_{10}(\frac{r_{ik}}{d_0}) + X_{\sigma RSS_{ik}}, \tag{2}$$

where γ is the path-loss exponent, $PL(d_0)$ is the power loss in dB at a reference distance d_0 and $X_{\sigma RSS_{ij}}$, $X_{\sigma RSS_{ik}}$ in dB are the shadowing random variables representing the noise in the measured RSSs. Contrarily to time varying noise sources, the errors induced by shadowing can not be averaged out by taking multiple measurements and can be modeled in logarithmic scale by a zero mean Gaussian distribution with variance $\sigma_{RSS_{ij}}, \sigma_{RSS_{ik}}$.

With this in mind, the RSS-based range measurement of the ith BN to the jth RN (respectively the kth BN), separated by the true LOS distance Rij (respectively rik) from the ith BN, denoted by Lij (respectively l_{ik}) is represented as

$$L_{ij} = k10^{(-RSS_{ij})/10\gamma}, \tag{3}$$

$$l_{ik} = k10^{(-RSS_{ik})/10\gamma}. \tag{4}$$

The true ranges can be written in terms of the measured ones as [9]

$$R_{ij} = \alpha_{ij} L_{ij}, \tag{5}$$

$$r_{ik} = \beta_{ik} l_{ik}, \tag{6}$$

where, for NLOS propagation, $0 < \alpha_{ij} \leq 1$, $j = 1, ..., N$ and $0 < \beta_{ik} \leq 1$, $k = 1, ..., M$. The values of α_{ij} and β_{ik} are restricted since the NLOS error is a large positive bias that causes the measured ranges to be greater than the true ones.

The goal of the proposed algorithm is to compute values for the scale factors or weights α_{ij}, $j = 1, ..., N$ and $\beta_{ik}, k = 1, ..., M$ so that the LOS ranges to the nodes can qbe estimated. From the definitions of α_{ij} and β_{ik}, we find that the approximation of the true range is simply

$$\widehat{R}_{ij} \approx \zeta_{ij} L_{ij}, \tag{7}$$

$$\widehat{r}_{ik} \approx \xi_{ik} l_{ik}, \tag{8}$$

where ζ_{ij} and ξ_{ik} can be deduced from the estimated values of either α_{ij} and β_{ik}. Once the scale factors are determined, then the adjusted ranges $\widehat{R}_{ij}$ and $\widehat{r}_{ik}$ are determined. These ranges indeed adjust the NLOS-corrupted range measurements to near their LOS values and they can be used in any traditional LOS based RSS location algorithm.

Next, only the four higher RSS measurements, among the N remaining RNs of the cell are considered. Without loss of generality, let the selected best RSS measurements RNs be indexed by $j = 1, 2, 3$ and 4. Given the NLOS corrupted range measurements and RN (respectively BN) locations, the scale factors, α_{ij} , $j = 1, 2, 3, 4$, (respectively $\beta_{ik}, k = 1, ..., M$) , can be derived. Because the NLOS error is always positive, the measured ranges are greater than the true ranges and the ith BN location must lie in the region of overlap of the range circles (region enclosed by U, V, W, Z) as shown in figure 1. The details of finding the boundaries of α_{ij} , $j = 1, 2, 3, 4$, are given by [9]

$$\alpha_{i1,min} = \max \left\{ 1 - \frac{\overline{AB}}{L_{i1}}, 1 - \frac{\overline{CD}}{L_{i1}}, 1 - \frac{\overline{EF}}{L_{i1}} \right\} = \left\{ \frac{T_{12} - L_{i2}}{L_{i1}}, \frac{T_{13} - L_{i3}}{L_{i1}}, \frac{T_{14} - L_{i4}}{L_{i1}} \right\}. \tag{9}$$

Similarly, the lower bounds on α_{ij} , $j = 2, 3, 4$, are given by

$$\alpha_{i2,min} = \max \left\{ \frac{T_{12} - L_{i1}}{L_{i2}}, \frac{T_{23} - L_{i3}}{L_{i2}}, \frac{T_{24} - L_{i4}}{L_{i2}} \right\},$$

$$\alpha_{i3,min} = \max \left\{ \frac{T_{32} - L_{i2}}{L_{i3}}, \frac{T_{13} - L_{i1}}{L_{i3}}, \frac{T_{34} - L_{i4}}{L_{i3}} \right\},$$

$$\alpha_{i4,min} = \max \left\{ \frac{T_{14} - L_{i1}}{L_{i4}}, \frac{T_{24} - L_{i2}}{L_{i4}}, \frac{T_{34} - L_{i3}}{L_{i4}} \right\},$$

where $T_{jl} = \sqrt{(X_j - X_l)^2 + (Yj - Y_l)^2}$ is the distance between the j th and l th RNs.

Similarly, the lower bound on $\beta_{im}, m \in \{1, ..., M\}, (m \neq i)$ are given by

$$\beta_{im,min} = \max \left\{ \frac{r_{1m} - l_{i1}}{l_{im}}, ..., \frac{r_{(m-1)m} - l_{i(m-1)}}{l_{im}}, \frac{r_{(1+m)m} - l_{i(m+1)}}{l_{im}}, ..., \frac{r_{Mm} - l_{iM}}{l_{im}} \right\},$$

For NLOS RNs, the weighted circles do not intersect at the same point, which results in the following inconsistent equations

$$\alpha_{ij}^2 L_{ij}^2 = s_i + K_j - 2X_j x_i - 2Y_j y_i, \tag{10}$$

$$\beta_{ik}^2 l_{ik}^2 = s_i + k_k - 2x_k x_i - 2y_k y_i, \tag{11}$$

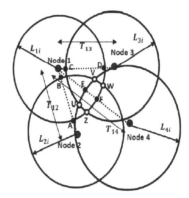

Fig. 1. Geometry of RSS-based location showing measured range circles and the region of overlap in which the ith BN lies

where

$$s_i = x_i^2 + y_i^2, \tag{12}$$

$$K_j = X_j^2 + Y_j^2, \tag{13}$$

$$k_k = x_k^2 + y_k^2. \tag{14}$$

If the location estimation of the ith BN $\widehat{\theta}_i = [\widehat{x}_i, \widehat{y}_i]$ is got, then the corresponding residual is defined as

$$R_{es}\left(\theta_i\right) = \sum_{j=1}^{4} \left(\alpha_{ij} L_{ij} - \left\|\widehat{\theta}_i - \Phi_j\right\|\right)^2, \tag{15}$$

where $\alpha_{ij,\min} \leq \alpha_{ij} \leq 1$.

There are 4 equations in (10), we can get other 3 linear equations by fixing the rth equation (supposed $r = 4$) and subtracting it from the rest equation for $j = 1, ..., 4, (j \neq r)$. Then after some manipulations, we obtain the following linear equation

$$2A\theta_i = P, \tag{16}$$

where

$$A = \begin{bmatrix} X_1 - X_4 & Y_1 - Y_4 \\ X_2 - X_4 & Y_2 - Y_4 \\ X_3 - X_4 & Y_3 - Y_4 \end{bmatrix}, P = \begin{bmatrix} \alpha_{i4}^2 L_{i4}^2 - \alpha_{i1}^2 L_{i1}^2 - K_{4,1} \\ \alpha_{i4}^2 L_{i4}^2 - \alpha_{i2}^2 L_{i2}^2 - K_{4,2} \\ \alpha_{i4}^2 L_{i4}^2 - \alpha_{i3}^2 L_{i3}^2 - K_{4,3} \end{bmatrix},$$

where $K_{4,j} = K_4 - K_j, j = 1, 2, 3$.

The Eq. (16) has a LS solution given by [3]

$$\widehat{\theta}_i = \frac{1}{2}(A^T A)^{-1} A^T P. \tag{17}$$

3   Selective Weighting Iterative LS with Residual Weighting-Reference Selection (RWGH-RS) for Cooperative Localization

In [7], they consider an iterative version of the LS based TOA location algorithm to exploit cooperation among targets. It requires selecting one of fixed terminals (FTs) $(FTs = RNs+M-1BNs = RNs+RNs\ virtual)$ as a reference FT (RFT) for obtaining a linear set of expressions. A two-step LS positioning algorithm incorporating the WED (wall extra delay) model was introduced to correct the range measurements in NLOS conditions when the layout of the environment is known.

In this paper, we study the cooperative localization accuracy enhancement obtained by combining a weighting procedure (using scale factors or weights), which aims to mitigate the NLOS range bias where contrarily to [7], the layout of the environment is not necessarily known (see figures 2 and 3). The region enclosed by the four RSS circles (the area enclosed by $UVWZ$), as illustrated in figure 2, determined by [4], [7] is replaced in this algorithm by the area enclosed by $ABCD$, as illustrated in figure 3. In addition, the choice of the reference node in the selective weighting iterative LS approach is investigated, it is an important aspect that can have a significant impact on localization accuracy. In the following, we first detail the cooperative Rwgh-RS technique used for the RFT selection. Then, the selective weighting iterative estimator with the Rwgh-RS technique is described.

3.1   Cooperative Rwgh-RS Algorithm

The recent reference selection method Rwgh-RS [4] is here adapted to the frame of cooperative localization. The procedure resulting follows these steps

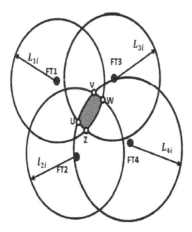

Fig. 2. The geometric layout of the four RSS circles

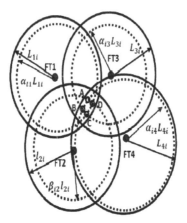

Fig. 3. The geometric layout of the four RSS weighted circles

- Step 1. Given $U - 1$ measured distances from $U - 1$ different fixed terminals $(FTs = RNs + M - 1 BNs = 4 + RNs Virtual)$ to form $W = \sum_{p=1}^{U-1} U - 1p$ measured distance combinations. Each combination is represented by an index set $\{S_q, q = 1, ..., W\}$.
- Step 2. For each combination, compute the location estimation of the ith BN with cooperative MR-RS algorithm [4], which is denoted as $\widehat{\Theta}_q, q = 1, ..., W$ and the normalized residual $R_{es}^q, q = 1, ..., W$

$$R_{es}^q = \frac{R_{es}\left(\widehat{\Theta}_q, S_q\right)}{sizeof\, S_q}.$$

when the recent reference selection method MR-RS [4] is here adapted to the frame of cooperative localization. The procedure follows these steps

- Step I. Each of the $U - 1$ FTs $(U - 1 = 4 + M - 1)$ can be set as the reference FT, so we can get $U - 1$ location estimations of the ith BN by the selective weighting iterative LS estimator, which can be expressed as $\widehat{\theta}_u, u = 1, ..., U - 1$.

$$R_{es}^u(\theta) = \sum_{j=1}^{4}\left(\alpha_{uj}L_{uj} - \left\|\widehat{\theta}_u - \Phi_j\right\|\right)^2 + \sum_{k=1, k\neq u}^{M-1}\left(\beta_{uk}l_{uk} - \left\|\widehat{\theta}_u - \widehat{\theta}_k\right\|\right)^2.$$
(18)

- Step II. For each $\widehat{\theta}_u$, the corresponding residual is computed, which is denoted as $R_{es}^u, u = 1, ..., U - 1$.
- Step III. The index of the RFT is given by $r = \arg\min_u \{R_{es}^u\}, u = 1, ..., U - 1$.
- Step IV. The final location estimation of the ith BN can be obtained by the selective weighting iterative LS estimator.

– Step 3. The final location estimation of the ith BN is the weighted linear combination of the intermediate estimation [4] from step 2.

$$\widehat{\theta}_i = \frac{\sum_{q=1}^{W} \widehat{\Theta}_q \left(R_{es}^q\right)^{-1}}{\sum_{q=1}^{W} \left(R_{es}^q\right)^{-1}} \tag{19}$$

3.2   The Selective Weighting Iterative LS Algorithm with Rwgh-RS

To make use of the range measurements between different BNs, the following cooperative selective weighting of iterative LS with Rwgh-RS algorithm is proposed.

Without loss of generality, we can consider that the RFT is the same for step 1 and step 2. Denote the coordinates of the RFT as (X_r, Y_r) .

– Step 1. set $n = 1$. Using (17) with the cooperative Rwgh-RS (with $U - 1 = N = 4$), determine the position estimates $\widehat{\theta}_i^{(1)}$ for the BNs, that is, $i = 1, ..., M$.
– Step 2. set $n = n + 1$. For each BN $i = 1, ..., M$, the selective weighting LS algorithm with the cooperative Rwgh-RS algorithm is applied by treating the other $M - 1$ BNs as additional "virtual" RNs located at the estimated positions $\widehat{\theta}_i^{(n)}$ obtained during the previous step. Specifically, the matrices $A^{(n,i)}$ and $P^{(n,i)}$ at step n and for the ith BN are now

$$A^{(n,i)} = \begin{bmatrix} X_1 - X_r & Y_1 - Y_r \\ \vdots & \vdots \\ X_N - X_r & Y_N - Y_r \\ \widehat{x}_1 - X_r & \widehat{y}_1 - Y_r \\ \vdots & \vdots \\ \widehat{x}_{i-1} - X_r & \widehat{y}_{i-1} - Y_r \\ \widehat{x}_{i+1} - X_r & \widehat{y}_{i+1} - Y_r \\ \vdots & \vdots \\ \widehat{x}_M - X_r & \widehat{y}_M - Y_r \end{bmatrix}, P^{(n,i)} = \begin{bmatrix} \alpha_{ir}^2 L_{ir}^2 - \alpha_{i1}^2 L_{i1}^2 - K_{r,1} \\ \vdots \\ \alpha_{ir}^2 L_{ir}^2 - \alpha_{iN}^2 L_{iN}^2 - K_{r,N} \\ \alpha_{ir}^2 L_{ir}^2 - \beta_{i1}^2 l_{i1}^2 - \widehat{k}_{r,1} \\ \vdots \\ \alpha_{ir}^2 L_{ir}^2 - \beta_{ii-1}^2 l_{ii-1}^2 - \widehat{k}_{r,i-1} \\ \alpha_{ir}^2 L_{ir}^2 - \beta_{ii+1}^2 l_{ii+1}^2 - \widehat{k}_{r,i+1} \\ \vdots \\ \alpha_{ir}^2 L_{ir}^2 - \beta_{iM}^2 l_{iM}^2 - \widehat{k}_{r,M} \end{bmatrix}, \tag{20}$$

where $\widehat{k}_{r,v} = K_r - \widehat{k}_v = K_r - \left(\widehat{x}_v^2 + \widehat{y}_v^2\right)$.

In equations (20) all nodes are accounted for. However, when the selective aspect is used, only the 4 higher RSS measurements, among the $U - 1$ remaining FTs ($FTs = RNs + RNsvirtual$), corresponding nodes are considered.

The selective weighting LS position estimate for the ith BN at step n is therefore

$$\widehat{\theta}_i^{(n)} = \frac{1}{2}(A^{(n,i)T} A^{(n,i)})^{-1} A^{(n,i)T} P^{(n,i)}. \tag{21}$$

– Step 3. If $n \geq N_{iter}$ (maximal number of iterations) stop; else go to step 2.
– Step 4. The ith optimal BN position is determed as the mean of the last iterations (near N_{iter}) obained positions values.

4   Simulation Results

This section presents the simulation results for the cooperative (with and without selection of the best RFT) and noncooperative (with selection of the RFT) localization problem. We consider a network with $N = 9$ RNs and $M = 3$ BNs. The nine RNs are located at $(0,0)$, $(866, 1500)$, $(1732, 0)$, $(866, 750)$, $(866, 0)$, $(433, 750)$, $(433, 0)$, $(1299, 0)$ and $(1299, 750)$ and the three BNs are randomly positioned inside the triangle region formed by the points $(0,0)$, $(866, 1500)$ and $(1732, 0)$. All units are in meters. The path loss exponent is fixed to $\gamma = 2$. The maximal number of N_{iter} (if not specified otherwise) is fixed to 5. The results are averaged over 1000 Monte-Carlo trials. A scenario where the standard deviation of the RSS nodes depends on the distance between the emitter and the receiver was simulated, where for $d \in [0, 144m[$, $\sigma_{RSS} = 1dB$ and an increase of $1dB$ per additional distance of $144m$.

The improvement in location accuracy provided by the selective weighting iterative LS (ILS) with Rwgh-RS technique for cooperative system can be seen in the Cumulative Distribution Function (CDF) curves of the location error as shown in figure 4. An improvement in performance can be observed with respect to conventional technique in [7] thanks to the use of the Rwgh-RS technique. Then, we observe that the selection of the best reference RN in the sense of minimizing the residual (see Eq. (18) can further improve the positioning accuracy. Thus, it is clear that adding selective aspect (in terms of the selection of the 4 higher RSS) with weighting aspect allows better estimation of the position of the BN than schemes using selective aspect only. It can be seen that the proposed selective weighting ILS with Rwgh-RS technique always providesz much better location estimate compared to the ILS of [7] .

Figure 5 depicts the CDF of the average location error for two scenarios (cooperative and non cooperative systems). It can be seen for the two scenarios, with the choice of the reference node, selective aspect and without use of the weighting aspect, that cooperation is not always advantageous. In fact, it was shown that the geometric configuration of the devices may have a stronger impact than the quality of the intertarget range estimates on the localization accuracy. This is an important consideration when deriving guidelines for cooperation in positioning algorithms. We can conclude that the correction of the range measurements using the weighting aspect leads to a significant performance improvement for many locations.

Figure 6 was performed to study how the average radiolocation error is affected by the number of NLOS FTs among the four selected ones when the proposed selective weighting schemes are employed and compared to the non selective unweighting schemes. As expected, it is observed from figure 5 that the performance of the proposed selective weighting schemes, outperforms the non selective un-weighting schemes. For all considered weighting algorithms, the average radiolocation error decreases slightly when all FTs are NLOS as compared to the case when two or three FTs are NLOS (which is not the case with the version not including range weighting).

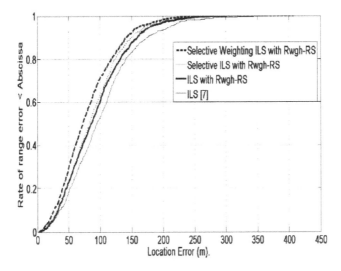

Fig. 4. CDF plots of the average radiolocation error for the different methods

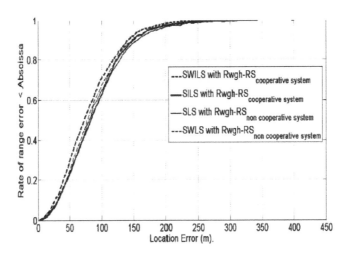

Fig. 5. CDF plots of the average radiolocation error for the cooperative and non cooperative systems

The next simulation compares the performance of the selective weighting schemes and non selective un-weighting schemes, against the RSS standard deviation. Twelve scenarios, which differ in the standard deviation σ_{RSS} of the RSS nodes, were simulated. The standard deviation σ_{RSS} of the RSS nodes ranged from $1dB$ to $12dB$ in increments of $1dB$. The simulation results are shown in figure 7. As expected, the performance of any location algorithm deteriorates when the standard deviation σ_{RSS} of the RSS nodes increases. The least average location error is that obtained with the SW ILS where cooperation among nodes is used.

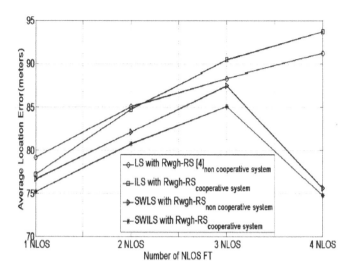

Fig. 6. Average location error versus the number of NLOS FTs for the different methods

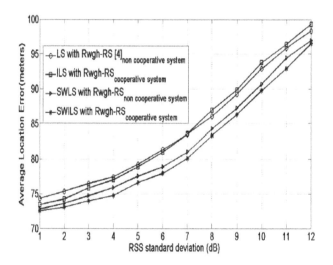

Fig. 7. Average location error versus the standard deviation of the RSS FT for the different methods

5   Conclusion

We here considered RSS based wireless localization problem. To circumvent the degradation of the performance because inappropriate choice of the reference fixed terminal (RFT) and in order to mitigate the NLOS effect, we have proposed a selective weighting ILS for iterative LS and/or LS which incorporates the Rwgh-RS technique for reference node selection. Both non cooperative and cooperative localization problems were investigated. Simulation results demonstrate that : 1) in NLOS environment, the ILS- Rwgh-RS algorithm can indeed mitigate the effect of NLOS error, and the algorithm only has better performance when the number of LOS FTs is more than two. 2) the choice of the RFT in the ILS approach is an important aspect that can have a significant impact on localization accuracy. 3) cooperation is not always advantageous without weighting aspect and Rwgh-RS technique. 4) our proposed SWILS and SWLS with Rwght-RS techniques outperformed existing algorithms in RSS-based wireless localization framework.

We can conclude that combining the selective aspect with correction of the range measurements through range weighting, and the choice of the best reference node RFT, using the Rwgh-RS technique, leads to a significant performance improvement for both cooperative and non cooperative localization schemes.

References

1. Vossiek, M., Wiebking, L., Gulden, P., Wieghardt, J., Hoffmann, C., Heide, P.: Wireless local positioning. IEEE Microw. Mag. 4, 77–86 (2003)
2. Al-Jazzar, S., Ghogho, M.: Ajoint TOA/AOA constrained minimization method for locating wireless devices in non-line-of-sight environment. In: Proc. IEEE 66th VTC-Fall, pp. 496–500 (2007)
3. Venkatraman, S., Caffery, Jr., J.J.: Hybrid TOA/AOA techniques for mobile location in non-line-of-sight environment. In: Proc. IEEE WCNC, vol. 1, pp. 274–278 (2004)
4. Wu, S., Li, J., Liu, S.: Improved Localization Algorithms Based on Reference Selection of Linear Least Squares in LOS and NLOS Environments. Wireless Pers Commun. 14 p. (January 2013), doi:10.1007/s11277-011-0446-9
5. Patwari, N., Ash, J.N., Kyperountas, S., Hero III, A.O., Moses, R.L., Correal, N.S.: Locating the nodes: Cooperative localization in wireless sensor networks. IEEE Signal Processing Magazine 22(4), 54–69 (2005)
6. Dardari, D., Conti, A.: A sub-optimal hierarchical maximum likelihood algorithm for collaborative localization in ad-hoc network. In: Proceedings of the 1st Annual IEEE Communications Society Conference on Sensor and Ad Hoc Communications and Networks (SECON 2004), Santa Clara, Calif, USA, pp. 425–429 (October 2004)
7. Dardari, D., Conti, A., Lien, J., Win, M.Z.: The Effect of Cooperation on Localization Systems Using UWB Experimental Data. Hindawi Publishing Corporation EURASIP Journal on Advances in Signal Processing, 11 p. Article ID 513873 (2008), doi:10.1155/2008/513873
8. Chen, P.C.: A non-line-of-sight error mitigation algorithm in location estimation. In: Proc. IEEE WCNC, vol. 1, pp. 316–320 (Septemper 1999)
9. Venkatraman, S., Caffery, J., Heung-Ryeol: A Novel TOA Location Using LOS Range Estimation for NLOS Environments. IEEE Transactions on Vehicular Technologies (September 2004)

Q-POINT: QoE-Driven Path Optimization Model for Multimedia Services

Ognjen Dobrijevic[1,*], Andreas J. Kassler[2],
Lea Skorin-Kapov[1], and Maja Matijasevic[1]

[1] University of Zagreb, Faculty of Electrical Engineering and Computing
Unska 3, 10000 Zagreb, Croatia
{ognjen.dobrijevic,lea-skorin.kapov,maja.matijasevic}@fer.hr
[2] Karlstad University, Department of Mathematics and Computer Science
Universitetsgatan 2, 65188 Karlstad, Sweden
andreas.kassler@kau.se

Abstract. When delivering multimedia services over Internet, different media types are impacted by resource limitations in a different way. While an interactive audio service calls for low-latency communication, video streams should be routed over network paths with sufficient capacity. However, in current networks flows towards the same destination follow the same path, which may lead to a suboptimal resource utilization that effectively penalizes end-users' quality of experience (QoE). This paper proposes Q-POINT, a QoE-driven path optimization model to fairly maximize aggregated end-user QoE for competing clients' service flows by calculating the best path for each flow, subject to resource constraints. We formulate the problem as a mixed integer linear program integrating QoE models for audio, video and data transfer. Such an approach can be leveraged within the software-defined networking paradigm, which provides a control plane to orchestrate path set-up. We evaluate our model and illustrate its benefits over shortest path selection.

Keywords: Multimedia services, quality of experience, software-defined networking, network-wide optimization, mixed integer linear program.

1 Introduction

The Internet is transforming from a data-centric network towards a network that delivers diverse services, accessed by fixed and mobile users. In addition, novel services such as cloud computing or multi-player online gaming lead to a significant increase in traffic demands, which might result in network congestion, thus calling for new resource management mechanisms. When delivering multimedia services over heterogeneous networks, the impact of resource limitations manifesting themselves as, e.g., packet loss or delay depends on the service type and the end-users' quality expectations. For example, dropping an I-frame for a video session might lead to more adverse effects then dropping a few TCP packets for

---

* Corresponding author.

A. Mellouk et al. (Eds.): WWIC 2014, LNCS 8458, pp. 134–147, 2014.

a Cloud-delivered system upgrade. Researchers are looking into new ways that enable flexible, yet efficient optimization of multimedia delivery under resource constraints, while considering user quality, or quality of experience (QoE) [1].

Let us consider a network operator and its network. The operator's goal is to dynamically allocate network resources across all users and services in such a way that the total QoE is maximized over all ongoing sessions, while also considering given resources constraints. However, such an optimization is difficult to achieve because different services may have different resource demands, be impacted differently by resource limitations, and, finally, end-users may have different preferences. This requires metrics that quantify expected QoE of an end-user with regards to a given service and a specific network configuration, and functions that map network resource limitations to service metrics. Once these metrics and mapping functions are in place, the network operator can perform an optimization that guides the resource allocation and leads to, e.g., network path selection for given flows and queue configuration. Such a QoE-based optimization may consider user-, network-, and service-related constraints, but must also regard multiple sessions, service flows, and the whole network domain [2]. A preliminary approach for a multi-user domain-wide optimization has been presented in [3], but was treating the network as a "black box". This has the disadvantage that no control over the resource allocation could be exercised.

In current networks, all flows for a source-destination pair typically follow the same path, which might be a suboptimal decision. Rather, a flow should be routed over a path which has the least impact on QoE degradation for given resource constraints. For example, an audio flow should be delivered over a path that offers low latency. This calls for a mechanism that calculates the "best available path", in terms of the impact on overall QoE, for each service flow and enables per-flow routing conformed to given QoE constraints. Software-defined networking (SDN) [4] proposes an efficient means to decouple data forwarding from the control in network devices. Using, e.g., the OpenFlow protocol, routers can be configured by a centralized control ("SDN controller") to forward flows along certain paths and treat the flows according to quality of service (QoS) rules. As an outcome, SDN-based routing is beneficial for QoE-based optimization [5].

In this paper, we tackle the problem of finding the best path for each media flow by developing Q-POINT, a QoE-driven path optimization model. Our goal is to maximize the aggregated user-expected QoE value over all users and service flows in a network domain, subject to resource constraints and network topology. We use different QoE functions that map resource limitations (i.e., QoS parameters) to the QoE values in terms of mean opinion score (MOS). We formulate the problem as a mixed integer linear program and use linearization techniques to cope with the non-linearity of, e.g., buffering latency. A preliminary evaluation for different network topologies and different number of flows shows that our approach increases the overall QoE over shortest path selection.

The rest of the paper is organized as follows. We review related work in the areas of QoE-based routing and SDN in Section 2. Section 3 presents the proposed path optimization model, along with its mathematical formulation, while Section 4 gives a brief overview of our model implementation. Q-POINT is evaluated in Section 5, followed by the conclusion and future work plans.

2   Related Work

2.1   Path Assignment Based on QoS/QoE Metrics

QoS-based routing has been an active research area going back over the past two decades [6,7], focused on solving multi-constrained path and constrained shortest path problems. In recent approaches, Kumar *et al.* [8] present multi-objective optimization algorithms aimed at finding optimal routes for service flows belonging to different QoS classes, which is based on the importance of QoS parameters for a specific flow. Given that QoS-based routing as a multi-constrained path problem is known to be NP-complete [9], the authors propose an evolutionary algorithm that considers prioritized QoS requirements. Further, Lu *et al.* propose a genetic algorithm for solving multi-constrained routing problem with QoS guarantees, shown to be efficient in dynamic environments [10].

While QoS-based solutions consider media flows in terms of different QoS parameters and classes, QoE-driven approaches generally incorporate application-level knowledge (e.g., application state or codecs used) which provides more accurate insight to impacts on user quality. Amram *et al.* [11] present network-level mechanisms that support optimization of video transfer in cellular networks. Their goal is to maximize QoE for video flows by calculating needed transmission rate and identifying the optimal network path from video sources, and they equalize QoE among the flows that are delivered through a congested network part. A QoE optimization approach based on overlay networks that routes traffic around link failures and congestion is proposed by De Vleeschauwer *et al.* [12], while Venkataraman *et al.* [13] adapt to video QoE degradations by selecting one-hop, by-pass paths in overlay network that support application demands.

2.2   SDN-Based Approaches

SDN offers centralized control of data forwarding and has been used in recent approaches to optimized path assignment. SDN solutions are more light-weight and flexible than overlay networks, the former not depending on overlay structures.

Egilmez *et al.* [14] propose an analytical framework for dynamic routing of video traffic over QoS-optimized network paths. Unlike in the current Internet, where routes are not changed on a per-flow basis, SDN provides mechanisms for dynamic route management and calculation to meet different flow requirements (e.g., in terms of QoS). The authors mathematically formulate a constrained shortest path problem, for which the cost metric is based on packet loss and jitter. Focusing on scalable video coding, their approach supports QoS delivery of a video base layer, while enhancement layers can be assigned QoS-aware routes pending available capacity. OpenQoS, an SDN controller design based on dynamic QoS-driven routing that utilizes previously outlined optimization framework is described in [15]. Results have shown that OpenQoS outperforms existing approaches for RTP video streaming and HTTP adaptive streaming.

Jarschel *et al.* [16] present an SDN approach that utilizes different path selection schemes to enhance YouTube QoE. The most advanced scheme, application-aware path selection, leverages on application-level information about YouTube pre-buffered playtime to decide on a particular path. The actual path assignment is based on choosing one of the available links between two switches, whereas in contrast we will provide problem specification considering multi-hop paths.

In summary, a number of approaches have addressed path assignment with the goal of improving service quality. While most solutions tackle this problem from a QoS perspective, limited recent work (primarily focused on video streaming) has taken on a user-driven QoE perspective, relying on an understanding of the relationships between QoE and QoS. SDN is a viable approach in offering QoE-driven control of the path selection process, by providing an interface between application-level information and the network. Going beyond existing approaches, we propose a novel QoE-driven solution for the optimal routing of different service flows based on QoE models and user preferences. Previous work on path optimization has either neglected QoE aspects, or has assumed that all flows belonging to a session are routed along the same path between a given source and destination. We build on our generic approach proposed in [5] by formulating and solving the multi-user domain-wide QoE optimization problem.

3   The QoE-Driven Path Optimization Model

3.1   Model Overview

A high-level view of the previously proposed multimedia service delivery that leverages on the Q-POINT model and SDN [5] is given in Figure 1. It employs the Session Initiation Protocol (SIP) [17] to negotiate parameters for multimedia sessions that are to be established. The negotiation is assisted by an SIP application server with a QoS Matching and Optimization Function (QMOF) (introduced in our past work [18]), which calculates a set of configurations for each session that incorporate information such as feasible media flows, media codecs and bit rates, and user preferences in terms of favored media type(s). Session configurations include one optimal and several suboptimal configurations with regards to user- and service-imposed constraints (e.g., the configurations may differ in number of supported media flows and codec types). Calculated session and media flow parameters are passed to an SDN controller, which provides the obtained information to the Q-POINT optimization engine. The latter is run to determine which media flows should be routed along which paths in order to maximize the aggregated QoE. In its current design, Q-POINT focuses on planning flow routes by executing a single optimization process for multiple sessions, assumed to be entering the network, before they are established. We will extend our model so as to control the path optimization with regards to new sessions and flows being added and removed on a dynamic basis. The optimization output is finally translated into a set of forwarding rules, which are then installed

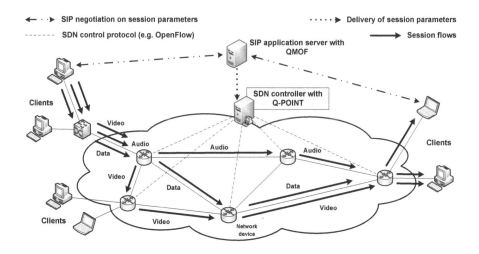

Fig. 1. Multimedia service delivery based on Q-POINT and SDN

on network devices using, e.g., OpenFlow. Other technical and implementation-related specifics of the overall system, as well as its extensive evaluation and discussion on advantages it brings, will be presented as a part of future work.

When assigning a network path to a session flow, the optimization model implementation needs to specify all the constituent nodes and links for the given path. To achieve this objective, Q-POINT utilizes (a) an optimal configuration of each session that is to be established, (b) QoE-QoS mapping functions for different media types (e.g., for audio, video, and data), (c) network topology and link capacities, and (d) average end-to-end delay and packet loss probability.

We use a *session configuration* which includes information about media flows, such as their type, source and destination nodes, negotiated codec type and bit rate, minimum QoE value requested (which can be specified based on the chosen codec and bit rate for each flow), and weight factor, which indicates the importance of a flow within a session (e.g., audio being more important than video). In this work we will assume that audio flows belong to Voice over IP (VoIP)-based conversations, video flows to high-definition IPTV sessions, while data flows are generated by File Transfer Protocol (FTP)-based delivery.

As QoE is a multi-dimensional concept and is affected, among others, by session parameters and measurable QoS metrics, QoE models are used to capture the relationship between user-perceived quality and the considered influence factors. While other methods are possible, here we use the MOS metric with values on a scale from 1 to 5 in order to quantify quality for a media flow in the scope of the path selection process. For audio, the following model estimates MOS [19]:

$$MOS_{audio} = T - \alpha * p_{e2e} + \beta * d_{e2e} - \gamma * (d_{e2e})^2 + \delta * (d_{e2e})^3, \qquad (1)$$

where d_{e2e} and p_{e2e} are end-to-end (E2E) path delay and packet loss probability, respectively, while T, α, β, γ, and δ are function-specific values. T denotes maximum MOS value, specific for a chosen voice codec and bit rate, which is achievable when no packet loss and delay exist. All the chosen QoE models are representative parametric models for in-service MOS estimation. Q-POINT employs a parametric model that calculates video quality based on the video codec type (e.g., H.264), its bit rate, and E2E packet loss degradation [20]:

$$MOS_{video} = 1 + P(c_f, o_f) * \exp(-\frac{p_{e2e}}{Q(c_f)}), \qquad (2)$$

where $P(c_f, o_f)$ and $Q(c_f)$ are model-specific functions of the codec type (c_f) and codec bit rate (o_f) to approximate influence of these parameters on MOS value. To assess QoE for the data transfer, the presented optimization model utilizes a logarithmic function that is described in [3]:

$$MOS_{data} = a * \log(b * o_f * (1 - p_{e2e})), \qquad (3)$$

where o_f is average data traffic rate, while a and b are model-specific constants.

One of the key issues in the problem specification regards modeling network delay and packet loss probability. In this model, E2E delay for a given path considers propagation delay of the path's links and buffering delay of its "transit nodes", while average E2E loss probability takes into account loss at the path's transit nodes due to possible congestion (link loss is assumed zero). As values for link propagation delay are input parameters of the model, average buffering delay and loss probability in the nodes are calculated during the optimization process based on the incoming traffic rate, buffer configuration at a node, and link capacity. We assume that network nodes are configured to have one incoming buffer per each media type, i.e. one for audio, one for video, and one for data, while each buffer is modeled based on an $M/M/1/K$ queuing system. This allows us to calculate average delay and loss probability at node i as follows:

$$d_i = \frac{\frac{x}{b} * (1 + K * (\frac{x}{b})^{K+1} - (K+1) * (\frac{x}{b})^K)}{\frac{x}{e} * (1 - \frac{x}{b}) * (1 - (\frac{x}{b})^K)}, \qquad (4)$$

$$p_i = \frac{(1 - \frac{x}{b}) * (\frac{x}{b})^K}{1 - (\frac{x}{b})^{K+1}}. \qquad (5)$$

Parameter K represents the buffer size in number of packets, x overall incoming traffic rate for a specific buffer, e mean packet length, while b denotes the buffer processing rate (which corresponds to link capacity). While $M/M/1/K$ is a common way of modeling network node buffers, we note here that our aim is to extend Q-POINT so as to include other queuing system types and be able to approximate a wider range of traffic characteristics with regards to the inter-arrival time and service time distributions (e.g., assuming bursty traffic).

3.2   Mathematical Formulation

We use the *generalized network flow model* with multi-commodity flows [21] to specify an integer linear optimization model as fast solution algorithms are available for such model type. The complete model notation is given in Table 1.

Table 1. Model notation

Model component	Symbol	Data type
Nodes	$N = \{i\}, |N| = n$	Integers
Links	$L = \{(i,j), i,j \in N\}, |L| = l$	Pairs of integers
Link delay, loss and capacity	$d_{ij} > 0, p_{ij} = 0, b_{ij} > 0$	Floats
Node delay and loss	$d_{iq} \geq 0, p_{iq} \geq 0, q \in \{1,2,3\}$	Floats
Multimedia sessions	$S = \{s\}, |S| = h$	Integers
Session MOS value	$u_s > 0$	Float
Media flows	$M = \{f\}, |M| = m$	Vectors of floats and integers
Flow source and destination	$src(f) = i^f_{src}, i^f_{src} \in N,$ $dst(f) = j^f_{dst}, j^f_{dst} \in N$	Integers
Flow type, bit rate and codec	$t_f, o_f > 0, c_f$	String, float and string
Flow weight factor	$1 \geq w_f \geq 0$	Float
Flow MOS minimum	$v_f > 0$	Float
Flow MOS value	$u_f > 0$	Float
Node rates	$R_i = \{r^f_i = o_f : src(f) = i\},$ $i \in N, f \in M$	Vectors of floats

Let $G = (N, L)$ be a directed network specified by the set of *nodes* N and the set of *links* L (Figure 2). Each node $i \in N$ associates the cost per buffer $q \in \{1, 2, 3\}$ in terms of delay, d_{iq}, and loss probability, p_{iq}, which are calculated with functions (4) and (5), respectively. Each link $(i, j) \in L$ has the cost in terms of delay, d_{ij}, and it is assumed that the cost does not vary with the flow amount. Moreover, a link specifies capacity b_{ij}, the maximum flow amount on the link.

Let S be the set of h *multimedia sessions* that are to be established over network (N, L). Each session s may involve multiple *media flows*. A media flow

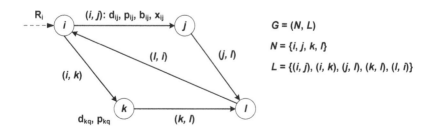

Fig. 2. Network graph illustration for the path optimization problem

$f \in M$ is specified with its source $i^f_{src} \in N$, destination $j^f_{dst} \in N$, type t_f, codec c_f (if applicable, e.g., PCM for audio or H.264 for video), which also influences the accompanying mean packet size, bit rate o_f (e.g., 5 Mbit/s), weight factor in a session w_f, and defined MOS threshold, or minimum quality requested, v_f (e.g., 3.8 for audio with PCM and 80 kbps). MOS value for a flow, u_f, is predicted in the path selection process, based on formulas (1), (2) and (3) for a specific flow type, and then used to calculate MOS value for a session, u_s. Depending on session configurations, node $i \in N$ may be the source or the destination for multiple flows, or just act as a transit node on their paths. If i is the source for flow f, then node rate $r^f_i = o_f$, while R_i references rates of all the associated flows. If i is a transit node for flow f, then $r^f_i = 0$.

Model Parameters. While one group of the Q-POINT input parameters relates to session configurations, the second group encompasses MOS functions g, as given by equations (1), (2) and (3), which map application-level parameters (c_f, o_f) and network QoS parameters (d_{e2e}, p_{e2e}) to an MOS value. The last parameter group refers to network topology, which specifies how the nodes are interconnected and what are link characteristics (b_{ij}, d_{ij}).

Decision and Auxiliary Variables. We choose two types of decision variables for this problem formulation: (a) x^f_{ij} denotes rate of flow $f \in M$ on link $(i, j) \in L$, which may be different from the original rate due to possible losses, and (b) $y^f_{ij} \in \{0, 1\}$ indicates whether link (i, j) is selected for the path of flow f or not.

If path loss probability p^f_{e2e} is calculated based on loss probability of each node (p_{iq}) on the path, then the derived loss formula incorporates a product of decision variables y^f_{ij} (to select network segments that contribute to the E2E loss), which makes the mathematical formulation non-linear. Figure 3 illustrates the applied solution to this issue by introducing a virtual network node Z and an auxiliary variable z^f_i. Node Z represents the sink for packets being lost at the path's nodes, while z^f_i holds loss rate of flow f at node i (if packet loss occurs). All network nodes $i \in N$ are connected to Z with virtual links, which are characterized by $b_{iZ} = \infty$, delay $d_{iZ} = 0$, and loss probability $p_{iZ} = 0$.

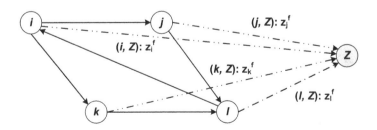

Fig. 3. Network graph with virtual node Z as the "lost packets' sink"

Building on the applied solution, average loss probability for flow $f \in M$ can then be calculated as the sum of loss rates at nodes that are included in the flow's path over original flow rate (note that the path loss is not additive with respect to node loss probability, p_{iq}):

$$p_{e2e}^f = \frac{\sum_{i \in N : i \neq dst(f)} z_i^f}{o_f}; \qquad z_i^f = \sum_{\substack{\{i \in N: \\ i = tail(i,j), (i,j) \in L\}}} x_{ij}^f * \frac{p_{iq}}{1 - p_{iq}}. \qquad (6)$$

To calculate E2E delay for flow $f \in M$, on the other hand, delays on each node and link of the flow's path are summed up:

$$d_{e2e}^f = \sum_{\substack{\{(i,j) \in L: \\ i = tail(i,j), i \neq dst(f), \\ i \in N\}}} y_{ij}^f * (d_{iq} + d_{ij}). \qquad (7)$$

Objective Function. As per the problem specification, the Q-POINT objective is to maximize the sum of MOS values over all multimedia sessions:

$$maximize \sum_{s \in S} u_s, \qquad (8)$$

where MOS value for a session is calculated as a weighted sum of MOS values for the comprising (one or more) media flows:

$$u_s = \sum_{\{f \in M : session(f) = s\}} w_f * u_f. \qquad (9)$$

Model Constraints. Table 2 depicts mathematical formulation of the model constraints. The *Minimum MOS* constraint forces Q-POINT to select a path that provides, at least, MOS value v_f for flow f, thus satisfying minimum quality requirements for a specific flow and also guaranteeing a certain fairness among all end-users. *Maximum link rate* denotes that link $(i, j) \in L$ can admit flow f only if its link rate x_{ij}^f does not exceed the link capacity. Similarly, the *Maximum sum of link rates* constraint imposes that the sum of link rates for flows following the same link cannot exceed the link capacity. *Maximum link rate* is specified so as to simplify the mathematical formulation and facilitate the problem solving.

The *Flow conservation* constraint for each flow specifies that incoming link rate x_{ij} at node j is divided between outgoing link rate x_{jk} and loss rate z_j^f. If j is the source for flow f, then incoming link rate equals to node rate r_j^f. *Link selection* forces a flow to follow only one outgoing link from its source, one incoming and one outgoing link at a transit node, and only one incoming link at the flow's destination. This means that flows are non-splittable and cannot use concurrent paths to reach their destinations, leading to a complex-to-solve model. Finally, the *Loop-back links* constraint requires Q-POINT to avoid choosing links that would send flows back towards their source nodes.

Table 2. Model constraints

Model constraint	Mathematical formulation
Minimum MOS	$u_f \geq v_f \, , \forall f \in M$
Maximum link rate	$x_{ij}^f \leq y_{ij}^f * b_{ij} \, , \forall f \in M \, , \forall (i,j) \in L$
Maximum sum of link rates	$\sum_{f \in M} x_{ij}^f < b_{ij} \, , \forall (i,j) \in L$
Flow conservation	$\sum_{\{k:k=head(j,k)\}} x_{jk}^f + z_j^f = r_j^f \, ,$ $\forall f \in M \, , \forall j \in N : j = src(f)$ $\sum_{\{k:k=head(j,k)\}} x_{jk}^f + z_j^f - \sum_{\{i:i=tail(i,j)\}} x_{ij}^f = 0 \, ,$ $\forall f \in M \, , \forall j \in N : (j \neq src(f)) \wedge (j \neq dst(f))$
Link selection	$\sum_{\{k:k=head(j,k)\}} y_{jk}^f = 1 \, ,$ $\forall f \in M \, , \forall j \in N : j = src(f)$ $\sum_{\{k:k=head(j,k)\}} y_{jk}^f - \sum_{\{i:i=tail(i,j)\}} y_{ij}^f = 0 \, ,$ $\forall f \in M \, , \forall j \in N : (j \neq src(f)) \wedge (j \neq dst(f))$ $\sum_{\{i:i=tail(i,j)\}} y_{ij}^f = 1 \, ,$ $\forall f \in M \, , \forall j \in N : j = dst(f)$
Loop-back links	$y_{ij}^f + y_{kl}^f \leq 1 \, , \forall f \in M \, ,$ $\forall (i,j) \in L, \forall (k,l) \in L : (((i,j) > (k,l)) \wedge (i = l) \wedge (j = k))$

4   Model Implementation

We use the IBM Optimization Programming Language [22] to formulate our model. One of the major issues regarding model implementation was the existence of non-linear functions in the initial formulation (e.g., equations (4) and (5) incorporate decision variable x_{ij}). Equation (7) for calculating E2E delay on a path includes a non-linear product of binary variable y_{ij} and continuous function d_{iq}. To linearize it, we apply a technique that introduces substitute decision variables. In this case, d_{iq} is defined as a new decision variable, which in turn creates a product of binary and continuous variable. The latter product can be replaced by a new continuous decision variable, which we refer to as yd_{ijq}. To be able to employ this substitution, additional constraints need to be defined:

$$yd_{ijq} \geq 0, \quad yd_{ijq} \leq y_{ij} * M, \quad yd_{ijq} \leq d_{iq}, \quad yd_{ijq} \geq d_{iq} - (1 - y_{ij}) * M, \quad (10)$$

where M is the upper bound on value of d_{iq}. Similarly, equation (6) includes a product of continuous variable x_{ij} and continuous function p_{iq}. This product is linearized by using the one-dimensional method from [23], which introduced five continuous decision variables, two binary decision variables and several of the accompanying constraints to our initial formulation.

5   Model Evaluation

In this section, we present an initial evaluation of the proposed model. The evaluation examines the problem solving time with respect to different number of flows to be routed and network topologies. It also analyzes overall QoE gains of Q-POINT over the shortest path approach typically used in current networks.

We use IBM ILOG CPLEX Optimization Studio 12.5 [22], CPLEX Optimizer's mixed integer solver and the branch-and-cut algorithm with default settings. The solver is run in Debian Linux 6.0.8 on a workstation with an Intel Xeon CPU @ 2.6 GHz and 32 GB of RAM. To obtain numerical results for the evaluation, m flow requests are generated: $\frac{2m}{5}$ audio flows, $\frac{2m}{5}$ video flows, and $\frac{m}{5}$ data flows. Flows of the same type are generated with the same characteristics (Table 3). For each flow we randomly choose its source and destination, but in a way that each network node serves as the source and the destination to a similar portion of m flows. After flow generation, the Q-POINT model is run.

The evaluation network topologies are shown in Figure 4. The first one is a random topology, while the other one is modeled against the Croatian National and Research Network (CARNet), i.e. a part of its core network. For both topologies capacity of each link is set to 1 Gbps, while link delay is randomly chosen from {10 ms, 20 ms, 30 ms}. Each network node is pre-configured with 3 buffers. Audio buffer size is set to 1000 bytes (i.e., 5 audio packets), video buffer size to 28800 bytes (i.e., 20 packets), while data buffer size is set to 30000 bytes. The weighted fair queuing discipline is assumed at network nodes, which all serve as source and destination to flows of different type, with buffer weights set to 0.3, 0.5 and 0.2 for audio, video and data flows, respectively. The chosen network values were empirically derived and impact of their variations on the optimization result will be analyzed in future work, as well as impact of more complex network topologies. All results are obtained over 10 test runs for each topology and flow number m, which is specified from {100, 200, 300, 400, 500}.

With respect to the CARNet-like topology, Table 4 shows the sum of QoE values over all flows for Q-POINT and the shortest path selection, which is based on the "hop-count" metric. While Q-POINT achieves higher aggregate QoE for each m value, a notable difference occurs for $m = 500$, when overall traffic increases link utilization considerably (for some links to above 50%). Our model consequentially aims to distribute video and data paths so as to "balance" traffic load per node, thus minimizing QoE degradations. For $m = 500$, Q-POINT

Table 3. Flow characteristics for the Q-POINT evalution

Flow type	Codec	Bit rate [Mbps]	Maximum MOS	Mean packet length [bytes]	Generated no. of flows
Audio	PCM	0.08	4.3	200	$\frac{2m}{5}$
Video	H.264	5.0	4.7	1440	$\frac{2m}{5}$
Data	-	5.0	4.5	1500	$\frac{m}{5}$

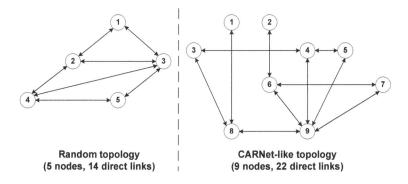

Random topology
(5 nodes, 14 direct links)

CARNet-like topology
(9 nodes, 22 direct links)

Fig. 4. Network topologies for the Q-POINT evaluation

obtains, e.g., video loss probability under 0.15% at each node, with all video flows over two-hop paths facing loss probability of 0.23% on average and achieving MOS of 4.56 on average. With the same flow configuration, the shortest path selection results in, e.g., video loss probability at node 9 of 0.87%. Moreover, 66 video flows are assigned two-hop routes with loss probability of 1.12% on average, leading to their average MOS value of 3.99. Although this preliminary evaluation shows some encouraging results on QoE gains of Q-POINT over the shortest path, a thorough analysis needs to be performed to derive general conclusions.

Table 4. Comparison of the sum of QoE values over all flows

$CARNet\text{-}like\ topology$	$m = 100$	$m = 200$	$m = 300$	$m = 400$	$m = 500$
Shortest path selection	448.5	892.9	1330.3	1754.2	**2147.4**
Q-POINT model	449.0	895.6	1338.8	1775.1	**2200.7**

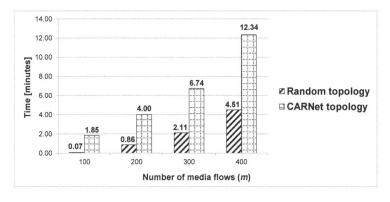

Fig. 5. The solver execution time

Average execution time of the solver is shown in Figure 5. While Q-POINT yields acceptable performance for the random network, which is of a simpler topology than the CARNet-like network, and $m = \{100, 200\}$, it is evident that running a single optimization of paths for that many flows in a network would be too time consuming to apply the model for dynamic network reconfiguration.

6   Conclusion

In this paper, we have presented Q-POINT, a QoE-driven path optimization model for multimedia services. In contrast to traditional networks, where flows with the same destination typically follow the same path, Q-POINT calculates the best path for each service flow so as to maximize the aggregated QoE for a whole network domain. The key contribution of this paper is the presented mathematical model, which is formulated as a mixed integer linear program. The preliminary evaluation shows that our model increases the overall QoE, which means that end-users will be more satisfied with the delivered service.

Our work opens up several interesting research aspects. First is to evaluate impact of different QoE-QoS mapping functions on resource utilization and of using multi-path transfer, with the latter simplifying the model complexity since flows become splittable. As end-users frequently establish new sessions and flows, we are currently extending Q-POINT to control optimization for given traffic dynamics, while trying to keep the number of path reconfigurations for the existing flows to a minimum. We also plan to address the applicability and benefits of our approach in the context of additional service types (e.g., adaptive video streaming over HTTP and on-line gaming) and more complex traffic mixes. A step further will be to explore heuristics that will allow us to achieve a satisfactory QoE result in minimal (or acceptable) execution time. Finally, we have also started to implement the model within the SDN framework by developing an SDN controller application to run Q-POINT.

Acknowledgments. This work has been supported by the European Community's 7th Framework Programme under grant agreement no. 285939 (ACROSS), and the research projects 036-0362027-1639 and 071-362027-2329 funded by the Ministry of Science, Education, and Sports of the Republic of Croatia. Additional support was provided by the KK-stiftelsen under the READY project.

References

1. Schatz, R., Hoßfeld, T., Janowski, L., Egger, S.: From Packets to People: Quality of Experience as New Measurement Challenge. In: Biersack, E., Callegari, C., Matijasevic, M. (eds.) Data Traffic Monitoring and Analysis. LNCS, vol. 7754, pp. 219–263. Springer, Heidelberg (2013)
2. Thakolsri, S., Khan, S., Steinbach, E.G., Kellerer, W.: QoE-Driven Cross-Layer Optimization for High Speed Downlink Packet Access. J. Communications, North America. 4, 669–680 (2009)

3. Brajdic, A., Kassler, A., Matijasevic, M.: Quality of Experience based Optimization of Heterogeneous Multimedia Sessions in IMS. In: 2011 BCFIC, pp. 25–32 (2011)
4. Open Networking Foundation: Software-Defined Networking. White paper (2012)
5. Kassler, A., Skorin-Kapov, L., Dobrijevic, O., Matijasevic, M., Dely, P.: Towards QoE-driven Multimedia Service Negotiation and Path Optimization with Software defined Networking. In: 20th SoftCOM, pp. 1–5 (2012)
6. Wang, Z., Crowcroft, J.: Quality-of-service Routing for Supporting Multimedia Applications. IEEE J. Selected Areas in Communications. 14, 1228–1234 (1996)
7. Lorenz, D.H., Orda, A.: QoS Routing in Networks with Uncertain Parameters. IEEE/ACM Trans. on Networking. 6, 768–778 (1998)
8. Kumar, D., Kashyap, D., Mishra, K.K., Mishra, A.K.: Routing Path Determination Using QoS Metrics and Priority based Evolutionary Optimization. In: 13th IEEE HPCC, pp. 615–621 (2011)
9. Kuipers, F., Van Mieghem, P., Korkmaz, T., Krunz, M.: An Overview of Constraint-based Path Selection Algorithms for QoS Routing. IEEE Communications Magazine 40, 50–55 (2002)
10. Lu, T., Zhu, J.: A Genetic Algorithm for Finding a Path Subject to Two Constraints. Applied Soft Computing 13, 891–898 (2013)
11. Amram, N., Fu, B., Kunzmann, G., Melia, T., Munaretto, D., Randriamasy, S., Sayadi, B., Widmer, J., Zorzi, M.: QoE-based Transport Optimization for Video Delivery over Next Generation Cellular Networks. In: 2011 IEEE ISCC, pp. 19–24 (2011)
12. De Vleeschauwer, B., De Turck, F., Dhoedt, B., Demeester, P., Wijnants, M., Lamotte, W.: End-to-end QoE Optimization Through Overlay Network Deployment. In: 2008 ICOIN, pp. 1–5 (2008)
13. Venkataraman, M., Chatterjee, M.: Effects of Internet Path Selection on Video-QoE: Analysis and Improvements. IEEE/ACM Trans. on Networking, 14 p. (2013)
14. Egilmez, H.E., Civanlar, S., Tekalp, A.M.: An Optimization Framework for QoS-enabled Adaptive Video Streaming over OpenFlow Networks. IEEE Trans. on Multimedia. 15, 710–715 (2013)
15. Egilmez, H.E., Dane, S.T., Bagci, K.T., Tekalp, A.M.: OpenQoS: An OpenFlow Controller Design for Multimedia Delivery with End-to-end Quality of Service over Software-Defined Networks. In: 2012 APSIPA, pp. 1–8 (2012)
16. Jarschel, M., Wamser, F., Hoehn, T., Zinner, T., Tran-Gia, P.: SDN-based Application-Aware Networking on the Example of YouTube Video Streaming. In: 2nd EWSDN, pp. 87–92 (2013)
17. Rosenberg, J., Schulzrinne, H., Camarillo, G., Johnston, A., Peterson, J., Sparks, R., Handley, M., Schooler, E.: SIP: Session Initiation Protocol. IETF (2002)
18. Skorin-Kapov, L., Matijasevic, M.: Modeling of a QoS Matching and Optimization Function for Multimedia Services in the NGN. In: 12th IFIP/IEEE MMNS, pp. 55–68 (2009)
19. Moura, N., Vianna, B., Albuquerque, C., Rebello, V., Boeres, C.: MOS-Based Rate Adaption for VoIP Sources. In: 2007 IEEE ICC, pp. 628–633 (2007)
20. Yamagishi, K., Hayashi, T.: Parametric Packet-Layer Model for Monitoring Video Quality of IPTV Services. In: 2008 IEEE ICC, pp. 110–114 (2008)
21. Ahuja, R.K., Magnanti, T.L., Orlin, J.B.: Network Flows: Theory, Algorithms, and Applications. Prentice Hall, New Jersey (1993)
22. IBM ILOG CPLEX Optimization Studio, http://www-03.ibm.com/software/products/us/en/ibmilogcpleoptistud/
23. D'Ambrosio, C., Lodi, A., Martello, S.: Piecewise Linear Approximation of Functions of Two Variables in MILP Models. Operat. Research Letters. 38, 39–46 (2010)

Least Path Interference Beaconing Protocol (LIBP): A Frugal Routing Protocol for The Internet-of-Things

Lutando Ngqakaza[1] and Antoine Bagula[2]

[1] ISAT Laboratory, Department of Computer Science, University of Cape Town, Private Bag
X3 Rondebosch, Cape Town, South Africa
[2] ISAT Laboratory, Department of Computer Science, University of Western Cape, Private Bag
X17, Bellville 7535, Cape Town, South Africa
`ngqlut003@myuct.ac.za, bbagula@uwc.ac.za`

Abstract. This paper presents a frugal protocol for sensor readings dissemination in the Internet-of-Things (IoT). The protocol called Least Path Interference Beaconing (LIBP) is based on a lightweight path selection model that builds a routing spanning tree rooted at the sink node based on information disseminated through a periodic beaconing process. LIBPs frugality results from a routing process where the sensor nodes select the least path interfering parents on the routing spanning tree with the expectation of flow balancing the traffic routed from nodes to the sink of a sensor network. The simulation results produced by Cooja under the Contiki operating system are in agreement with previous results obtained under the TinyOS operating system. They reveal that LIBP outperforms different versions of the RPL protocol and the CTP protocol in terms of power consumption, scalability, throughput and recovery from failure as well as its frugality as a routing protocol.

1 Introduction

A new form of modern communication is emerging where sensing, identification and many other types of processing devices are combined with the objective of interacting pervasively with the physical world to provide to different users various services. It is predicted that these devices will be deployed in our daily living environment in thousands of heterogeneous computing elements building multi-technology and multi-protocol platforms that provide access to the information not only *"anytime"* and *"anywhere"*, but also using *"anything"* in a first-mile of the Internet referred to as the *"Internet-of-the- Things" (IoT)* [1]. The next generation IoT infrastructure is expected to include millions of interconnected islands of sensing/identification networks spread around the world to provide services that would not be possible to provide with current generation sensor networks. Such network islands will be using multi-hop routing to avoid the need for the high communication power that might be required from the lightweight IoT devices for communication with each other directly. They will be operating on either an m-to-1 or an m-to-n routing model where where all the nodes will be collecting from their environments sensor readings carrying the information to be sent to either a unique sink node (m-to-1 mono-sink architecture) or multiple sinks (m-to-n multi-sink architecture).

A. Mellouk et al. (Eds.): WWIC 2014, LNCS 8458, pp. 148–161, 2014.

1.1   Routing over the Lightweight IoT Devices

The routing of sensor readings in IoT settings can be formulated as a problem of finding a set of paths for routing the traffic flows carrying these readings from their points of collection to sink nodes which are tasked to deliver these readings to gateways for further processing. When applied to a mono-sink architecture, the traffic packets carrying the sensor readings are routed from nodes to neighbours along the path to the unique sink node following a multi-hop process usually aimed at reducing the energy that each node would spend if it had to send its data traffic directly to the sink. The process can be constrained by spatio-temporal and different other constraints depending on the IoT settings and the application. The solutions to the routing problem above may differ but are usually expected to be self-organized, self-repairing and frugal routing protocols in terms of storage, processing and communication requirements on the lightweight devices that are used in IoT deployments. In a typical mono-sink IoT deployment, the information carried by the sensor readings would typically be aggregated from the nodes towards a unique sink that forms the root node of a tree which is connected to the gateway by the sink with most of the leaf nodes present in the network sending their sensor readings upwards towards the root/sink node for storage, analysis or further processing.

1.2   Contribution and Outline

The LIBP protocol [2, 3] was previously implemented for TinyOS using the Tossim emulator [4]. This paper presents a Contiki [5] implementation of LIBP and evaluates its performance compared to CTP [6] and different versions of the RPL protocol [7] with the objective of assessing the frugality of LIBP and its efficiency compared to these two other routing protocols. While the LIBP implementation presented in this paper has been implemented from scratch following the model proposed in [2], the RPL and CTP implementations considered in this paper are widely available in open-source format on a wide variety of platforms. They did not require any new implementation in the platform of choice for this paper. The remainder of this paper is organized as follows: Section 2 presents the proposed LIB protocol while 3 describes related routing protocols used in IoT settings. The results obtained through comparative simulation study are presented in Section 4, and finally Section 5 draws the conclusions and provide avenues for future work.

2   Least Path Interference Beaconing Protocol (LIBP)

2.1   Protocol Description

LIBP [2, 3] is an implementation of the LIBA algorithm. This routing protocol, like CTP, uses a beaconing process initiated by the source (sink) node. When the process is initiated nodes incident to the sink node will be the first to recognize that a sink node is within one hop distance. This process is then initiated by these nodes to their neighbours and this process is repeated thereafter. This results in a network where each node is aware of its neighbours. The least interference paradigm is integrated into the process by which nodes select parent nodes which have the smallest number of (supporting) children, which is the parent of least traffic flow interference. This configuration is especially powerful in the situation where sensors are periodically sensing information (which is a very popular sensor use case). LIBP basically aims to provide a way to balance traffic flow in such a way that it results in energy efficiency by having a network where nodes support less traffic. The network building process is highly detailed in the paper by Bagula et al [2].

2.2   LIBP Implementation

RPL and CTP are already implemented in ContikiOS [5], however LIBP is not, this resulted in having LIBP implemented for Contiki. Following the successful methodology of adapting CTP to conform to the LIBP model and ideas [2], this approach was used to preserve the same interfaces that CTP has implemented with the simulation environment (Cooja). At a very high level the link-estimate module for CTP found in Contikis network library was modified to conform to LIBP ideas. This means that the ETX link metric was altered to rather conform to interference represented by the amount of supporting children nodes. Features not required for LIBP were removed (trickle algorithm code for example). It should be noted that since LIBP in its Contiki implementation is forked from CTPs implementation in Contiki, it inherited the same underlying communications stack, Rime [8].

2.3   LIBP Network Building Process

The LIBP network building owes its power to simplicity that builds upon an ad-hoc routing protocol that is also structurally similar to RPL in structure. LIBP uses two control plane messages for network configuration, one being the beacon message, and the other is the acknowledgement (ACK). In the scenario where the network is initialized, the root node will broadcast a beacon at a given interval where the beacon includes important routing information regarding the senders identity and weight. Once the root node advertises the beacon, nodes within the immediate vicinity of the root would have received the beacon. The root node advertises a weight of 0 which prompts the nodes within its vicinity to use that node as a parent. The parent is alerted to the new nodes dependence by the acknowledgement packet. When a node sends an acknowledgement packet to a parent then that parent must increase its weight since that parent is supporting an extra node.

2.4   LIBP Maintenance and Recovery

From the network configuration stage of LIBP (shortly after network epoch) each node keeps a linked list of neighbouring nodes. This list holds an object which characterizes the neighbouring nodes address and its weight (interference) along with its route metric.

Maintenance - Since each node accounts for each of its neighbours in a linked list, it is then possible for nodes to perform rudimentary operations for local network maintenance, and in the event of parent failure, network repair is achievable. The age attribute is there to keep track how long that particular LIBP Neighbour has been in the list, whenever the LIBPNeighbour linked list is updated then the age attribute is incremented. The route metric attribute describes the precedence in which nodes are tiered by how far they appear to be from the root node, nodes with a low route metric are closer to the sink node. RPL uses a similar metric which can be described as node depth [7].

Recovery - When a node is compromised in such a way that its ability to communicate is impaired then recovery is required. Such a node would have to be removed from the network as a whole. This usually happens when a particular node is unable to acknowledge sent data messages, the main event which alludes to this conclusion is that a node would have retransmitted the same packet for an amount that is equal to the programmed max retransmits. If this happens then the compromised node is removed from the sending nodes LIBP Neighbour list. This in effect removes the parent of the sending node, which requires the sending node to pick a new parent.

3 Related Routing Protocols: RPL and CTP

3.1 Collection Tree Protocol (CTP)

CTP [6] is a routing protocol which extends the Trickle algorithm [9]. It does so because the assumption can be made that data aggregation is one of the primary goals of a WSN. CTP promises to be reliable, efficient, robust, and hardware independent. CTP relies on data packets to validate the routing topology and loop detection. This routing protocol also utilizes adaptive beaconing (an application of Trickle) to dynamically setup and adapt to network changes. Every node implementing CTP maintains an estimate of the cost of its route to a collection point (namely, the sink node). This metric is typically called expected transmissions (ETX).

CTP Network Building Process. CTP (and RPL) employ a similar strategy for network construction. CTP extends the use of the trickle algorithm [9] by sending out control messages at a rate which is dependent on how dynamic the network is. In summary when the routing is empty (the network has just been deployed), A set number of nodes in a network advertise themselves as network roots. Thereafter, nodes form a set of routing trees to these roots. In CTP each node selects one parent as a next-hop link and that parent is closer to the root node than the node is.

CTP Maintenance and Recovery. CTPs strength lies in the fact that its network maintenance is implied by its adaptive control messaging implementation.

Maintenance - The adapted trickle algorithm used in CTP also counts for the handling of network inconsistencies. These inconsistencies include node addition, the significant change in link ETX and loop avoidance. The adapted trickle algorithm counts for the ability for CTP to maintain the network. Even if a network is heavily degraded, due to the adapted trickle algorithm, the network should relax to a near-optimum state.

Recovery - CTP employs a simple strategy for detecting node failure. In the case of node failure, all nodes which are dependent on the failed node will find another parent (usually the next best local parent). Node failure is usually recognized when a node cannot unicast a message to its parent, this is when the node uses up all its retransmissions for a given packet. Once node failure is established then a node will do a lookup in its routing table to find the best replacement if possible.

3.2 Routing Protocol for LLNs (RPL)

RPL [7] is a direct result of The Internet Engineering Task Force (IETF) which recognized the need to form a standardized IPv6-based routing solution for LLNs. The IETF formalized a working group specific for this problem called ROLL (Routing over Low power and Lossy). The direct outcome of this workgroup was RPL.

RPL Network Building Process. RPL is a Distance Vector IPv6 routing protocol for LLNs that specifies how to build a Destination Oriented Directed Acyclic Graph (DODAG) using an objective function and a set of metrics and constraints. RPL basically builds a logical communications graph over a physical network that conforms to satisfying a set of objectives and conforms to a set of constraints which can be set by a network administrator. The graph building process is initiated at the root (or sink) node, multiple roots can exist in the same network. The root(s) start advertising the information about the graph using messages outlined in its RFC and other literature [7].

RPL Objective Functions. An objective function (OF) allows for RPL to optimize, constrain, or scale the routing metric or link metric of a path. It is entirely possible to have multiple objective functions operating on the same node or same network. Objective functions allow network administrators to impose a set of rules which affect the traffic flow of the network. For example, on one subsection of a network one could implement a rule that specifies that paths with the best Expected Transmissions (ETX) must be used and that the paths must be non-encrypted, or that paths with lowest latencies must be used while avoiding battery operated nodes.

Objective Function ETX - The ETX Objective function (OF-ETX) [6] is a widely popular link metric in the field of WSN. It is a link metric that in some way encompasses link congestion and link latency. ETX is simply defined as the expected number of transmissions required to successfully transmit and acknowledge a packet on a wireless link. In practical terms the ETXroot = 0 (the root node is not expected to send data packets) and the ETXnode = ETXparent + ETXlinktoparent. The objective for OF-ETX is to (greedily) choose the route with the lowest ETX. It should be noted that OF-ETX is standardized and thus can be considered as a modular addition to RPL.

Objective Function Zero - The Objective function Zero (OF-0) is a relatively new objective function proposed by the IETF. In comparison to ETX, OF-0 is not highly established since ETX is considered a mature link metric in the field of WSNs. The goal of OF-0 is for a node to select a parent in such a way that it provides or contributes good enough connectivity to a specific set of nodes or to a larger routing infrastructure. OF-0 is described as being an OF which guides nodes in their parent selection using a metric called node rank. The rank computation of OF-0 has a set of constraints and norms which can be seen in its RFC [10].

RPL Maintenance and Recovery. RPL tries to limit the control plane traffic in the network to minimize the impact that control plane traffic has on the network. Some protocols use periodic keep alives (often called beacons) [2]. RPL uses a different paradigm when attempting to maintain and recover the network.

Maintenance - Instead of using a periodic keep alive for network node maintenance, RPL uses an adaptive timer mechanism called the trickle timer. This algorithm dictates the sending rate of control messages. In essence the trickle timer treats the network as a distributed system that suffers from a consistency problem. A set of events confirms graph inconsistency, for example if a node detects a loop then the network is considered inconsistent, or when a node joins a network, or when a node leaves a network. The more inconsistencies that are detected the more control messages that are sent in the network. The more consistent the network is then the less control messages that are sent.

Recovery - RPL employs two techniques in order to recover the network from node and link failure. In essence RPL uses both local and global repair to initiate graph recovery. When a link or parent node failure is detected, the child node will quickly find an alternative route that conforms to the rules of the OF upon it. This is local repair, given enough local repairs, the graph may diverge from optimum setup. At this point it may be necessary for the graph to be rebuilt using global repair. Global repair is the rebuilding of the graph as if the network was newly deployed as outlined in the RPL Network Building Process section of this paper. Thus global repair is costly as that imposes a high flow of control traffic in the network.

4   Performance Evaluation

Testing Environment - These experiments will be conducted on the Contiki [5] platform. The mote that will be emulated in Cooja for this experiment will be the Tmote sky mote. In the case that emulation is not required; Cooja motes will be used for simulation. The experiment will be conducted in a simulation environment in which UDGM (Distance Loss) will be the radio medium of choice. RPL and CTP are already implemented in Contiki. LIBP was implemented by forking the CTP code found in Contiki and modifying it in order to meet the LIBP requirements.

Data Collection - Metrics in the experiment were collected by implementing the energest [11](Energy Estimation) module in Contiki, energest is used for obtaining per-component power consumption. This module gives metrics which are related to the amount of power required by certain modes of operation. The metrics that can be obtained from energest is the count of power utilized for radio RX and TX, Low Powered Mode(LPM), and Normal Powered Mode (NPM) also known as awake mode. By using the Tmote sky datasheet. The power utilized is described below.

To calculate the power we need an intermediary function which helps us calculate the power utilized.

$$f(x,y) = ((x \times 64) + (y \times 64)/1000) \tag{1}$$

And to calculate the power utilized given the energest RX TX LPM and APM values we calculate the power.

$$P = 3 \times \frac{APM \times f(1,800) + LPM \times f(0,545) + TX \times f(17,700) + RX \times f(20,0)}{64 \times (APM + LPM) \div 1000}$$

(2)

Cooja also has an online data collection application called the shell collect view. The shell collect view gives a comprehensive breakdown of node specific status variables and meta-data. Cooja has another nice feature which comes in a Cooja application called PowerTracker. PowerTracker is an online real-time radio duty cycle monitoring tool. PowerTracker can be used to deduce the amount of time that a node spends in a particular state with regards to its radio.

Testing Variables - RPL will be run as two experiment instances since RPL can be run with various objective functions (OF). As a result RPL will be run with OF-0 and OF-ETX and thus for the rest of the paper RPL will be referred to either RPL-0 or RPL-ETX to refer to RPL coupled with their objective functions respectively. RPL itself cannot be tested as a routing protocol rather RPL and an objective function needs to be tested against CTP and LIBP respectively. Since there are implementations for OF-0 and OF-ETX on Contiki already, the experiment variables will be CTP, LIBP, RPL-0, and RPL-ETX.

Table 1. Simulation Setup

Test Attributes	Test Value
Topology	175mx175m grid of 30 randomly placed nodes (density 30m2/node)*
Beacon Interval	30 seconds (LIBP), Adaptive (CTP, RPL)
Messaging Interval	30 seconds
Message Contents	Hello from node
Simulation Runtime	10 minutes (2 minutes for network self organization)*
(LIBP)	1
TX/INT Range	50m/100m

4.1   Methodology

The table above outlines the experiment runtime. In short, unless otherwise specified, the networks are each given a 2 minute period to allow for the network to settle; thereafter the network is run for 8 minutes to give a total simulation runtime of 10 minutes. Each node will periodically send a packet containing the string Hello from node as its packet data. Since each node is given 8 minutes to send the data at a period of 30 seconds, the nodes will each send 16 packets data to be collected by the sink. For the various experiments, all of Coojas existing profiling tools were used as experimentation tools. Simulation timers and node real-time timers were used as experimentation tools for time sensitive experiments. For discerning between control plane traffic and data plane traffic the packets were flagged accordingly, the packets would then trigger a counter which would hold a value that shows how many times a packet of that particular classification occurred as traffic during simulation runtime. Routing protocols have to be tested in terms of scalability. 10 random topologies were generated ranging from a topology sizes of 10 to 100 (in increments of 10). Each topology had the same node density. The benefit of having all these network topologies is so that metrics related to the routing protocols can be observed while the topology size increases.

4.2   Results and Evaluation

In this section, CTP, and RPL (alongside its OFs) is evaluated against the new implementation of LIBP on Contiki.

Energy Profile. The average power consumption in Figure 1 (a) was taken by averaging the power consumption amounts of each node. RPL seems to be significantly more power hungry on average when compared to CTP and LIBP. This could be put down to the fact that the radio in the sink node in RPL is always on, in addition to that, RPL is built on top of a slightly more capable but heavyweight communications protocol.

The graph of Figure 1 (b) shows the average radio duty cycle. It should be noted that the duty cycles represents the percentage of time that the radio was in a particular stage during the 10 minute simulation runtime. The TX and RX power draw are roughly the same on many motes.

RPL makes the assumption that the sink nodes are typically well powered. This is shown in the graph Figure 1 (c), the radios in the sink nodes for RPL are always turned on, which results in a very power hungry sink. The sink nodes in RPL would consume in the region of 60 mW, whereas the sink nodes in CTP and LIBP would consume power in the region of 4mW. In effect the sink nodes in RPL consume more than 1 order of magnitude more energy than the CTP and LIBP sink nodes. This can mostly be put down to the always on radio.

Table 2. Power Distribution

Routing Protocol	Mean (mW)	Standard Deviation (mW)
CTP	4.06	0.474
LIBP	3.24	0.278
RPL-0	5.01	10.81
RPL-ETX	5.43	10.73

The standard deviation of the power consumption presented in Table 4.2 for the routing protocol can describe how well distributed the energy consumption will be in the topology. This is a very important metric in figuring out the amount of time that a network can be deployed before requiring a battery change. Having a energy usage low mean and a low energy usage standard deviation shows that the protocol is energy efficient in its distribution and energy efficient in its implementation.

Routing Profile. The routing metrics of each routing protocol include the amount of supporting children per node, the average path length and the agility of the protocol.

Figure 3 (a) shows the path interference (contention) in terms of average amount of children that a node would support. This value was obtained by counting the amount of times each node referenced a parent and then averaging those values. Having a smaller number of average children is a desirable metric because it can help with energy distribution in the network which helps with leaving all the nodes at more or less the same battery life. Having a high contention undesirable since it may also introduce a higher rate of packet loss or interference into the network. LIBP being the protocol which tries

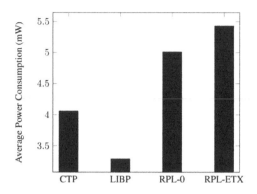

(a) Average Power Consumption (mW)

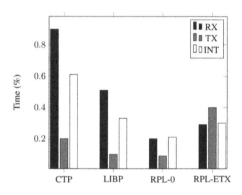

(b) Radio Duty Cycle

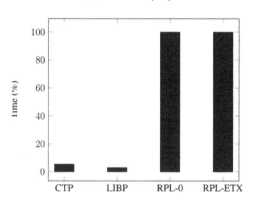

(c) Radio Duty Cycle For Sink nodes

Fig. 1. Power consumption: average consumption and duty cycles

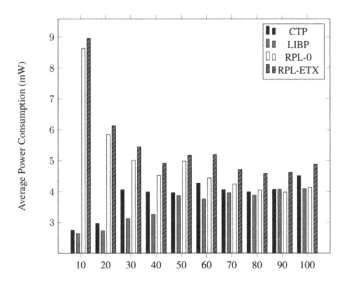

Fig. 2. Scalability for Average Power Consumption

to minimize the average amount of children in the pursuit for better energy distribution does better in this experiment.

The average path length depicted in Figure 3 (b) was obtained by computing the TTL like attributes in the protocol control plane packets. LIBP and RPL use TTL (time to live) however CTP uses time has lived (which is TTL_MAX TTL). Once the number of hops was obtained they were averaged to give an average path length metric for each protocol respectively. Depending on the application, A high average path length is desirable for better for energy distribution but a lower average path length can result in a lower latency between the leaf nodes and sink nodes.

Recovery from Failure. The graph in Figure 4 (a) shows how quickly the protocols can come up with contingency routes if a node with high contention fails. To simulate this event, a node with a high degree of children (4 children) was chosen and deleted at the 10 minute mark. The times represented in the graph above shows the amount of time required for all 4 of the children to find alternate parents/routes. The data above shows how agile the routing protocols are in terms of how they deal with catastrophic failure.

The graph of Figure 4 (b) demonstrates how agile the routing protocols are in the ad-hoc sense. The experiment was set up by running a normal collect experiment of 30 nodes, except 1 node would be out of reach from the network (thus not part of the network). At the 10 minute mark from the start of the simulation the secluded node would be introduced to the network. The times in the above graph represent the time it took for that node to have acknowledged a parent (to become part of the network).

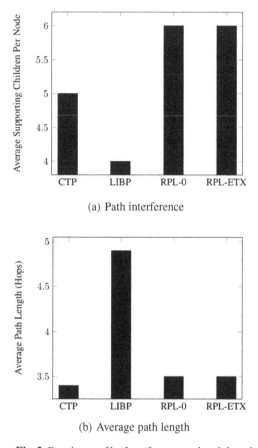

(a) Path interference

(b) Average path length

Fig. 3. Routing profile: Interference and path length

Traffic Profile. It is a worthwhile effort to see how much energy is spent on the control plane as opposed to the data plane. It should be noted that in the case of CTP, since beacon information piggybacks on data transmission, it counts as a beacon sent.

Table 3. Successful Transmission Rate

Protocol	Success Rate
CTP	99.7%
LIBP	99.7%
RPL-0	100%
RPL-ETX	100%

The table above describes the percentage of data packets that were collected by the sink node. Most packets were successfully collected by CTP and LIBP by achieving a higher than 99% transmission to the sink node. RPL achieved a 100% transmission rate. This astounding transmission rate could be attributed to how complete the communications protocol that RPL is built on top of is. Whereas CTP and LIBP are built on top of Rime [8].

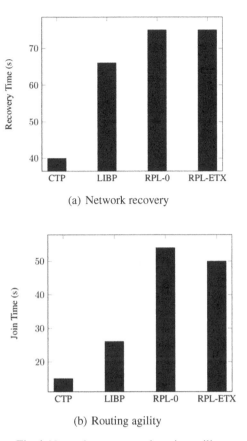

(a) Network recovery

(b) Routing agility

Fig. 4. Network recovery and routing agility

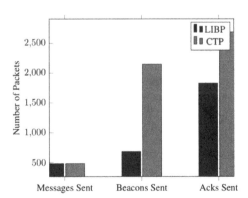

Fig. 5. Control Packets Sent

5   Conclusion and Future Work

This paper presents a comparison between routing protocols. Experiments were conducted between CTP, LIBP and RPL. The simulations revealed that CTP and LIBP are relatively light in their implementation and goals but lack a few features that RPL has like mote to mote communication. RPL also can utilize the full stack of security mechanisms present in IPv6. The inherent heaviness of RPL can be attributed to its underlying protocol and how the underlying protocol uses larger more feature rich packets. CTP and LIBP are very similar in their performance metrics, this could be attributed to the fact that they both use the same underlying communications stack. CTPs strength lies in its very agile nature. CTPs trickle timer allows it to react to adverse changes in the network very quickly. One of LIBPs main goals was to have a routing protocol that was more efficient in its global energy consumption. This resulted in a protocol that is very efficient in how each node in the network consumes a similar amount of energy. LIBP is a very compelling routing protocol to use for battery powered deployed sensor networks since this routing protocol evidently seems to be better adapted for that scenario. Future work may include testing the topology lifespan to see how long these topologies last before requiring a re-charge or battery replacement. Examining the security mechanisms of RPL has also been reserved for future work.

IoT networks and connected-oriented share the same routing paradigm of setting traffic flows from source to destination. Building upon the least path interference principle previously implemented for connection-oriented networks in [12–14, 16], the LIBP protocol presented in this paper reveals that traffic engineering techniques previously designed for traditional networks can be revamped to be applied to the emerging IoT. Similarly, there is room for revamping some of the techniques previously intended for gateway design [15] and quality of service (QoS) support [17] and long distance IoT deployment [18] for deployment in 6LoWPAN settings to enable flexibility and heterogeneity in IoT settings.

References

1. Vasseur, J., Dunkels, A.: Interconnecting Smart Objects with IP, The Next Internet. Morgan Kaufmann (July 2010) ISBN: 9780123751652
2. Bagula, A., Djenouri, D., Karbab, E.B.: Ubiquitous sensor network management: The least interference beaconing model. In: Proceedings of the IEEE 24th International Symposium on Personal Indoor and Mobile Radio Communications (PIMRC), September 8-11, pp. 2352–2356 (2013) ISSN 2166-9570
3. Bagula, A.B., Djenouri, D., Karbab, E.: On the Relevance of Using Interference and Service Differentiation Routing in the Internet-of-Things. In: Balandin, S., Andreev, S., Koucheryavy, Y. (eds.) NEW2AN 2013 and ruSMART 2013. LNCS, vol. 8121, pp. 25–35. Springer, Heidelberg (2013)
4. Levis, P., Lee, N., Welsh, M., Culler, D.: TOSSIM: Simulating large wireless sensor networks of tinyos motes. In: Proc. of ACM SenSys 2003, Los Angeles, CA, pp. 126–137 (November 2003)
5. Dunkels, A., Gronvall, B., Voigt, T.: Contiki - a lightweight and flexible operating system for tiny networked sensors. In: 29th Annual IEEE International Conference on Local Computer Networks, pp. 455–462 (2004)

6. Gnawali, O., Fonseca, R., Jamieson, K., Moss, D., Levis, P.: Collection Tree Protocol. In: Proc. of ACM SenSys 2009, Berkeley, CA/USA, November 4-6 (2009)
7. Winter, T., et al.: RPL: IPv6 Routing protocol for Low-Power and Lossy Networks, RFC 6550 (March 2012)
8. Dunkels, A.: Poster Abstract: Rime: A Lightweight Layered Communication Stack for Sensor Networks. In: European Conference on Wireless Sensor Networks (EWSN), Delft, The Netherlands (January 2007)
9. Levis, P., Patel, N., Culler, D., Shenker, S.: Trickle: A self regulating algorithm for code maintenance and propagation in wireless sensor networks. In: Proc. of the USENIX NSDI Conf., San Francisco, CA (March 2004)
10. Thubert, P.: Objective Function Zero for the Routing Protocol for Low-Power and Lossy Networks (RPL). Internet Engineering Task Force (IETF), Request for Comments 6552, 1–14 (2012)
11. Dunkels, A., Osterlind, F., Tsiftes, N., He, Z.: Software-based Online Sensor Node Energy Estimation. In: ACM Proceeding of the 4th Workshop on Embedded Networked Sensors (EmNets 2007), pp. 28–32 (2007)
12. Bagula, A.: On Achieving Bandwidth-aware LSP/LambdaSP Multiplexing/Separation in Multi-layer Networks. IEEE Journal on Selected Areas in Communications (JSAC): Special issue on Traffic Engineering for Multi-Layer Networks 25(5) (June 2007)
13. Bagula, A.: Hybrid traffic engineering: the least path interference algorithm. In: Proc. of ACM Annual Research Conference of the South African Institute of Computer Scientists and Information Technologists on IT Research in Developing Countries, pp. 89–96 (2004)
14. Bagula, A.B.: Hybrid routing in next generation IP networks. Elsevier Computer Communications 29(7), 879–892 (2006)
15. Zennaro, M., Bagula, A.: Design of a flexible and robust gateway to collect sensor data in intermittent power environments. International Journal of Sensor Networks 8(3/4) (2010)
16. Bagula, A., Krzesinski, A.E.: Traffic engineering label switched paths in IP networks using a pre-planned flow optimization model. In: Proceedings of the Ninth International Symposium on Modelling, Analysis and Simulation of Computer and Telecommunication Systems (MASCOTS 2001), pp. 70–77 (August 2001)
17. Bagula, A.: Modelling and Implementation of QoS in Wireless Sensor Networks: A Multiconstrained Traffic Engineering Model. Eurasip Journal on Wireless Communications and Networking 2010, Article ID 468737, doi:10.1155/2010/468737
18. Bagula, A., Zennaro, M., Inggs, G., Scott, S., Gascon, D.: Ubiquitous Sensor Networking for Development (USN4D): An Application to Pollution Monitoring. MDPI Sensors 12(1), 391–414 (2012)

Analyzing Impacts of Coexistence between M2M and H2H Communication on 3GPP LTE System

Irina Gudkova[1], Konstantin Samouylov[1], Ivan Buturlin[1], Vladimir Borodakiy[2], Mikhail Gerasimenko[3], Olga Galinina[3], and Sergey Andreev[3]

[1] Peoples' Friendship University of Russia (PFUR), Russia
{igudkova,ksam}@sci.pfu.edu.ru, ivan_buturlin@mail.ru
[2] JSC "Concern Sistemprom", Russia
bvu@systemprom.ru
[3] Tampere University of Technology (TUT), Finland
{mikhail.gerasimenko,olga.galinina,sergey.andreev}@tut.fi

Abstract. In this paper, we consider 3GPP LTE cellular system where machine-to-machine (M2M) devices and human-to-human (H2H) users transmit their data into the network. By contrast to previous studies which primarily focused on M2M overload protection and respective control mechanisms, this work concentrates on system operation when M2M and H2H data flows coexist in the network. In particular, we propose an integrated simulation-analytical framework to evaluate relevant performance characteristics (data transmission delays, blocking probabilities, etc.) with both Markov process based analysis and system-level simulations. Our results indicate that the proposed methodology demonstrates acceptable levels of convergence between analytical and simulations components, as well as becomes useful to characterize impacts of M2M/H2H coexistence on radio resource allocation in 3GPP LTE across a number of important M2M-centric scenarios.

1 Introduction and Background

Machine-to-machine (M2M) communication is believed to reshape the Internet as we know it today, as billions of unattended devices (sensors, actuators, smart meters, etc.) become connected and send their data into the network [1]. Such massive connectivity offers novel attractive services, but also raises significant challenges to manage large number of devices, typically transmitting only small data fragments, across a wide range of emerging applications [2]. This is especially true for current cellular technology (e.g., 3GPP LTE [3]), which has been historically optimized for human-to-human (H2H) traffic and therefore creates inefficiency at every step of M2M communication, from initial network entry to actual data transmission [4].

Cellular industry, and in particular 3GPP standards community, has recently been very active with several study and work items identified on M2M communication [5]. These primarily focused on overload protection, when a large number of M2M devices attempt to connect to the network in a correlated manner [6].

A. Mellouk et al. (Eds.): WWIC 2014, LNCS 8458, pp. 162–174, 2014.
© Springer International Publishing Switzerland 2014

Such scenarios may be characteristic for modern smart grid deployments, where a high density of metering devices transmit their "last gasp" signaling in case of a massive power outage event. In some situations, this excessive messaging quickly deteriorates available capacity of LTE signaling channels (i.e., PRACH: physical random access channel and PDCCH: physical downlink control channel) and results in significant outage when meters cannot access the network with their data [7], [8]. Furthermore, at these periods, conventional H2H users suffer from denial of service by the network as well, as they share the same signaling channels with M2M devices.

The above overload protection research resulted in respective control mechanisms (e.g., EAB: extended access barring) standardized for LTE Release-11 and designed to mitigate initial network entry peaks by barring some of the (delay-tolerant) M2M devices from accessing the network for predefined periods of time [9]. These simple mechanisms, whereas offer an immediate solution to the problem, do not help control regular system operation when both M2M devices and H2H users already coexist in the network. Little is known about such coexistence with only a few research works mainly addressing improved scheduler design by taking into account the typical properties of M2M traffic [10]. These single-issues papers are primarily build on computer simulations and do not offer comprehensive understanding of M2M/H2H coexistence.

In this work, we bridge the indicated gap by proposing an adequate simulation-analytical framework to capture the main impacts of M2M communication on the conventional H2H traffic. In particular, we mathematically characterize the key performance characteristics of M2M and H2H communications, such as data transmission times and blocking probabilities [11], and confirm our results by extensive system-level evaluations across a number of important M2M-centric scenarios. Our framework allows to optimize radio resource allocation procedures in a cellular network and achieve understanding of resulting system performance to reach good balance between M2M and H2H communication. The rest of the text is organized as follows. Section 2 details our mathematical model and introduces its core assumptions. Further, in Section 3, we conduct numerical analysis of representative M2M-centric scenarios and derive the key performance characteristics. Section 4 introduces our M2M-aware system-level simulator and offers some initial performance evaluation results, primarily, for the purposes of verification of the analytical framework.

2   System Model of LTE Cell with H2H and M2M Traffic

Consider a single cell of LTE network (see Figure 1) with the peak capacity of C *units of channel resource* (UCR), measured in bps. All users employ identical H2H-service, such as voice telephony or video streaming. Additionally, the cell supports transmission of M2M *data fragments* of a particular type from many M2M devices. The system reserves C_h UCR to offer H2H-services to users. Hereinafter, the indexes "m" and "h" in mathematical expressions differentiate if a specific parameter applies to M2M or to H2H traffic, respectively. Consequently, not more than $C_m = C - C_h$ UCR are available for M2M devices, while not less than C_h UCR are available for H2H devices.

A minimum of b_m UCR is required to transmit M2M data fragments. Correspondingly, in order to transmit the current number of the data fragments, UCR are grouped into fixed *transmission zones* comprising c UCR. Then $M = \lfloor c/b_m \rfloor = \max\{y \in \mathbb{N} : y \leq c/b_m\}$ is the maximum number of data fragments which may be transmitted in one such fixed zone. Further, we assume that the cell might allocate $S = \lfloor C_m/c \rfloor$ transmission zones to serve M2M user traffic.

The arrival flow of requests from M2M devices to transmit their data is assumed to be Poisson with the rate of λ_m [1/time-unit = 1/s], whereas the length of each data fragment is exponentially distributed with the mean θ [UCR×time-unit = bit]. Denote $a = \lambda_m\theta$ [UCR] as the corresponding offered load rate. These simplifying assumptions are made for the sake of analytical tractability and provide a first-order insight into the performance of the considered system.

Further, H2H-services require b_h UCR. We consider the arrival flow of requests from the users demanding H2H-service to be Poisson with the rate of λ_h [1/time-unit], while the duration of H2H-service is exponential with the mean of $1/\mu$ [time-unit]. Denote as $\rho = \lambda_h/\mu$ [Erlang] the respective offered load rate by H2H users.

The considered model is a combination of First Come – First Served streaming model and Egalitarian Processor Sharing (EPS) elastic traffic model.

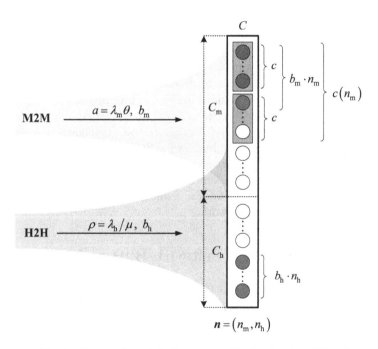

Fig. 1. Proposed model of resource distribution in LTE cell

In our model, three different scenarios are possible when a new data fragment transmission request is generated by an M2M device:

1. The request is accepted for service and additional resources are not allocated. This scenario corresponds to the situation when at the moment of the request generation the number of data fragments is such that the decrease in their transmission rate (but not less than b_m) *allows* to serve this new data fragment.
2. The request is accepted for service and a new fixed transmission zone is allocated for its service. This scenario corresponds to the situation when at the moment of the request generation the number of data fragments is such that the decrease in their transmission rate (but not less than b_m) *does not allow* to serve this new data fragment. At the same time, there are at least c UCR of free (unallocated) resources available for M2M service out of the maximum C_m to allocate a new transmission zone.
3. The request is blocked without any impact on the rate of the spawning Poisson process.

Similarly, two different scenarios are possible when a new service request is generated by an H2H device:

1. The request is accepted for service when at the moment of its generation there are at least b_h of C_h UCR of free resource.
2. The request is blocked without any impact on the rate of the spawning Poisson process.

Let $N_m(t)$ be the number of M2M data fragments transmitted at the moment $t \geq 0$, and $N_h(t)$ be the number of users which at the moment $t \geq 0$ are receiving H2H-service. Then the operation of the considered LTE cell model featuring both H2H and M2M traffic can be described by the compound random process $\{(N_m(t), N_h(t)), t > 0\}$, over the state space

$$\mathcal{X} = \{(n_m, n_h) : n_h b_h \leq C - c(n_m), n_m b_m \leq C_m, n_m \geq 0, n_h \geq 0\},$$
$$|\mathcal{X}| = \sum_{n_m=0}^{\lfloor (S \cdot c)/b_m \rfloor} \left(\left\lfloor \frac{C - c(n_m)}{b_h} \right\rfloor + 1 \right), \tag{1}$$

where $c(n_m) = c \cdot \lceil n_m/M \rceil = c \cdot \min\{y \in \mathbb{N}, y \geq n_m/M\}$ is the number of UCR allocated for the transmission of n_m M2M data fragments.

For the considered model, we may derive a system of balance equations. The equation corresponding to the state $(n_m, n_h) \in \mathcal{X}$ is given as follows:

$$p(n_m, n_h) \times [\lambda_m \cdot 1\{(n_m, n_h) \notin \mathcal{B}_m\} + (c(n_m)/\theta) \cdot 1\{n_m > 0\} +$$
$$+\lambda_h \cdot 1\{(n_m, n_h) \notin \mathcal{B}_h\} + n_h \mu_h] = p(n_m - 1, n_h) \cdot \lambda_m \cdot 1\{n_m > 0\} +$$
$$+p(n_m + 1, n_h) \cdot (c(n_m + 1)/\theta) \cdot 1\{(n_m, n_h) \notin \mathcal{B}_m\} +$$
$$+p(n_m, n_h - 1) \cdot \lambda_h \cdot 1\{n_h > 0\} + p(n_m, n_h + 1) \cdot (n_h + 1) \mu_h \cdot 1\{(n_m, n_h) \notin \mathcal{B}_h\},$$

where the boundaries of the state space may be defined by means of the sets:

$$\mathcal{B}_m = \{(n_m, n_h) \in \mathcal{X} : n_h b_h > C - c(n_m + 1) \vee (n_m + 1) b_m > C_m\}, \tag{2}$$

$$\mathcal{B}_h = \{(n_m, n_h) \in \mathcal{X} : (n_h + 1) b_h > C - c(n_m)\}. \tag{3}$$

The random process $\{(N_m(t), N_h(t)), t > 0\}$ constitutes a reversible Markov process with the stationary probability distribution:

$$p(n_m, n_h) = G^{-1}(\mathcal{X}) \left(\frac{a}{M \cdot b_m}\right)^{n_m} \left(\prod_{i=1}^{n_m} \left\lceil \frac{i}{M} \right\rceil\right)^{-1} \times \frac{\rho^{n_h}}{n_h!}, (n_m, n_h) \in \mathcal{X}, \tag{4}$$

where $G(\mathcal{X})$ is the constant obtained from the normalizing condition.

Further, we consider the primary time-probability characteristics of the proposed LTE cell model and introduce analytical expressions to derive these. To this end, we write the state space $\mathcal{X}$ as follows:

$$\mathcal{X} = \bigcup_{s=0}^{S} \mathcal{X}_s, \ \mathcal{X}_s = \{(n_m, n_h) \in \mathcal{X} : c(n_m) = s \cdot c\}. \tag{5}$$

Knowing the distribution (4) and using the state space partitioning in (5), we arrive at the expression for the M2M request blocking probabilities B_m as well as those for H2H devices B_h, respectively:

$$B_m = \sum_{(n_m, n_h) \in \mathcal{B}_m} p(n_m, n_h) = \sum_{s=0}^{S-1} \sum_{n_h = \lfloor (C-(s+1)\cdot c)/b_h \rfloor + 1}^{\lfloor (C-s\cdot c)/b_h \rfloor} p(s \cdot M, n_h) + \sum_{n_h=0}^{\lfloor C_h/b_h \rfloor} p(S \cdot M, n_h), \tag{6}$$

$$B_h = \sum_{(n_m, n_h) \in \mathcal{B}_h} p(n_m, n_h) = p\left(0, \left\lfloor \frac{C}{b_h} \right\rfloor\right) + \sum_{s=1}^{S} \sum_{n_m=(s-1)\cdot M+1}^{s \cdot M} p\left(n_m, \left\lfloor \frac{C - s \cdot c}{b_h} \right\rfloor\right). \tag{7}$$

The resulting formula for the mean M2M data fragment transmission time may be given as:

$$T_m = \frac{\sum_{n_m=0}^{\lfloor C_m/b_m \rfloor} \sum_{n_h=0}^{\lfloor (C-c(n_m))/b_h \rfloor} n_m \cdot p(n_m, n_h)}{\lambda_m (1 - B_m)}, \tag{8}$$

where the upper part determines the mean number of the transmitted M2M data fragments N_m.

Further, we continue by numerically analyzing the operational characteristics of the considered resource distribution model with the fixed transmission zone for M2M traffic in LTE cell with H2H users.

3   Numerical Analysis of the Proposed Model

As an example, we consider a single cell of LTE with the peak capacity of $C = 52.8$ Mbps, which is distributed between H2H users and M2M devices. For the H2H user service, the system reserves $C_h = 10.56$ Mbps of its capacity. Let every M2M data fragment of $\theta = 0.88$ Mbit require a minimum of $b_m = 0.88$ Mbps. As a numerical illustration of an H2H-service, we consider streaming video, which has a requirement of $b_h = 2.64$ Mbps on the minimum throughput. Assume the H2H offered load rate to be $\rho = 5$ Erlang. Let up to $S = 2$ fixed transmission zones can be allocated for M2M data fragments transmission, each of which comprising $c = 20$ Mbps.

Figure 2 introduces plots illustrating H2H request blocking probabilities B_h calculated as given by formula (7), M2M data fragment blocking probabilities B_m (6), and mean fragment transmission time T_m (8) on increasing M2M offered load. The figure indicates that the mean fragment transmission time varies significantly with the changing offered load. In order to explain the main reasons behind the observed effects let us consider the plots of other probability-time characteristics in our model.

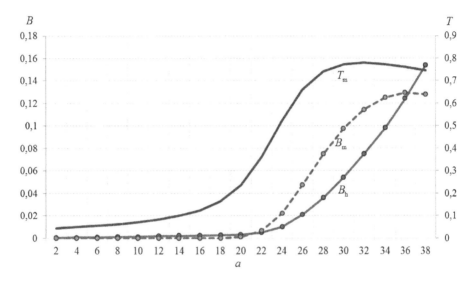

Fig. 2. Blocking probabilities and mean data fragment transmission time

Together with the mean number of transmitted M2M data fragments N_m, we also consider the following characteristics:

1. Mean number of the allocated fixed transmission zones for M2M devices:

$$\bar{s} = \sum_{(n_m,n_h)\in X} \left\lceil \frac{n_m}{M} \right\rceil \cdot p(n_m,n_h) = \sum_{n_m=0}^{\lfloor S\cdot c/b_m \rfloor} \sum_{n_h=0}^{\lfloor (C-c(n_m))/b_h \rfloor} \left\lceil \frac{n_m}{M} \right\rceil \cdot p(n_m,n_h). \quad (9)$$

2. Mean number of UCR allocated for the transmission of a single data fragment:

$$\bar{b}_1 = \sum_{(n_m,n_h)\in X, n_m\neq 0} \left(\frac{c(n_m)}{n_m}\right) \times p(n_m,n_h) =$$
$$= \sum_{n_m=1}^{\lfloor S\cdot c/b_m \rfloor} \sum_{n_h=0}^{\lfloor (C-c(n_m))/b_h \rfloor} \left(\frac{c(n_m)}{n_m}\right) \times p(n_m,n_h). \quad (10)$$

3. Probability that at least one data fragment is being transmitted:

$$P_1 = P\{n_{\mathrm{m}} = 1\} = \sum_{(n_{\mathrm{m}},n_{\mathrm{h}})\in X, n_{\mathrm{m}}\neq 0} p\left(n_{\mathrm{m}}, n_{\mathrm{h}}\right) = \sum_{n_{\mathrm{m}}=1}^{\lfloor S\cdot c/b_{\mathrm{m}}\rfloor} \sum_{n_{\mathrm{h}}=0}^{\lfloor (C-c(n_{\mathrm{m}}))/b_{\mathrm{h}}\rfloor} p(n_{\mathrm{m}}, n_{\mathrm{h}}). \quad (11)$$

4. Probability that two fixed transmission zones have been allocated for serving M2M devices:

$$P\{s = 2\} = \sum_{(n_{\mathrm{m}},n_{\mathrm{h}})\in X_{s=2}} p\left(n_{\mathrm{m}}, n_{\mathrm{h}}\right). \quad (12)$$

The plots for the aforementioned characteristics of the LTE cell model are shown in Figures 3 and 4.

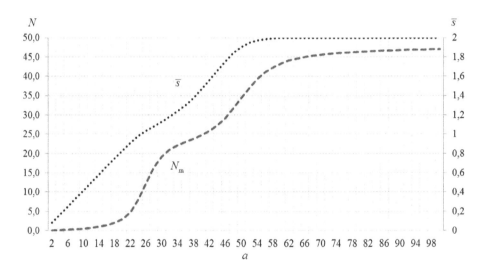

Fig. 3. Time-probability characteristics $\bar{s}$ and N_{m}

Let us now consider again the primary parameter for the performance evaluation of our model operation, which is the mean time T_{m} of the M2M data fragment transmission (see Figure 5). We may further identify three intervals of the M2M offered load, within which the mean number of fixed transmission zones $\bar{s}$ belongs to the following ranges: $0 \leq \bar{s} \leq 1$, $1 \leq \bar{s} \leq 2$, and $\bar{s} \to 2$.

Over the first interval of the offered load for serving M2M devices, one fixed transmission range is allocated on average and, correspondingly, $0 \leq \bar{s} \leq 1$. It is important to emphasize that with the growth of the offered load from $a = 16$ UCR, the mean transmission time T_{m} is showing non-uniform behavior. Over the second interval, all UCR of the first fixed transmission zone have been used for the data fragments transmission $1 \leq \bar{s} \leq 2$, and the probability increases that two fixed zones will be allocated $P\{s = 2\} \to 1$. When the offered load

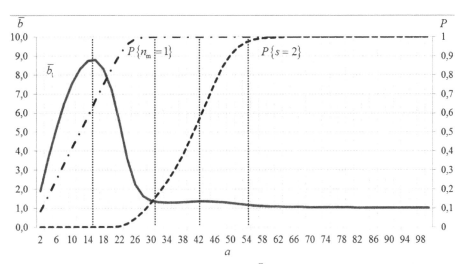

Fig. 4. Time-probability characteristics $\bar{b}_1$, $P\{n_m = 1\}$, and $P\{s = 2\}$

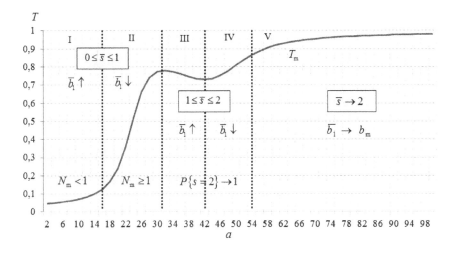

Fig. 5. Mean data fragment transmission time

reaches the value of $a = 55$ UCR, all available UCR are used to transmit M2M data fragments and $\bar{s} \to 2$.

In what follows, we consider variation in the mean data fragment transmission time over each of the indicated M2M offered load intervals:

1. Over the interval $a = [2, 16]$ UCR, the value of T_m grows insignificantly as the number of data fragments in the system is small, $P_1 < 1$, and they arrive at the low rate of $N_m < 1$. Accounting for the fact that M2M service follows the EPS discipline, the amount of resources taken by one M2M device

increases up to $\bar{b}_1 \leq 9$ UCR. Therefore, we observe minimal values of T_m in this interval.

2. Over the interval $a = [16, 30]$ UCR, the value of T_m grows faster and reaches the value of $T_m \approx 0, 8$ seconds. Data fragments begin to arrive with higher rate and their mean number exceeds one, $N_m \geq 1$. Therefore, the amount of resources allocated for the transmission of one fragment decreases down to $\bar{b}_1 \leq 2$. Accounting for such decrease together with increase in the offered load, the value of T_m grows significantly.

3. Over the interval $a = [32, 44]$ UCR, when one more fixed transmission zone has been allocated to serve M2M traffic, the value of T_m decreases slightly. Probability that an additional fixed transmission zone is available tends to one $P\{s = 2\} \to 1$, and the mean number of UCR allocated for the transmission of one data fragment is $\bar{b}_1$.

4. Over the interval $a = [44, 55]$ UCR, almost all of the available UCR allocated across two fixed transmission zones are used for data fragments transmission. Therefore, the amount of UCR allocated for the transmission of one fragment decreases further and the value of T_m grows.

5. Over the interval $a = [55, 98]$ UCR, the allocated fixed transmission zones are completely filled with M2M data fragments, and $40 \leq N_m \leq 48$. The mean amount of resources allocated for the transmission of one data fragment tends to the allowed minimum of $\bar{b}_1 \to b_m$. Within this interval of the offered load, it is typical to observe the maximum data fragment transmit times T_m and high loss probabilities B_m.

We proceed with detailing our simulation methodology to extend the above mathematical analysis.

4   Simulation Methodology, Results, and Conclusions

In our past M2M work [12], [13], we were mostly concentrated on the particular features of IEEE 802.16 and 3GPP LTE technology related to signaling channel simulations and analysis. For those purposes we employed a simplified Protocol Level Simulator (PLS) to abstract away many realistic system features for the sake of simulation speed. By contrast, in this paper we are considering a more detailed simulation methodology incorporating most of the practical 3GPP LTE features. Our approach is based on detailed System Level Simulator (SLS) which has been developed and applied successfully in our recent publications on next-generation wireless networks [14] focusing H2H traffic. However, this work extends our SLS tool to enable characteristic M2M scenarios.

The core capabilities of the considered simulator are: detailed LTE MAC-layer features (according to 3GPP LTE Release-10 specifications, fully calibrated), dynamic channel modeling, different traffic types, user and eNodeB directivity and location modeling, as well as many others (see Figure 6). In particular, the basic features of the LTE implementation inside our SLS tool are: realistic 10 ms FDD frame structure, inter-cell interference, support for several scheduling schemes (round-robin, proportional-fair, etc.). Instead of modeling the control channels explicitly, the respective control signaling overhead is taken into account to speed-up the simulations. However, necessary channel procedures could be easily integrated into the SLS, if required.

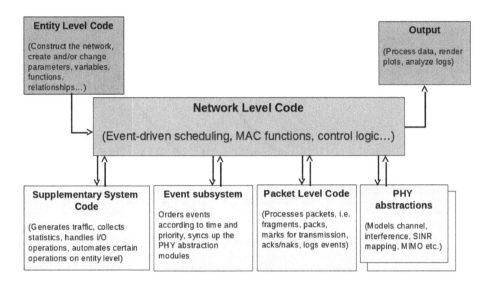

Fig. 6. High-level structure of our system-level simulator

Regarding channel models implementation, the most challenging aspects are interference and pathloss characterization [15]. Basic ITU models (Urban Macro, Urban Micro, ITU-R M.2135) have been realized and used in the SLS. Interference calculation has been somewhat simplified to speed-up simulations further. Instead of per-RB (resource block) calculations, only the percentage of intersections between the same time-frequency domain user requests (of different cell in a sector) is accounted for. Large-scale and small-scale parameters are modeled employing random variables with a certain deviation and mean; the numbers are taken from ITU-R M.2135 document.

More advanced Spatial Channel Model (SCM, 3GPP TR25.996), which is based on multiple ray clusters is currently under implementation. As a conclusion, we emphasize that the methodology behind our SLS tool simplifies physical-layer implementation to enable better support for MAC-layer features and procedures across a large-scale system deployment. Furthermore, our abstractions result in a profound decrease in simulation complexity, which, in combination with efficient code structures written in Python and C++, delivers attractively short simulation times: one second of the real-time in a typical 19-cell (3 sector) deployments with 30 users per cell could be simulated with only around 100 seconds of simulation time.

As a first step in this paper, we calibrate the simulation results with the above analysis. Along these lines, we choose to disregard realistic interference,

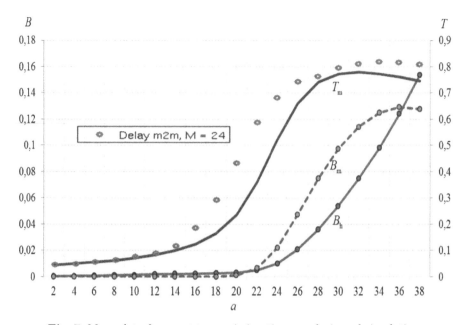

Fig. 7. Mean data fragment transmission time: analysis and simulation

pathloss, and other complex channel effects. However, we account for the actual LTE frame structure to verify that simulation results fall well near our analytical expectations. We further assume that the resource allocated to the H2H and M2M devices is employing all available frequencies, so that the scheduler is working in a time-division manner. Additionally, to account for some channel degradation factors, we enable a simple physical-layer pathloss model described in [14]. For the purposes of initial calibration and testing, we focus on a tagged sector of our one-cell scenario. Users are deployed in a 288m-area around eNodeB (typical for Urban macro model, ISD = 500).

User arrivals and departures are modeled according to the above analysis in Section 3. At this stage, the interference between the users is considered insignificant, due to the absence of other cells (which may be also the consequence of appropriate network planning). More advanced interference and channel modeling will be given in our future publications. In Figure 7, we overlay our simulation results on top of the previously obtained analysis (see Figure 2). Hence, we observe that simulated mean data fragment transmission times are reasonably close to the analytical prediction, but they also remain slightly higher due to the increasing influence of the realistic LTE performance factors not captured by the current analysis. Our ongoing work is to extend the reported analytical framework towards the inclusion of practical performance degradation factors explicitly [16], as well as to build a number of more insightful simulation scenarios mindful of upper-layer protocols [17]. However, already now we can conclude that the constructed simulation-analytical framework is a very useful tool to characterize M2M/H2H coexistence and understand the resulting LTE system behavior.

Acknowledgment. The reported study was partially supported by RFBR, research projects No. 13-07-00953 a and No. 14-07-00090, GETA, and the Internet of Things program of Digile, funded by Tekes.

References

1. David, K., Vinodrai, V., Yao, J.: WWRF Introduction and Vision (2010)
2. Wu, G., Talwar, S., Johnsson, K., Himayat, N., Johnson, K.: M2M: From mobile to embedded Internet. IEEE Communications Magazine 49(4), 36–43 (2011)
3. 3GPP LTE Release 10 & beyond (LTE-Advanced)
4. Gotsis, A., Lioumpas, A., Alexiou, A.: M2M scheduling over LTE: Challenges and new perspectives. IEEE Vehicular Technology Magazine 7(3), 34–39 (2012)
5. Study on RAN Improvements for Machine-Type Communications. 3GPP Technical Report (TR) 37.868 (2011)
6. Cheng, M.-Y., Lin, G.-Y., Wei, H.-Y., Hsu, A.: Overload control for machine-type-communications in LTE-Advanced system. IEEE Communications Magazine 50(6), 38–45 (2012)
7. Andreev, S., Larmo, A., Gerasimenko, M., Petrov, V., Galinina, O., Tirronen, T., Torsner, J., Koucheryavy, Y.: Efficient small data access for machine-type communications in LTE. In: Proc. of the IEEE International Conference on Communications, pp. 3569–3574 (2013)
8. Dementev, O., Galinina, O., Gerasimenko, M., Tirronen, T., Torsner, J., Andreev, S., Koucheryavy, Y.: Analyzing the overload of 3GPP LTE system by diverse classes of connected-mode MTC devices. In: Proc. of the IEEE World Forum on Internet of Things (2014)
9. Hasan, M., Hossain, E., Niyato, D.: Random access for machine-to-machine communication in LTE-Advanced networks: Issues and approaches. IEEE Communications Magazine 51(6), 86–93 (2013)
10. Zheng, K., Hu, F., Wang, W., Xiang, W., Dohler, M.: Radio resource allocation in LTE-Advanced cellular networks with M2M communications. IEEE Communications Magazine 50(7), 184–192 (2012)
11. Borodakiy, V.Y., Buturlin, I.A., Gudkova, I.A., Samouylov, K.E.: Modelling and analysing a dynamic resource allocation scheme for M2M traffic in LTE networks. In: Balandin, S., Andreev, S., Koucheryavy, Y. (eds.) NEW2AN 2013 and ruS-MART 2013. LNCS, vol. 8121, pp. 420–426. Springer, Heidelberg (2013)
12. Andreev, S., Galinina, O., Koucheryavy, Y.: Energy-efficient client relay scheme for machine-to-machine communication. In: Proc. of the IEEE Global Telecommunications Conference (2011)
13. Gerasimenko, M., Petrov, V., Galinina, O., Andreev, S., Koucheryavy, Y.: Impact of MTC on energy and delay performance of random-access channel in LTE-Advanced. Transactions on Emerging Telecommunications Technologies 24(4), 366–377 (2013)
14. Andreev, S., Pyattaev, A., Johnsson, K., Galinina, O., Koucheryavy, Y.: Cellular traffic offloading onto network-assisted device-to-device connections. IEEE Communications Magazine 52(4), 20–31 (2014)
15. Andreev, S., Koucheryavy, Y., Himayat, N., Gonchukov, P., Turlikov, A.: Active-mode power optimization in OFDMA-based wireless networks. In: Proc. of the IEEE Global Telecommunications Conference Workshops (2010)

16. Moltchanov, D., Koucheryavy, Y., Harju, J.: Loss performance model for wireless channels with autocorrelated arrivals and losses. Computer Communications 29, 2646–2660 (2006)
17. Dunaytsev, R., Koucheryavy, Y., Harju, J.: TCP NewReno throughput in the presence of correlated losses: The slow-but-steady variant. In: Proc. of the IEEE International Conference on Computer Communications, INFOCOM (2006)

Agent-Based Content Retrieval
for Opportunistic Content-Centric Networks

Carlos Anastasiades, Wafaa El Maudni El Alami, and Torsten Braun

Institute of Computer Science and Applied Mathematics
University of Bern,
3012 Bern, Switzerland
{anastasiades,elmaudni,braun}@iam.unibe.ch

Abstract. In this paper, we describe agent-based content retrieval for opportunistic networks, where requesters can delegate content retrieval to agents, which retrieve the content on their behalf. The approach has been implemented in CCNx, the open source CCN framework, and evaluated on Android smart phones. Evaluations have shown that the overhead of agent delegation is only noticeable for very small content. For content larger than 4MB, agent-based content retrieval can even result in a throughput increase of 20% compared to standard CCN download applications. The requester asks every probe interval for agents that have retrieved the desired content. Evaluations have shown that a probe interval of 30s delivers the best overall performance in our scenario because the number of transmitted notification messages can be decreased by up to 80% without significantly increasing the download time.

1 Introduction

Information-centric networks (ICN), e.g., [1], [2], [3], [4], have attracted much attention in recent years as a new network paradigm replacing host-based Internet communication. Routing and forwarding is based on content names instead of host identifiers. The exchanged messages do not contain any source or destination address supporting caching in any node. Nodes can express Interests to receive corresponding Data from any nearby node that provides the content.

Therefore, ICN can support opportunistic networking, where connectivity and contact durations between devices are unpredictible and intermittent. Content discovery can be performed using multicast to quickly detect available content sources [5] in the vicinity. Nodes transmit requests if they are looking for content and content transmissions are only triggered if the desired content can be found in the vicinity of the requester. If a requester moves inside the network, the recipients of request messages will change and new content sources or forwarders are discovered automatically. No device discovery is required, because content availability may be independent of specific neighboring devices.

In this work, we base our investigations on the content-centric networking (CCN) approach proposed by Van Jacobson et. al. [4]. Earlier work [6] has shown that short-term caches can be extended to support delay-tolerant networking

A. Mellouk et al. (Eds.): WWIC 2014, LNCS 8458, pp. 175–188, 2014.
© Springer International Publishing Switzerland 2014

without significant processing and storing overhead. However, if a node does never meet a content source directly, it needs to forward the requests to other nodes. Multi-hop forwarding is challenging due to intermittent connectivity and asymmetric forwarding paths. Interests in individual segments of content may be forwarded by different nodes in mobile ad-hoc networks. Since CCN requires symmetric forwarding, i.e., Data needs to travel the reverse path back to the requester, segments may not be forwarded all the way back to the requester and parts of content may be stored in different nodes making it difficult to retrieve the complete content. Additionally, if forwarded over multiple hops, Interests may time out at intermediate nodes so that content can never reach the requester. In this work, we describe agent-based content retrieval, where requesters can delegate content retrieval to one-hop neighbor nodes, which will retrieve the complete content on their behalf. Earlier studies [7] have shown that human mobility exhibits temporal and spatial periodicity. People tend to have strong location preferences in their daily mobility and meet other individuals regularly. Agents with different mobility patterns as requesters can, therefore, increase the search coverage by requesting content in locations the requester would never visit. Requesters can then retrieve the content from agents as soon as they have found the content. We assume a decentralized communication network using the 802.11n interface and not considering any cellular communication.

The remainder of this paper is organized as follows. Related work is reviewed in Section 2. In Section 3, we describe our design and implementation on Android smart phones. Evaluation results are shown in Section 4. Finally, in Section 5 we conclude our work and give an outlook on future work.

2   Related Work

Content-Centric networking (CCN) [4] is based on two messages: *Interest* and *Data*. Content is composed of multiple segments and users need to express Interests in every segment, which is included in a Data message, to retrieve the complete content. CCNx [8] provides an open source reference implemenation of CCN. The core element of the implementation is the CCN daemon (CCND), which performs message processing and forwarding decisions. Links to other nodes are performed via faces, which are defined by TCP/IP or UDP/IP sockets. Interests are forwarded based on information stored in the Forwarding Information Base (FIB). If an Interest is forwarded, it is included in the Pending Interest Table (PIT). The PIT is used to avoid forwarding of duplicate Interests over the same face. If an Interest retrieves a Data packet, it follows the reverse path back to the requester based on information in every forwarder's PIT. The content store (CS) is used as cache in a CCN router to store received Data packets temporarily for a short time. Content is persistently stored and shared with others in repositories. The Interest header comprises four fields that are relevant for this approach. First, the *Interest lifetime* determines the maximum time an Interest stays in the PIT. Second, the *AnswerOriginKind* determines from where a Data message needs to be received, e.g., someone's cache or a repository. Third, the *Scope* determines where Interests are forwarded to, e.g. only to applications on the local hosts or also to neighbors. Fourth, the *Exclude* field includes all components that have already been received and do not need to be retrieved again.

Mobility in CCN has been the topic of several investigations. Early works [9] investigated the applicability of existing MANET routing protocols for mobile CCN based on analytical models. The Listen-First-Broadcast-Later (LFBL) algorithm limits forwarding of Interests at every node based on its relative distance to the content source [10]. Both works assume continuous network connectivity and do not consider intermittent connectivity. Other works consider mobility in CCN based on locator-name splits or redirection points [11], [12], [13]. But these works are based on a static core network and cannot solely rely on opportunistic contacts in distributed networks.

Earlier work [14] has already identified the potential of CCN for delay-tolerant networking, such as opportunistic networking. The Bundle protocol [15] describes a delay-tolerant protocol stack to support intermittent connectivity. The destinations of messages, i.e., bundles, are identified by endpoint identifiers. To receive bundles, nodes can register in endpoint identifiers and these registrations are exchanged when two devices meet. Thus, content bundles are transmitted in bursts and stored locally until the next forwarding opportunity arises. To reduce the burden of caching content, nodes delegate responsibility for storage and retransmission to custodians on the path.

Haggle [16] describes a data-centric network architecture for opportunistic networks. The platform targets point-to-point communications between devices. Data is decribed by keywords and users express and forward Interests in these keywords. All files that match the keywords are forwarded to the requesting node by a push-based dissemination model. The successor project of Haggle, called SCAMPI [17], developed a service-oriented platform for mobile and pervasive networks. Routing and opportunistic networking is hidden from applications through a middleware. It contains a communication subsystem, which is responsible for detecting neighbouring peers and exchanging messages. Direct peer sensing mechanisms are applied to discover peers and services within communication range based on IP multicast or static IP discovery. To discover nodes further away, the platform defines transitive peer discovery, where nodes exchange information about other nodes they have discovered. Routing of messages in the network is based on discovered peers and controlled by the routing subsystem.

Agent-based content retrieval described in this paper does not rely on point-to-point connections and peer discovery. Thus, no hello beacons are required to find neighbors and subsequently connect to them. Instead, a requester transmits a content request via multicast addressing all available nearby content sources at once. If one or multiple content sources are available, the requester can select one of the nodes directly.

3   Agent-Based Content Retrieval

In this section we describe the motivation and phases of agent-based content retrieval.

3.1   Motivation

In DTN protocols such as the Bundle protocol [15], nodes exchange so-called Bundle packets upon encounter. Combining the Bundle protocol with CCN is difficult due to potentially long delays between encounters that may result in the expiration of CCN Interests. Increasing the Interest lifetime to obtain long-living Interests may enable the integration with existing protocols but it would result in two major drawbacks:

1. Since content is organized in segments and content transmissions are pull-based, multiple Interests in segments are required to obtain the complete content. In general, a requester does not know the length of the requested content until it receives the last segment. Therefore, proactive Interest transmissions to request all segments are not possible. Simply assuming a very high number of segments may obviously result in many unnecessary Interest transmissions and inefficient resource utilization if the content has much fewer segments. Since all entries are valid for a long time, the PIT size would drastically degrade lookup performance.
2. Long-living Interests in the PIT prevent forwarding of similar Interests because the request is already pending. Forwarding and retransmission is blocked for the entire lifetime, even if the environment has changed due to mobility and the content would be available.

Since opportunistic content-centric communication is based on one-hop connections, requests can be quickly answered by content sources. As earlier work has shown [6], short Interest lifetimes result in larger multicast throughput because retransmissions due to packet collisions can be performed faster. Therefore, Interest lifetimes should be rather short and only used to reexpress Interests in case of collisions. If multiple immediate reexpressions are not successful, it can be assumed that no content source is available in the current environment and the retrieval is postponed by the time t_r. In current DTN approaches, nodes exchange hello beacons to learn about their neighbors and subsequently connect to each neighbor to discover and exchange content. This is not required in CCN, because the existence of a host may not imply the existence of desired content. If a multicasted Interest is not answered by a neighboring node, no matching content is available, which - in terms of content retrieval - is equivalent to the unavailability of neighboring devices.

However, if the requester never meets a content source, simply postponing content retrieval to a later time will not be successful. Therefore, in this paper, we describe agent-based content retrieval, a mechanism that enables requesters to delegate content retrieval to other nodes that may have a higher probability to meet the content source. Figure 1 shows the exchanged messages during agent-based content retrieval. The approach comprises three phases, which are explained in the following subsections. In the agent delegation phase (Phase I), the requester needs to find an agent and delegate the content retrieval to it. In the content retrieval phase (phase II), the agent is looking for the content and retrieves the content. It is followed by the notification phase (phase III) in which the requester asks available agents whether they retrieved the complete content. The requester can then retrieve content from the agent node (not shown in the figure). All parameters that are used in the three phases are listed in Table 1.

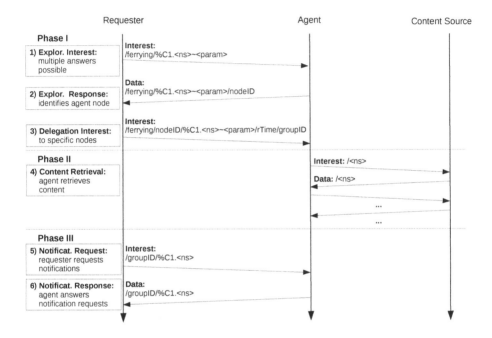

Fig. 1. Agent-based content retrieval performed in three phases

3.2   Phase I: Agent Delegation

If a requester cannot find the desired content in its environment, content retrieval can be delegated to an agent. In phase I, the requester finds an available agent. It is based on a three-way handshake protocol to find potential agents and delegate content retrieval to only one of them. An agreement between requester and agent could be enforced by signing the exchanged Interest and Data messages with the sender's private key so that both nodes know the identity of each other. This helps to implement incentives and avoid denial of service attacks. Because available agents in the neighborhood are not known and can change, agent discovery and delegation is performed via multicast. As a requirement, every requester and agent needs to register the application specific prefix */ferrying*

Table 1. Time parameters for agent-based content retrieval

parameter	description
t_r	request interval: time after which a requester/agent will probe the environment again for content if the content has not been found.
t_p	probe interval: time after which the requester probes for a content notification from an assigned agent.
t_a	agent interval: time after which the requester assigns a new agent if no notification has been received from existing agents.

to the multicast face so that these Interests can be received and forwarded on the multicast face. A similar approach of using service-based name components has been proposed in [18]. The requester transmits an *Exploration Interest* in the namespace */ferrying/%C1.<ns>~<param>*. Every agent application will listen for Interests in */ferrying*. Commands can be delegated by using extensible command markers *C1* [19] followed by the namespace */ns* that needs to be requested and optional parameters *param* if required for content retrieval. The parameters may describe an area, where content retrieval should be performed and agents can decide whether to respond based on locally collected mobility traces. Agents respond by an *Exploration Response*, which is a Data message including the requested prefix name and appending their */nodeID*. Optionally, the agent can also include information in the payload of the Data message, such as regularly visited locations, to facilitate agent selection at the requester.

Exploration Responses have a short lifetime of only a few seconds to avoid usage of old information from the cache. Exploration Interests that are transmitted via multicast will trigger potentially many answers from different agents. Since every Interest can pull at most one Data message, only the first answer will be forwarded to the agent delegation application on the requester. To consider all received answers, the requester needs to poll its content store subsequently for other responses by reexpressing the Exploration Interest with the Interest Scope set to 0 and excluding nodeIDs of already received answers. Because these follow-up requests are answered locally, all answers are received immediately.

The requester can then create an agent list that includes all available agents and select one for delegation. The agent selection can be performed randomly or based on optional parameters that are included within the payload of the Exploration Response such as recently visited locations or planned destinations. However, agent selection algorithms are outside the scope of this paper. The requester assigns an agent by transmitting a *Delegation Interest* with the name prefix */ferrying/nodeID/%C1.<ns>~<param>/rTime/groupID*. The nodeID is included right after the */ferrying* prefix so that all agents receive it and know whether they have been selected or not. *rTime* defines the remaining time, i.e., how long the requester is still interested in the content. This is an upper limit for content retrieval and after this time has passed, the agent does not look for the content anymore. *groupID* is a random nonce, which is created by the requester for every delegation of content retrieval in order to create a multicast group of agents. Assigned agents will register and listen to Interests with the */groupID* to receive notification requests from the requester as explained later in Subsection 3.4.

If the requester does not receive a notification within an agent interval t_a, agent delegation can be repeated and another agent will be selected.

3.3   Phase II: Content Retrieval

After receiving the Delegation Interest in step 3 of phase I, the agent registers the namespace */ns* to the multicast face in the FIB using a lifetime that equals *rTime* included in the Delegation Interest (explained above). Then, it can start probing the environment for the availability of a content source by periodically sending Interests in the content name. It is repeated after every time interval t_r until a matching Data message is received in a response. An agent needs to store the received Data including all CCN header information and original signatures in its mobile repository, which is an another application running on the same mobile device as the agent, so that the requester can retrieve the content and verify it as authentic. Therefore, the agent needs to instruct its mobile repository via the start write command *C1.R.sw* to individually request and store all content segments. For simplicity, this is not shown in Figure 1. The start write command is included in an Interest with the following name structure *ccnx:/<full content name>/%C1.R.sw*. The scope of the Interest is set to 1 so that only applications on the local node, such as the repository, will receive the Interest but other hosts do not. The repository will then extract the full content name from the Interest and independently request all segments of the content. Because the content source is not known, the repository requests all segments via the multicast face. Communication in opportunistic networks may be completely distributed and nodes may never be connected to the Internet. Therefore, requesters need to meet their agents again to retrieve the content.

However, if both requester and agent would occasionally connect to the Internet, content retrieval and notification could be facilitated. Agents could synchronize retrieved content with *home repositories*, which are repositories running in the users' home network and are continously connected to the Internet. Content sharing via home repositories is similar to custodian-based information sharing [20] with the difference that users do not only synchronize their own personal content but also content retrieved from others. This would support communication in disruptive and delay-tolerant networks similar to DTN throwboxes [21], which are static nodes placed in DTNs to increase contact opportunities and network performance. In contrast to throwboxes, home repositories are continously connected to the Internet and agents can synchronize content on their mobile devices with home repositories only if connected to the Internet. Requesters could then obtain the content from the agents' home repositories, if they do not have a direct connection to the agents. If the content transfer is complete, the agent can answer notification requests in phase III.

3.4 Phase III: Notification and Content Distribution

Agents indicate to requesters via notifications that content has been found and is ready for retrieval. Since CCN is pull-based, notifications can only be transmitted in response to Interests. Therefore, the requester needs to request a content notification from any agent in the vicinity that has retrieved the content completely. The pull-based approach is advantageous in opportunistic networks with multiple agents. Since only requesters periodically ask for notifications instead of multiple agents transmitting beacons, fewer notification messages need to be transmitted, i.e. only one periodic request from a requester looking for content in its vicinity. If notifications would be pushed-based, agents would transmit notifications even if they are not near requesters and not knowing whether requesters have already completed content retrieval such that no further notifications would be required. The pull-based approach enables a requester to quickly find other agents in case of mobility and intermittent connectivity as well as stop requesting notifications if content retrieval has been completed.

The *Notification Request* is transmitted periodically after a probe interval t_p until a *Notification Response* is received. The Notification Request is an Interest in the name */groupID/<ns>*. By using the groupID, all assigned agents in the requester's transmission range receive the request and only agents that have completed phase II will respond with a Notification Response, which is a generated Data message that uses the same name as the Notification Request. The payload of the Notification Response comprises the current node identifier of the agent, e.g., an IP or MAC address, such that requests can be directly addressed to the corresponding node. The node identifier can be viewed as temporary locator of content, which is not part of the signed Data packet, similar to existing designs [11], [12]. However, in contrast to these approaches, it is only used to identify a content source in the local broadcast environment and it can not be used for global routing. The node identifier is required to create a unicast face at the requester to the agent's mobile repository to avoid multicast communication, which has a significantly lower throughput than unicast. After the requester creates a new unicast entry with a short lifetime in the FIB, the content can be requested via the newly generated unicast face. The final content retrieval between the requester and the agent is not shown in Figure 1.

Alternatively, in networks with occasional Internet connectivity, requesters and agents could make use of their home repositories to synchronize retrieved content. However, even in this case, mobile requesters would need to periodically check the home repository for new content.

4 Evaluation

We implemented the agent-based content retrieval in CCNx 0.7.1 [8] and evaluated it on Google Nexus devices running with Android 4.2. We evaluated it in a network of three nodes: one smart phone acting as the requester, one smart phone acting as agent or forwarder and one laptop acting as content source. All communication is performed via 802.11n, i.e., no cellular communication, and the nodes use private IP addresses as temporary node locators. Requester and agent have configured a multicast face for the prefix */ferrying* on UDP port 59695. To avoid requesters fetching overheard content between agent and content source from their local cache, we set the AnswerOriginKind field in Interests to 0 indicating that no answer from the content store is accepted. This is only necessary in our evaluations. In practice, if a requester would be in communication range of the content source, it could retrieve the content directly without an agent. In all evaluations, we assume that if the agent detects the content source, it has enough time to retrieve all segments subsequently without disruptions. The unicast face to retrieve content from the agent is generated automatically by the requester upon the reception of the Notification Response. Additionally, the requester automatically creates the */groupID* and registers it to the multicast face before transmitting the Delegation Interest to the first agent. We also perform evaluations with *ccngetfile*, a standard CCNx content transfer application, for reference purposes. To have the same conditions as with agent-based content retrieval when using ccngetfile, every Interest is transmitted via unicast on the first hop and then forwarded via multicast on the second hop to the content source. Therefore, only a unicast face is configured at the requester and a multicast face is configured at the forwarder and the content source. Consequently, the requester cannot overhear multicast communication between forwarder and content source and needs to send Interests to the forwarder.

4.1   Agent-Based Content Retrieval

Agent-based content retrieval is performed via two hops. As explained in Section 3, all communication during agent-based content retrieval is performed via multicast except the content retrieval between requester and agent, which is unicast. The reason for this is that content sources and agents are not known and may change. Only after the agent tells the requester its current IP address, the requester can create a unicast face for direct content retrieval. In this subsection, we compare agent-based content retrieval with *ccngetfile* over two hops. Agent-based content retrieval comprises all three phases including agent delegation, content retrieval and notification as explained above while ccngetfile only comprises content retrieval over two hops. In both cases, content transmission on the first hop between requester and forwarder/agent is performed via unicast and on the second hop between forwarder/agent and content source via multicast.

   Figure 2 shows the measured throughput of both transmissions for different content sizes. The x-axis shows the different content sizes and the y-axis the throughput. Agent-based content retrieval uses a probing interval t_p of 5s. This means that every 5 seconds the requester transmits a multicast request to every reachable agent asking whether it has retrieved the desired content. For content transmissions of 1MB, the throughput of ccngetfile is 20% higher than agent-based content retrieval and for 200KB it is even 80% higher. Since

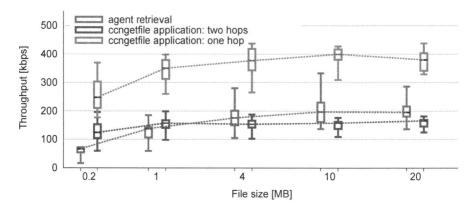

Fig. 2. Throughput of agent-based retrieval vs. ccngetfile

no agent delegation and notification is required with ccngetfile, the throughput when transferring small content is higher due to lower overhead. However, agent-based content retrieval results in higher troughput for content transmissions of 4MB or larger although every segment is retrieved from the agent's repository and not from the cache as with ccngetfile. For content sizes of 10MB and 20MB, throughput is even 20% higher than with ccngetfile. As explained above, with ccngetfile, every Interest is transmitted by the requester via unicast on the first hop and then forwarded via multicast to the content source on the second hop. Since the number of concurrently transmitted Interests is limited by the pipeline size at the requester, new Interests can only be transmitted if matching Data for previously transmitted Interests has been received. Therefore, the unicast transfer rate on the first hop is limited by the multicast transfer rate on the second hop, which is lower than the unicast transfer rate. With agent-based content retrieval, content transfers are performed subsequently. First, the agent retrieves the content via multicast from any unknown content source and stores it in its repository. Then, the requester can request the content via unicast from the agent using the full unicast transfer rate.

In practice, multi-hop unicast forwarding with ccngetfile is not feasible in opportunistic networks because forwarders are not known and, thus, can not be configured in the FIB. Even if it would be possible, to reach a content source that is far away, forwarding over many hops would reduce overall throughput. Figure 2 shows that throughput of ccngetfile over two hops is halved compared to the throughput over one hop. Earlier studies have shown that in unicast multi-hop communication, the throughput degrades with the number of n hops by $1/n$ [22] or worse [23]. Furthermore, it is challenging to set an appropriate fixed value for the Interest lifetime because nodes closer to the requester would need to wait longer for a reply than nodes closer to the content source. In contrast to this, the agent-based approach can exploit the mobility of agent nodes to reach a content source via multiple subsequent one-hop transmissions.

4.2 Impact of the Probe Interval

A requester transmits a notification request after every probe interval t_p to check whether a neighboring agent has retrieved the content. As soon as the requester detects the desired content on an agent, it can start content download from the agent. The larger t_p is, the more coarse is the notification granularity. With increasing content size, the number of received Notification Requests increases, because more time is required until content retrieval is completed and a Notifcation Response can be transmitted. An appropriate value for the probe interval may, therefore, also depend on the requested content size. However, it is currently not possible in CCNx to know the content size until receiving the last segment. In this subsection, we investigate the influence of different t_p values on the number of transmitted Notification Requests and the transfer time. The transfer time is measured from the transmission of the first Exploration Interest at the requester until the requester has completely received the content from the agent. Therefore, the transfer time also depends on the time until an agent retrieves the content from a content source. In practice, depending on the mobility and connectivity of the nodes, there may be a delay until an agent meets a content source, retrieves the content and meets the requester again to answer a Notification Request. For simplicity, we ignore this delay in this evaluation and assume that an agent can instantly reach a content source and reply to Notification Requests as soon as the download is finished.

Figure 3 shows the number of transmitted Notification Requests when using a probe interval of 1s, 5s, 30s, 60s and 120s during content transmissions of 1MB, 4MB and 10MB. As expected, the shorter the probe interval t_p is, the more Notification Requests need to be transmitted. In Table 2 we list the differences of transmitted notification requests in percent when using a probing interval of 30s, 60s or 120s instead of 5s. During a 10MB content transmission, 76% fewer Notification Requests are required with a probe interval of 30s and 85% fewer requests with a probe interval of 60s.

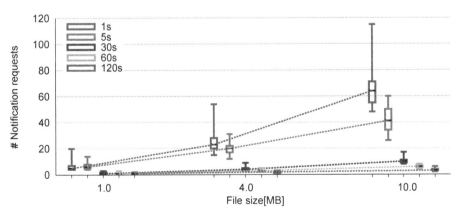

Fig. 3. Number of transmitted notification requests for different probe intervals

Table 2. Percentages relative to number of notification requests with probe interval of 5s

File size	30s	60s	120s
4MB	-80%	-85%	-90%
10MB	-76%	-85%	-92%

Table 3. Percentages relative to transfer time with probe interval of 5s

File size	30s	60s	120s
4MB	+3.7%	+26.7%	+59.9%
10MB	+6.5%	+8.4%	+11.6%

Figure 4 shows the transfer times when using different probe intervals. The figure shows that the transfer time increases with increasing content size but the differences between different probe intervals decrease with increasing content size. In Table 3 the differences of the transfer times are shown in percentages compared to a probe interval of 5s. For a 4MB file, only 3.7% more time is needed with a probe interval of 30s and 26.7% more time with a probe interval of 60s. For transfer times of 10MB content or larger, the median transfer times are similar because the overall transfer time is much larger than the differences in the probe interval. Therefore, a good probe interval value seems to be 30s, because compared to a probe interval of 5s, the Notification Requests decrease by 76-80% but the transfer time increases only by 3.7-6.5%. When transmitting content of 10MB or larger, the probe interval could also be set to larger values such as 60s, because the number of Notification Requests could be decreased even more at the expense of only a small increase in transfer time. However, a probe interval of 60s results in significantly longer transfer times for content transmission of 4MB or less.

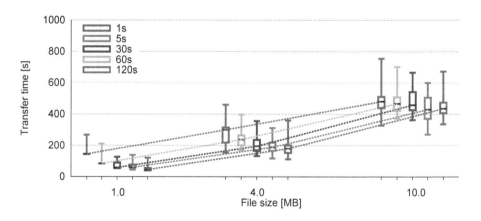

Fig. 4. Transfer time for different probe intervals

5   Conclusion

In opportunistic networks, a requester may never meet the content source directly. Forwarding Interests over multiple hops may not be possible due to intermittent connectivity between the network nodes or only at a very low rate. In this paper, we described agent-based content retrieval where requesters can delegate content retrieval to agent nodes, which can find the content on behalf of the requester. Since neighbor nodes are not known, Interests need to be transmitted via multicast. If the requester detects an agent that has retrieved the complete content, it can retrieve the content from the agent via unicast. We have implemented and evaluated agent-based content retrieval on Android smart phones. Evaluations have shown that the overhead for agent delegation and notification is only measurable for very small content. For content larger than 4MB, agent-based content retrieval results in 20% higher throughput than with multi-hop forwarding, although the content is stored at intermediate nodes on secondary storage and not in the cache. Because the maximum number of concurrently transmitted Interests is limited by the pipeline size, the overall transfer rate during multi-hop forwarding is limited by the slowest link. With agent-based retrieval, content is transmitted subsequently over both hops and, thus, every link can reach its maximum capacity. A probe interval of 30s showed the best performance in our scenario since the number of transmitted notification requests decreased by 76-80% compared to a probe interval of 5s but the overall transfer time increased only by 3.7-6.5%. However, probe and agent intervals may also depend on the mobility and the density of the network nodes.

Acknowledgments. The work presented in this paper was partially supported by the Swiss State Secretariat for Education and Research under grant number C10.0139.

References

1. Caesar, M., Condie, T., Kannan, J., Lakshminarayanan, K.: ROFL: Routing on Flat Labels. In: ACM SIGCOMM, Pisa, Italy, pp. 363–374 (September 2006)
2. Koponen, T., Chawla, M., Chun, B.G., Ermolinskiy, A., Kim, K.H., Shenker, S., Stoica, I.: A Data-Oriented (and Beyond) Network Architecture. In: ACM SIGCOMM, Kyoto, Japan, pp. 181–192 (August 2007)
3. Särelä, M., Rinta-aho, T., Tarkoma, S.: RTFM: Publish/Subscribe Internetworking Architecture. In: ICT-Mobile Summit, Stockholm, Sweden, pp. 1–8 (June 2008)
4. Jacobson, V., Smetters, D.K., Thornton, J.D., Plass, M.F., Briggs, N.H., Braynard, R.L.: Network Named Content. In: 5th ACM CoNEXT, Rome, Italy, pp. 1–12 (December 2009)
5. Anastasiades, C., Uruqi, A., Braun, T.: Content Discovery in Opportunistic Content-Centric Networks. In: 5th IEEE WASA-NGI, Clearwater, FL, USA, pp. 1048–1056 (October 2012)
6. Anastasiades, C., Schmid, T., Weber, J., Braun, T.: Opportunistic content-centric data transmission during short network contacts. In: IEEE WCNC, Istanbul, Turkey (April 2014)

7. Gonzalez, M.C., Hidalgo, C.A., Barabasi, L.: Understanding individual human mobility patterns. Nature 453(5), 779–782 (2008)
8. CCNx (April 2014), http://www.ccnx.org/
9. Varvello, M., Rimac, I., Lee, U., Greenwald, L., Hilt, V.: On the Design of Content-Centric MANETs. In: 8th WONS, Bardonecchia, Italy, pp. 1–8 (January 2011)
10. Meisel, M., Pappas, V., Zhang, L.: Listen First, Broadcast Later: Topology-Agnostic Forwarding under High Dynamics. In: ACITA, London, UK, pp. 1–8 (September 2010)
11. Hermans, F., Ngai, E., Gunningberg, P.: Global source mobility in the content-centric networking architecture. In: 1st ACM Workshop NOM, Hilton Head Island, South Carolina, USA (June 2012)
12. Ravindran, R., Lo, S., Zhang, X., Wang, G.: Supporting Seamless Mobility in Named Data Networking. In: IEEE FutureNet V (2012)
13. Lee, J., Kim, D.: Proxy-assisted content sharing using content-centric networking (CCN) for resource limited mobile consumer devices. IEEE Consumer Electrics Journal (2011)
14. Tyson, G., Bigham, J., Bodanese, E.: Towards an Information-Centric Delay-Tolerant Network. In: 2nd IEEE NOMEN (2013)
15. Scott, K., Burleigh, S.: Bundle Protocol Specification (November 2007), http://tools.ietf.org/html/rfc5050
16. Su, J., et al.: Haggle: Seamless networking for mobile applications. In: Krumm, J., Abowd, G.D., Seneviratne, A., Strang, T. (eds.) UbiComp 2007. LNCS, vol. 4717, pp. 391–408. Springer, Heidelberg (2007)
17. Pitkänen, M., Karkkainen, T., Ott, J., Conti, M., Passarella, A., Giordano, S., Puccinelli, D., Legendre, F., Trifunovic, S., Hummel, K., May, M., Hegde, N., Spyropoulos, T.: SCAMPI: Service platform for soCial Aware Mobile and Pervasive computIng. In: Mobile Cloud Computing (MCC), Helsinki, Finland (August 2012)
18. Braun, T., Hilt, V., Hofmann, M., Rimac, I., Steiner, M., Varvello, M.: Service-Centric Networking. In: Fourth International Workshop on the Network of the Future, FutureNet IV (2011)
19. CCNx Name Conventions (April 2014), http://www.ccnx.org/releases/latest/doc/technical/NameConventions.html
20. Jacobson, V., Braynard, R.L., Diebert, T., Mahadevan, P., Mosko, M., Briggs, N., Barber, S., Plass, M., Solis, I., Uzun, E., Lee, B., Jang, M.W., Byun, D., Smetters, D.K., Thornton, J.D.: Custodian-based information sharing. IEEE Communications Magazine 50(7), 38–43 (2012)
21. Zhao, W., Chen, Y., Ammar, M., Corner, M., Levine, B., Zegura, E.: Capacity Enhancement using Throwboxes in DTNs. In: IEEE International Conference on Mobile Ad hoc and Sensor Networks (MASS) (October 2006)
22. Hofmann, P., An, C., Loyola, L., Aad, I.: Analysis of UDP, TCP and Voice Performance in IEEE 802.11b Multihop Networks. In: 13th European Wireless Conference (2007)
23. Gupta, P., Gray, R., Kumar, R.: An experimental scaling law for ad hoc networks. Technical report. University of Illinois (2001)

NextServe Framework: Supporting Services over Content-Centric Networking

Dima Mansour, Torsten Braun, and Carlos Anastasiades

Communication and Distributed Systems, University of Bern
Neubruckstrasse 10, 3012 Bern, Switzerland
{mansour,braun,anastasi}@iam.unibe.ch
http://cds.unibe.ch

Abstract. The future Internet architecture aims to reformulate the way the content/service is requested to make it location-independent. Information-Centric Networking is a new network paradigm, which tries to achieve this goal by making content objects identified and requested by name instead of address.

In this paper, we extend Information-Centric Networking architecture to support services in order to be requested and invoked by names. We present *NextServe* framework, which is a service framework with a human-readable self-explanatory naming scheme. *NextServe* is inspired by the object-oriented programming paradigm and is applicable with real-world scenarios.

Keywords: Service-Centric Networking, Content-Centric Networking, Information-Centric Networking, Future Internet Architecture.

1 Introduction

The design of the Internet architecture relies on the fact that every node has an IP address. The sender's packet should contain the IP addresses of the source and the destination. The increasing use of the Internet and the expanding content volume prompt the researchers to think about new designs for the Internet architecture to be compatible with the new requirements like mobility and security [1].

There are many questions about the next-generation of the Internet architecture. Some of them are related to the way the content objects are requested, some are related to the optimal routing scheme for the content object requests, and others investigate the capability to build a suitable architecture for the current use case scenarios of the Internet.

Information-Centric Networking (ICN) [2] proposes some answers for those questions by giving content objects names instead of addresses. There are many implementations of ICN like Content-Centric Networking (CCN) [2], Publish-Subscribe Internet Routing Paradigm (PSIRP) [3], and Data-Oriented Network Architecture (DONA) [4] . These projects differ in design and implementation, but agree on the concept that content is the first-class citizen in the network.

A. Mellouk et al. (Eds.): WWIC 2014, LNCS 8458, pp. 189–199, 2014.
© Springer International Publishing Switzerland 2014

There is one main limitation with those projects. They all support static content only and there is no natural support for services. By taking a look at the current Internet applications and user needs, we can see that a high percentage of user requests is for services. Some are simple like "user sign up" services, and others are complex like financial transaction services. So, we believe that future ICN projects and architectures should support dynamic services as well as static content.

In this paper we extend an ICN architecture and naming scheme to support services. Our approach allows services to be requested and invoked by their names to reach the concept of Service-Centric Networking (SCN), where services are also first-class citizens of the network. Our service naming scheme is inspired by the object-oriented programming paradigm and takes into consideration simple and complex service characteristics. *NextServe* is the implementation of our approach to support services over ICN. Our implementation is based on the CCNx project [5], which is an implementation of the Content-Centric Network (CCN) protocol [6]. We explain the architecture and the naming scheme of the *NextServe* framework and discuss the advantages and the limitations of our approach.

The rest of the paper is organised as follows: In section 2, we introduce the necessary technical information regarding the CCN protocol. In section 3, we explain our approach and its architecture. We demonstrate a detailed example and motivate our design decisions. In section 4, we discuss the naming schemes of previous projects in Service-Centric Networking and show the advantages of *NextServe* over those projects. Finally, we conclude this paper in section 5 and discuss the future work in section 6.

2   Technical Background

Content-Centric Networking (CCN) deals with content objects as separate entities regardless of the hosts'IP addresses. The elements of the CCN architecture and the CCN communication model is shown in Figure 1. Content publishers publish their content objects by advertising them to the content router. The CCN communication model relies on two types of packets rather than IP packets. The consumer sends an Interest packet containing the content name. The producer sends a Data packet containing the corresponding data. The content router processes the request using three tables:

1. The Content Store (CS): It is a cache memory that stores the retrieved data mapped with the corresponding content name.
2. The Forwarding Information Base (FIB): It is a table of outbound faces for Interests. The FIB table is a standard routing table used for Interest forwarding based on content names rather than IP addresses.
3. Pending Interest Table (PIT): This table matches between the content name and all faces that are interested to reach the corresponding data. Then the router can remember the outstanding Interests.

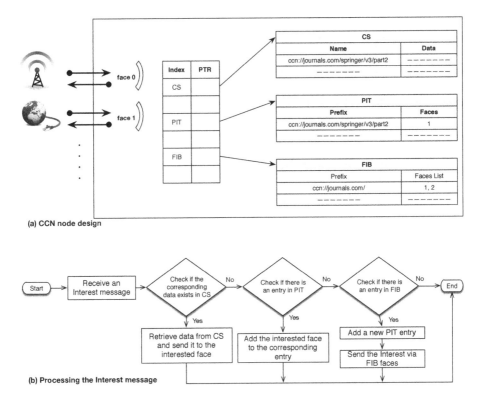

Fig. 1. A general overview of the CCN protocol

When a client sends an Interest packet, the content router looks it up in the CS to retrieve the corresponding data directly. When there is no corresponding entry in CS, the router searches the PIT looking for an entry that has the same content name to add the interested interface or to add a new entry with the content name and the corresponding interested interface. Finally, the router searches in the FIB. If there are matching prefixes in the FIB, it will forwards the Interest to the corresponding faces. Otherwise (no matching prefixes in FIB), there is no way to reach the corresponding data.

The names in CCN are arranged in a hierarchical structure to facilitate aggregation, management, and discovery. Each name consists of multiple components, which in turn can be any string of arbitrary length. These names have also information like versions and chunks of data. For instance, the name *ccn://Journals/springer/v3/part2* is to ask for the second part of the third version of the content *ccn://Journals/springer*.

3 The *NextServe* Framework

3.1 Naming Scheme

The naming scheme in *NextServe* is very similar to the method invocation style in modern programming languages like Java or C#. Service names follow the grammar in Figure 2. From those production rules, we can see that services have exactly the hierarchical names as content objects in CCN, but with the following additions:

- Services can accept parameters.
- Service parameters can be primitive values (string, integer, *etc.*), content objects, and other services.
- The returned result from one service can be a parameter to another service. This allows for service composition easily.
- The service parameters are contained between "/(" and "/)".
- The service parameters are separated using ",".
- When the parameters are primitive values, they are contained within double quotations.

To summarize, the service name is: */prefix1/prefix2/.../ServiceName/(param1, param2,.../)*. The parameters can be simple scalar values ("2", "3.14", "Hello World", *etc.*), content objects (*e.g.*,/unibe/iam/cds/schedule), or other services.

```
<CompleteName>     ::= / <ServicePrefix> <ServiceName> <Parameters>
<ServicePrefix>    ::= identifier/ | identifier/ <Component>
<Component>        ::= identifier/ | identifier/ <Component>
<ServiceName>      ::= identifier
<Parameters>       ::= /(<Params>/) | epsilon
<Params>           ::= epsilon | <ParamValue> | <ParamValue>,<Param>
<Param>            ::= <ParamValue> | <ParamValue>,<Param>
<ParamValue>       ::= <LocalParam> | <CompleteName>
<LocalParameter>   ::= "<Value>"
<Value>            ::= text
```

Fig. 2. The grammar of the naming scheme in *NextServe*

3.2 Architecture

The layered architecture of our approach is shown in Figure 3. The topmost layer contains the services. These services contain the application-specific business logic. The middle layer contains the necessary components for publishing services, handling requests, responses, and service parameters, as well as invoking service implementations. The lowest layer contains the CCN core.

The "CCN Connector" component handles the communication with the CCN core. It manages the Interest and Data messages. The "Name Parser" component parses the service requests according to the grammar in Figure 2 to determine the service implementation and the parameter values. When a parameter is a content object or another published service, the "Parameter Retriever" fetches the corresponding content data or service reply through the "CCN Connector". All the aforementioned functionality is encapsulated and abstracted from the "Services" layer through the "Service Publisher" component, which is responsible for publishing and un-publishing services.

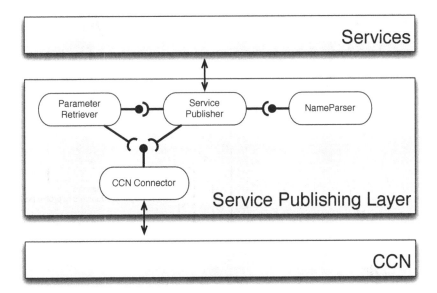

Fig. 3. The layered architecture of *NextServe*

3.3   Concrete Example

To better explain the approach, we give a concrete example. This example is completely implemented using CCNx and *NextServe*. The setting of the test scenario is as follows (as in Figure 4):

- There are three content routers. Each one has a running "ccnd" daemon (the executable of CCNx).
- There are two service providers. Each one is running a "ccnd" daemon and *NextServe*.
- There is one content provider running a "ccnd" daemon.
- Each node in the setting is running on a separate virtual machine. All virtual machines are connected via a network exactly as in Figure 4.

There is an encryption service called */scn/encrypt*. This service takes two parameters. The first one is the encryption password. The second parameter is the content object to encrypt. Then the service encrypts the content object using the password. There is another service called */fileManager/zip*. This service takes a content object as a parameter and compresses it. A possible client might submit the request */scn/encrypt/("P@ssw0rd",/fileManager/zip /(/university/profile.pdf/)/)*. This request can be read exactly like a method invocation in Java or C#. This means that the client wants to compress the file */university/profile.pdf* and then encrypt it using the password "P@ssw0rd".

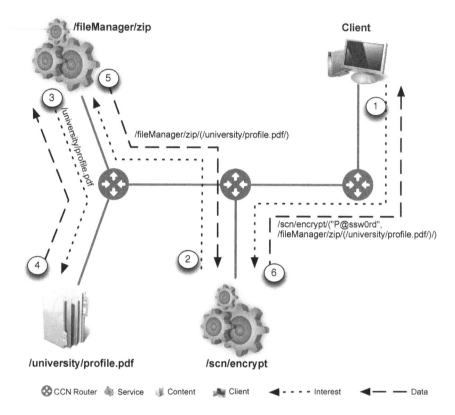

Fig. 4. The process of handling the request */scn/encrypt/("P@ssw0rd",/fileManager /zip/(/university/profile.pdf/)/)*

There are few points to notice here:

- The encryption service is published under the name */scn/encrypt*.
- The compression service is published under the name */fileManager/zip*.
- The profile content object is published under the name */university /profile.pdf/*.

Figure 4 shows the process of handling the service request using *NextServe*. When the CCN router receives a request for */scn/encrypt/("P@ssw0rd", /fileManager/zip/(/university/profile.pdf /)/)*, it performs name-based routing based on the maximum component match. In this case it is */scn/encrypt*. The CCN router does not understand the components in the parameter part. The perception of the rest of the request is the responsibility of the "Service Publishing" layer in the encryption service node. When the request reaches the service encryption node, the service publisher component receives the request and uses the "Name Parser" to parse the service parameters. In this case, the service publisher extracts two parameters. The first one is the password "P@ssw0rd" and the second one is "*/fileManager/zip/(/university/profile.pdf/)*". Then the service publisher uses the "Parameter Retriever" component to retrieve the second parameter from the CCN network by sending a request for "*/fileManager/zip/(/university/profile.pdf/)*". Again, when the CCN router receives that request, it forwards it to the compression service node by maximum name component matching, which is in this case "*/fileManager/zip*". In the same way, the service publishing layer parses the request name and extracts the parameter for the compression service. This parameter in this case is "*/university/profile.pdf*". Then, the "Parameter Retriever" component places a request for that content from the CCN network. When the Data message for "*/university/profile.pdf*" is received, the "Service Publisher" invokes the "zip" service on that content object data. Then, it sends the result in a Data message to the CCN network that routes it to the requester, which is the encryption service node. After receiving the result, the "Service Publisher" component in the compression service node invokes the service "encrypt" using the password and the content parameters. Then it sends back the result in a Data message to the client via the CCN network.

3.4   Implementing and Publishing Services

Publishing services is easy since the only interface that has to be dealt with is the *Service Publisher*. Service publisher has a method called *publish* that takes two parameters: The first one is the name of the published service as a string (*e.g.*,/scn/encrypt). The second parameter is an object that has a method called *execute*, which takes an list of byte arrays, which represent the parameter values. So when a request for a service is received, the "Service Publisher" fetches the parameter values from the request and transforms them to a list of byte arrays. Then it invokes the *execute* method over that ArrayList.

So, the service owner only needs to implement the parameter mappings to the desired types and then invokes whatever business logic that needs to be invoked. Of course this mapping can also be automated through Java Reflection but this is not done yet.

3.5   Motivating Our Design Decisions

We chose the layered architectural style because it is very appropriate for network applications and protocols. It also achieves the separation of concerns design principle allowing each layer to evolve separately without affecting other layers.

The decision of putting the responsibility of handling services, service names, and service parameters in the application side or service provider side is based on the discussion in [7]. The authors in [7] discuss three approaches to implement services over CCN: One of them is to implement services in the core of CCNx.

In this case some modifications are needed in the existing infrastructure of CCNx core. Another approach is to implement services at the publisher side. Then, all publishers have to be modified to serve the conversion service to all clients. The third approach is to implement services as a separate application. In this case, there is no need to touch the CCNx core.

NextServe follows the third approach and uses the CCN infrastructure as it is without any modification. Also our approach follows the CCN protocol guidelines regarding naming that specifically states that "CCNx content names are not interpreted in the operation of the CCNx protocol itself, just matched" [8]. In this way, our approach allows for caching because the parameters are components in the Interest name. So, if two clients ask for the same service on the same parameters, the CCN routers will only fetch one and forward the answer to both clients. If a third client asks for the same service on the same parameters, the CCN router gets the result from its Content Store.

4   Related Work and Discussion

There are many projects that aim at supporting services over ICN. CCNxServ[9] is also built on top of CCN. It adopts the same hierarchical structure of the names as CCN. The naming scheme is *ContentName + ServiceName*, where *ContentName* is exactly as in CCN. *ServiceName* is the name of the service module that should be invoked on the requested content. CCNxServ assumes that services are implemented as separate Java JAR files. So CCNxServ retrieves the service file (as a JAR file) and the content file, then it executes the service on the content. The CCNxServ architecture has three main components. The first component is the CCN network. It is responsible for handling Interest and Data messages. The second component is the *ServiceProxy*. It is responsible for interpreting the name in the Interest message to get the service name and the content name. ServiceProxy intercepts the Interest message and creates two Interest messages instead. The first one is for the service file and the second one is for the content file. After getting the files, ServiceProxy deploys and executes the service on a service execution framework called NetServ[10], which is the third component. NetServ is responsible for executing the service and returning the result to the ServiceProxy, which in turn, returns the result to the client.

NextServe has the following advantages over CCNxServ:

– *NextServe* allows any number of parameters.
– *NextServe* allows for parameters to be sent from the client itself.
– *NextServe* allows for service composition.
– *NextServe* does not make any assumption about how the service is implemented as long as it provides a compatible interface.

Named-Function Networking (NFN)[11] is another project that is built on top of CCN to support services. Service naming in NFN is inspired by the λ-expression language. For instance, the corresponding grammar for the λ-expression: f(g(data)) has the following CCN name: *[ccn:nfn | /name/of/data | /name/of/g*

| /name/of/f]. This is a request for applying function "f" on the result of applying function "g" on "data". NFN is a promising approach but it still does not support local parameters as in *NextServe* and its naming scheme is not as user-friendly as the naming scheme in *NextServe* especially when the request is complicated.

Another important project in Service-Centric Networking is Serval[12]. Serval changes the TCP/IP protocol stack to provide special interfaces to deal with service allocation and connection. In Serval, every service has an ID, which consists of three parts: *Provider-Prefix + Provider-Specific + Self-Certification*. The *Provider-Prefix* can be the company name (*e.g.*, Apple). The *Provider-Specific* can be the service name (*e.g.*, iMessage). The *Self-Certification* is the hash of the public key and the service name allowing the services to be self-authenticating without relying on a central certifying authority. Serval introduces a new kind of routers called "Service Routers", which combine the functionality of load balancers, proxies, and DNS. When a client asks for a certain service, the service routers are responsible for finding the best service replica to serve the request. Serval has many advantages in its architecture. It allows for load balancing, mobility, sessions, and fault tolerance.

NextServe differs from Serval in the following points:

- *NextServe* does not change the underlying TCP/IP protocol stack. This allows for easier adoption and integration into the current Internet architecture.
- *NextServe* supports caching naturally.
- Serval has been mainly developed to support data centers. *NextServe* can be adopted by any service provider or service client.

As mentioned in section 3, *NextServe* does not change the implementation of CCN. Hence, any evaluation results of CCN can be applied on *NextServe*. It is shown in [6] that CCN performs better than TCP and also scales to numbers of requests of exponential magnitude of nowadays needs. Similar results in [13] show that CCN introduces an overhead of 19% when compared with TCP/IP. But as the number of consumers increases, CCN outperforms TCP/IP and the download time in CCN is 25% less than it is in TCP/IP. In [14], it is stated that network topology has no effect on the efficiency of CCN but multi-path routing plays an important role in the performance of CCN. The main advantage of CCN is coming from the caching mechanism. *NextServe* inherently supports caching because of the naming scheme design. This leads to the fact that the evaluation results of CCN can be extended to cover also *NextServe*.

5   Conclusions

In this paper, we introduce the field of Service-Centric Networking (SCN) and the necessary background. Then we demonstrate *NextServe*, which is an SCN framework to support services over Content-Centric Networking (CCN). We show that *NextServe* overcomes most of the problems and shortcomings of the previous projects by applying a naming scheme that is inspired from object-oriented languages. *NextServe* is implemented in a way that does not put any limitations on service implementations. *NextServe* does not change the underlying CCN network but rather implements services in the application layer on the service provider side.

6   Future Work

In CCN there might be redundant content retrievals when the router FIB table has no entry for that specific content object and uses broadcast to find the content object, or the content object is not in the router Content Store (CS), and the router FIB table has many route entries for the content object. In those cases the Interest packet might reach many content item replicas, all of them will respond with Content packets but only one will reach the client. This redundancy becomes very expensive when we deal with services. There are few attempts to overcome this issue [15]. In the future we are going to investigate how we can find an optimal or near-optimal routing solution in *NextServe*. Also *NextServe* does not support sessions. But after solving the routing problem, session support comes for free because a client can connect to the best service replica from the beginning and keep sending the following requests to the same replica. We also plan to use Java Reflection to allow the automatic mapping between the parameters in the Interest packet and the actual parameters in a Java method. In this way, we decrease the amount of effort needed to publish any Java method as a service over *NextServe*. Another important direction in the future is to evaluate the efficiency and performance of *NextServe* in comparison with current service technologies like web services.

References

1. Pan, J., Paul, S., Jain, R.: A survey of the research on future internet architectures. Communications Magazine, IEEE 49, 26–36 (2011)
2. Jacobson, V., Smetters, D.K., Thornton, J.D., Plass, M.F., Briggs, N.H., Braynard, R.L.: Networking named content. In: Proceedings of the 5th International Conference on Emerging Networking Experiments and Technologies, CoNEXT 2009, pp. 1–12. ACM, New York (2009)
3. Fotiou, N., Trossen, D., Polyzos, G.: Illustrating a publish-subscribe internet architecture. Telecommunication Systems 51(4), 233–245 (2012)
4. Koponen, T., Chawla, M., Chun, B.-G., Ermolinskiy, A., Kim, K.H., Shenker, S., Stoica, I.: A data-oriented (and beyond) network architecture. SIGCOMM Comput. Commun. Rev. 37, 181–192 (2007)
5. Ccnx project official website, http://www.ccnx.org/ (last Checked, December 6, 2013)
6. Jacobson, V., Smetters, D.K., Thornton, J.D., Plass, M.F., Briggs, N.H., Braynard, R.L.: Networking named content. In: Proceedings of the 5th International Conference on Emerging Networking Experiments and Technologies, CoNEXT 2009, pp. 1–12. ACM, New York (2009)

7. Cheriki, E.: Design and implementation of a conversion service for content centric networking. Master's thesis. Institute of Computer Science and Applied Mathematics University of Bern (2012)
8. Ccn protocol overview, http://www.ccnx.org/releases/latest/doc/technical/CCNxProtocol.html (last Checked: January 6, 2014)
9. Srinivasan, S., Singh, A., Batni, D., Lee, J., Schulzrinne, H., Hilt, V., Kunzmann, G.: Ccnxserv: Dynamic service scalability in information-centric networks. In: 2012 IEEE International Conference on Communications (ICC), pp. 2617–2622 (2012)
10. Lee, J.W., Francescangeli, R., Song, W., Janak, J., Srinivasan, S.R., Kester, M.S., Baset, S.A., Liu, E., Schulzrinne, H.G., Hilt, V., Despotovic, Z., Kellerer, W.: Netserv framework design and implementation 1.0. technical report. Columbia University (May 2011), http://academiccommons.columbia.edu/catalog/ac:135424
11. Tschudin, C., Sifalakis, M.: Named functions for media delivery orchestration. In: 2013 20th International Packet Video Workshop (PV), pp. 1–8 (2013)
12. Nordström, E., Shue, D., Gopalan, P., Kiefer, R., Arye, M., Ko, S.Y., Rexford, J., Freedman, M.J.: Serval: An end-host stack for service-centric networking. In: Proceedings of the 9th USENIX Conference on Networked Systems Design and Implementation, NSDI 2012, Berkeley, CA, USA, pp. 8–7. USENIX Association (2012)
13. Guimaraes, P.H.V., Ferraz, L.H.G., Torres, J.V., Mattos, D.M., Murillo, P., Andres, F., Andreoni, L., Martin, E., Alvarenga, I.D., Rodrigues, C.S.: Experimenting content-centric networks in the future internet testbed environment. In: Guimaraes, P.H.V., Ferraz, L.H.G., Torres, J.V., Mattos, D.M., Murillo, P., Andres, F., Andreoni, L., Martin, E., Alvarenga, I.D., Rodrigues, C.S. (eds.) 2013 IEEE International Conference on Communications Workshops (ICC), pp. 1383–1387. IEEE (2013)
14. Rossi, D., Rossini, G.: Caching performance of content centric networks under multi-path routing (and more). Relatório técnico, Telecom ParisTech (2011)
15. Shanbhag, S., Schwan, N., Rimac, I., Varvello, M.: Soccer: services over content-centric routing. In: Proceedings of the ACM SIGCOMM Workshop on Information-centric Networking, ICN 2011, pp. 62–67. ACM, New York (2011)

A Peer-to-Peer Overlay System for Message Delivery in Wide Intermittently-Connected Hybrid Networks

Armel Esnault, Nicolas Le Sommer, and Frédéric Guidec

IRISA Laboratory, Université de Bretagne-Sud
Bâtiment ENSIBS, Campus de Tohannic
56017 Vannes Cedex, France
{Armel.Esnault,Nicolas.Le-Sommer,Frederic.Guidec}@univ-ubs.fr

Abstract. With the emergence of the Internet of Things, billions of new devices will be wirelessly-connected to the Internet in the next decade, thus yielding a growth of the data traffic, especially in the network infrastructures maintained by mobile operators. Intermittently-connected hybrid networks (ICHNs), which combine an infrastructure part and loosely-connected mobile ad hoc parts, offer interesting perspectives to cope with the growing data traffic.

This paper presents a decentralized unstructured peer-to-peer overlay system that aims at supporting communications in ICHNs deployed in wide geographical areas. It also presents the simulation results we obtained for our system for an ICHN composed of a few hundreds of fixed stations (with Internet access) and thousands of mobile devices used by people to exchange data while roaming a medium-size city.

Keywords: Opportunistic networking, intermittently-connected mobile ad hoc networks, peer-to-peer overlay.

1 Introduction

Every day, billions of people use their smartphones to access the Internet either through a 3G, a 4G or a Wi-Fi connection. With the evolution of the Internet towards an Internet of Things, the number of communicating devices in our daily environment will increase tremendously in the next decade, thus entailing a growth of the data traffic generated by these many devices in the future. This growth will undoubtedly be more important in the networks deployed by mobile operators, because people will want to access and to control their things from anywhere at anytime using their smartphones or their tablets. Yet the spectrum available for mobile data traffic is limited, and recent radio access technologies (such as LTE) are reaching the limits of Shannon's law. Progress made at the physical layer to increase the capacity of cellular networks may therefore prove insufficient in the future. One of the most relevant solution in terms of cost-effectiveness and deployment facilities is based on Wi-Fi mesh networks.

Several mesh networking projects, such as RoofNet [1], Serval [5], OpenGarden[1] and and Commotion[2] have shown that it is possible to provide nomadic users in cities with

---

[1] http://opengarden.com/
[2] https://commotionwireless.net

A. Mellouk et al. (Eds.): WWIC 2014, LNCS 8458, pp. 200–213, 2014.

broadband multi-hop connectivity to the Internet, thanks to a set of Wi-Fi access points acting as mesh routers and forming a backbone infrastructure with a limited number of wired links to the Internet. Yet, these mesh networks have some limitations. When such networks involve mobile devices, and when these devices are distributed sparsely or irregularly in the environment, network partitions can occur. Maintaining end-to-end connectivity between all network nodes then becomes quite a challenge, as dynamic routing protocols designed especially for MANETs (Mobile Ad hoc NETworks), such as OLSR, B.A.T.M.A.N. or AODV, prove unable to ensure message forwarding in such conditions.

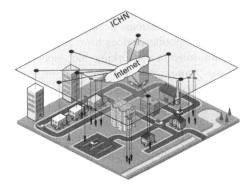

Fig. 1. Illustration of an intermittently-connected hybrid network (ICHN)

An interesting evolution of mesh networks is what we refer to as intermittently-connected hybrid networks (ICHNs), which unlike traditional mesh networks can tolerate network partitions. In an ICHN, communications rely on the "store, carry and forward" principle. This principle is the foundation of Opportunistic Networking [3]. The basic idea is to take advantage of radio contacts between devices to exchange messages, while exploiting the mobility of these devices to carry messages between different parts of the network. Two devices can thus communicate even if there never exists any temporaneous end-to-end path between them. Recent experiments conducted in real conditions have shown that applications that do not require end-to-end routes to work, such as voice-messaging, e-mail, or data sharing, can indeed perform quite satisfactorily in networks that rely on this principle [13,4,6,15,10].

We argue that ICHNs can be an interesting option for mobile operators to cope with the growth of the data traffic inherent in the emergence of the Internet of Things, even for Internet service providers or local authorities to provide nomadic people with ubiquitous services without resorting to any expensive infrastructure equipment. In this paper, we present Nephila, a decentralized and unstructured peer-to-peer overlay system we have designed to support communications in a wide ICHN, such as that illustrated in Figure 1. Nephila offers an homogeneous view of the network by hiding the connectivity disparities between mobile and fixed devices. It implements scalable mechanisms to perform neighbor discovery, and it provides a utility-based function to define message forwarding strategies. The "store, carry and forward" principle is used to deal with connectivity disruptions.

The remainder of the paper is organized as follows. Section 2 presents works pertaining to communication in intermittently-connected networks, and shows their limitations for wide ICHN. Section 3 gives an overview of Nephila, and details some of its salient features. Section 4 describes the neighbor discovery process implemented in Nephila. Section 5 shows how message forwarding paths are computed in Nephila. Section 6 presents evaluation results. Nephila is here compared with two other well-known opportunistic forwarding protocols: Spray-and-Wait [14] and PRoPHET [9]. Finally, Section 7 summarizes our contribution, and gives perspectives for future work.

2   Related Work

Communications in intermittently-connected networks composed only of mobile devices or of both stationary and mobile devices have been studied in research works dealing with delay/disruption-tolerant networking and opportunistic networking [18]. These works implement the "store, carry and forward" principle and devise several strategies and optimizations to control the replication of messages, and thus to avoid an epidemic dissemination of messages in the network [16]. The Spray-and-Wait routing protocol [14] provides a drastic way to reduce the number of message copies that are disseminated in the network. It relies on a two-phase message delivery mechanism. During the spray phase, the source node and first carriers of the message spread multiple copies of the same message over the network. Then, in the wait phase, each relay node maintains its copy in its cache and eventually delivers it to the final destination if it encounters this one. Nevertheless, this protocol relies on a random-based forwarding, and as such is not really suited to route messages efficiently in wide ICHNs. In order to improve message delivery in intermittently-connected networks, several research works have investigated deterministic approaches. For instance, the Message Ferrying approach [19] exploits the non-randomness mobility behavior of specific nodes (the message ferries) to carry messages between the different partitions of the network with the aim of increasing the delivery rate and of reducing the message propagation delays.

Some works go beyond the Message Ferrying approach by considering the recurrent social mobility patterns of users and by investigating solutions relying on probabilistic and prediction techniques in order to choose among a set of nodes the best carrier(s) for each message that must be forwarded. The probabilities and the predictions of future contacts are computed using context properties and history of contacts. PRoPHET [9] takes it routing decisions according to the delivery probabilities it computes based on the frequency of encounters. When a node wants to forward a message to another node, it looks for the neighbor node that has the highest frequency of direct or transitive contacts with the destination. Where PRoPHET relies on the history of encounters, the Context-Aware Routing protocol (CAR) [11] exploits some contextual properties using utility functions and Kalman filters to compute the message delivery estimation. HiBOp [2] and Propicman [12] investigate a social and history-based approach in order to predict the future movements of the nodes and to route the messages according to this prediction. HiBOp and Propicman can be considered as more general than CAR, because unlike the latter, they do not suppose the existence of an underlying routing protocol, and they can process context information provided by the message emitters in order to take their routing decisions.

History-based algorithms can offer a good performances in terms of delivery ratio and delivery delay, but have the major drawback of assuming that a node is able to store locally a large amount of contact information. Such an assumption is somewhat optimistic since the majority of the devices forming ICHN are small portable devices with limited capabilities and capacities. Processing contact histories and predicting movement patterns is also a tricky problem, especially in environments composed of numerous mobile devices that move following irregular patterns, such as those carried by pedestrians in a city. Moreover, unlike the RoofNet, Commotion, Serval and OpenGarden projects, the above-mentioned works focus only on communication between mobile devices, and they do not exploit the communication capacities offered by a mesh networking infrastructure. This point can be considered as a limitation to support communication between mobile devices in wide ICHNs. However it must be noticed that the disruption-tolerant communication solutions proposed in these works are more efficient than those implemented in projects Commotion and Serval (RoofNet and OpenGarden projects do not offer such communication means). Indeed, in Serval and Commotion, the text messaging and file sharing applications are developed over a file distribution system that implements an epidemic file dissemination model based on the "store, carry and forward" principle in order to tolerate the communication disruptions. In Commotion and Serval, no precautions are taken to limit the number of messages that are exchanged and forwarded by the devices. Messages or files are thus disseminated in the network and replicated on every encountered node. Consequently in in high-density regions, some network congestions can happen.

In the next section, we present a peer-to-peer overlay system that provides efficient communications between devices in wide ICHNs by tolerating communication disruptions and network partitions, and by exploiting mesh network infrastructures.

3 Overview of Nephila

An ICHN can be complex, can cover a wide area (e.g., a city), and can be composed of numerous fixed and mobile devices (see Figure 1). Mobile devices can be carried and used by people, or can be embedded in vehicles. Fixed devices can be connected to the Internet or to corporate intranets through wired or wireless links. Our approach aims at proposing a versatile system. We do not make any assumption about the management and the location of fixed devices, about the global number of devices in the network, or about how mobile devices move in the network. Mobile devices can therefore be distributed irregularly in the environment. Fixed devices can be operated by mobile operators, by local authorities, or they can be simply managed by private companies or citizens (e.g., residential gateways). Mobile and fixed devices can appear in, and disappear from, the network at any time.

Nephila is a decentralized and unstructured peer-to-peer overlay system that offers an homogeneous view of wide ICHNs (see Figure 2), and that is meant to support the communications between devices in these networks. It implements a set of mechanisms and provides several functions that allows to devise various event-based message forwarding strategies in a simple way. The main mechanisms and functions are the following:

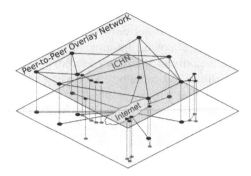

Fig. 2. A peer-to-peer overlay system for an ICHN

Neighbor Discovery. Nephila performs a proactive discovery of fixed and mobile nodes. It can provide each node with a list of its neighbors, and can notify these nodes about any change in their neighborhood. This discovery process is an original feature of Nephila, and consequently it is detailed afterward in a specific section.

Backbone Management. Nephila creates and maintains logical links between devices that act as gateways between the infrastructure part and loosely-connected mobile ad hoc parts of the IHCN in order to form a backbone (see Figure 2). This backbone helps cover a wide area and support communications between numerous mobile devices. The scalability of our system mainly resides in the existence of this backbone.

Disruption Tolerant Networking. The messages received from the local applications or from the neighbor nodes are stored locally in a cache until they expire, or until they are delivered directly to their destination. When a mobile node encounters another one, they can exchange the messages they have in their local cache, thus implementing the "store, carry and forward" principle, and supporting the connectivity disruptions and the network partitions.

Computation of Message Forwarding Paths. In order to devise efficient message forwarding algorithms, Nephila provides a list of so-called "trail values" (TV). The trail value of a node reflects its capacity to reach a given destination, either directly or through intermediate nodes. The computation and the dissemination scheme of trail values are key features of our proposition, and consequently they are described more precisely later in Section 5.

Message Forwarding. In Nephila, the message forwarding can be conditioned by a preliminary exchange of summary vectors. A vector includes the ID of messages a node has locally, and for which it considers the neighbor with which it performs an exchange as a best forwarder than itself based on the trail values of this one. When a node receives such a summary vector, it compares the ID of the messages it has locally with those contained in the summary vector, and request the message(s) that it does not have yet.

Event-Based Message Forwarding Algorithms. Several events are generated in Nephila, such as the arrival of a new neighbor, the disappearance of a neighbor, the reception of trail values from neighbors, the reception of summary vectors and the reception of requests for a message (or a list of messages). Based on these events, several message forwarding strategies can be easily devised in Nephila. Currently, Nephila implements a message forwarding algorithm that exploits all the above-described features and implements the "store, carry and forward" principle. This algorithm is called BTSA (for Best Trail Selection Algorithm). With BTSA, each mobile node receiving a message is expected to forward a copy of this message to one or several of its neighbors. When no forwarding opportunity exists (e.g., no neighbor is available, or all current neighbors are considered as being unsuitable as carriers for this message) the node stores the message and waits for future contacts with other devices. A message can thus be delivered to a destination node, even if the source and destination never get close to each other, and even if they are never present simultaneously in the network. In addition with BTSA, each node takes a local decision based on its own trail values and on those sent by its neighbors. When a node receives a message from a neighbor node, or from a local application, it forwards this message to the neighbor that has the greatest trail value for the destination, provided that this value is greater than its own value. Sometimes it might be risky to forward message copies exclusively to good carriers, especially in sparse network where the contact with a good carrier is uncertain. To address this issue BTSA has a stock of a few number of copies dedicated to bad neighbors. This number of copies is limited in order to avoid network overload and resource consumption on mobile devices.

4   Neighbor Discovery

In an ICHN, it is difficult to forward the messages towards their destinations based on the IP address of the devices, especially in the ad hoc parts of the network due to the mobility of the nodes. In order to address this issue, Nephila assigns to each node a unique ID at the installation time, and forwards the messages according to these IDs. The neighbor discovery mechanisms maintain a mapping between the ID of nodes and their IPv6 address. It must be noticed that the IPv6 address of a node is only known by the neighbors of this one.

Nephila implements two distinct neighbor node discovery mechanisms: one for the mobile ad hoc parts of an ICHN, and another one for the backbone part of this ICHN. The neighbor discovery of mobile devices is achieved by a standard beaconing system, while in backbone the neighbors of nodes are discovered using a peer sampling service based on Cyclon [17]. With Cyclon, the nodes forming the backbone exchange each other lists of neighbors periodically. In order to initiate the discovery we assume, in the current implementation of this service, the existence of a limited set of fixed nodes. This set is a parameter of Nephila. It is used by Cyclon in order to discover the nodes that are always present in the backbone. Cyclon allows to define the maximum size of the list of neighbors exchanged periodically by the nodes. Thus, each fixed node only knows a limited number of the nodes forming the backbone, thus reducing the computation time needed to evaluate the next suitable message forwarder(s). Cyclon provides a fast dissemination of routing tables thanks to gossiping techniques.

5 Computation of Forwarding Paths

The trail values computed by Nephila are meant to be used by a forwarding algorithm in order to select, for each message, the most relevant next forwarder(s). The nodes share their respective trail values with their neighbors through the discovery process. The values are included in beacon messages, and are provided by the Cyclon-based service we have developed. Disseminating such pieces of information can be costly in terms of traffic because the nodes can have trail values for a large number of devices. In order to address this issue, we use a modified version of the Exponential Decay Bloom Filter (EDBF [8]). EDBF is an extension of the traditional Bloom filter. EDBF allows to encode probabilistic forwarding tables in a highly compressed manner. It was originally designed to store and propagate in unstructured peer-to-peer networks information about content hosted in the neighborhood of a node. EDBF has been coupled with a query routing mechanism in order to locate content in such networks. The modified version of the EDBF we designed allows to store and disseminate efficiently the trail values of each node in the overlay system. This version of EDBF will be called TBF (for Trail Bloom Filter) in the remainder of this paper. Based on the values included in TBFs, a message can reach its destination in a small number of hops and with a high probability.

A TBF is defined as an array of m floating point elements noted $[tbf_0, ..., tbf_{m-1}]$. It uses k hash functions (assumed to be independent) noted $h_0, h_i, ..., h_{k-1}$. Hash functions are used to insert trail values of nodes into a TBF. These function are also used to retrieve a trail value from a TBF. When inserting a given node x in a TBF, all k functions $h_0, h_i, ..., h_{k-1}$ are evaluated simultaneously over x and the floating point elements $tbf_0, ..., tbf_{m-1}$ in the TBF indexed by $h_i(x)$, with $i \in [0, m-1]$ are set to the trail value of x. A query for node y in a TBF looks at the floating elements in the TBF indexed by $h_i(y)$, with $i \in [0, m-1]$ and returns the trail value for node y.

In order to take into account the loss of confidence in the routing information (i.e., in trail values) over time and hops, a function *decay* is applied by a node on its TBF periodically. When a node detects the disappearance of one of its neighbors, it deletes the TBF it received from this neighbor previously, and it applies the *decay* function on its local TBF in order to reflect the loss of capacity to forward messages to this node. When a node detects another node in its neighborhood, it calls the *reinforce* function on its local TBF. This function sets to the maximum trail value (i.e., to 1), the value of all floating point elements $tbf_0, ..., tbf_{m-1}$ returned by the hash functions for this new neighbor node. When a node receives the TBF of a neighbor, it stores this TBF locally and it merges a decayed version of this TBF with its own TBF. The periodic decaying applied on the local TBF is compensated for each neighbor by the frequent invocation of the *reinforce* function triggered by the discovery process. Function *merge* keeps the maximum of each element of two TBF tbf and $rtbf$, where tbf is the local TBF structure and where $rtbf$ is a TBF sent by a neighbor node.

In order to retrieve the trail value for a given node from a TBF, we have defined a function called *query*. By applying this function on its own TBF and on the TBFs received from its neighbors, and by comparing the values returned by this function, a node can determine if it is a better forwarder than its neighbors, or otherwise can select the best one among them. This function *query* can be assimilated to the utility-based functions introduced by Musolesi and Mascolo, in [11]. Functions *decay, reinforce, merge* and *query* rely on the hash functions associated with the TBF. These functions are defined as follows:

Parameters:

df is the decaying factor

n is the identity of a node

tbf TBF of the local node or a remote node

$rtbf$ TBF of a remote node

mv is a minimum trail value

Functions:

$decay(tbf, df, mv) : tbf_i \leftarrow max(mv, tbf_i * (1 - df)); \forall i, 0 \leq i \leq m - 1$

$reinforce(tbf, n) : tbf_{h_i(n)} \leftarrow 1; \forall i, 0 \leq i \leq k - 1$

$merge(tbf, rtbf) : tbf_i \leftarrow max(tbf_i, rtbf_i); \forall i, 0 \leq i \leq m - 1$

$query(tbf, n) : min(tbf[h_0(N_n)], tbf[h_1(N_n)], ..., tbf[h_{m-1}(N_n)])$

TBFs allow to propagate trail values transitively in the network. The trail values decrease proportionally with the number of hops and the time. The trail value for a given destination reachable in n hops is defined as $(1 - df)^n * (1 - df)^{\left\lfloor \frac{e-a}{p} \right\rfloor}$, where e and a are respectively the emission date of a TBF sent by a node located at $n - 1$ hops and the reception date of a TBF sent by a neighbor node, and p the decaying period.

By assigning to the devices forming the backbone a default trail value greater than that assigned to mobile devices, one can favor the forwarding of messages via the backbone. Thus, the forwarding of a message whose destination is unknown at the emission time could all the same be triggered. The message will indeed be forwarded towards a device of the backbone, and will be stored in the latter until discovering the destination. It is expected that the nodes of the backbone will be more able to deliver the message than the initial emitter itself, especially when the destination is not in the close neighborhood of the emitter. Since this message will be stored, carried and forwarded by intermediate nodes, it can obviously be delivered directly by one of them if it encounters the destination.

6 Simulation and Results

In order to evaluate the overlay system described in the previous sections, we have developed a prototype in Java, and we performed simulations using the ONE [7], a discrete event simulator written in Java. In this section, we present the scenario, the simulation setup we used, and the results we obtained.

6.1 Scenario and Simulation Setup

The scenario we consider in the simulations is meant to be as realistic as possible. It involves a number of pedestrians carrying smartphones who walk freely in the streets of the city of Vannes, a French city covering about 25 km². We assume that pedestrians move at a speed that varies between 1 m/s and 1.6 m/s, and that 100 pedestrians use their smartphone to communicate periodically. They send several messages, and then stop to use their smartphones. After a few minutes they repeat the same process. For the sake of comparison, the number of people using their smartphone is kept constant, while the total number of pedestrians increases. The smartphones of the other pedestrians only act as relays. We performed simulations with 100, 500, 1000 and 2000 pedestrians. The environment is additionally populated by either 0, 100 or 200 fixed access points. These access points are interconnected through the Internet, and form the backbone in Nephila. They were chosen among residential gateways deployed in the city of Vannes on the basis of geographic and random criteria. An illustration of this environment is given in Figure 3.

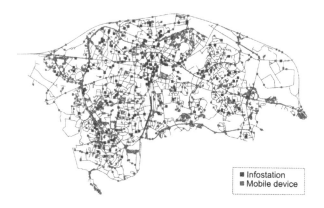

Fig. 3. Illustration of the simulation environment

By considering an environment devoid of fixed access points, an environment populated with 100 fixed access points, and another one populated with 200 fixed access points, we want to evaluate the performances of Nephila (with BTSA), and the impact of the number of access points on the message delivery (i.e., the impact of the size of the backbone). In the simulation results presented hereafter, these three configurations will be referred as BTSA 0, BTSA 100 and BTSA 200 respectively.

The simulation duration is 1 hour and 20 minutes. During the first 10 minutes, both fixed and mobile devices perform a discovery of their neighbors, and compute and disseminate Trail Bloom Filters (TBFs). After this warm-up period, mobile devices start to send messages. The emission of messages is stopped 10 minutes before the end of the simulation. The other simulation parameters are defined in Tables 1 and 2. The Nephila's parameters were determined empirically through extensive experiments.

Table 1. Simulation parameters

Parameter	Value
Size of the cache of messages of mobile devices	10 MBytes
Size of the cache size messages of access points	40 MBytes
Bitrate of wired links	20 Mbit/s
Bitrate of wireless interfaces	10 Mbit/s
Communication range of the wireless interface	50 meters
Number of hops	30
Maximum size of messages	200 kBytes

6.2 Simulation Results

The objectives of these simulations is to know how our proposition works when only opportunistic communications are feasible, and to study the impact of the backbone and of the size of this one on the message delivery. For comparison purposes, we run in an environment devoid of fixed access points, the PRoPHET and the Spray-and-Wait protocols. A maximum of 10 copies of a given message can be replicated by Spray-and-Wait in our simulations. PRoPHET has been configured with its default parameters [9].

The performances of Nephila (with BTSA) are compared with those of PRoPHET and Spray-and-Wait following three metrics, namely the average delay and the ratio of message delivery, and the network load. The delivery ratio is the number of messages delivered over the total number of messages sent by the 100 emitters. It reflects the ability of the protocol to eventually forward messages to their destination before they expired. It must be noticed that during a single simulation run, approximatively 2600 messages have been generated by the 100 pedestrians. The network load is the overall number of messages exchanged between nodes during the simulation. On the wireless parts of the ICHN, only messages carrying data related to the protocols were counted, because the beaconing process is not implemented in the versions of PRoPHET and Spray-and-Wait in the ONE simulator.

Figures 4a and 4b show, according to the number of pedestrians involved in the simulation, the average delay and the percentage of messages that have been delivered successfully. The average number of hops needed to forward a message to its destination

Table 2. Nephila's parameters

	Parameter	Value
TBF	Decay period	20 s
	Decay factor	0.2
	Strengthen period	20 s
	Broadcast period	30 s
	Pedestrian min trail value	0.1
	Infostation min trail value	0.3
	Number of elements	600
	Number of hash functions	2
BTSA	Best threshold	0.1
	Number of copies	10
Cyclon	Neighborhood size	13
	Fanout	3
	Shuffling period	120

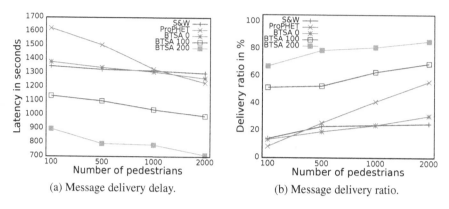

(a) Message delivery delay.   (b) Message delivery ratio.

Fig. 4. Message delivery performances

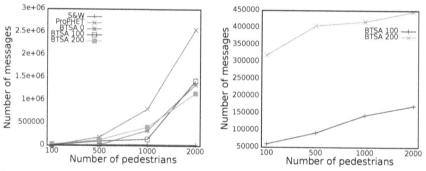

(a) Number of messages forwarded in the   (b) Number of messages forwarded in the
wireless parts of the network.   backbone.

Fig. 5. Number of messages forwarded in wireless and wired parts of the network

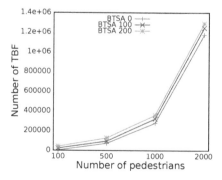

Fig. 6. Amount of TBF exchanged in the wireless parts of the network

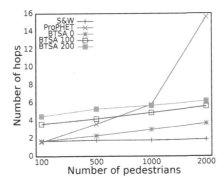

Fig. 7. Number of hops needed to reach the destination

is given in Figure 7. Figures 5a, and 5b show the number of messages disseminated in the wireless and wired parts of the network respectively.

BTSA 0 (BTSA without access points) and Spray-and-Wait have very close performances in terms of delivery delay and ratio. However, where the number of copies remains constant with Spray-and-Wait, it increases with BTSA 0 according to the number of nodes in the network (see Figure 5a). Indeed, as we do not have assigned a time to live to messages, in order to evaluate only the behavior of our forwarding algorithm, the messages are replicated in the network even after the deliverance of the first copy to the destination. This number of messages can be reduced by assigning a time to live to messages and by implementing a healing mechanism in BTSA. Both BTSA 0 and Spray-and-Wait perform better than PRoPHET from 100 up to 500 pedestrians. The main reason lies in the fact that in sparse networks, the radio contacts are not frequent, and therefore the delivery probabilities estimated by PRoPHET on the basis of the frequency of encounters are not useful. With PRoPHET many messages are actually delivered to their destination by the initial emitters themselves. BTSA 0 and Spray-and-Wait do not have this limitation, as they can forward several copies of a message to "potentially bad" carriers. These carriers can in turn forward a copy of the message to other nodes, thus increasing the probability of encountering good carriers later. When the number of pedestrians increases, the number of radio contacts increases as well, and the probabilities of finding good carrier(s) increase accordingly. PRoPHET provides a better delivery ratio than BTSA 0 and Spray-and-Wait from 1000 up to 2000 pedestrians, but with the major drawback of increasing the number of copies disseminated in the network. Spray-and-Wait does not benefit as much as PRoPHET of the increase of the number of pedestrians because the number of copies that can be disseminated remains limited. The delivery ratio remains relatively constant due to the limited number of copies disseminated in the network (see Figure 5a).

Figure 6 shows the overhead induced by the TBF exchanges in the wireless parts of the network. This overhead depends of the number of contacts and of their duration. The overhead is thus more important in a dense network than in a sparse one. In the simulation we made for 2000 pedestrians, the average of the additional amount of data generated by each device of the wireless part of the ICHN during the simulation is about 2Kbits/s per nodes. In the wired part, the amount of data related to the TBF exchanges depends of the number of access points. It is about $3.2 * 10^8$ bytes for BTSA 100 and about $6.6 * 10^8$ bytes for BTSA 200. It represents on average 770bits/s per fixed node.

Figures 4a and 4b show the benefit provided by the backbone. This one allows to drastically reduce the message delivery delay and to strongly increase the delivery ratio without increasing the number of messages disseminated in the wireless parts of the network. A greater number of fixed nodes allows to cover a wider geographical area, and therefore to increase the probability of delivering a message to a remote destination, as well as to reduce the delivery delay. When the number of radio contacts increases, this effect is attenuated gradually. Figure 5b shows that an important amount of messages is transmitted through the backbone.

7   Conclusion and Future Work

In this paper we have presented Nephila, a system that can support opportunistic message forwarding in wide intermittently-connected hybrid networks (ICHN). Nephila builds and maintains a peer-to-peer overlay structure that interconnects fixed nodes at reasonable cost, while relying on the "store, carry and forward" principle to tolerate connectivity disruptions on mobile nodes. It implements a scalable neighbor node discovery mechanism, and defines a utility-based function that is meant to help select the next message forwarders based on so-called trail values. These values reflect the capacity of a node to reach a given destination directly, or via intermediate nodes. In this paper, we have also compared the performance of our system with those of protocols Spray-and-Wait and Prophet. Simulation results confirm that communications between mobile devices in wide ICHN can indeed be achieved with good performances, using a limited number of fixed interconnected access points.

In the future, we plan to implement Nephila on Android-based smartphones and tablets, and on Raspberry Pi-based access points. These devices will be used to run experiments in real conditions. We also plan to devise new forwarding algorithms that can take into account contextual properties such as the power budget, location, speed, and trajectories of the mobile devices.

References

1. Aguayo, D., Bicket, J., Biswas, S., Judd, G., Morris, R.: Link-level measurements from an 802.11b mesh network. In: Proceedings of the 2004 Conference on Applications, Technologies, Architectures, and Protocols for Computer Communications, SIGCOMM 2004, pp. 121–132. ACM, New York (2004)
2. Boldrini, C., Conti, M., Jacopini, J., Passarella, A.: HiBOp: a History Based Routing Protocol for Opportunistic Networks. In: Conti, M. (ed.) International Symposium on a World of Wireless, Mobile and Multimedia Networks (WoWMoM 2007), pp. 1–12. IEEE CS, Helsinky (2007)
3. Conti, M., Giordano, S.: Multihop Ad Hoc Networking: The Reality. IEEE Communications Magazine 45(4), 88–95 (2007)
4. Farrell, S., McMahon, A., Weber, S., Hartnett, K., Lynch, A., Meehan, E.: Report on DTN Applications During Arctic Summer 2010 Trial. In: 1st International Workshop on Opportunistic and Delay/Disruption-Tolerant Networking (October 2011)

5. Gardner-Stephen, P., Palaniswamy, S.: Serval mesh software-wifi multi model management. In: Proceedings of the 1st International Conference on Wireless Technologies for Humanitarian Relief, pp. 71–77. ACM (2011)
6. Islam, M.T., Turkulainen, A., Kärkkäinen, T., Pitkänen, M., Ott, J.: Practical Voice Communications in Challenged Networks. In: 1st Extreme Workshop on Communications (August 2009)
7. Keränen, A., Ott, J., Kärkkäinen, T.: The ONE Simulator for DTN Protocol Evaluation. In: SIMUTools 2009: Proceedings of the 2nd International Conference on Simulation Tools and Techniques, ICST, New York, NY, USA (2009)
8. Kumar, A., Xu, J., Zegura, E.: Efficient and scalable query routing for unstructured peer-to-peer networks. In: INFOCOM 2005. 24th Annual Joint Conference of the IEEE Computer and Communications Societies. Proceedings IEEE, vol. 2, pp. 1162–1173. IEEE (2005)
9. Lindgren, A., Doria, A., Schelén, O.: Probabilistic Routing in Intermittently Connected Networks. In: Dini, P., Lorenz, P., de Souza, J.N. (eds.) SAPIR 2004. LNCS, vol. 3126, pp. 239–254. Springer, Heidelberg (2004)
10. Mahéo, Y., Le Sommer, N., Launay, P., Guidec, F., Dragone, M.: Beyond Opportunistic Networking Protocols: a Disruption-Tolerant Application Suite for Disconnected MANETs. In: 4th Extreme Conference on Communication (ExtremeCom 2012), pp. 1–6. ACM, Zürich (2012)
11. Musolesi, M., Mascolo, C.: CAR: Context-Aware Adaptive Routing for Delay Tolerant Mobile Networks. IEEE Transactions on Mobile Computing 8(2), 246–260 (2009)
12. Nguyen, H.A., Giordano, S., Puiatti, A.: Probabilistic Routing Protocol for Intermittently Connected Mobile Ad hoc Network (PROPICMAN). In: International Symposium on a World of Wireless, Mobile and Multimedia Networks (WoWMoM 2007), pp. 1–6. IEEE CS, Helsinky (2007)
13. Ntareme, H., Zennaro, M., Pehrson, B.: Delay Tolerant Network on Smartphones: Applications for Communication Challenged Areas. In: 3rd Extreme Workshop on Communications (September 2011)
14. Spyropoulos, T., Psounis, K., Raghavendra, C.S.: Spray and Wait: an Efficient Routing Scheme for Intermittently Connected Mobile Networks. In: 2005 ACM SIGCOMM Workshop on Delay-tolerant Networking (WDTN 2005), pp. 252–259. ACM, Philadelphia (2005)
15. Tziouvas, C., Lambrinos, L., Chrysostomou, C.: A Delay Tolerant Platform for Voice Message Delivery. In: 1st International Workshop on Opportunistic and Delay/Disruption-Tolerant Networking, pp. 1–5 (2011)
16. Vahdat, A., Becker, D.: Epidemic Routing for Partially Connected Ad Hoc Networks. Tech. rep., Duke University (April 2000)
17. Voulgaris, S., Gavidia, D., Van Steen, M.: Cyclon: Inexpensive Membership Management for Unstructured P2P Overlays. Journal of Network and Systems Management 13(2), 197–217 (2005)
18. Zhang, Z.: Routing in Intermittently Connected Mobile Ad Hoc Networks and Delay Tolerant Networks: Overview and Challenges. IEEE Communications Surveys and Tutorials 8(1), 24–37 (2006)
19. Zhao, W., Ammar, M., Zegura, E.: A Message Ferrying Approach for Data Delivery in Sparse Mobile Ad Hoc Networks. In: Proceedings of ACM Mobihoc 2004, Tokyo, Japan (May 2004)

A Solution for the Naming Problem for Name-Centric Services

Torsten Teubler, Mohamed A. Hail, and Horst Hellbrück

Lübeck University of Applied Sciences, Electrical Engineering and Computer Science,
Mönkhofer Weg 239, 23562 Lübeck, Germany
{teubler,hail,hellbrueck}@fh-luebeck.de
http://www.cosa.fh-luebeck.de

Abstract. In recent past name-centric or content-centric networking (CCN) has gained substantial attention in the networking community. In a further development step name-centric service architecture enables the flexible placement and distribution of services in the network especially in a heterogeneous environment of wired and wireless (sensor) networks. However, the problem of structuring and creating hierarchies for names in name-centric networks is not solved yet. E.g. there is no configuration of service names in name-centric service WSN, no concept of unsolicited names or link-local names in CCN. In IP networks, DHCP or IPv6 auto-configuration is available, but no equivalent technique exists for CCN. We analyze the naming problem in the software development life cycle for name-centric services in WSN and propose a structure, hierarchy, and configuration mechanism for names. The paper introduces the overall concept and preliminary steps of implementation.

Keywords: Content-Centric Networking, Wired/Wireless Environments, Service Development, Service Management.

1 Introduction

The Internet has evolved in the last decades from a network of devices with a handful of standardized protocols and applications to a service platform for numerous applications. In the recent past the focus of the Internet has evolved from devices to services and content delivery. Todays Internet business is concentrated on content and applications running on wireless devices.

The challenge for the future development of the Internet is a seamless integration of sensor networks that provide content and services where the devices delivering these services are not of importance at all. Therefore, new paradigms like content-centric networking (CCN) and name-centric networking (NCN) are proposed for an alternative architecture of the future Internet [8]. CCNx is a reference implementation for content-centric networking from Palo Alto Research Center that received attention in the CCN community [2]. CCNx provides a powerful API and a well-designed core engine called daemon. In a recent paper we have presented a way to develop name-centric services with CCNx and a

A. Mellouk et al. (Eds.): WWIC 2014, LNCS 8458, pp. 214–227, 2014.

lightweight CCN implementation for wireless sensor networks (WSN) [6]. However, one of the most basic problems for applications and services in CCN is not solved. CCNx neither provides a name configuration mechanism nor suggests a consistent naming scheme.

In this paper, we address the naming problem in a structured way from the design and development of services, via the deployment of these services on the platform until the startup of the services during runtime. Different requirements and naming parts need to be assigned during this software development life cycle.

In summary, the contributions of the paper are as follows:

- We analyze the naming problem for name-centric services in the software development life cycle for name-centric services in mixed wired wireless topologies.
- We propose a structure and hierarchy for names and introduce unsolicited names or link-local names in a naming concept.
- We present the usage of alias names and mapping at gateways at the boundaries between wired and wireless topology.
- We describe the overall concept and implementation details.

The rest of the paper is organized as follows: Section 2 presents related work for name-centric approaches and auto-configuration mechanisms. Section 3 presents background information and motivates the naming problem more specific. In Section 4 we perform a structured analysis of the naming problem and develop the solution. Section 5 presents some implementation details with focus on the gateway between wired and wireless topologies. The gateway provides a name configuration and a name alias service. The paper concludes with a summary and a discussion of future work.

2   Related Work

This section first discusses related work on name or content-centric approaches. In the second part, we introduce automatic configuration approaches in Id-centric networks as they are related to our configuration approach for name-centric services.

A well-known approach of content-centric networking for WSN is Directed Diffusion [7]. Directed Diffusion uses an addressing scheme tightly coupled to the application. Therefore, a standardized addressing convention is hard to implement with Directed Diffusion. The same holds for SPIN [9], another content-centric networking protocol for WSN. It uses also an addressing scheme tightly coupled to the application.

The authors of "Service-Centric Networking" [4] propose a consistent naming convention for services and content. They give examples of content and service names but do not classify the parts of the name. Configuration mechanisms are not part of this work.

In the recent past, CCNx [8,2] gained attention. With CCN-WSN [12] we developed a CCNx derivate for WSN and wireless networks. In CCNx content is addressed by name not by its location or host, where it is stored. CCNx allows a maximum flexibility for names without limitations or semantics of names. However, a semantic meaning of names for name-centric services is desirable.

In Id-centric networking, configuration of addresses and networking parameters is ubiquitous. DHCP [5] is a prominent example for configuration of nodes in a network. The fact that automatic configuration is important in large networks is seen in the further development of the IP protocol. In Version 6 (IPv6) auto-configuration protocol standard [10] nodes integrate automatically in a local network.

The NFN project [11] introduces a lambda expression inspired naming scheme for functions and computation tasks. With this approach names are semantically bound to functions or tasks. Functions and computation tasks are orchestrated by concatenating the names of each function or task. Automatic name configuration for functions and computation tasks seems not to be addressed by the NFN project by now. In our current work we propose a generic naming approach and we also address the name configuration problem. Orchestration of services is not part of our current work. We briefly introduced a concept for service orchestration in [6] which goes in a similar direction as in NFN.

In summary, recent approaches in name-centric networking do not cover generic naming conventions. In our opinion, a generic naming convention is the key for automatic configuration. Our approach targets name-centric services in a mixed wired and wireless topology. To the best of our knowledge, we are the first to present a naming concept together with a configuration mechanism for service names in name-centric networks.

3   Name-Centric Services

In this section we introduce CCN and how name-centric services can be implemented with CCN. This introduction is needed to prepare for the discussion of the naming problem in the last subsection.

3.1   CCN

In content-centric networking (CCN) content is addressed by names. We will introduce only the most basic concept of CCN which are needed to understand the naming problem and our solution. More detailed information is available on CCNx technical documentation web page [1] and [12].

CCN follows a hierarchical naming scheme following the URI syntax [3]. It is recommended that the first component is a registered unique DNS name to avoid name clashes among different service providing authorities. Message types in CCN are *interests* and *content objects*. Interests request content by name. Content objects carry service responses to an interest back to the requester.

A CCN node comprises the daemon and its three storages: *Content Store* (CS), *Pending Interest Table* (PIT), and *Forward Information Base* (FIB). The daemon is the protocol processing unit. Applications using CCN communicate via the daemon using *faces*. Faces in CCNx are a generalization of an interface comparable to TCP/IP sockets. When an interest arrives, the daemon looks up the content store if it contains a content object matching the interest name. An interest name matches a content name, if the interest name equals the prefix of the content name and the prefix is the longest prefix among all compared content names (longest prefix match). If no content object matches in the content store, the pending interest table is searched. If an interest in the pending interest table matches, the incoming face of the recent interest is associated with this entry. If no entry matches, the interest is forwarded to a suitable face and an entry is created in the PIT. Content objects are sent only as a response to an interest. They are stored in a content store and arrive through faces generated by services.

3.2 Services with CCN

CCN is a powerful general purpose protocol that can be the basis for name-centric services. In [6] we introduced a name-centric service architecture. Interests can contain service requests by using so called *command marker* in CCN. Content objects contain service responses from the service provider. The advantage is that with the name-centric service oriented architecture (SOA), transparent access to services is achieved independent of their location (wireless networks or wired network in the Internet/Cloud). Our future vision is an easy-to-use SOA programming paradigm based on a name-centric service engine. For this goal, a standardization of service names is inevitable. Consequently, we propose a solution for this problem in this work.

3.3 The Naming Problem

Names in CCN can be chosen arbitrarily, following institutional or global conventions. The only restriction is that names describing the content must be unique. A typical solution to this restriction is a naming scheme according to the directory structure of a file system. The first name component is a global unique domain name. Further name components are the directory names of a file system. This name hierarchy or folder structure has contextual semantic meaning to users.

Assignment of names for services is different. Different parts of service names must be configured at different phases of the software life cycle which is not yet considered in CCN. During service development names are assigned to service methods by the developer of the service and should reflect the purpose of the method. During the service deployment in the next phase, contextual information needs to be added to the service name describing the context of the service. It is important to stress that the structure of the contextual information in a service name has not been considered in the past.

Thus, CCN does not specify any semantics on names there are no predefined valid names for limited access comparable to *link-local*, *unsolicited*, and *multi-* or *unicast* addresses. Such predefined addresses are necessary for automatic configuration and are also missing in name-centric networks.

A second severe problem with CCN naming is that names are usually verbose. Verbose names are useful for humans but not for resource constrained wireless devices. Verbose names waste memory on constrained devices and messages sent over wireless links become considerably large wasting bandwidth and energy. Name components can be mapped to shorter name components for example at the transition from the wired to the wireless network. For mapped name components, it is necessary that they preserve the shortlex order of names as explained in the CCNx technical documentation [1]. The shortlex order of names is necessary because in CCN a content object with the longest prefix match on the name is returned in response to a request. Well-known compression techniques for strings will not work because they do not preserve shortlex ordering. An important additional requirement is that this mapping must be generated a runtime without reconfiguring whole service names and content object names in the wireless network.

4   Naming Approach for Name-Centric Services

In order to solve the naming problem introduced in Section 3.3 systematically we introduce and analyze the software development life cycle for name-centric services with the focus on service names. Then, we present our naming concept for name-centric services. We conclude this section with a discussion of the necessary architectural changes of the basic architecture of wireless networks integrated in the wired Internet.

4.1   Life Cycle for Name-Centric Services

One can compare the software development life cycle of name-centric services to the software development life cycle of distributed applications running on an office PC of a company. In this life cycle of an application different institutions are involved. First a software manufacturer develops the application software. This software is then deployed by an IT-support company according to the wishes of the end-user. Finally, the end-user integrates the PC with the software in his company network. In summary, the life cycle can be roughly divided into three phases. The same life cycle phases exist for name-centric services in a wireless network, depicted in Figure 1.

During the first phase named *service development* a manufacturer–service developing institution—assigns names for commands or methods of services. The second phase is the *service deployment* where services are deployed to the wireless devices for example by another institution. Services on a wireless device can be grouped into categories during this service deployment phase. During the third phase named *service integration*, the "end-user" deploys the wireless devices and

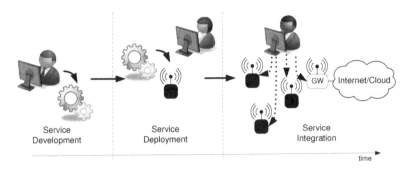

Fig. 1. Life Cycle of Wireless Devices

configures the gateway and thus, integrates the services in the company's wireless network. Deployment and configuration is depicted as dotted arrows in Figure 1. Each of the phases introduced above will assign parts of a name for our service. In the next section we will introduce a concept that will reflect this assignment of the names in the different phases.

4.2 Naming Concept for Service

In this section we develop the naming concept for services by a dedicated example. The example is based on the following name: `/fh-luebeck.de/building-18 /floor-2/room-14` This name addresses services on a sensor node placed on university campus of Lübeck University of Applied Sciences, building 18, second floor, room 14. The first component is a global unique domain name of the institution. Further components address the *site*. The addressing scheme for sites follows an individual institutional naming scheme. In this example the site describes a physical location on a campus but a site can be any generic, logical addressing as well.

As a suffix of the site addressing components we propose one or more components which semantically group the category of services. This can be for example "climate" describing a category of climate related services like temperature and humidity. The last component of the service name is a command beginning with a command marker. For details of command marker we refer to the CCNx technical documentation [1] due to space restrictions here. A command represents a service method (see [6]).

Domain name, site, category of service, and command together form a *fully-qualified service name* (e.g. `/fh-luebeck.de/building-18/floor-2/room-14 /climate/%C1.de.manufacturer.sensors.humidity`).

Each life cycle phase (see Figure 1) maps to a part of a service name. Figure 2 shows three parts of the service name and the phase in the life cycle where they are assigned.

During service development the so called *manufacturer-provided service name* is assigned. A manufacturer—service developing institution—assigns names for

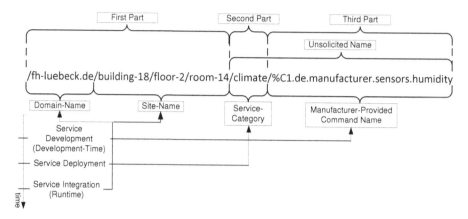

Fig. 2. Example Service Name

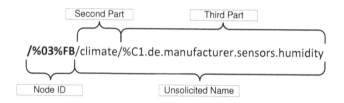

Fig. 3. Example Link-Local Service Name

commands or methods. Manufacturer-provided command names are the *third part* of the service name.

During service deployment, services are deployed on the node and grouped together in categories. These names of the categories are the *second part* of the service name.

With the second and the third part of the name set, services are accessible but only in a local network, not in the name-centric Internet. We term service names with second and third part set *unsolicited service names* (see Figure 2 for an example). There are maybe many nodes with the same unsolicited service name in a local network. It is not clear which node answers a request with an unsolicited service name.

To send a request to a node with a certain node-Id in a local network, a so called *link-local name* is necessary. A link local name is the unsolicited service name prefixed by a name component representing the node-Id (see Figure 3 for an example). The node-Id in the first component is highlighted. The so called *link-local name service* on a node answers requests addressed to link-local names. At first glance, link-local names contradict to the name-centric paradigm but nodes are entities like services and therefore, they should be addressable by CCN. Furthermore, link-local names are necessary for configuration and maintenance.

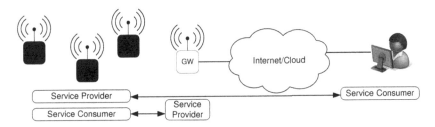

Fig. 4. Overview of the Architecture

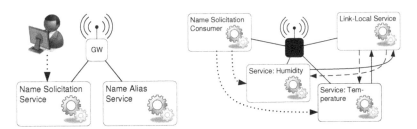

Fig. 5. Gateway Architecture   **Fig. 6.** Sensor Node Architecture

The *first part* of a service name consists of *domain* and *site* name. It is assigned by the "end-user" institution who runs a wireless network. This institution integrates ready-to-use nodes in the company's wireless network and configures the first part of the service name. A name with first part (domain and site name), second part, and third part set is a fully-qualified service name. Note that only services with a fully-qualified service name are accessible from the name-centric Internet

4.3   Architecture

In the last sections we introduced name-centric services as well as the naming concept for these services with focus on wired and wireless networking topologies. In this part of the work we describe the system architecture for our suggested solution. Figure 4 depicts the wired and wireless devices as well as the name-centric services running on these devices. Wireless devices, for example sensor nodes, provide services to give consumers actual context information about real-world phenomenon via the Internet/Cloud. For the naming-concept suggested in this work the architecture needs to be extended by additional services for configuration and the support for link-local names. We will explain the services for the most important device in the architecture namely the gateway that connects the wired and wireless topology first.

Gateway. The gateway ("gw") provides transition between wired/wireless networks and it provides services to the wireless network (see Figure 4). For this purpose the gateway performs a protocol conversion from the wired to the wireless protocol and vice versa for each service request and service response.

The gateway additionally provides the important configuration services to the name-centric wireless network. The *name solicitation service* provides name configuration for the third phase of our life cycle during the runtime of the name-centric service. In Figure 5 the gateway runs such a name solicitation service. Additionally, a *name alias service* for mapping verbose names from the Internet to alias names used in the wireless network topology runs on this gateway. We will explain details of these services in the next section.

Wireless Devices. Figure 6 shows the extended architecture of a wireless device. In the middle of Figure 6 the wireless device and around software components like services or service consumers are depicted. This software is executed on the wireless device (indicated by solid lines in Figure 6).

Counter-clockwise the service solicitation consumer, services for sensor data (humidity and temperature), and link-local service are depicted.

The name solicitation service configures the first part of the service names during service integration. Before the wireless devices can be integrated the name solicitation service has to be configured by the institution who operates the wireless network (dotted arrow in Figure 6). Details of the name solicitation service will be explained in Section 5.2.

The link-local service receives service link-local named requests over the network. If the first component matches the node-Id from the wireless device, the link-local service sends a request with the unsolicited service name to the local services (dashed arrows in Figure 6). One of the services on the node responds and sends a response back to the link-local service (solid arrows in Figure 6). The link-local service then adds the node-Id to the response and forwards it on the wireless network.

5   Implementation

In this section we describe some implementation aspects of the naming concept introduced in the previous sections. We start with the gateway implementation. Then, we describe the implementation of the *name solicitation service* and *name alias service* in more detail. As our current work is in a preliminary state we cannot present a quantitative evaluation.

5.1   Gateway

In contrast to many monolithic approaches our gateway is implemented as modular collection of individual services which provides a high degree of flexibility. All services are implemented as *CCN applications*. CCN applications communicate with each other via the CCN daemon exchanging requests and replies as shown in Figure 7. On the left side the CCN daemon is depicted. On the right side, name solicitation and name alias service are shown as an example.

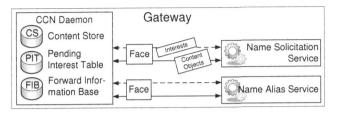

Fig. 7. Schematic Overview of the Gateway

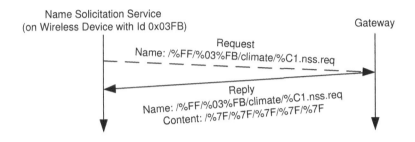

Fig. 8. Message Exchange during Name Solicitation

Our gateway is based on the Java CCNx implementation [2]. Consequently gateway services are implemented in Java where each service is a collection of Java classes. To enable the gateway the CCNx daemon has to be started first and then the services.

The gateway hardware comprises a low power industrial PC with Intel Atom 1.6 GHz CPU, 1 GB DDR2 RAM, and a 30 GB solid state hard disk running Windows operating system. For communication with the wireless sensor nodes the gateway contains an IEEE 802.15.4 transceiver attached to a USB port.

5.2   Name Solicitation Service

The name solicitation service listens for requests sent from the name solicitation consumers in the wireless network. On the gateway the name solicitation service responds with the first part of the service name. Message exchange between a wireless device and the gateway is shown in a path-time diagram in Figure 8.

A name solicitation request from a name solicitation consumer from a wireless device with Id 0x03FB has the name /%FF/%03%FB/climate/%C1.nss.req. Requests from name solicitation consumers are broadcasted through the network. The first component %FF is the service name for the name solicitation service. Then, a component containing the node-Id and a component containing the service category (second part of the service name) follows. The last component is the service method for name requests (req) of the name solicitation service (nss).

To assign the first part of service name to a service, the name solicitation service needs to know the first part of the service name. The first part is configured in an XML file which is stored in the configuration section of the gateway in a file which is read by the name solicitation service during startup. Listing 1 shows an example XML configuration for two wireless devices. Node 0x03FB runs climate monitoring services and node 0x03FC runs services for light and window control. The grouping of tags—from general-to-specific—follows the form general-to-specific semantics of the service name.

Listing 1. XML Name Solicitation Configuration

```
<Configuration>
 <Domain name="fh-luebeck.de">
  <Site name="building-18">
   <Site name="floor-02">
    <Site name="room-14">
     <LinkLocal name="%03%FB">
      <Category name="climate"/>
     </LinkLocal>
     <LinkLocal name="%03%FC">
      <Category name="light"/>
      <Category name="window"/>
     </LinkLocal>
    </Site>
   </Site>
  </Site>
 </Domain>
</Configuration>
```

With the information the name solicitation service gets from the name solicitation consumer the necessary information can retrieved from the configuration file. The first part of the name for services under the category "climate" of node 0x03FB is /fh-luebeck.de/building-18/floor-2/room-14.

5.3 Alias Service

Verbose service names are a problem in wireless networks as discussed in Section 3.3. Therefore, a mapping is implemented between the verbose name of the wired topology and an alias name used in the wireless topology. These alias names are only used in the wireless network exclusively. At the gateway the alias service maps verbose names to alias names and vice versa.

A mapping of a verbose name to an alias is stored in a dictionary or hash map. To ensure that the aliases follow the shortlex order of names a simple scheme consisting of numbers can be used as aliases and assigned to the verbose names accordingly. For example, the name "my-verbose-name" maps to alias "1" and name "my-other-verbose-name" maps to alias "2". In this simple example the aliases follow the shortlex ordering of CCN. This is because in shortlex order "my-verbose-name" comes before "my-other-verbose-name" and "1" comes before "2".

The mapping presented above is not extendable if the aliases should follow name shortlex ordering. For example if one want to add the name "my-verbose-name-two" to the dictionary containing "my-verbose-name" and "my-other-verbose-name". This name is placed according to the canonical ordering between "my-verbose-name" and "my-other-verbose-name". The mapping of "my-other-verbose-name" has to be changed to alias "3" because "my-verbose-name-two" now maps to alias "2".

Therefore, we implemented an algorithm for the alias service, that maps the names to alias numbers independently and allows adding new aliases at runtime while the aliases follow the name shortlex ordering.

This basic algorithm is shown in pseudo code style in Listing 2. To insert a new name in the dictionary addAlias(name,MAX_NUMBER/2,0,MAX_NUMBER) is called, where MAX_NUMBER is the largest number assigned for aliases. The dictionary is a collection of tuples (alias, name).

Listing 2. Algorithm for adding Alias Numbers

```
addAlias(name, piv, lo, up) {
 tempName = dictionary.alias(piv)
 if (tempName == "") {
  dictionary.add(piv, name)
  SUCCEEDED
 }
 if (lo >= up || lo + 1 == up) {
  FAILED: "Number-Range exceeded!"
 }
 if (tempName > name) {
  addAlias(name,(lo + piv)/2,lo,piv)
 } else if (tempName < name) {
  addAlias(name,(up + piv)/2,piv,up)
 } else {
  FAILED: "Name already inserted!"
 }
}
```

The algorithm fails, if the range of numbers exceeds. The efficiency of the alias number assignment depends on the sequence the names are inserted into the system.

It is possible to add aliases to each component of a service name independently under consideration of the position in the service name. This works because components of service names follow a tree hierarchy. An example tree hierarchy is shown in Figure 9. An alias—shown as hexadecimal number above each node—is mapped for each component in that tree. Numbers on edges in the tree graph

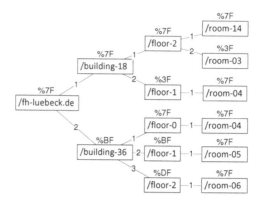

Fig. 9. Service Name Tree

Figure 9 indicate the time the components were configured. For example, service name /fh-luebeck.de/building-18/floor-2/room-14 maps to /%7F/%7F /%7F/%7F.

The name solicitation service requests the aliased service name during name solicitation and assigns the aliased name to the service. If a request from the Internet is received at the gateway, the alias service maps the service name to the shorter alias service name and forwards it to the wireless network.

Advantages of the alias algorithm are that new components can be added without changing the aliases of the other components. This is beneficial if names are configured ad-hoc and the sequence of the names is not known in advance. Furthermore, alias names do not need explicitly configured, and alias names follow the canonical order of the aliased names. One drawback is that only a limited number of names can be aliased.

6   Conclusion and Further Work

In this work, we motivated the need and the advantages of name-centric services based on concepts of content-centric networking (CCN). However, the problem of naming is neither solved for CCN nor for name-centric services. Therefore, we developed and introduced a solution to the naming problem based on an analysis of the software development life cycle of name-centric services for wired and wireless topologies. The naming concept divides a service name into several name parts which are assigned at different phases of the service development and deployment. The implementation of a name solicitation service running on the gateway between the wired and the wireless topologies shows the configuration mechanism of service names during runtime. Additionally, an alias service maps verbose names to short-length alias names in wireless networks and thereby demonstrates the flexibility and benefits of this naming approach. The name solicitation service is about to be finished on the gateway. In the future we will implement service orchestration and an exemplary application together with a name-centric service engine and provide evaluation results on our sensor network testbed.

Acknowledgments. This work was funded by the Federal Ministry of Education & Research of the Federal Republic of Germany (17PNT017, DataCast) and the Federal Ministry for Economic Affairs & Energy (035SX361C, BOSS). The authors alone are responsible for the content of this work.

References

1. CCNx Project: CCNx Technical Documentation,
   `http://www.ccnx.org/releases/latest/doc/technical/`
2. CCNx Project: Homepage, `http://www.ccnx.org/`
3. Berners-Lee, T., Fielding, R., Masinter, L.: Uniform Resource Identifiers (URI): Generic Syntax (1998)
4. Braun, T., Hilt, V., Hofmann, M., Rimac, I., Steiner, M., Varvello, M.: Service-Centric Networking. In: 2011 IEEE International Conference on Communications Workshops (ICC), pp. 1–6 (2011)
5. Droms, R.: Dynamic Host Configuration Protocol. RFC 2131 (Draft Standard) (March 1997), `http://www.ietf.org/rfc/rfc2131.txt`, updated by RFCs 3396, 4361, 5494, 6842
6. Hellbrück, H., Teubler, T., Fischer, S.: Name-Centric Service Architecture for Cyber-Physical Systems (Short Paper). In: 2013 6th IEEE International Conference on Service-Oriented Computing and Applications, SOCA. p. tbd (2013)
7. Intanagonwiwat, C., Govindan, R., Estrin, D.: Directed Diffusion: A Scalable and Robust Communication Paradigm for Sensor Networks. In: Proceedings of the 6th Annual International Conference on Mobile Computing and Networking, MobiCom 2000, pp. 56–67 (2000)
8. Jacobson, V., Smetters, D.K., Thornton, J.D., Plass, M.F., Briggs, N.H., Braynard, R.L.: Networking Named Content. In: Proceedings of the 5th International Conference on Emerging Networking Experiments and Technologies, CoNEXT 2009, pp. 1–12. ACM, New York (2009)
9. Kulik, J., Heinzelman, W., Balakrishnan, H.: Negotiation-Based Protocols for Disseminating Information in Wireless Sensor Networks. Wirel. Netw. 8(2/3), 169–185 (2002)
10. Narten, T.: Neighbor Discovery and Stateless Autoconfiguration in IPv6. IEEE Internet Computing 3(4), 54–62 (1999), `http://dx.doi.org/10.1109/4236.780961`
11. Tschudin, C., Sifalakis, M.: Named functions and cached computations. In: 11th Annual IEEE Consumer Communications and Networking Conference (to appear, 2014)
12. Zhong, R., Hail, M.A., Hellbrück, H.: CCN-WSN - A lightweight, flexible Content-Centric Networking Protocol for Wireless Sensor Networks. In: 2013 IEEE Eighth International Conference on Intelligent Sensors, Sensor Networks and Information Processing (IEEE ISSNIP 2013), Melbourne, Australia (April 2013)

Predicting Queueing Delays in Delay Tolerant Networks with Application in Space

Nikolaos Bezirgiannidis and Vassilis Tsaoussidis

Space Internetworking Center,
Democritus University of Thrace, Greece
{nbezirgi,vtsaousi}@ee.duth.gr

Abstract. In this paper we present a study of queueing delays experienced in Delay Tolerant Networks with topology based on deterministic contact plan schedules. We examine a generic scenario and propose a sampling procedure that extracts measurements of queueing rates and queue lengths. Sampling queueing information is transmitted to network nodes, which then form time series and can be used to forecast future queueing rates. Through simulations we show that the introduced method can be useful for DTNs with predetermined contact schedules, such as the Interplanetary Internet, providing accurate end-to-end delivery delay predictions.

Keywords: Delay Tolerant Networking, Queueing Delay, Interplanetary Internet, Space Communications, Contact Graph Routing.

1 Introduction

Although transmission rates in space communications increase, space application data increase even faster: high-quality images and vast volumes of telemetry data are expected to be delivered daily. Therefore, data volumes transmitted may increase disproportionally to the number of launched space assets. Beyond that, space assets cannot be upgraded to match the evolution of network bandwidth capacity. Therefore, queueing delay, which is in essence the waiting time until all data ahead of the current data item is forwarded, becomes significant in space, for three main reasons: first, it can become a considerable part of the total delay in planetary networks where propagation delay is not prohibitive; second, in networks with common disruptions, as in space environments, even a small queueing delay may lead to the loss of a transmission opportunity, thus postponing the data transmission for a significant amount of time until line-of-sight and transmission opportunity have returned; third, by observing queueing lengths and delays we can foresee when the space asset resources (e.g., buffer space) may be exhausted, which could be a potential disaster for some space applications.

In this work, we attempt to predict queueing delay in Delay-Tolerant Networks (DTNs). DTN [11] has been designated as the technology of choice for

A. Mellouk et al. (Eds.): WWIC 2014, LNCS 8458, pp. 228–242, 2014.

inter-agency cross-support operations, Solar System Internet (SSI) [1] and deep-space missions. In [2] we have made a preliminary step towards predicting the delivery time of a bundle (i.e., DTN Protocol Data Unit [8]) by presenting a method to forecast propagation and transmission delay in data transmissions, assuming high data priority and therefore zero queueing delay. The latter, however, can be an important component of the total delay and its calculation may be really challenging, especially in complex topologies where a number of nodes are transmitting data concurrently.

In this context, we examine a generic scenario and study the outbound queue of a network node that receives unicast data simultaneously and/or successively from a number of nodes and enqueues it in an outbound queue for transmission to the next node. Even though the production and delivery rates of data cannot be foreseen, past measurements include valuable information that can assist in estimation of the corresponding future rates via time-series forecasting. The rationale for this argument is that, in space environments, data transmission flows follow a time-dependent scheme, since: a) mission data availability follows a time-dependent (rather than random) pattern, b) periodicity is imposed by planet rotations, satellite orbital movements and occasional high or low data rate passes [14], and c) linear dependency is inflicted by spaceship movements, as well as linearly evolving space weather phenomena. In a similar way, the authors in [5] use a time series to accurately model the requests received by a www server.

We present a simple method in which all nodes extract queueing rate measurements in a per-contact (i.e., per-transmission opportunity) granularity. Extracted measurements are then disseminated to all neighbours, and are stored in each node's contact plan, composing different time series between each pair of network nodes. The available time series information are then used to forecast future queueing rates and the predictions are combined with the contact plan schedules to estimate the queueing delay for the bundles to be transmitted. We evaluate the proposed method through simulations with different sets of parameters and the results show that it provides accurate information of the queueing delay, thus improving the overall precision of the estimated end-to-end bundle delivery delay.

The introduced method is, to the best of our knowledge, the first work to attempt a forecast of queueing delays in deterministic DTNs (including Space DTNs) with topologies based on contact plans. Although it was designed to apply in space internetworks, it may also cover other contact-plan-based DTNs in a similar way. Our technique can be used as a standalone tool to provide accurate information on the end-to-end delivery delays in transport- or service-layer protocols of the DTN stack (e.g. [16], [17]). It can also be incorporated into the administrative Bundle Delivery Time Estimation tool [2], to enhance the prediction of the total delay required for a bundle to reach its destination.

The rest of the paper is structured as follows: In Section 2 we discuss a number of related studies on queueing delay, both in earlier internetworks and in DTNs. In Section 3 we briefly present the space internetworking background which is used as the base for our analysis, and in section 4 we present our approach, including the generic scenario that we target, and the methods we use for measurements extraction, information dissemination, and forecasting. In section 5 we describe the simulation methodology that we used, and in section 6 we present the simulation results. In section 7 we discuss the possible ways to extend our method, and, finally, we conclude the paper in Section 8.

2   Related Work

Packet queueing delay in computer networks has been concerning the scientists since the early stages of Internet, and numerous research papers have been published on the topic. In as early as 1985, Takagi and Kleinrock [20] study a CSMA-CD system and analytically calculate the average queueing delay of packets. In 1989, Demers et al. [9] suggest the use of the average queueing delay as a metric to control traffic in datagram networks, as opposed to flow control algorithms. End-to-end delay of Internet packets has also been thoroughly studied in the past 30 years. Bolot [6] analyses end-to-end packet delay using a probing process and discusses, among others, the queueing delay distribution. In the same context, Karam and Tobagi [15] discuss voice traffic over the Internet and emphasize the queueing component of the delay, as the only source of jitter, whereas Garetto and Towsley [12] study TCP traffic generated by file transmissions and its significant impact on queueing delays in the Internet.

In the DTN paradigm, on the other hand, queueing delay modelling and analysis differ from Internet-based internetworks. The main motivation for scientists to study queue lengths and the corresponding delays in DTNs has been their impact in routing efficiency. In [13], the authors present and compare different source routing algorithms based on the amount of knowledge that is available at the transmission initiation node. They exalt the knowledge of queueing occupancies in network nodes and state that, amongst all "oracles" that provide different types of information, (e.g., contact plan, buffer/queueing occupancies, traffic demand), the "queueing oracle" is the most difficult to realize, in order to achieve a complete knowledge of the queue occupancies in network nodes. In [10], a DTN-based link-state algorithm is applied on wireless networks in developing regions. The used link information includes queue occupancy, among others, and routing decisions incorporate the queueing delay that is calculated based on the most recent cached copy of the link information. Queueing delay has also been used as part of a performance metric in [19]; Seligman et al. propose a DTN routing scheme with push and pull functions and measure its congestion control effectiveness with a time-weighted network storage metric. This metric is the product of the storage used by all queued messages and the amount of time they remain queued.

In the typical routing algorithm that targets Interplanetary Internet, namely Contact Graph Routing (CGR - [7]), the arrival time computation does not take into account the queueing component of the delivery latency. In [3] we have proposed a modification of the CGR algorithm with the use of Earliest

Transmission Opportunity (ETO) parameter, which incorporates the available information on already enqueued data in the computation of bundle delivery delay. Queue information for the local node's outducts (based only on already queued bundles) are incorporated in the delivery delay estimation and can be disseminated to other network nodes via Contact Plan Update Protocol (CPUP). However, queue length increase will generate a CPUP message only when it exceeds some predefined threshold and the message is transmitted only when there are available contact opportunities before information gets obsolete. Therefore, ETO updates with CPUP might sometimes prove inadequate for timely updates and, thus, queue length information through the path to destination might be inaccurate. In this work we exploit the queue length information in the local outducts as introduced in [3] and we move a step forward: besides measuring queue lengths, we attempt to forecast future queueing rates and delays. In section 6, the reactive computation of queueing delays with the use of CPUP is compared to its proactive equivalent with the use of forecasting, introduced in this work.

3   Background

The future SSI Architecture, which is a fundamental part of our analysis, involves cooperation of different agencies under a common framework. The overlay layer protocol that attempts to unify different internetworks and infrastructures (e.g., Interplanetary Network, Near-Earth Network, Deep-Space Network, satellite communications, planetary surface networks including the Internet, ad-hoc or opportunistic networks, etc.) is the Bundle Protocol (BP) [18]. A bundle, the BP's protocol data unit of operation, is created whenever an application initiates a data unit transmission the next neighbour is selected by the routing algorithm to forward it. The bundle is then enqueued in the outbound queue that corresponds to the selected neighbouring node and to the bundle's priority, until the underlying convergence layer protocol [18] initiate its transmission. Consecutively received bundles that are routed to the same neighbour are being enqueued in the same outbound queue, provided they have the same priority. BP comprises three different priority classes, namely bulk, normal and expedited, which characterize bundles according to the application service requirements. These classes suggest a relative prioritization that forwarding policies take into consideration to decide on the bundle to be forwarded.

In space environments, communication is not always possible between any two nodes. It requires line-of-sight between the space assets, as well as adequate provisioning by the owner agency, since for example ground stations are responsible for receiving data from multiple space missions and the distinct reception intervals for each mission have to be configured in advance. The transmission opportunities among the network nodes are also referred to as *contacts* and the complete list of future contacts form the *contact plan*. A typical space contact plan follows a periodic pattern due to the periodic nature of space asset movements.

Routing decisions for next neighbour has not been standardized yet in the framework of SSI operations. However, basic routing functionality involves the exploitation of the detailed knowledge of contacts amongst space assets well in advance [7]. A space internetwork topology is thus deterministic and configured using a contact plan, and BP routing decisions are based on the predefined contact schedules. Our method covers all networks that exhibit such predictability and base routing decisions on contact plan configurations; in this context, it may apply to other forms of disruptive internetworks as well.

The sampling procedures and queue information extraction can be part of the DTN management framework, in the context of instrumentation statistics that are periodically taken from all network nodes in order to examine the health of space assets and avoid system malfunctions. The dissemination of the extracted information can be achieved either via DTNMP [4] or with CPUP [3], both protocols compatible with the DTN architecture.

4   Queueing Delay Estimation Method

4.1   Generic Scenario

We study the queues and queueing delays in a BP outduct queue by considering a generic scenario with topology as depicted in Fig. 1. In this topology, N sender nodes are transmitting data to destination node D via node A. Thus all data sent from nodes $1, 2, ..., N$ to D or beyond need to be stored in the relay node A and then forwarded to D. This store-and-forward procedure inevitably imposes extra waiting time for any bundle enqueued in the outduct from A to D, until all previously enqueued bundles are forwarded. The corresponding generic contact plan is illustrated in Fig. 2, where a single period of transmission opportunities is depicted. The period starts from the end of the previous $A - D$ contact and ends at the next $A - D$ contact. Note that nodes $1 - N$ may have more than one communication opportunity with A during a cycle. Our primary interest is in the bundle queueing delay and, consequently, in the total end-to-end bundle delivery latency, from bundle creation time until arrival at destination D. We initially consider a simple case where all bundles are transmitted with equal priority and, thus, there is a single outbound queue for the A-D outduct.

4.2   Queueing Rate Measurements and Dissemination

In order to study the queue length and all queueing rates through time, we apply a sampling process in a per-contact granularity. When a contact from node k to A ends, the number of bytes that arrived over this contact and were enqueued for delivery to D are counted. This amount is then divided by the contact duration to obtain the average queueing rate r_{kAD} that node k imposes into outduct $A - D$. Note that this queueing rate typically differs from the $k - A$ transmission rate, due to transmission and retransmission overhead and since some of the delivered bundles may not be forwarded to this outduct to D. Furthermore, upon the end

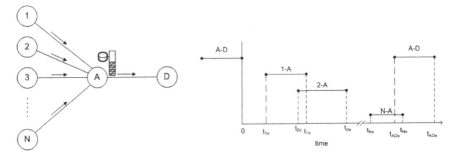

Fig. 1. Scenario Topology   **Fig. 2.** Contact Plan

of the $A - D$ contact, node A calculates the remaining queue length $Qrem_{AD}$ at the specific outduct. Information about the extracted queueing rates and the remaining queue is transmitted to all neighbouring nodes other than the outduct destination (i.e. D in this example) at the next available opportunity, via CPUP. The dissemination mechanism of CPUP is responsible to relay the information PDUs to all network nodes. In our two-hop scenario, PDUs are transmitted from A to nodes $1..N$ and no further transmissions occur.

Measurement granularity for the queueing rates could be improved, if sampling occurred in a number of time intervals during each contact. This would impose serious overhead, however, and would increase the complexity of historic rates management.

4.3   Prediction of Future Queueing Rates

Following the dissemination of the measurements, all network nodes have received past values of queueing rates and remaining queue lengths. The past rate values comprise a time series for each distinct pair of neighbouring links. For example, for links $k \to A$ and $A \to D$, the time series contains past average values of r_{kAD}, i.e. data transmitted during contacts $k \to A$ and enqueued in the outduct $A \to D$.

Due to the mainly deterministic and periodic nature of Space communications, we argue that the past observations can be useful to predict future values such as queueing rates, with some accuracy. Time series may incorporate periodicity and/or a linear trend. In this context, a number of different forecasting techniques might apply in our model. The procedure used in [2], for example, utilizes a triple exponential smoothing method, which incorporates possible trends and/or periodicities in the BER time series under study. In this initial work we do not focus on the optimization of the time series forecasting method, but make a first step into proving the applicability of our proposal. Therefore we choose a simple exponential moving average (EMA) forecasting method for low complexity and low processing overhead purposes. For any contact j, the EMA S_j is calculated recursively, by computing $S_j = \alpha r_j + (1 - \alpha)S_{j-1}$, where r_j is the measured rate for contact j, and α the constant smoothing parameter,

$0 < \alpha \leq 1$. The forecast rate is set equal to the EMA of the previous time step (i.e., contact): $\hat{r}_{j+1} = S_j$. In our simulations we examine different values for the smoothing parameter α, including $\alpha = 1$, which is equivalent to a random walk model. When the time series include missing values, due to delays in the arrival of information updates, the last computed EMA is reused.

Queue length at the end of contacts $A - D$, noted as $Qrem_{AD}$, also form a time series and a similar forecasting procedure applies.

4.4 Bundle Delivery Delay Calculation

The introduced method applies on the output of any contact-plan-based routing algorithm, that is the path to destination, and calculates the total delay from bundle creation time to the arrival at destination. In our generic scenario, a bundle is created in node k and the routing algorithm selects path $k \rightarrow A \rightarrow D$. The transmission from k to A comprises the following components: i) propagation delay $d_{pr.k-A}$, ii) transmission delay $d_{tr.k-A} = (bundle\_size + overhead)/Bandwidth_{k-A}$, iii) processing delay, iv) queuing delay $d_{q.k-A}$, and v) total waiting time $d_{w.k-A}$ until transmission opportunity is available. Queueing delay for the first transmission hop is calculated based on the queue information that is available for the local outduct and may exceed the duration of a single contact. Waiting time is extracted from the contact plan and may also span across more than one time periods, if the data ahead have filled the capacity of the next contact(s). In contact plans where contacts are not often, the waiting time can be the most significant part of the total delay. Based on the aforementioned delay components and assuming trivial processing delays, expected arrival time at node A is calculated as follows, if t_{cr} the bundle creation time:

$$t_{arr.A} = t_{cr} + d_{w.k-A} + d_{q.k-A} + d_{pr.k-A} + d_{tr.k-A} \tag{1}$$

For the next transmission hop, the total delay has the same, aforementioned components, with starting time equal to $t_{arr.A}$. Calculation of the queueing delay $d_{q.A-D}$ exploits the contact plan information, the queueing rates $\hat{r}_{iAD}, i = 1..N, i \neq k$, as well as the remaining data in-queue $\hat{Q}rem_{AD}$ at the end time t_0 of the most recent $A - D$ contact before $t_{arr.A}$. All these values can either be the actual measurements, if the corresponding information has already arrived at k, or the values predicted using the proposed forecasting procedure. Queueing delay for the bundle in outduct $A - D$ is computed as follows:

$$d_{q.AD} = \frac{\hat{Q}rem_{AD} + \sum_i \hat{r}_{iAD} \times \tau_i}{Bandwidth_{A-D}}, \tag{2}$$

where i represents all contacts that may cause backlog, or, in other words contacts that are active during the time interval from the end time t_0 of the last contact A-D, until the expected bundle arrival time at node A, $t_{arr.A}$, and τ_i the contacts' duration. The waiting time $d_{w.A-D}$ for the bundle is the interval between the arrival time $t_{arr.A}$ and the next available contact $A - D$, plus all intervals between consecutive $A - D$ contacts that the bundle waits in queue. Using these calculations and eq. 2, bundle arrival time at destination node D, which is the output of our method, becomes:

$$t_{arr.D} = t_{arr.A} + d_{w.A-D} + d_{q.A-D} + d_{pr.A-D} + d_{tr.A-D} \qquad (3)$$

5   Simulation Methodology

For the evaluation of our prediction method, we have used a Java discrete-event simulator designed for Space-based scenarios, used initially in [3]. Our simulator utilizes the BP functionality and different routing algorithms apply on the contact plan simulation input.

We conducted a variety of simulations with different sets of parameters and with periodic contact plans with period equal to half day and total duration equal to one week. Contacts were randomly put during this time period and followed a periodic pattern afterwards. For each set of parameters we performed 100 repetitions to have a statistically adequate sample. The topology used is the one depicted in Fig. 1, with different number of input nodes and varying parameters displayed in Table 1.

We define λ as the ratio of the sum of all first-hop $(1..N - A)$ contact volume capacities divided by the sum of all second-hop $(A - D)$ contact volume capacities:

$$\lambda = \frac{N \times r_1 \times \tau_1}{r_2 \times \tau_2}, \qquad (4)$$

where r_1 is the transmission rate of the first-hop links, r_2 is the transmission rate of the second-hop links, τ_1 is the duration of contacts $1..N - A$ and τ_2 is the duration of contacts $A - D$. The value of λ is practically the ratio of the capacities of the two transmission hops. When $\lambda > 1$, the queueing system is unstable and can potentially lead to storage exhaustion and node failures. In our simulations we have used three different values of λ, 0.1, 0.5, and 0.9 and we set $\tau_1 = 600s$. The respective durations of the second-hop contacts are calculated using (4).

We have also examined different data production levels, with respect to the maximum amount of data that each of the first N nodes can transmit during the total simulation time. Bundle creation times are uniform for the total simulation period.

In order to evaluate the prediction accuracy of our method, we measure the *Bundle Delivery Delay Prediction Error*, both as an absolute time unit (*BDDPredErr*), and as a percentage (*BDDPredErr*) of the *Bundle Delivery Delay* (*BDD*):

$$BDDPredErr = BDD - BundleDeliveryDelayEstimation \qquad (5)$$

$$NormalizedBDDPredErr = \frac{BDD - BundleDeliveryDelayEstimation}{BDD} \qquad (6)$$

Furthermore, in each simulation we calculate *RelativeOverhead*, which is the total number of bytes of the measurement information messages, divided by the total number of data payload bytes.

In the next section we provide comparisons of four different prediction methods: i)the *BDD* estimation implemented in CGR [7], mentioned also as No Forecasting ii)the delivery time estimation method that reactively exploits the queue data based on CPUP update messages presented in [3] and mentioned here as Reactive Estimation with CPUP, iii) the prediction method proposed in this work, mentioned as Forecasting with Exponential Smoothing, and iv) a prediction method similar to ours, but where there are no network updates on the queueing rates and future lengths and rates are not forecast but, instead, are set equal to the nominal link transmission rates. The latter is mentioned as Forecasting with Nominal Rate.

$$RelativeOverhead = \frac{\text{Total Overhead Bytes}}{\text{Total Data Payload Bytes}} \qquad (7)$$

Table 1. Simulation Parameters

Parameter	Value(s)
Number of Producing Nodes N	2, 5, 10, 20
Bundle Size N	64 Kbytes
Capacities Ratio λ	0.1, 0.5, 0.9
Transmission Rate $1..N - A$	64 Kbps
Transmission Rate $A - D$	512 Kbps
Propagation Delay $1..N - A$	0.01s
Propagation Delay $A - D$	1s
Contact Duration $1..N - A$	600s

6   Simulation Results

An initial observation of the simulation results was that the occurrence of the contacts during the time period had significant impact on the total bundle delivery delay. The reason for this is the fact that the most significant portion of the total bundle delivery delay was the waiting time, in the order of tens of thousands of seconds, since contacts occur twice per day. So, when a bundle arrives at A and there is enough backlog ahead, it may be queued for a period of time longer than the contact duration, and thus it has to wait for the next transmission opportunity (i.e., half a day in our simulations). We observed that, depending on the contact occurrences, the simulations were divided into two groups. In the first and most common one, all bundles were transmitted during the contacts predicted by CGR; in other words, there were no queueing delays large enough to cause any bundles to miss the transmission opportunity and wait for a total transmission cycle. In these simulations, to which we will refer from now on as *Case 1* simulations, the *BDDPredErr* (i.e. the error in bundle delivery delay prediction) does not exceed the duration of a contact, and comprises a small percentage of the total delivery delay. In the second observed group of simulations (referred to from now on as *Case 2* simulations), on the other hand, queueing delays caused loss of transmission opportunities for a portion of the transmitted bundles, resulting in a significant $BDDPredErr$.

The percentage of the *Case 2* simulations depends heavily on the number of network nodes and the contact plan. Table 2 shows the percentage of *Case 2* simulations for different number of nodes, and the corresponding average percentage of bundles (in these simulations) that miss the contact opportunities due to queueing delays.

Table 2. *Case 2* simulations as a percentage of total simulations and average percentage of bundles that missed contact opportunities, in *Case 2* simulations

N	*Case 2* Simulations (%)	Bundles that missed transmission opportunity (%)
2	3.33	24.75
5	4	7.6
10	12	6.66
20	23.67	2.42

For example, when $N = 10$, 11.33% of the conducted simulations were *Case 2*, and an average of 6.66% of the bundles in each simulation was actually transmitted during a different contact than the one that CGR predicted. Even though this percentage of bundles seems small, $BDDPredErr$ calculated by CGR approaches the time period, i.e. half day. This may have significant impact on the performance of the application or service layers residing on top of BP, such as unnecessary retransmissions due to timeout expirations and delayed in-order delivery, when the Delay-Tolerant Payload Conditioning protocol [16] is used. In Fig. 3 we present the average $BDDPredErr$ for different values of capacity ratio λ, with $N = 10$ producing nodes. The bundles that have lost a transmission window are reflected in the significant error observed in Fig. 3b, when no forecasting is used. In our simulations we have observed that both the reactive queue estimation method with CPUP, and the proactive forecasting method are able to predict this deviation for all bundles, that is 100% of the bundles for all set of parameters, resulting in a major $BDDPredErr$ decrease and resolving the aforementioned misbehaviour.

Nevertheless, due to the large fluctuation in the bundle delivery delay prediction, average values is not the most appropriate statistical function. In order to capture the whole range of prediction errors we use the $NormalizedBDDPredErr$ percentiles: all bundle delivery delay prediction errors are sorted in an ascending order and the k-th percentile corresponds to the $NormalizedBDDPredErr$ that is greater than the $k\%$ of all bundle delivery delay prediction errors. In Figures 5 and 6 we depict the $NormalizedBDDPredErr$ percentiles for sample simulations of different parameter sets, for $N = 20$ and $N = 2$, respectively. In the former (Fig. 5) we

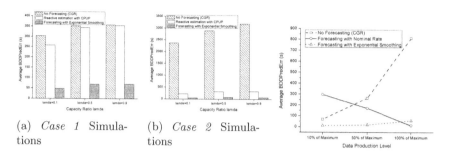

(a) *Case 1* Simula-   (b) *Case 2* Simulations   tions

Fig. 3. Average $BDDPredErr$ versus the ca-   **Fig. 4.** Average $BDDPredErr$
pacity ratio λ, with $N = 10$ versus the data production level

compare our method with CGR and a forecasting method with the use of nominal transmission rates, rather than predictions. In the latter (Fig. 6) we compare
our exponential forecasting method with CGR, and with the reactive estimation
with the use of CPUP. In Fig. 5 all algorithms achieve small prediction errors
for the majority of bundles; there is, however, a 2%-3% of the bundles that all
algorithms err. The CGR prediction error reaches 90% of the bundle delivery
delay, for the *Case 2* simulation, and 40% of the bundle delivery delay, for the
Case 1 simulation. For our exponential smoothing method, the respective errors are less than 20%, whereas the forecasting with nominal rates provides an
overall good prediction, leaving a tail of overestimation for 4 % of the bundles.
For $N = 2$ (Fig. 6), $NormalizedBDDPredErr$ is significantly improved for a
larger percentage of all bundles, with both reactive CPUP estimation and our
forecasting method. Fig. 6a shows that in a *Case 1* simulation, the prediction
accuracy can be improved with the exponential smoothing forecasting method
for all bundles. However, since the queueing component is a tiny portion of the
total end-to-end delivery delay, $NormalizedBDDPredErr$ does not exceed the
amount of 0.4%.

So far, we have used a uniform data production rate, equal to the maximum
rate that the network can serve. The prediction method with the use of nominal
transmission rates provides good accuracy, as depicted in 5. However, in cases
where network nodes produce less data than the network can serve, its performance degrades. In Fig. 4 we measure the Average $NormalizedBDDPredErr$
for different production levels, presented as a percentage of the maximum amount
of data that can be served. Although forecasting with nominal rates outperforms
the other algorithms for large data rate productions, its results for 10% of the
maximum production rate become even worse than with CGR. In our method,
despite the fact that network nodes have no prior knowledge of the production
rates of other nodes, they achieve a good estimation for all production rates, due
to the past queueing values obtained through update messages. Note that in Fig.
4, the average $BDDPredErr$ represents the mean of absolute values, whereas
in the percentiles figures we also provided the negative, overestimated values.

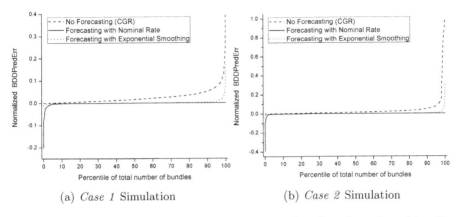

(a) *Case 1* Simulation   (b) *Case 2* Simulation

Fig. 5. *NormalizedBDDPredErr* versus the percentiles of total number of bundles for sample simulations with N=20 and λ=0.9

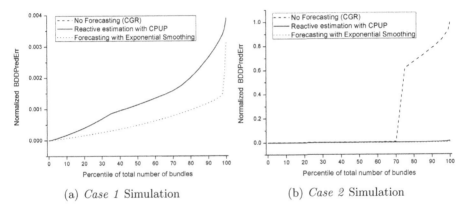

(a) *Case 1* Simulation   (b) *Case 2* Simulation

Fig. 6. *NormalizedBDDPredErr* versus the percentiles of total number of bundles for sample simulations with N=2 and λ=0.9

In Fig. 7 we illustrate the overall overhead caused by the update messages in relevance to the transmitted amounts of data payloads. The amount of overhead bytes span from 11.7 Kbytes for simulations with data transmissions of 137 Mbytes (N=2), to 818 Kbytes for simulations with data transmissions of 1.37 Gbytes (N=20).

Finally, we study the impact of the exponential smoothing parameter by using the different values $\alpha = 0.1, 0.5, 0.9, 1$. Figure 8 illustrates that the predictions are more accurate for values of α near 1, (i.e., more sensitive to changes), which shows larger dependency on the recent values than on the history observations. This behaviour is justified by the use of a uniform production rate in our simulations: the resulting transmission rates increase gradually from zero to the steady-state rate, stay there till the end of bundle productions and decrease

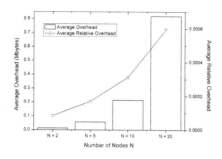
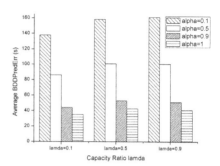

Fig. 7. Total Overhead versus the number of nodes N

Fig. 8. Average $BDDPredErr$ for different values of the smoothing parameter α, with $N = 5$

gradually to zero again. Different production rates than the uniform we used in this work might require less sensitivity to fluctuations and more weight on the history values.

7   Future Work

As mentioned in the description of our method, in this initial work we do not focus on the optimization of the queueing rates forecasting procedure. Instead, we describe the proof-of-concept and attempt an initial evaluation with a simple exponential smoothing forecasting method. A potential future expansion of our work is the analysis of different time series forecasting methods, such as triple exponential smoothing or ARMA/ARIMA, and the assessment of the trade-off between the practicality of the prediction accuracy and the computational overhead that time series calculation will impose on the energy-sensitive Space assets.

We also intend to study the performance of our method when there are bundles with different priority levels, such as the three priority classes defined in [18] (i.e., bulk, normal and expedited), For that, the proposed method should be modified with respect to the forwarding policy that is applied on the DTN nodes. With a typical routing scheme (Contact Graph Routing [7]) that defines three different outbound queues for each neighbouring node depending on bundle priorities, our method can be easily adjusted: queue lengths and queueing rates will be stored, disseminated and forecast for each of the three outbound queues separately.

Furthermore, the proposed forecasting method has not been incorporated into any contact-plan-based routing algorithm. It is merely a tool to estimate end-to-end delivery delay on the bundle route extracted by the routing algorithm. It is in our future plans to study the applicability of an optimized version of the proposed forecasting method in routing algorithm decisions, and to examine the complexity inflicted by this incorporation.

8   Conclusion

In this paper, we introduced a novel method to predict queueing rates and queueing delays in contact-plan-based DTNs with application in Space communications. Queue length statistics are extracted in a per-contact granularity and is disseminated to the network nodes. These historical data are then used to predict future queueing rates via time series forecasting and, ultimately, improve the estimation of bundle queueing delays en route to destination. Through extensive simulations we showed that it outperforms both the calculation of end-to-end delays provided in CGR and the reactive updates of queue lengths with the use of update messages, without inflicting any significant transmission overhead.

Our method can assist the configuration of higher layer protocols and services, providing a more accurate end-to-end delivery delay estimate (e.g. configuration of retransmission timers, etc.). It can also be used as an administrative tool to analyse queue length distributions and queueing delays in DTNs with deterministic contact schedules.

Acknowledgments. The research leading to these results has received funding from the European Community's Seventh Framework Programme ([FP7/2007-2013, FP7-REGPOT-2010-1, SP4 Capacities, Coordination and Support Actions) under Grant Agreement n. 264226 (Project title: Space Internetworking Center - SPICE). This paper reflects only the authors' views and the Community is not liable for any use that may be made of the information contained therein.

References

1. Sisg operations concept for ssi - final version. Interagency Operations Advisory Group, Space Internetworking Strategy Group (January 2011)
2. Bezirgiannidis, N., Burleigh, S., Tsaoussidis, V.: Delivery time estimation for space bundles. IEEE Transactions on Aerospace and Electronic Systems 49(3), 1897–1910 (2013)
3. Bezirgiannidis, N., Tsapeli, F., Diamantopoulos, S., Tsaoussidis, V.: Towards flexibility and accuracy in space dtn communications. In: ACM MobiCom CHANTS 2013, pp. 43–48. ACM, New York (2013)
4. Birrane, E., Ramachandran, V.: Delay tolerant network management protocol. Tech. rep., Delay-Tolerant Networking Research Group (2013)
5. Bolot, J.C., Hoschka, P.: Performance engineering of the world wide web: application to dimensioning and cache design. Comput. Netw. ISDN Syst. 28(7-11), 1397–1405 (1996)
6. Bolot, J.C.: End-to-end packet delay and loss behavior in the internet. In: SIGCOMM 1993, pp. 289–298. ACM, New York (1993)
7. Burleigh, S.: Contact graph routing. Tech. Rep. draft-burleigh-dtnrg-cgr-01, Network Working Group (July 2010)
8. Cerf, V., Burleigh, S., Hooke, A., Torgerson, L., Durst, R., Scott, K., Fall, K., Weiss, H.: Delay-Tolerant Networking Architecture. RFC 4838 (Informational) (April 2007), http://www.ietf.org/rfc/rfc4838.txt
9. Demers, A., Keshav, S., Shenker, S.: Analysis and simulation of a fair queueing algorithm. SIGCOMM Comput. Commun. Rev. 19(4), 1–12 (1989)

10. Demmer, M., Fall, K.: Dtlsr: delay tolerant routing for developing regions. In: NSDR 2007, pp. 5:1–5:6. ACM, New York (2007)
11. Fall, K.: A delay-tolerant network architecture for challenged internets. In: ACM SIGCOMM 2003, New York, NY, USA, pp. 27–34 (2003)
12. Garetto, M., Towsley, D.: Modeling, simulation and measurements of queuing delay under long-tail internet traffic. In: ACM SIGMETRICS 2003, pp. 47–57. ACM, New York (2003)
13. Jain, S., Fall, K., Patra, R.: Routing in a delay tolerant network. SIGCOMM Comput. Commun. Rev. 34(4), 145–158 (2004)
14. Jennings, E., Segui, J., Gao, J., Clare, L., Abraham, D.: The impact of traffic prioritization on deep space network mission traffic. In: 2011 IEEE Aerospace Conference, pp. 1–6 (2011)
15. Karam, M., Tobagi, F.: Analysis of the delay and jitter of voice traffic over the internet. In: Proceedings of IEEE INFOCOM 2001, vol. 2, pp. 824–833 (2001)
16. Papastergiou, G., Alexiadis, I., Burleigh, S., Tsaoussidis, V.: Delay tolerant payload conditioning protocol. Computer Networks 59, 244–263 (2014)
17. Papastergiou, G., Bezirgiannidis, N., Tsaoussidis, V.: On the performance of erasure coding over space dtns. In: Koucheryavy, Y., Mamatas, L., Matta, I., Tsaoussidis, V. (eds.) WWIC 2012. LNCS, vol. 7277, pp. 269–281. Springer, Heidelberg (2012)
18. Scott, K., Burleigh, S.: Bundle Protocol Specification. RFC 5050 (Experimental) (November 2007), http://www.ietf.org/rfc/rfc5050.txt
19. Seligman, M., Fall, K., Mundur, P.: Storage routing for dtn congestion control. Wireless Communications and Mobile Computing 7(10), 1183–1196 (2007)
20. Takagi, H., Kleinrock, L.: Mean packet queueing delay in a buffered two-user csma/cd system. IEEE Transactions on Communications 33(10), 1136–1139 (1985)

ICPN: An Inter-Cloud Polymorphic Network Proposal

Nihed Bahria El Asghar[1], Omar Cherkaoui[2],
Mounir Frikha[1], and Sami Tabbane[1]

[1] University of Carthage, High School of Communication of Tunisia, Tunisia,
{nihed.bahria,m.frikha,sami.tabbane}@supcom.rnu.tn
[2] University of Quebec in Montreal, Canada

Abstract. Inter-Cloud virtual machine (VM) migration is of great interest today to fulfill the applications' and services' requirements for ubiquitous resources availability anywhere and on-demand. But to migrate large volume operating systems, we will need huge network resources trough the best-effort underlying Internet. To deal with this impractical requirement, we have chosen the pre-copy migration strategy. We have proven, however, that we still need a *high bandwidth* for the beginning of the migration process and a *low latency* link for the final downtime phase. As a solution, we propose an Inter-Cloud Polymorphic Network (ICPN) design combining packet and circuit switching paradigms to meet the conflicting migrations' network requirements. To ensure the migration transparency, we propose an admission control strategy based on the VMware vMotion downtime delay value.

Keywords: Polymorphic network, inter-Cloud migration, liveliness.

1 Introduction

VM migration is a useful technology that better allocates server resources and maintains application performance. It works great in the Datacenter (DC) and it sounds to be a good idea for distributed resource management optimization and continuous availability when applied between DCs. Multiple use cases (outlined in Tab.1) can justify the need for an Inter-Cloud Migration (ICM).

In practice, this is not as simple as it sounds. A huge volume of workload, with specific characteristics, should be transferred via the best-effort Internet. The main inhibiting factors for the process of an ICM are (1) the migrated data characteristics and (2) the network characteristics (Tab. 2). In the context of seamless migration requirement, the migration should be processed as fast as the VM's user cannot perceive it. In case of insufficient network resources and/or fickle migrated data, the migration process will never end, and all the existing traffic will suffer the consequences. From a network perspective, a transparent VM migration means that the source and destination VMs' IP addresses remain unchangeable so that the migrated VM is indistinguishable from the original when the migration is achieved. While this is easily achieved in a shared LAN

A. Mellouk et al. (Eds.): WWIC 2014, LNCS 8458, pp. 243–256, 2014.

Table 1. Inter-Datacenter VM migration use cases

Use case	Description	Need for ICM
Outages [1]	Complete DC outages: - Planned (maintenance) - Unplanned (disasters)	When the whole site is damaged, we need to move the data to another DC
Cloudbursting [2], [3]	Resources in an enterprise network are augmented with resources in "the cloud"	Workloads are migrated from the enterprise DC to the provider's DC when they exceed the available resources
Follow-the-sun [2]	Teams, spanning multiple continents, are collaborating on a common project	Workloads are moved from one DC to another based on time of the day

environment (by means of VLANs), extending Layer-2 connectivity to WAN environment is a real challenge since different Datacenters and Cloud sites support different IP address spaces.

Table 2. Practical constraints of ICM

(1)Migrated data	- Huge volume - Fickle and unpredictable
(2)Network	- High latency - Low available bandwidth - reconfigurable (change in IP addresses)
(3)Migration process	- Must be fast/seamless - Must have an end / finish

Table 2 summarizes the practical constraints of inter-Cloud VM migration. It indicates that for seamless ICM, two features should be addressed :

1. Reduce the volume of data to be transferred;
2. Provide a convenient "layer-2", low latency and high bandwidth WAN network.

The first point has been over-much studied for intra-Datacenter migrations (cf. sub-sec 2.2). We will show later that some proposed solutions could be applied to inter-Cloud context. However, to our knowledge, there is no prior work addressing the networking requirements evoked above, for seamless inter-Cloud migration (ICM). Our concern in this paper is to propose a network that can meet both bandwidth and latency requirements of the ICM and preserve VM's IP address. It will be a utility network or, in other words, a network as a service.

Our proposal is based on a new characterization of the migrated traffic pattern; that will be the object of section 3. This characterization is based on the state-of-the-art outlined in section 2. Our inter-Cloud network service solution, responding to the latter elaborated requirements, will be introduced in section 4. Finally, the evaluation of our proposition using OMNET++ simulator will be drawn in section 5.

2   Background and Related Work

In this section, we are giving an insight on the different enabling techniques for the live VMs migration when those span a wide area network for inter-Datacenters interoperability. We will start with an overview of some proposed interconnecting infrastructures adapted for the WAN migration case. A state-of-the-art on migration algorithms is given in the second subsection.

2.1   Inter-Cloud Network Platforms

A critical network design requirement for deployment of distributed Cloud computing environment is to have all servers (even if they belong to different Cloud providers) in the same layer-2 virtual network. Cisco was a leader to propose a proprietary solution for this case. Then, some research groups have proposed and/or tested other methods to federate the Clouds:

Cisco OTV Datacenter Interconnect Platform [4] is the new Datacenter interconnect (DCI) solution that Cisco have developed on their Cisco Nexus 7000 Series Switches. It's based on MAC routing scheme. Each Cisco Nexus 7000 series aggregation switch maintains a MAC-address table for every device across the Cisco OTV domain. When a Cisco OTV edge device identifies a layer-2 frame targeted for a remote destination, it encapsulates the frame in an IP packet and transmits it across the layer-3 network. After it arrives at the remote Datacenter, its edge device entraps the layer-2 frame and seamlessly forward it to its ultimate destination. This provides an overlay that enables layer-2 connectivity between separate layer-2 domains while keeping these domains independent [5].

F5&VMware Datacenter-to-Cloud Network [6]. This solution moves vMotion from the binds of the local Datacenter (DC) and enables live migration of both VMs and the back-end storage across the WAN between DCs and Clouds. It is based on BIG-IP solutions. An iSessions tunnel is first set-up between the DCs creating the infrastructure to support the storage and VMs migrations. After successful completion of the vMotion migration event to the secondary DC, the primary DC will start routing existing connections through the iSessions tunnel to the VM now running at the secondary DC. As the remaining user connections naturally terminate, all application traffic will be directly routed to the secondary DC. A re-registration to the secondary DC management tool is required. The IP addresses in the primary DC can be reclaimed and reused for other applications.

CloudNet Platform [7]. Focusing on a way to manage enterprises' resources across Datacenters, Wood et al. [7] propose CloudNet, a Cloud platform architecture which utilizes virtual private networks to securely and seamlessly link Cloud and enterprise sites.

Dynamic and Distributed Cloud Infrastructure [8]. This infrastructure proposes first to leverage virtualization and multiple Cloud Computing infrastructures to build distributed large scale computing platforms. They experiment using the ViNe [9] virtual network overlay and the Nimbus [10] IaaS (*Infrastructure-as-a-Service*) Cloud toolkit.

All the above proposed inter-Clouds enabling architectures focus primary on the manner to provide a layer-2 virtual/overlay network in order to translate the layer-3 WAN problem into a layer-2 LAN problem. None has explained how this infrastructure could support at least one of the state-of-the-art migration algorithms. In our work, we deeply believe that the migration network platform is closely linked to the migration process. A summary statement of the most cited migration algorithms is given in the next subsection.

2.2 VM Migration Algorithms

In order to migrate a virtual machine, all its state should be transferred from source to destination host. A VM's state consists of its memory/storage and CPU. The researchers community propose some ideas for live storage and memory migration. Particularly, J. G. Hansen and E. Jul [11] use *shared disk storage* for intra-Cloud VM migration in order to reduce the amount of data to be transferred and therefore reduce migration and downtime delays. In the case of inter-Cloud migration (ICM), however, this approach cannot achieve the maximum availability of VM hosting services, due to unexpected failures in storage servers and WAN latencies. T. Hirofuchi et al. [12] have, however, focused on the use of shared storage for live migration over the WAN. They proposed xNBD, a proxy for VM storage relocation based on blocks caching. To read a not-yet-cached block, the destination host proxy fetches the block from the source disk, returns the block to the VM and saves it to local storage. This will consume huge storage capacity since the source storage should remain intact until it is entirely relocated to the destination site. Furthermore, the authors have dealt only with storage migration and have not focused on CPU and dirtied pages transfer; discarding the liveliness problem of a VM migration.

In [13] and [14], the authors propose freeze-and-copy, post-copy and pre-copy methods for VM's whole-system state transfer for seamless VM migration. The simpler is the *freeze-and-copy* strategy [13] that freezes the VM to avoid file system consistency hazards, copies its hole system state, and then restarts the VM at the destination host. The problem here is that the operating system of the migrating VM will be stopped during the *freeze* phase and the migration may be perceived by end users specially for large workloads (which is usually the case in WAN migrations) since they will take more transfer delay.

The *post-copy* strategy ([14], [15]) first transfers memory and CPU state only, and delays the storage migration. It then fetches storage data on-demand. The main restriction of this approach is the perceivable downtime since the VM will be stopped twice: first for CPU transfer and then for dirtied memory pages and remaining data synchronisation. The migrated machine/application might, so, suffer a significant slow-down. Since post-copy technique has not been thoroughly evaluated for scientific workloads [16], we haven't been motivated for it.

The *pre-copy* strategy is the traditional live migration approach [15]. Pre-copy is the default migration algorithm for Xen [17]. It is also implemented on KVM [16]. The pre-copy algorithm consists of copying first the storage state to the target host while the VM continues running at the source host. Then, the VM should be paused for a while to ensure data synchronisation, and finally stopped at the source host to start execution on the destination host. In addition to Xen and KVM use of this solution, a wide range of researchers ([12], [13], [16] - [19]) have based their works on the pre-copy strategy, which showcase the promise of this algorithm for live migration. This method has been studied ([13], [12], [20]) and even patented for wide area optical networks [21] too. For all these reasons, we will use the pre-copy migration algorithm as a reference to study and analyse the migration process steps over the WAN. This will be helpful for a better understanding of the inter-Cloud migration (ICM) network requirements.

3   Network Requirements for ICM

Adopting the *pre-copy migration strategy*, we will focus, particularly, on the steps involving network: Upon receiving confirmation of the existence of a path between the source and destination computing systems (a lightpath in US patent 7761573 [21]), the VMTC (*Virtual Machine Turnable Control*) issues a *migrate* command to the source computing system. In response, the source and destination computing systems engage in an *iterative copy process* for transferring a copy of the state of the VM to the destination computing system. When the iterative copy process *converges to data synchronization*, the VMTC reconfigures the IP tunnel (VM-to-user IP tunnel), thereby seamlessly redirecting and connecting the client-side application to the VM, now executing on the destination computing system.

The flowchart of Fig. 1 describes the pre-copy migration steps. During the first step, all the data of the virtual machine to migrate is saved in cache and copied to the target computing system where the new VM is instantiated. Then, iteratively, the dirtied data (the memory pages that have changed) since the previous iteration (saved in the cache) is sent to the target VM. These iterations are repeated until the dirtied data comes down a prefixed threshold. All this phase is told a *pre-copy phase* during which the VM is still running on the initial computing system. Therefore, there will not be any delay constraint during this phase. However, since the amount of transferred data is very high during this phase, it will require high bandwidth migration links. We define therefore this phase as a **bandwidth-sensitive phase**. The bandwidth-sensitive phase will work optimally if data pages can be copied to the target computing system faster than they are dirtied by the migrating virtual machine. But this will require very large bandwidth paths that the substrate network may not offer, or that may restrict the network availability.

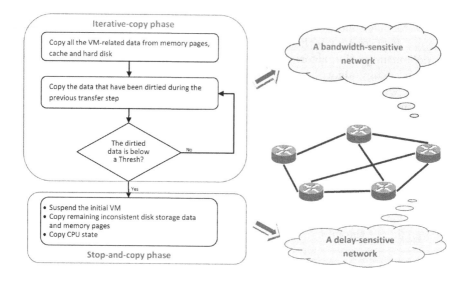

Fig. 1. Network requirements for inter-Cloud live migration

The synchronization step (Fig. 1) starts with suspending the VM execution on the source computing system. Then the remaining inconsistent disk and memory pages are sent to the target VM with the CPU state. The duration of this transfer is called the *downtime delay* since it corresponds to the suspension of the VM on the initial computing system. For transparent and live VM migration, this *stop-and-copy phase* should be executed at very low latency. We call it therefore, a **delay-sensitive migration phase**.

Our idea is so to design the migration network as a service offering for each migration request a migration path which will be carried through (Fig. 1):

- *A **bandwidth-sensitive** network during the iterative copy phase;
- *A **delay-sensitive** network during the stop-and-copy phase.

We believe that our proposition will not only achieve live/seamless VM migration due to the delay-sensitive phase, but it will also reduce the total migration delay due to the bandwidth-sensitive phase. In fact, the bandwidth-sensitive path can rapidly carry the migrated data which reduces the amount of dirtied data. Furthermore, the switching between two different-object migration networks will increase network resources availability. Our goal in this paper will be, therefore, to find a network model able to offer a multi-criteria networks mix. The proposed model should be able to dynamically switch the migration process from the bandwidth-sensitive network to the delay-sensitive one. The switching instant is also a key parameter to achieve unperceived application's downtime. The next section will explain our network model proposal.

4   Polymorphic Network Service (PNS) Design

To deal with the increasingly large volume of transferred data across networks, a big interest was given to the resource management mechanisms for better network performance. However, the different natures of the traffic and services carried by nowadays networks cannot fit all with a single network architecture. In this context polymorphic networks were first introduced.

We start this section with a brief insight about polymorphic networks. Then, we propose a polymorphic architecture that can achieve the bandwidth-sensitive and delay-sensitive migration phases.

4.1   Polymorphic Networks: Overview

A *polymorphic network* is a combination of two or more networking concepts. It was first proposed for optical networks which architectures rely each on a different switching paradigm. The framework of polymorphic optical networks has its origin in the concept of polymorphic control introduced by Qiao et al. [22]. The authors propose a network architecture sliced into several virtual optical networks (VONs), each one designed to support a different class of service. For each VON, a dedicated set of resources is allocated and a different kind of control is employed, thereby introducing the concept of polymorphic control.

Miguel et al. [23] propose also a polymorphic multi-service optical network (PMON) as an integrated architecture that combines several switching paradigms in a single physical network, allowing (as long as possible) resource re-utilization between all the supported paradigms. Each switching paradigm is selected to best serve a certain traffic type, thereby providing service differentiation at the optical layer.

Ben Mnaouer et al. [24] propose an optimized, polymorphic, hybrid multicast routing (OPHMR) protocol for MANET. OPHMR combines both proactive and reactive paradigms depending on the underlying context. It is a hybrid routing protocol that attempts to discover balance between the two; such as proactive for neighbourhood, reactive for far away.

Recently, there is a common thought ([25], [26]) that the future Internet has to be flexible enough to accommodate different cooperation models simultaneously (the so called Multi-layer Networks). The multidisciplinary concept of networking science is therefore imperative to better understand and analyse the future Internet. Thanks to virtualization, which enables the parallel execution of different networking systems, it will be possible to conciliate different architectural paradigms. The way could be so opened for a polymorphic future Internet.

4.2   Inter-Cloud Polymorphic Network (ICPN) Design

In order to answer the ICM network requirements suggested in section 3, the interconnection network should be a cooperative architecture of a bandwidth-sensitive network for the first migration phase requirements and a delay-sensitive network for the downtime phase requirements. This is consistent with the definition of polymorphic networks. The heterogeneous nature of polymorphic networks would provide new possibilities and challenges for the efficient support of the smart virtual machine migration application. It only remains to find the most adequate network technologies providing respectively high bandwidth and low latency performances for a seamless VM migration process. An other important issue is to adequately choose the switching threshold to move the migrated data from the bandwidth-sensitive network to the delay-sensitive one. This latter should be available and should ensure the transparency of the downtime phase with regard to the application's users. If the remaining network resources are not enough for the last delay-sensitive phase, the seamless migration request should be rejected since the beginning. The migration requests that have no liveliness requirements are considered as a background workload and are not covered by the migration's admission controller.

If we take into account the architecture of the future Internet, we will assume a multi-layered WAN substrate supporting different networking technologies and various switching paradigms.

Packet switching technologies have been identified as flexible and promising solutions to deal not only with the increased volume of data-centric traffic but also with the bursty/dynamic variation of traffic patterns ([27], [28]). A packet switched network will therefore best serve the bandwidth-sensitive migration phase requirements.

To best serve the downtime phase, however, we need to establish end-to-end circuits with no electronic conversion at any of the intermediate nodes across the migration path. The migration path should be established on-demand and released just when the migration is ended. The best solution here is the use of a lightpath circuit switching technology which can be dynamically reconfigured (setup or released). Such a circuit-switched path could be configured so that the configuration of network settings of the migrated VM remain the same (layer-2 VPN). The migration would not cause, so, any service disruption when the VM starts running on its new hosting system. For the bandwidth-sensitive migration network, it is not necessary that the source and destination hosting systems of the VM keep their network configuration unchangeable. In fact, during the bandwidth-sensitive iterative pre-copy phase, the VM is still running on the initial computing system and the destination VM is still idle.

To enjoy the benefits of the previously mentioned network technologies, we propose a polymorphic network architecture combining **packet switching** and **circuit switching** technologies. Such a network would be able to transport bandwidth-critical data (using the packet switching) together with delay-sensitive data (using circuit switching). The use of a polymorphic network is safe since each network technology will deal with a different kind of workload; and since the migration phases are segregated through the VM's withholding. But the question is: how to decide when to go through the packet switched bandwidth-sensitive network and when to go through the circuit switched delay-sensitive network?

The migration switching from the bandwidth-sensitive network to the delay-sensitive one is performed when the dirtied pages to transfer reach a prefixed threshold value (Fig. 1). This switching threshold should be adequately chosen to guarantee the transparency of the downtime phase.

VMware has somewhat examined this threshold value. The tests performed by the VMWare vMotion team assert that a maximum latency of $5ms$ can ensure transparent vMotion migration through a Cisco Datacenter Interconnect (DCI) WAN [29]. We will therefore take this latency value as input and compute the corresponding memory pages' dirtying rate. For each migration request that the dirtied pages' threshold volume can be supported by the remaining resources on the delay-sensitive network, the migration request is performed. Otherwise, the migration request is delayed until the necessary network resources become available. This admission control procedure is used to avoid VM migration breaking, which could not only cause a time lost, but also the ineffective network resources usage. Figure 2 illustrates the VM migration admission control and the polymorphic network establishment flowchart.

5   Implementation and Results

5.1   Implementation

We have used the OMNET++ simulator since it is a complete tool providing easy network elements creation and simple code extension.

The network edge nodes (Fig. 3) should support both circuit and packet switching paradigms. We have, so, extended the packet header for packet switched networks, and added an APPLICATION module that generates messages for the circuit establishment on the delay-sensitive migration network. The APPLICATION module also generates the delay-sensitive traffic to be carried through the established circuit. A QUEUE module is added to the OMNET++ simulator to schedule the migrations' requests for a delay-sensitive circuit.

Based on the VMware vMotion migration infrastructure requirements [29], we have chosen to test the Inter-Cloud Polymorphic Network service (ICPN) on the National Science Foundation (NSF) network [31]. The reference model of the NSF network consists of 14 nodes and 21 bidirectional links whose propagation delay goes from 1 to 14ms (Fig. 4). The details of the underlying infrastructure are introduced, through a text file, to the OMNET++ Netbuilder module.

For each VM migration request, the availability of a delay-sensitive circuit achieving $5ms$ latency is required to initiate the migration process. This circuit is reserved until the pre-copy bandwidth sensitive phase is achieved.

The APPLICATION module is first called to send circuit connexion request from the source to the destination host. When a migration request is admitted,

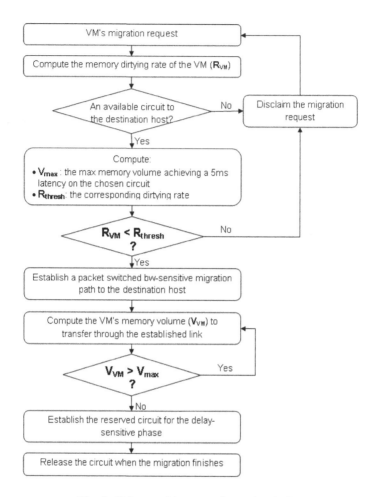

Fig. 2. Polymorphic network service design

a link-state routing protocol is used to establish the bandwidth-sensitive migration path. When the source host receives an acknowledgement of the processed iteration, it (1) keeps a snapshot of the VM's state, (2) computes the dirtied data volume V_{VM} and (3) processes it over the bandwidth-sensitive packet switched network. This process is iteratively repeated until the dirtied data volume (V_{VM}) comes down to the threshold value V_{max} (achieving a $5ms$ latency). At this point, the reserved circuit is accessed to send all the remaining data after shutting down the VM on the source host.

We have tested the admission control of VM's migration requests when all the available links are $1Gbps$ load (Fig. 5). The migration request cannot be admitted for dirtying rates higher than $250000pages/s$. This value corresponds to R_{thresh} for the $1Gbps$ link.

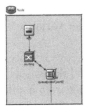

Fig. 3. Edge node design

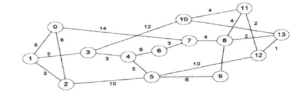

Fig. 4. The NSF simulation model

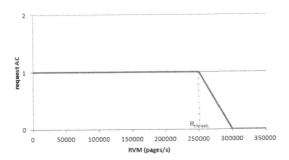

Fig. 5. Impact of the dirtying rate on the migration admission by the PNS-IC

5.2   Evaluation

In order to test the polymorphic network service efficiency in achieving long distance live migrations under various conditions, we investigate three live migration scenarios. Each scenario invokes the migration of different VMs' workloads going from large background workload to relatively small live workload. It is not required to perform the migration process end-to-end. Only a Datacenter-to-Datacenter workload transfer across the PNS network could evaluate the migration network performance. Recently, Chen et al. [30] characterize the inter backbone-Datacenters (Yahoo!'s Datacenters in particular) traffic as background traffic (backup traffic) in its majority with some client-triggered "live" workload (web search, on-line chat, gaming, video, etc.).

The Inter-Datacenters migration's performance is highly dependent on the WAN links capacity. According to data from the National Science Foundation (NSF) [31], 59% of academic institutions are nowadays (2011) mostly interconnected via at least 1*Gbps* optical links. We assume, therefore, that all the invoked Datacenters are interconnected via 1 to 3*Gbps* optical links. The experiments were executed for the three following scenarios:

1) **On-Line Chat.** In this scenario we deal with live workload that exhibits varying trends over the day but does not require a lot of storage.
2) **Data/Storage Backup.** Data backup workload represents the majority of the inter-Datacenters traffic. In [30], the authors call it a "background" traffic

consisting mostly of periodic data backup and search indexing. Their measurement assert that the background workload has smaller variance with no
significant trends over the day.

3) **Video Streaming.** Some surgical operations are nowadays remotely performed and require live video streaming with no perceived delay. such workload is not only voluminous, but also extremely varying over a relatively
short time of the day.

For each of these scenarios, the VM's mean dirtying rate and the initial workload volume to transfer, used in simulations, are given in table 3.

Table 3. Evaluation scenarios

Scenario	Initial volume V_{VM}^0	Mean dirtying rate $\overline{R}_{VM}$
Chat	500Kb	50000 pages/s
Backup	10Gb	12000 pages/s
Streaming	512Mb	3000000 pages/s

Table 4. Migration's admission parameters

Migration Src→Dest	min bw circuit	V_{max}	R_{thresh}
1→6	1Gbps	5Mb	1250 pages/5ms
4→10	3Gbps	15Mb	3750 pages/5ms
6→13	2Gbps	10Mb	2500 pages/5ms

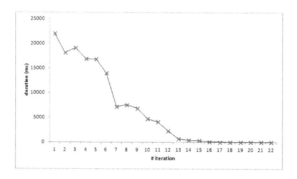

Fig. 6. Delay of each BW-sensitive iteration of a streaming application migration

Let's assume that the chat workload is migrated from Datacenter 1 to Datacenter 6, the backup workload is going from DC 4 to DC 10 and that the
streaming workload interconnects DCs 6 and 13. The minimal bandwidth value
of the circuit-switched link chosen by simulation for each migration request is
fixed in table 4. The admission control parameters V_{max} and R_{thresh} are then
computed for the NSF network model estimating 4Kb memory pages volume.

It is obvious from the comparison of tables 3 and 4 that the chat and backup
workloads could be seamlessly transferred (with no downtime) on the chosen
circuit-switched links. These migrations processes are therefore accepted by the
PNS-IC network. However, since the mean dirtying rate of the streaming application is much higher than the threshold pre-calculated for achieving $5ms$ latency,
a qualitative comparison is not sufficient for deciding whether the workload could

be migrated through the proposed network platform or not. The simulation results show that the bandwidth-sensitive phase was achieved after 22 iterations and has taken a total duration of about $40s$ (Fig. 6).

6   Conclusion

In this paper, we studied live migration behaviour in pre-copy migration architectures. The analysis of the whole migration process and its partitioning in a bandwidth-sensitive phase for the pre-copy steps and a delay-sensitive phase for the downtime step, gave us the idea of choosing a different switching paradigm for each of the conflicting phases of the same process. To deal with this problem, we proposed ICPN, a Polymorphic Network service for inter-Cloud VM migration. The indicated network service offers a packet-switched network for the large workload transfer and a circuit-switched lightpath ensuring transparent downtime phase to the VM's end user. The transparency of the pause-time is ensured by choosing a lightpath circuit achieving the $5ms$ latency approved by vMotion for seamless VM migration. Three test workloads were defined to be executed on the ICPN network. Some initiative results where given assuming a single migration process once and an unused network. This have shown extremely fast migration realisation even for the highly changeable streaming traffic.

For future work, we intend to simulate more realistic substrate network for better showing the impact of ICPN model on a loaded network. We intend also to integrate an SLA based choice of the migration threshold value to enable flexible management of the migrations' requests.

References

1. Ramakrishnan, K.K., et al.: Live data center migration across WANs: a robust cooperative context aware approach. In: SIGCOMM Workshop, ACM (2007)
2. Van der Merwe, J., et al.: Towards a ubiquitous cloud computing infrastructure. In: 17th IEEE Workshop on Local and Metropolitan Area Networks, LANMAN (2010)
3. Hajjat, M., et al.: Cloudward bound: planning for beneficial migration of enterprise applications to the cloud. ACM SIGCOMM Comp. Comm. Review 40(4) (2010)
4. Cisco Systems, Technology Comparison: Cisco Overlay Transport Virtualization and Virtual Private LAN Service as Enablers of LAN Extensions, White paper (2010)
5. Cisco Systems, Cisco Overlay Transport Virtualization Technology Introduction and Deployment Considerations, Whitepaper (last updated January 12, 2011)
6. Murphy, A.: Enabling Long Distance Live Migration with F5 and VMware vMotion, F5 Networks, Inc. (2001)
7. Wood, T., et al.: The case for enterprise-ready virtual private clouds. In: USENIX HotCloud (2009)
8. Riteau, P.: Building Dynamic Computing Infrastructures over Distributed Clouds. In: IEEE Int. Sym. on Parallel and Distributed Processing Workshops, Shanghai (2011)
9. Tsugawa, M., Fortes, J.: A virtual network (ViNe) architecture for grid computing. In: Int. Parallel and Distributed Processing Symposium (2006)

10. Nimbus Project, Nimbus, http://www.nimbusproject.org/
11. Hansen, J.G., Jul, E.: Lithium: virtual machine storage for the cloud. In: Proc. of the 1st ACM Sym. on Cloud computing (SoCC 2010), USA (2010)
12. Hirofuchi, T., et al.: A live storage migration mechanism over wan for relocatable virtual machine services on clouds. In: Proc. of the 9th IEEE/ACM Int. Symposium on Cluster Computing and the Grid (2009)
13. Bradford, R., et al.: Live Wide-Area Migration of Virtual Machines Including Local Persistent State. In: ACM/Usenix Int. Conf. On Virtual Execution Environments (VEE 2007), USA, pp. 169–179 (2007)
14. Hines, M.R., Gopalan, K.: Post-Copy Based Live Virtual Machine Migration Using Adaptive Pre-Paging and Dynamic Self-Ballooning. In: ACM SIGPLAN/SIGOPS Int. Conf. on Virtual Execution Environments (VEE 2009), New York, USA (2009)
15. Hines, M.R., Deshpande, U., Gopalan, K.: Post-Copy Live Migration of Virtual Machines. ACM SIGOPS Operating Systems Review 43(3), 14–26 (2009)
16. Ibrahim, K.Z., et al.: Optimized pre-copy live migration for memory intensive applications. In: Int. Conf. for High Perf. Computing, Networking, Storage and Analysis. ACM (2011)
17. Zhang, X., et al.: Exploiting data deduplication to accelerate live virtual machine migration. In: 2010 IEEE Int. Conf. on Cluster Computing (CLUSTER). IEEE (2010)
18. Clark, C., et al.: Live migration of virtual machines. In: Symposium on Networked Systems Design and Implementation, vol. 2. USENIX Association (2005)
19. Nagarajan, A.B., et al.: Proactive fault tolerance for HPC with Xen virtualization. In: Proc. of the 21st Annual Int. Conf. on Supercomputing. ACM (2007)
20. Svärd, P., et al.: Evaluation of delta compression techniques for efficient live migration of large virtual machines. ACM Sigplan Notices 46(7), 111–120 (2011)
21. Travostino, F., Wang, P., Raghunath, S.: Seamless live migration of virtual machines across optical networks, US patent 7761573 (July 20, 2010)
22. Qiao, C., et al.: Polymorphic Control for Cost-Effective Design of Optical Networks. Eur. Tran. on Telecomm. 11(1), 17–26 (2000)
23. de Miguel, I., et al.: Polymorphic architectures for optical networks and their seamless evolution towards next generation networks. Photonic Network Communications 8(2), 177–189 (2004)
24. Manouer, A.B., et al.: OPHMR: an optimized polymorphic hybrid multicast routing protocol for MANETs. IEEE Tran. on Mobile Computing 6(5), 503–514 (2007)
25. Salamatian, K.: Toward a polymorphic future internet: a networking science approach. IEEE Comm. Magazine 49(10), 174–178 (2011)
26. Future Internet Assembly Research Roadmap, Framework 8: Towards Research Priorities for the Future Internet, A report of the FIARR WG., V.1.0 (2011)
27. Gonzalez, J.C., et al.: Polymorphic optical networks: a solution for service differentiation at the optical layer. In: Proc. of the 8th Eur. Conf. on Networks and Optical Comm. (NOC 2003), Austria, (2003)
28. Gauger, C.M., et al.: Hybrid optical network architectures: bringing packets and circuits together. IEEE Comm. Magazine 44(8), 36–42 (2006)
29. Cisco Systems and VMware, Virtual machine mobility with Vmware Vmotion and cisco data center interconnect technologies, Whitepaper (August 2009)
30. Chen, Y., et al.: A first look at inter-data center traffic characteristics via yahoo! datasets. In: IEEE INFOCOM, pp. 1620–1628 (2011)
31. Gibbons, M.: Computing and Networking Capacity Increases at Academic Research Institutions, National Center for Science and Engineering Statistics NCSES, National Science Foundation, NSF 13-329 (July 2013)

A Hybrid Cluster and Chain-Based Routing Protocol for Lifetime Improvement in WSN

Mourad Hadjila, Hervé Guyennet, and Mohammed Feham

UFR-ST, Computer Science Dept.,
25000 Besanon, France
mhadjila_2002@yahoo.fr,
herve.guyennet@femto-st.fr,
m_feham@mail.univ-tlemcen.dz

Abstract. The main challenge in the field of Wireless Sensor Networks (WSNs) is the energy conservation as long as possible. Clustering paradigm has proven its ability to prolong the network lifetime. The present paper proposes two algorithms using an approach that combines fuzzy c-means and ant colony optimization to form the clusters and manage the transmission of data in the network. First, fuzzy c-means is used to construct a predefined number of clusters. Second, we apply Ant Colony Optimization (ACO) algorithm to form a local shortest chain in each cluster. A leader node is randomly chosen at the beginning since all cluster nodes have the same amount of energy. In the next transmission, a remaining energy parameter is employed to select leader node. In the first algorithm, leader nodes transmit data in single hop to the distant base station (BS) while in the second the ACO algorithm is applied again to form a global chain between leader nodes and the BS. Simulation results show that the second proposed algorithm consumes less energy and effectively prolongs the network lifetime compared respectively with the first proposed and the LEACH algorithms.

Keywords: Wireless sensor network, fuzzy c-means, clustering, ant colony optimization, network lifetime.

1 Introduction

The progress made in recent decades in the fields of microelectronics, micromechanics, and wireless communication technologies, have produced at a reasonable cost components in volume of a few cubic millimeters, called sensor nodes. A sensor node is typically equipped with a sensing subsystem, a processing subsystem, a radio subsystem and a power supply subsystem [1]. Standalone deployment of several of them, to collect and transmit environmental data to one or more collection points form a wireless sensor networks (WSNs). Sensor networks can be very useful in many applications when it comes to collecting and processing information from the environment. Among the areas where these networks can offer the best contributions we quote the following areas: military, environmental, home, health, safety, etc.

A. Mellouk et al. (Eds.): WWIC 2014, LNCS 8458, pp. 257–268, 2014.
© Springer International Publishing Switzerland 2014

The constraints imposed by these networks are very well known: very limited computation, communication, storage capabilities, and energy resources. This last aspect, which limits the lifetime of the network and therefore its utility, has received considerable attention by the research community over the last several years. The design of energy-aware protocols, algorithms, and mechanisms, with the goal of saving as much energy as possible, and therefore extending the lifetime of the network, has been the topic of many research studies [3]. Since communication task consumes the most energy during the network operation, clustering is introduced to WSNs because it has proven to be an effective approach to provide better data aggregation and avoid longest link. Clustering consists to breakdown network into groups of entities called clusters by giving to network a hierarchical structure [2]. A cluster is composed of cluster-head and member nodes. Choosing cluster centers is a crucial to clustering. One of the most used approaches in this regard is Fuzzy C-Means (FCM), which assists to optimize the clusters based on minimizing the distance between the sensor node and the cluster center [4]. In addition to cluster-based protocols, chain-based protocols reduce against the total energy of the network [5–10]. An ant colony optimization (ACO) algorithm can be used to form a chain between multiple nodes [11]. As the energy is inversely proportional to the distance, the construction of short-chain is highly recommended while the ACO algorithm be the best suited for this kind of problem. In this paper in order to enhance network lifetime, we combine the above two approaches, cluster-based and chain-based, for routing data to the BS. We propose two protocols where the second protocol is an improvement of the first one. The rest of this paper is organized as follows: section 2 introduces related works. Section 3 describes the proposed protocols. The simulation is then analyzed in Section 4 in order to validate our approaches and this paper is concluded in Section 5.

2   Related Work

One of the fundamental problems in WSNs is how to prolong the network lifetime. In order to achieve this, many researchers proceed in grouping sensor nodes into clusters. Clustering routing protocols have been developed in order to reduce the network traffic toward the BS [12–19]. Low-Energy Adaptive Clustering Hierarchy (LEACH) [16] is one of the most common cluster routing protocols, which aims to achieve the load balancing in sensor nodes so it can prolong the network lifetime. Each sensor node elects itself as a cluster-head based on the probability model. Each sensor node will become cluster-head in every cycle to evenly distribute the works load. Hybrid Energy- Efficient Distributed (HEED) [19] clustering approach is one of the most recognized energy-efficient clustering protocols. It extends the basic scheme of LEACH by using residual energy and node degree or density. In HEED, the clustering process is divided into a number of iterations, and a node is selected as a cluster head depending on whether other cluster heads are its one hop neighbors and its own residual energy. Hoang et al in [4] proposed an approach based on fuzzy cmeans for clustering calculation, cluster head selection and data transmission.

Another family of solutions is chain-based protocols [5–10]. In this category, PEGASIS [5] was the first protocol. It forms a chain including all nodes in the network using a greedy algorithm so that each node transmits to and receives from a neighboring node. In each round, nodes take turns to be leader and transmit the aggregated data to the base station. Kemei Du et al. proposed a multiple-chain scheme [10] to decrease the total transmission distance for all-to-all broadcasting in order to prolong network lifetime. The key idea is to divide the whole network into four regions centered at the node that is closest to the center of the network. Also, the linear sub-chains in each region are constructed by minimum total energy algorithm.

3 Proposed Algorithms

Before explaining the proposed approaches, we briefly introduce the principle of the cluster formation using fuzzy cmeans algorithm and the formation of the chains using ant colony optimization algorithm.

3.1 Cluster Formation Using Fuzzy C-Means Algorithm

Fuzzy C-Means (FCM) is an unsupervised fuzzy classification algorithm. It introduces the concept of fuzzy set in the definition of clusters: each node in the deployed area belongs to each cluster with a certain degree, and all clusters are characterized by their center of gravity.

Like other non-supervised classification algorithms, it uses a criterion of minimizing intra-cluster distances and maximizing inter-cluster distances, but giving a degree of belonging to each cluster for each node. This algorithm requires prior knowledge of the number of clusters and generates clusters through an iterative process by minimizing an objective function. Thus, it provides a fuzzy partition of the environment by giving each node a degree between 0 and 1 in a given cluster. The cluster, which is associated with a node, is one whose degree of membership is the highest. FCM is based on minimizing the following objective function [20]:

$$J_m = \sum_{i=1}^{c} \sum_{j=1}^{N} \mu_{ij}^m . d_{ij}^2 \tag{1}$$

Where m is any real number greater than 1, μ_{ij} is node j's degree of belonging to cluster i, c is the number of clusters, N is the number of nodes and d_{ij} is the Euclidean distance between node j and the center of cluster i.

The algorithm is composed of the following steps:

1. Fix an arbitrary membership matrix.
2. Compute the centers of the clusters using the following equation:

$$z_j = \frac{\sum_{i=1}^{N} \mu_{ij}^m . o_i}{\sum_{i=1}^{N} \mu_{ij}^m} \tag{2}$$

3. The readjustment of the membership matrix according to the position of the centers is done according to the equation below:

$$\mu_{ij} = \frac{1}{\sum_{k=1}^{c} \left(\frac{d_{ij}}{d_{kj}} \right)^{\frac{2}{m-1}}} \tag{3}$$

4. Computes the minimization and return to step 2 if there is no convergence criterion.

3.2 Chains Formation Using Ant Colony Algorithm

The basic idea in ant colony optimization algorithms (ACO) is to imitate the cooperative behavior of real ants to solve optimization problems. ACO meta-heuristics have been proposed by M. Dorigo [21]. They can be seen as multia-gent systems in which each single agent is inspired by the behavior of a real ant. Traditionally, ACO have been applied to combinatorial optimization problems and they have achieved widespread success in solving different problems (e.g., scheduling, routing, assignment) [22].

To construct a local chain in each cluster, we use the ant colony algorithm. The idea is borrowed from the Traveling Salesman Problem (TSP) [23] where a shortest open chain is constructed in each cluster using the ant colony algorithm. Initially, each ant is randomly put on a node. During the construction of a feasible solution, ants select the following node to be visited through a probabilistic decision rule. When an ant k states in node i and constructs the partial solution, the probability moving to the next node j neighboring on node i is given by:

$$p_{ij}^{k}(t) = \begin{cases} \frac{\tau_{ij}(t)^{\alpha} . \eta_{ij}^{\beta}}{\sum_{l \in J_i^k} \tau_{il}(t)^{\alpha} . \eta_{il}^{\beta}} & \text{if } j \in J_i^k \\ 0 & otherwise \end{cases} \tag{4}$$

Where J_i^k is the list of possible moves for an ant k when it is on a node i, η_{ij} is the visibility which is equal to the inverse of the distance between two nodes i and j $(1/d_{ij})$ and $\tau_{ij}(t)$ is the intensity of the runway at a given iteration t. The two main parameters controlling the algorithm are α and β which controls the relative intensity and the visibility of an edge.

Once the tour nodes performed, an ant k deposits a quantity of pheromone $\Delta\tau_{ij}$ on each edge of the course:

$$\Delta\tau_{ij}^{k}(t) = \begin{cases} \frac{Q}{L^k(t)} & \text{if } (i,j) \in T^k(t) \\ 0 & otherwise \end{cases} \tag{5}$$

Where $T^k(t)$ is the tour done by ant k at iteration t, $L^k(t)$ the length of the path and a Q parameter setting.

At the end of each iteration of the algorithm, the pheromone deposited at previous iterations by ants evaporate from:

$$\rho\Delta\tau_{ij}^{k} \tag{6}$$

And at the end of the iteration, we have the sum of pheromones that have not evaporated and those who have just been laid.

$$\tau_{ij}(t+1) = (1-\rho) . \tau_{ij}(t) + \sum_{k=1}^{m} \Delta \tau_{ij}^{k} \tag{7}$$

Where m is the number of ants and ρ is an adjustment parameter.

At the end, when all tours are completed, we remove in each chain the longest distance between two nodes in order to obtain a shortest open chain.

3.3   Description of the Proposed Algorithms

In the present work, we combine different tools to deal with the problem of energy conservation in the field of WSNs. We propose two algorithms where we first applied FCM algorithm to form a predefined number of clusters. The number of clusters is chosen equal to square root of the total nodes. Second, an ACO algorithm is used to construct a local chain in each cluster. Figure 1 shows an example of cluster containing eight nodes interconnected to form a closed chain. This chain is obtained using the ant colony optimization algorithm as used in TSP. Then, we remove the longest distance between two consecutive nodes in order to obtain the shortest open chain. In Figure 2, the line between node 1 and node 8 is deleted. For routing data from nodes to the BS, we proceed as follows: At the beginning, a randomly node elects itself a leader node since all cluster nodes have the same amount of energy. For data gathering and fusion, each cluster member node senses and transfers data along the local chain to reach one particular node, which is leader node; the latter receives and aggregates data. When a node dies in a local chain, this latter is reconstructed by bypassing the dead node. The data transmission mode to the BS constitutes the difference between the two proposed approaches. In the first, the leader nodes send data directly to the BS meaning in one hop while in the second data transmission is performed in multiple hops by forming a global chain connecting all the leader nodes using again the ACO algorithm. Leader node rotation in each cluster is performed according to the remaining energy of nodes. The proposed algorithms are centralized controlled by the BS. Figure 3 and 4 illustrate the operating principles of our algorithms where the red lines represent the shortest chain that links nodes in each cluster while the blue dashed lines join the leader nodes and the BS respectively in single hop and multi-hop.

4   Simulation and Evaluation

In this section, we evaluate the performance of our proposed algorithms in Matlab. We consider 100 nodes randomly deployed in an area of $(100 \times 100)\,m^2$, the BS is located outside the area at the coordinate $(50, 150)$ so it is at least $50m$ from the closest sensor node. The following properties are assumed in regard to the sensor network being studied:

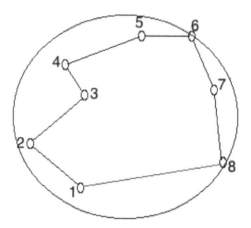

Fig. 1. Formation of closed chain

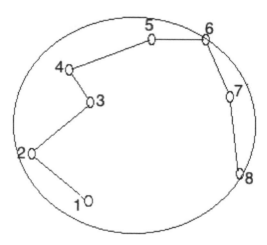

Fig. 2. Formation of the open chain

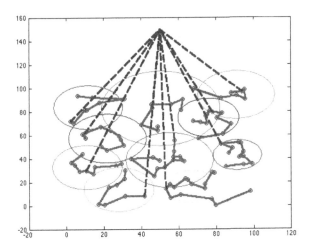

Fig. 3. Operating principle of the first algorithm

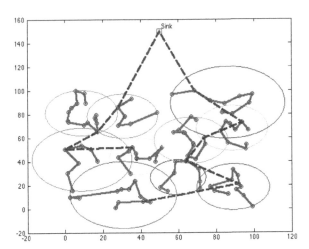

Fig. 4. Operating principle of the second algorithm

- The nodes are homogeneous and they are static.
- All the nodes have the same initial energy and the BS is not limited in terms of energy, memory and computational power.
- Links are symmetric so that the energy required to transmit a message from node i to node j is the same as energy required to transmit a message from node j to node i.

In the simulation part, we use the same radio model as introduced in [16] which is the first order radio model. This radio model uses both of the open space (energy dissipation d^2) and multi path (energy dissipation d^4) channels by taking amount the distance between the transmitter and receiver. So energy consumption for transmitting a packet of l bits in distance d is given by (8).

$$E_{TX}(l,d) = \begin{cases} l.E_{elec} + l.E_{fs}.d^2 \ if \ \ d < d_0 \\ l.E_{elec} + l.E_{mp}.d^4 \ if \ \ d \geq d_0 \end{cases} \tag{8}$$

Where d_0 is the distance threshold value, which is obtained by (9), E_{elec} is required energy for activating the electronic circuits. E_{fs} and E_{mp} are required energy for amplification of transmitted signals to transmit a one bit in open space and multi path models, respectively.

$$d_0 = \sqrt{\frac{E_{fs}}{E_{mp}}} \tag{9}$$

Energy consumption to receive a packet of l bits is calculated according to (10).

$$E_{RX}(l) = l.E_{elec} \tag{10}$$

The full simulation parameters are listed in table 1. where E_{DA} represents the energy required for data aggregation.

Table 1. Simulation parameters

Parameters	Values
Network size	(100×100) m^2
Number of nodes	100
Initial energy	0.1 J
Packet size	1000 bits
E_{elec}	50×10^{-9}
E_{fs}	10^{-11}
E_{mp}	1.3×10^{-15}
E_{DA}	5×10^{-9}

Two metrics are chosen in order to evaluate the proposed schemes, which are energy consumption and the number of alive nodes. Figure 5 illustrates the residual energy in the network for the three algorithms.

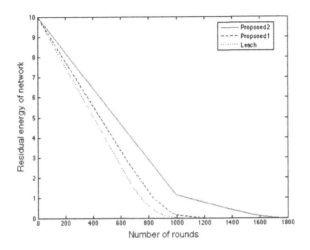

Fig. 5. Residual energy of the network vs. number of rounds

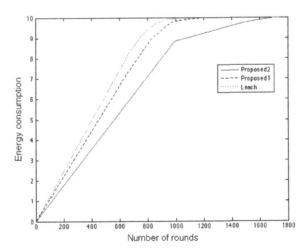

Fig. 6. Energy consumption vs. number of rounds

From the simulation results shown in figure 6, it was observed that the *proposed*2 algorithm consumes less energy than the *proposed*1. This is due to the presence of global chain, which reduces the long transmission from leader nodes to the remote BS. We see again that *proposed*1 is a few better than LEACH in term of energy consumption.

Figure 7 shows the evolution of the number of alive nodes per the number of rounds. We observe that the first node dies in LEACH after 653 rounds while in *proposed*1 and *proposed*2 first node dies after 654 and 964 rounds respectively. We also observe that the last node dies in LEACH after 1046 rounds while in *proposed*1 and *proposed*2 first node dies after 1213 and 1740 rounds respectively. Therefore, we note that *proposed*2 is about 30.28% more efficient in term of network lifetime than *proposed*1 and about 39.88% than the LEACH algorithm.

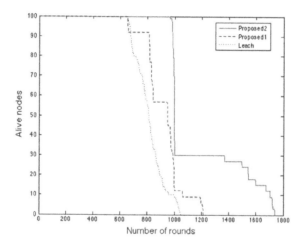

Fig. 7. Number of alive nodes vs. number of rounds

5   Conclusion

In this paper, we introduced two algorithms to address the problem of energy conservation in wireless sensor networks combining cluster-based and chain-based approaches. These algorithms are characterized by partitioning nodes in a predefined number of clusters using FCM and formation of local chain in each cluster. Inter-cluster communication is performed by chain-based approach using an ACO algorithm to find the shortest chain that links all cluster member nodes. The difference between the two proposed algorithms lies in the data transmission mode to the remote BS. The first uses direct transmission from leader nodes to the BS while the second constructs a global chain connecting the leader nodes and the BS. Also, these algorithms select leader node for each chain according to the remaining energy of nodes. Simulation results show that *proposed*2 prolong the network lifetime about 30.28% and 39.88% in comparison with the *proposed*1 and LEACH.

References

1. Anastasi, G., Conti, M., Di Francesco, M., Passarella, A.: Energy Conservation in Wireless Sensor Networks: A survey. Ad Hoc Networks 7, 537–568 (2009)
2. Wightmanl, P.M., Labrador, M.A.: Topology Maintenance: Extending the Lifetime of Wireless Sensor Networks. In: IEEE Latin-American Conference on Communications, pp.1–6. IEEE (2009)
3. Johnen, C., Nguyen, L.H.: Self-stabilizing weight-based clustering algorithm for ad hoc sensor networks. In: Nikoletseas, S.E., Rolim, J.D.P. (eds.) ALGOSENSORS 2006. LNCS, vol. 4240, pp. 83–94. Springer, Heidelberg (2006)
4. Hoang, D.C., Kumar, R., Panda, S.K.: Fuzzy C-Means Clustering Protocol for Wireless Sensor Networks. In: IEEE International Symposium on Industrial Electronics (ISIE), pp. 3477–3482 (2010)
5. Lindsey, S., Raghavendra, C.: PEGASIS: Power-efficient gathering in sensor information systems. In: IEEE Aerospace Conference Proceedings, pp. 1125–1130 (2002)
6. Yu, Y., Song, Y.: An Energy-Efficient Chain-Based Routing Protocol in Wireless Sensor Network. In: International Conference on Computer Application and System Modeling (ICCASM), pp. 486–489. IEEE (2010)
7. Guo, W., Zhang, W., Lu, G.: PEGASIS protocol in wireless sensor network based on an improved ant colony algorithm. In: Second International Workshop on Education Technology and Computer Science (ETCS), pp. 64–67. IEEE (2010)
8. Chen, Y., Lin, J., Huang, Y., Cheung, F., Lin, J.: Energy efficiency of a chain-based scheme with Intra-Grid in wireless sensor networks. In: International Symposium on Computer Communication Control and Automation (3CA), pp. 484–487. IEEE (2010)
9. Linping, W., Wu, B., Zhen, C., Zufeng, W.: Improved algorithm of PEGASIS protocol introducing double cluster heads in wireless sensor network. In: International Conference on Computer, Mechatronics, Control and Electronic Engineering (CMCE), pp. 148–151. IEEE (2010)
10. Du, K., Wu, J., Zhou, D.: Chain-based protocols for data broadcasting and gathering in the sensor networks. In: International Parallel and Distributed Processing Symposium, pp. 1926–1933. IEEE (2003)
11. Wen, Y., Chen, Y., Qian, D.: An Ant-based approach to Power-Efficient Algorithm for Wireless Sensor Networks. In: World Congress on Engineering, pp. 1546–1550 (2007)
12. Bandyopadhyay, S., Coyle, E.J.: An energy efficient hierarchical clustering algorithm for wireless sensor networks. In: Twenty-Second Annual Joint Conference of the IEEE Computer and Communications, pp. 1713–1723. IEEE Societies (2003)
13. Banerjee, S., Khuller, S.: A clustering scheme for hierarchical control in multi-hop wireless networks. In: Proceedings of Twentieth Annual Joint Conference of the IEEE Computer and Communications Societies, pp. 1028–1037. IEEE (2001)
14. Boukerche, A., Werner Nelem Pazzi, R., Borges Araujo, R.: Fault-tolerant wireless sensor network routing protocols for the supervision of context-aware physical environments. Journal of Parallel and Distributed Computing 4, 586–599 (2006)
15. Boukerche, A., Martirosyan, A.: An energy-aware and fault tolerant inter-cluster communication based protocol for wireless sensor networks. In: IEEE Global Telecommunications Conference, GLOBECOM 2007, pp. 1164–1168. IEEE (2007)
16. Heinzelman, W., Chandrakasan, A., Balakrishnan, H.: Energy-efficient communication protocol for wireless microsensor networks. In: Proceedings of the 33rd Annual Hawaii International Conference on System Sciences, pp. 3005–3014. IEEE (2001)

17. Manjeshwar, A., Agrawal, D.P.: TEEN: A Routing Protocol for Enhanced Efficiency in Wireless Sensor Networks. In: Proceedings of 15th International Parallel and Distributed Processing Symposium (IPDPS), pp. 2009–2015. IEEE, San Francisco (2001)
18. Manjeshwar, A., Agrawal, D.P.: APTEEN: A Hybrid Protocol for Efficient Routing and Comprehensive Information Retrieval in Wireless Sensor Networks. In: 2nd International Workshop on Parallel and Distributed Computing Issues in Wireless Networks and Mobile Computing, pp. 195–202 (2002)
19. Younis, O., Fahmy, S.: HEED: a hybrid, energy-efficient, distributed clustering approach for ad hoc sensor networks. IEEE Transactions on Mobile Computing, 1366–379 (2004)
20. Izakian, H., Abraham, A., Snasel, V.: Fuzzy clustering using hybrid fuzzy c-means and fuzzy particle swarm optimization. In: World Congress on Nature & Biologically Inspired Computing, pp. 1690–1694. IEEE (2009)
21. Dorigo, M., Blum, C.: Ant colony optimization theory: A survey. Theoretical Computer Science 344, 243–278 (2005)
22. Dorigo, M., Stutzle, T.: The ant colony optimization metaheuristic: Algorithms, applications, and advances. In: Handbook of Metaheuristics, pp. 250–285 (2003)
23. Dorigo, M., Gambardella, L.M.: Ant colonies for the travelling salesman problem. BioSystems 43, 73–81 (1997)

CARPOOL: Connectivity Plan Routing Protocol

Ioannis Komnios and Vassilis Tsaoussidis

Space Internetworking Center, Office 1, Building A, Panepistimioupoli Kimmeria,
Department of Electrical and Computer Engineering, Democritus University of Thrace,
67100, Xanthi, Greece
{ikomnios,vtsaousi}@ee.duth.gr

Abstract. Basic Internet access is considered a human right, however geographical, technological and socio-economic reasons set barriers to universal Internet access. To address this challenge, we have proposed an access method based on message ferrying that enables free delay-tolerant Internet access to all, and developed Connectivity plAn Routing PrOtOcOL (CARPOOL), a reference routing protocol for the proposed access method. In this paper, we describe CARPOOL in depth and evaluate its performance for increasing traffic load. Focusing on an urban scenario, where means of public transport, such as buses, follow predefined routes and schedules, CARPOOL utilises *a priori* knowledge about their current location to extend Internet access provided by hotspots to users and areas that are not typically covered. Our simulation results show that CARPOOL effectively exploits the existing connectivity plan of public transportation, achieving high delivery ratio with minimum overhead. This paper also discusses possible enhancements of the proposed routing protocol.

Keywords: Delay Tolerant Networking, DTN routing, Message ferries.

1 Introduction

The majority of people living in the developed world are already experiencing how access to the Internet is transforming their way of living. Internet has now become a critical infrastructure for the society with its availability levels increasing and its traffic volume constantly growing. Based on this consensus, in 2011 the United Nations declared Internet access itself a human right [1]. In a constantly evolving and expanding digital world, however, geographical isolation and socio-economic restrictions pose barriers to the invasion of the Internet to all parts of the society: remote regions demand significantly higher cost for Internet deployments due to infrastructure costs, while economic challenges exclude the under-privileged from accessing the Internet even in well-connected environments.

Delay/Disruption Tolerant Networking (DTN) architecture [2, 3] and its supporting Bundle Protocol (BP) [4] is an emerging technology to support the new era in interoperable communications by providing delay-tolerant access even when traditional continuous end-to-end connectivity fails. DTN has been frequently coupled with the concept of message ferrying, especially as far as remote areas are concerned, to facilitate data transfers through cars, buses, trams, trains etc.

A. Mellouk et al. (Eds.): WWIC 2014, LNCS 8458, pp. 269–282, 2014.

In this paper, we focus on metropolitan environments with an ultimate goal to provide free delay-tolerant Internet access to the under-privileged society that is currently excluded from today's digital world. To achieve that, we extend the existing free Internet access provided by public hotspots that are usually scattered around a city. Actually, we broaden connectivity options by deploying DTN nodes both on typical means of public transport (ferries), such as buses and trams, and their corresponding stops. Offline DTN gateways located near ferry stops collect Internet access requests from end-users in that area and DTN ferries act as relays between offline gateways or designated gateways that have access to the Internet and are capable of handling such requests. Through simulations, we have identified that existing DTN routing solutions underperform in such dense environments, due to their associated high overhead and their excessive energy needs.

Our novelty lies in the utilization of *a priori* knowledge of contacts between gateways and ferries, in an effort to achieve high delivery ratio with minimum overhead. First, we investigate the potential of existing DTN routing schemes to support free Internet access in high traffic load conditions and we observe that existing protocols are insufficient primarily because they fail to guarantee some level of service. Further, we describe and evaluate CARPOOL, a DTN routing protocol that utilises the connectivity plan between ferries and gateways (i.e. ferry stops) to compute routes to online gateways. CARPOOL was briefly described in [5]; here we describe and evaluate CARPOOL in detail, we discuss issues that may arise and we propose possible solutions. We also note that geographical extension of the Internet is here confined only within a metropolitan area: we do not include here ferries to reach isolated regions. However, this is our ultimate target and does not cancel the advantages of this standalone proposal. These are: (i) an easy-to-deploy access method that exploits information regarding the schedule of the ferries, which is already available and well-known in all major cities worldwide, (ii) free delay-tolerant access to the Internet for everyone, and (iii) energy-efficient design that delegates all expensive computing operations to gateways with increased computing and power capacity.

The remainder of this paper is structured as follows: in Section 2, we discuss related work in the field of DTN and free typically less-than-best effort Internet access. In Section 3, we describe in detail the proposed access method along with CARPOOL routing protocol, while in Section 4 we present our experimental results. In Section 5 we discuss CARPOOL and we propose mechanisms to enhance its performance. We conclude this paper in Section 6.

2   Related Work

In an effort to provide Internet access to all members of the society, several economic models, such as providing restricted Internet access during night at a lower price, have been proposed in the recent past. Nonetheless, these models are not affordable to all, leaving certain members of the society with the only alternative of using random hotspots when available. Several governments and local administrations have undertaken the initiative to deploy hotspots in points of interests, however cost-efficiency is a critical factor that hinders extended deployments [6]. An information-centric delay-tolerant networking architecture for the challenged is proposed in [7].

User-provided networks, where an Internet connection is shared freely and transparently among end-users in a way that is technically and legally independent of access or infrastructure providers, have been proposed as a solution [8]. Among others, the authors of [9] explore incentives and algorithms for broadband access sharing to support nomadic users. We have already investigated the performance of less-than-best-effort protocols in heavily shared backhaul links [10-11]. On the practical side, PAWS project [12] aims at providing free Internet for all by making the existing broadband connections in homes and public buildings publicly available. Similarly, BT FON initiative [13] encourages FON members to share their home broadband connection and get in return free access at millions of other FON hotspots, worldwide. Even though the aforementioned solutions can provide free Internet access in specific areas, they fail to provide extended coverage.

In recent years, Delay Tolerant Networking architecture has attracted the attention of the research community in an effort to provide Internet access to remote and disconnected regions. Routing has been one of the key challenges for DTNs, since an end-to-end path from the source to the destination might not exist in time. Epidemic routing [14] was one of the first proposals in this area by employing pair-wise exchanges of messages among all mobile hosts that connect to each other, maximizing delivery rate and minimizing overall latency. Naturally, the main disadvantage of epidemic routing is the extreme overhead it creates. Extending the idea of epidemic routing, the authors of [15] proposed a routing algorithm for Delay Tolerant Networks (PRoPHET) that exploits the non-randomness of real-world encounters by maintaining a set of probabilities for successful delivery to known destinations and replicating messages during opportunistic encounters only if the node that does not have the message appears to have a better chance of delivering it. In an effort to reduce the transmission overhead of epidemic routing while keeping delivery probability high, the authors of [16] proposed Spray-and-Wait routing protocol. In Spray-and-Wait, for each message originating at the source node, L copies are forwarded to the network. If the destination does not receive a copy of the message, each node that has received the message performs direct delivery to the destination.

As far as vehicular DTNs are concerned, MaxProp routing [17] is one of the most promising solutions based on prioritizing the schedules of packets to be transmitted and to be dropped. These priorities are built on path likelihood to peers according to historical data and some enhancement mechanisms. The concept of exploiting DTN ferries or data mules has been popular for data collection from sensors [18]. A few papers that consider message ferries for data transmission in DTN have also been presented in bibliography. KioskNet [19] was one of the first proposals on the field with a main goal to employ buses and cars as "mechanical backhaul" devices to carry data to and from a remote village and an Internet gateway. KioskNet was proposed at a period when DTN research was at its infancy, thus no clear routing solution was provided. ALARMS routing protocol [20] was later introduced to deliver bundles through message ferries. Ferries connect to gateways and pass information regarding their path for the next two rounds. Based on this information, gateways calculate the routing path that achieves earliest delivery. This work, however, does not consider global knowledge of the network and a path to the destination can only be found if a ferry exists to directly connect the source and the destination.

Our protocol differs from the aforementioned solutions, since CARPOOL utilizes *a priori* knowledge of future contacts between DTN ferries and stationary DTN gateways. Utilizing such knowledge, CARPOOL identifies all possible routes between two nodes and selects the one that achieves earliest delivery. Our aim is not to compare CARPOOL with DTN routing solutions that have no or partial knowledge of the network, but to highlight the inefficiency of these protocols in dense urban environments and propose a reference routing protocol that achieves high delivery ratio with minimum overhead. Our approach shares the philosophy of Contact Graph Routing [21], which is the most prominent routing solution in space internetworking. Similar to prescheduled contacts between ferries and gateways, Contact Graph Routing extracts a path for space data transmission utilizing *a priori* knowledge of contacts between space assets, which may include dynamic aspects as well [22]. Applications that can benefit from the proposed architecture include E-mail [23], fbDTN [24], Twitter [25] etc.

3   Architecture Overview

The proposed approach to free delay-tolerant Internet access aims at extending the existing access provided by public hotspots. Section 3.1 presents the access model we propose in order to achieve this goal, while Section 3.2 illustrates a specific realisation of the model within a DTN routing protocol that exploits known contacts.

3.1   Model

Our access model consists of two major components: *DTN gateways* that are responsible for handling requests from end-users within their radius and *DTN ferries* that are responsible for transferring messages across the gateways. While both components are crucial for our access model, we intentionally delegated all computational tasks to the gateways, since we assume that DTN ferries have restricted energy and computational capabilities. Typically, the travel plan of buses, trams and trains is predefined and only minor delays can occur. Therefore, in our model we assume that all gateways have global knowledge of the connectivity plan. Of course, in case of a major delay, the updated traffic schedule is flooded into the network through a central administrative node.

DTN gateways are resource-capable fixed nodes located near ferry stops. We assume that certain gateways have access to the Internet through a hotspot that exists in the area (*online DTN gateways*), while the majority is offline. All gateways have effectively enough buffer to store messages from several end-users and are equipped with network interfaces for data exchange with the mobile devices of the end-users and the DTN ferries. Once an end-user device discovers a DTN gateway in its radius, a request to/from the Internet is transferred from/to the relevant application.

When a bundle is received by an offline gateway, valid paths between this gateway and online gateways are calculated based on the connectivity plan and a path that achieves earliest bundle delivery is selected. Once a path is selected, the gateway extracts the ID of the next gateway on this path, the ID of the ferry that will transfer the bundle and the estimated forwarding time and stores the bundle in its buffer until a contact to the ferry becomes available, when it forwards the bundle. The procedure of selecting the next gateway is detailed in the next subsection.

In essence, instead of storing the end-to-end path through the network, we only store the next gateway on the path. This approach ensures that our model takes into consideration and proactively handles changes to the initial connectivity plan. If the full path to an online gateway were stored, the time-shift of an intermediate contact, even for a few seconds, would lead to a significant delay, let alone bundle expiration. The proposed method reacts to changes in the state of the network by re-evaluating the best route for a bundle at every gateway.

Unlike upload operations, downloading data from the Internet requires an additional publish/subscribe session layer (e.g. similar to the one presented in [26]), in order to allow for applications such as RSS content distribution and web access over DTN. For download requests, a user can explicitly state the gateway where data need to be delivered; this is not necessarily the same gateway that issued the request. The proposed routing protocol can function efficiently in both cases. We also note that the proposed model can be extended to support data transfers between end-users that are located near gateways, as well. Fig. 1 contains a sample topology corresponding to our model. We highlight that the majority of gateways do not have access to the Internet. Municipalities or local organisations can adopt this model, in order to extend the coverage area of the free Internet services they offer. Instead of installing new costly infrastructure all over a city to provide Internet access, a municipality can opt for this model, simply by installing the relevant components to bus stops (gateways) and buses (ferries).

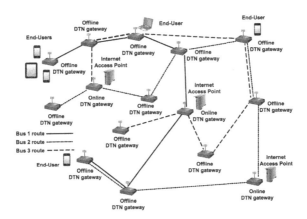

Fig. 1. Sample topology

3.2 CARPOOL Protocol

In order to support the proposed access model, we have designed and implemented CARPOOL, a DTN routing protocol that utilises *a priori* knowledge of the connectivity plan to deliver bundles among DTN gateways. The proposed routing protocol works as follows: all gateways hold the list of online gateways and the overall connectivity plan, which includes all contacts between gateways and ferries along with the scheduled start of each contact. In particular, the entries of the connectivity table for each ferry have the following 3-tuple structure (GatewayID, FerryID, ContactTime). When an offline gateway receives a new bundle from an end-user, CARPOOL identifies the most suitable next gateway for this bundle, in terms of estimated bundle delivery time to an online gateway. CARPOOL identifies paths between an offline gateway and an online gateway, starting from the destination, and moving towards the source in a hop-by-hop manner. The values required as input to the algorithm are PreviousGateway and NewArrivalTime. Initially, PreviousGateway is set to the ID of an online gateway and NewArrivalTime equals to bundle creation time plus TTL. The current gateway first identifies all contacts in the overall connectivity table that satisfy the following requirements:

- GatewayID equals PreviousGateway and

- ContactTime is greater than CurrentTime and less than the latest arrival time (NewArrivalTime).

For each of the aforementioned contacts, we store a set of 3-Tuples: the contact itself and the exact previous contact (in terms of time) between the same ferry and another gateway. When the previous gateway that this ferry has traversed becomes the current gateway, we have identified a direct contact, where the current gateway is only one hop away from an online gateway. Otherwise, the algorithm re-executes using as input the GatewayID and the ContactTime of the previous contact. Thus, we now search for valid contacts that are two hops away from an online gateway. This process is continued until a path is found.

In order to reduce the complexity and the associated computational overhead of our algorithm, instead of identifying all possible paths and selecting one that achieves earliest delivery, we first sort valid contacts to an online gateway starting from the earliest, prior to applying our selection algorithm. This way, we need not calculate all paths from the current gateway to all online gateways; instead we simply select the first plausible path to an online gateway, which is also a path that guarantees earliest delivery. Once a path has been discovered, the GatewayID of the next gateway on the path (NextGateway), the FerryID of the ferry that will transfer the bundle (NextFerry) and the TimeToForward that corresponds to the time that the bundle will be forwarded are added to the header of the bundle; the bundle is stored in the gateway buffer, until a connection between the gateway and *this* ferry exists. The CARPOOL Algorithm is presented in Algorithm 1.

When a connection is up, the gateway uploads bundles waiting to be forwarded through that ferry and downloads bundles from the ferry that are destined to that gateway. When an online gateway receives a new bundle, the bundle is forwarded to the receiving application through the Internet. When an offline gateway receives a bundle, the algorithm is re-executed and the corresponding fields in the header of the bundle are updated. Our access model faces two limitations: the finite buffer size of gateways and ferries, as well as the small window of communication opportunities between gateways and ferries. In the event that this window does not suffice for all bundles to be delivered at the gateway or the ferry respectively, the path for the unserviced bundles is re-calculated. Similarly, CARPOOL re-calculates the path for all bundles in the network with TimeToForward greater than CurrentTime aligned within a fixed threshold, set according to the arrival time of the next ferry to this gateway, in order not to miss this contact opportunity. This allows to cancel the impact of the schedule deviation and typically suffices to accommodate minor schedule drifts. In essence, CARPOOL recalculates routes each time a message misses its expected contact due to high load in the network or short connectivity time between gateways and ferries. As mentioned before, in case of a major delay, the updated traffic schedule is flooded into the network through a central administrative node.

It should be noted that, in contrast to most solutions proposed in literature, CARPOOL is not a replication scheme. Only a single copy of each bundle exists in the network at any given time, keeping overhead to minimum.

For each Ferry F **do**
　　　　For Contact C of ConnectivityTable$_F$ **do**
　　　　　　　　If (C.GatewayID = PreviousGateway) AND
　　　　　　　　(C.ContactTime $\geq$ CurrentTime) AND
　　　　　　　　(C.ContactTime $\leq$ NewArrivalTime) **then**
　　　　　　　　　　//A valid contact has been found. We store a set of 3-tuples: this
　　　　　　　　　　//contact and the previous contact the ferry has with another gateway
　　　　　　　　　　　　Add Set(C$_{prev}$,C) to ValidContacts
　　　　　　　　Endif
　　　　Endfor
Endfor
//Sort valid contacts starting from the earliest contact
C Sort ValidContacts
//Identify a path from source to destination
For Set(S$_{prev}$,S) of ValidContacts **do**
　　　　If (S$_{prev}$.Gateway = CurrentGateway) **then**
　　　　//Path found. Store header fields and exit algorithm
　　　　　　　　NextGateway = S.GatewayID
　　　　　　　　NextFerry = S.FerryID
　　　　　　　　TimeToForward = S$_{prev}$.ContactTime
　　　　　　　Exit
　　　　Else
　　　　//We have not found a path from current gateway to the online gateway.
　　　　//Re-run the algorithm moving one hop further from the online gateway
　　　　　　　　PreviousGateway = S$_{prev}$.GatewayID
　　　　　　　　NewArrivalTime = S$_{prev}$.ContactTime
　　　　　　　　Algorithm (PreviousGateway, NewArrivalTime)
　　　　Endif
Endfor

Algorithm 1. CARPOOL Algorithm

4   Evaluation

Through extensive simulations, we evaluate the performance of CARPOOL in a dense urban environment and study the impact of increased traffic load on its performance comparatively with four widely-used routing protocols, namely, Epidemic [14], PRoPHET [15], binary Spray-and-Wait with 10 message copies [16] and MaxProp [17].

4.1   Evaluation Methodology

The CARPOOL protocol has been implemented and evaluated using the Opportunistic Network Environment (ONE) simulator [27]. Initially, we created the connectivity plan for the entire simulation using as input:

(1) The ID and the coordinates of each gateway,

(2) The ID and the speed of each ferry, along with the gateways on the path of the ferry in the order it transverses them,

(3) The waiting time at each stop and

(4) The start times of each ferry.

We assume that all ferries follow the reverse path once they reach their destination. All gateways become aware of the connectivity plan.

We selected a topology for our simulations that corresponds approximately to an abstraction of the transport service of Thessaloniki, Greece, that includes both the city center and the suburbs. In total, our simulation environment covers an area of approximately 100 km^2 that includes 106 offline gateways (i.e. bus stops) and 15 online gateways. Our scenarios follow 60 ferries (i.e. buses) travelling on 20 routes. The speed of the ferries ranges from 5m/s to 14m/s. All gateways and ferries are equipped with 2GB storage size and wireless network cards at 10Mbps data rate and 50m communication radius. The overall duration of all simulations is 48 hours, including a sufficient training period for protocols to initialize themselves. The traffic load varies from 2500 to 50000 messages per 12 hours. Bundle size ranges from 500kB to 2MB. Given the delay-tolerant nature of the applications, bundle TTL is set to 20h, sufficiently large to accommodate all communication attempts by all protocols. The simulation topology is depicted in Fig. 2.

4.2   Evaluation Metrics

We evaluate performance using the following metrics:

1. *Delivery ratio* expresses the fraction of the total generated messages that are successfully delivered.

$$Delivery\ Ratio = \frac{\text{Number of messages successfully delivered}}{\text{Number of messages generated}}$$

2. *Overhead ratio* is calculated as the number of messages relayed minus the number of messages delivered to the number of messages delivered.

$$Overhead\ Ratio = \frac{Number\ of\ messages\ relayed-Number\ of\ messages\ delivered}{Number\ of\ messages\ delivered}$$

3. *Median latency* is computed as the numerical value separating the higher half of all message latencies from the lower half.

$$Median\ Latency = \frac{\sum_{i=1}^{Number\ of\ messages\ successfully\ delivered} Latency_i}{Number\ of\ messages\ successfully\ delivered}$$

Fig. 2. Simulation topology

4.3   Evaluation Results

Results in Fig. 3 illustrate the delivery ratio of the five routing schemes for increasing traffic load. We notice that in low traffic load conditions (less than 20000 messages in 12h) only CARPOOL and MaxProp manage to deliver all messages; the three other protocols fail to achieve maximum delivery ratio. CARPOOL achieves increased delivery ratio, since contacts between gateways and ferries are known *a priori* and in the event of unexpected delays, new paths to online gateways are being re-discovered. It should be noted that in contrast to other protocols, our current version of CARPOOL does not exploit short contacts between ferries. Through its scheduling tactics at the gateways and the ferries, MaxProp achieves high delivery ratio. Epidemic routing suffers from its excessive overhead and experiences worst performance. In high traffic load conditions (more than 25000 messages in 12h) the delivery ratio of all protocols decreases when traffic load increases. Even in the worst scenario, CARPOOL performs significantly better than all other protocols, managing to successfully deliver 82% of the created bundles despite heavy congestion. Unlike other protocols, the delivery ratio of CARPOOL, even in worst-case scenarios, suffices in its own right to guarantee some level of service. A user may feel confident that even if one attempt fails, most likely this will not be repeated. Several approaches to increase the delivery ratio of CARPOOL are proposed in Section 5.

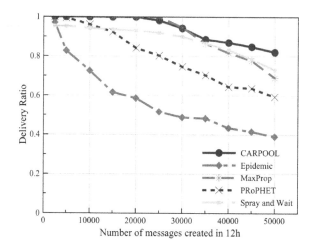

Fig. 3. Delivery ratio for increasing number of messages

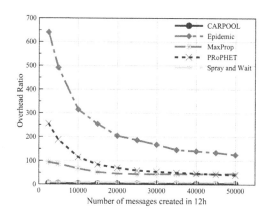

Fig. 4. Overhead ratio for increasing number of messages

In Fig. 4 we show the overhead ratio observed for each routing protocol for increasing traffic load. Given the density of the ferries and the gateways, along with the limited energy capacity of the ferries, overhead becomes important. As expected, CARPOOL presents minimum overhead, since there exists only one copy of each message in the network at any given time. Since CARPOOL keeps a single copy per message, it minimises energy consumption of battery-powered devices, but also allows for better bandwidth utilisation, which practically means our network can accommodate more users. Spray-and-Wait also keeps overhead low (as defined in its simulation settings), while the other three protocols suffer from increased overhead. As shown in Fig. 4, overhead decreases for the rest of the protocols when traffic load increases. This is justified by the protocols' failure to operate in regular mode, since they cannot create their typical number of copies. The result of this overhead reduction is their functional blackout as it appears in the corresponding heavy-traffic delivery ratio results in Fig. 3.

In Fig. 5 we show the median latency of each protocol for increasing traffic load. The median latency of all protocols presents a steady increase for increasing traffic load with the exception of MaxProp, which presents a rapid increase in latency as traffic load increases. CARPOOL performs sufficiently well. Spray-and-wait outperforms all other protocols at the expense of higher overhead and less delivery ratio. CARPOOL achieves exactly the same median latency with Spray-and-Wait in highly congested networks and manages to deliver 10% more packets with 1/10 of the overhead of Spray-and-Wait (i.e. CARPOOL keeps only one copy of each message in the network at any given time, while with Spray-and-Wait up to 10 copies of each message can co-exist in the network). When the network is not congested, Spray-and-Wait achieves lower median latency than CARPOOL by exploiting opportunistic contacts between ferries as well. We are confident that CARPOOL will outperform Spray-and-Wait even in median latency, when opportunistic contacts between ferries are also exploited. Several approaches to achieve that are described in the following Section.

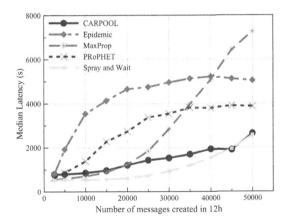

Fig. 5. Median latency for increasing number of messages

5   Discussion

The motivation behind this work was to design a platform for delay-tolerant Internet access that extends the existing coverage of free WiFi access points in an urban environment. Based on the simulation results in Section 4, we show that CARPOOL successfully exploits existing knowledge on the connectivity plan of typical means of public transport, in order to identify a route from the source node to a WiFi access point. From our evaluation results we observe that Spray-and-Wait with 10 copies achieves delivery ratio that approaches CARPOOL and smaller median latency when the network is not congested. This argues towards allowing a few copies to be sent over different paths in order to achieve increased delivery ratio (assuming that a node may fail to deliver its messages) and reduced delay. Towards this direction, we plan to incorporate a mechanism that injects two replicas of each message in the network that follow the two fastest paths, as calculated by the source gateway.

In order to further enhance the performance of CARPOOL, we plan to exploit opportunistic contacts between ferries. A simple approach would be for two ferries to exchange all messages when in range. However, this would lead to significant overhead and would not function properly given the small contact duration window. As a more sophisticated solution, during a contact between two ferries, both ferries can recalculate the estimated delivery time of all messages they hold through the other ferry; if the estimated delivery time of a message through the other ferry is smaller, then the message should be forwarded to the other ferry.

As mentioned before, in case of major delays, the updated traffic schedule is flooded into the network through a central administrative node. The proposed system sustains minor delays by scanning for transmission opportunities for a time period that ranges for a few seconds before and after the estimated arrival of each ferry at a gateway. In order for the system to remain sustainable when a significant bias is introduced in the connectivity table or major delays occur due to traffic or road accidents, we plan to enhance CARPOOL by allowing ferries to recalculate the estimated delivery time whenever a significant delay occurs. In particular, when a ferry reaches a gateway later than expected, it can download all messages destined to this gateway and, at the same time, recalculate the fastest route to an online gateway for all messages the ferry carries and are not destined to this gateway. This way, the overall latency will be significantly reduced. Major delays in ferry schedule can also lead to loops; to solve this problem we plan to include two new fields in message header: Last Ferry and Last Gateway. By holding and checking the values of the last ferry and gateway visited by the message, typical loops can be avoided.

Another optimization approach would be to prioritize small size packets, since large packets take long time to upload/download. Combining this with the restricted communication window, the transmission of a large file at the beginning of a contact can significantly delay the delivery of all other messages.

6   Conclusions

In this paper, we have described in detail an access model for urban environments suitable to extend existing free Internet access both in space and time. In particular, our communication model utilises means of public transport as message ferries that transfer messages between online and offline gateways located near ferry stops. Gateways are responsible for collecting and servicing Internet access requests from the end-users. To realize our communication model, we have employed delay-tolerant networking properties into our connectivity plan routing protocol. CARPOOL utilises existing knowledge on the schedule of ferries to extract the fastest route between a gateway that issues a request and an online gateway that will serve it. Our simulation results have shown that an acceptable level of service can be provided, since CARPOOL outperforms other DTN routing protocols in terms of delivery ratio (i.e. service probability) and overhead (i.e. potential to accommodate more users). Several enhancements of CARPOOL were also proposed. As future work, we plan to incorporate these mechanisms into CARPOOL and investigate its performance when large deviations to the predefined contact plan occur.

Acknowledgments. The research leading to these results has received funding from the European Community's Seventh Framework Programme ([FP7/2007-2013, FP7-REGPOT-2010-1, SP4 Capacities, Coordination and Support Actions) under Grant Agreement n° 264226 (Project title: Space Internetworking Center - SPICE). This paper reflects only the authors' views and the Community is not liable for any use that may be made of the information contained therein.

References

1. Rue, L.F.: Report of the Special Rapporteur on the promotion and protection of the right to freedom of opinion and expression. Human Rights Council, Seventeenth session Agenda item 3, United Nations General Assembly (2011)
2. Cerf, V., Burleigh, S., Hooke, A., Torgerson, L., Durst, L., Scott, K., Fall, K., Weiss, H.: Delay–Tolerant Networking Architecture, Internet RFC4838 (2007)
3. Fall, K.: A Delay-Tolerant Network Architecture for Challenged Internets. In: Proc. of ACM SIGCOMM (2003)
4. Scott, K., Burleigh, S.: Bundle protocol specification. RFC 5050 (2007)
5. Komnios, I., Tsaoussidis, V.: CARPOOL: Extending free Internet access over DTN in urban environment. In: Proc. of the 2013 ACM MobiCom Workshop on Lowest Cost Denominator Networking for Universal Access (LCDNet 2013), pp. 21–24. ACM, New York (2013)
6. Thraves, G., Urueta, A., Vidales, P., Solarski, M.: Driving the deployment of citywide ubiquitous WiFi access. In: Proc. of the Proceedings of First International Conference on Simulation Tools and Techniques for Communications, pp. 1–8 (2008)
7. Sathiaseelan, A., Trossen, D., Komnios, I., Ott, J., Crowcroft, J.: Information Centric Delay Tolerant Networking: An Internet Architecture for the Challenged. Computer Laboratory Technical Report, UCAM-CL-TR-841 (2013)
8. Sofia, R., Mendes, P.: User-provided networks: consumer as provider. IEEE Communications Magazine 46(12), 86–91 (2008)
9. Psaras, I., Mamatas, L.: On demand connectivity sharing: Queuing management and load balancing for user-provided networks. Computer Networks 55(2), 399–414 (2011)
10. Komnios, I., Sathiaseelan, A., Crowcroft, J.: LEDBAT Performance in Sub-packet Regimes. In: 11th IEEE/IFIP Annual Conference on Wireless On-Demand Network Systems and Services (WONS 2014), Obergurgl, Austria (2014)
11. Lenas, S.A., Tsaoussidis, V.: Enabling free Internet access at the edges of broadband connections: A hybrid packet scheduling approach. SIGMOBILE Mobile Computing and Communications Review (MC2R) 18(1), 55–63 (2014)
12. Sathiaseelan, A., Crowcroft, J., Goulden, M., Greiffenhagen, C., Mortier, R., Fairhurst, G., McAuley, D.: Public Access WiFi Service (PAWS). In: Digital Economy All Hands Meeting, Aberdeen (2012)
13. FON WIRELESS, http://www.fon.com

14. Vahdat, A., Becker, D.: Epidemic routing for partially connected ad hoc networks. Technical Report CS-200006, Duke University (2000)
15. Lindgren, A., Doria, A., Davies, E., Grasic, S.: Probabilistic routing protocol for intermittently connected networks. Internet Draft (2011)
16. Spyropoulos, T., Psounis, K., Raghavendra, C.S.: Spray and wait: An efficient routing scheme for intermittently connected mobile networks. In: Proc. ACM SIGCOMM Workshop on Delay Tolerant Networking (WDTN) (2005)
17. Burgess, J., Gallagher, B., Levine, B.N.: MaxProp: Routing for Vehicle-Based Disruption-Tolerant Networks. In: Proceedings of IEEE InfoCom (2006)
18. Ho, M., Fall, K.: Poster: Delay tolerant networking for sensor networks. In: The First IEEE Conference on Sensor and Ad Hoc Communications and Networks (SECON) (2004)
19. Seth, A., Kroeker, D., Zaharia, M., Guo, S., Keshav, S.: Low-cost communication for rural Internet kiosks using mechanical backhaul. In: Proc. of the MobiCom 2006, New York, NY, USA, pp. 334–345 (2006)
20. Xian, Y., Huang, C., Cobb, J.: Look-ahead routing and message scheduling in delay-tolerant networks. In: Proc. IEEE Conference on Local Computer Networks (LCN) (2010)
21. Burleigh, S.: Contact Graph Routing. Internet Draft (2010)
22. Bezirgiannidis, N., Burleigh, S., Tsaoussidis, V.: Delivery Time Estimation for Space Bundles. IEEE Transactions on Aerospace and Electronic Systems 49(3), 1897–1910 (2013)
23. Hyyrylainen, T., Karkkainen, T., Luo, C., Jaspertas, V., Karvo, J., Ott, J.: Opportunistic Email Distribution and Access in Challenged Heterogeneous Environments. In: Proc. of the ACM Workshop on Challenged Networks (CHANTS) (2007)
24. Lindgren, A.: Social Networking in a Disconnected Network: fbDTN: Facebook over DTN. In: Proc. of the 6th ACM Workshop on Challenged Networks (CHANTS), pp. 69–70 (2011)
25. Zaragoza, K., Thai, N., Christensen, T.: An implementation for accessing Twitter across challenged networks. In: Proc. of the 6th ACM Workshop on Challenged Networks (CHANTS), pp. 71–72 (2011)
26. Demmer, M., Fall, K.: The design and implementation of a session layer for delay-tolerant networks. Computer Communications 32(16), 1724–1730 (2009)
27. Keranen, A., Ott, J., Karkkainen, T.: The ONE simulator for DTN protocol evaluation. In: Proceedings of the 2nd International Conference on Simulation Tools and Techniques (SIMUTools), New York (2009)

Broadcasting Information
in Variably Dense Environment
Using Connectionless Data Exchange (CoLDE)

Osama Abu Oun[1], Wahabou Abdou[2],
Christelle Bloch[1], and François Spies[1]

[1] FEMTO-ST Lab. (CNRS) - University of Franche-Comte
1 Cours Leprince-Ringuet, 25200 Montbéliard, France
{oabuoun,christelle.bloch,francois.spies}@femto-st.fr
http://www.femto-st.fr/
[2] Univ. Bordeaux, LaBRI, UMR CNRS 5800
351 Cours de la Libération 33 405 Talence
wahabou.abdou@labri.fr
http://www.labri.fr

Abstract. Our main goal is to develop a new solution to use multi-tier broadcast in order to deliver messages to all the devices in certain areas, whether they are connected to different networks, or not connected to any network. We use beacons (management frames) in the IEEE 802.11 protocol to send data from the access point to the clients without an association, and we use the probe request/response to exchange small amounts of data without being connected to the same network and without threatening the security of any of them.

Keywords: Wi-Fi Beacons, Probe request/response, Connectionless, CoLDE, multi-tier broadcast.

1 Introduction

Broadcasting is a widely used communication mode in ad hoc networks. It allows sending an information from one node to all the nodes that are within its coverage area. This feature makes broadcasting a suitable mode for exchanging routing information in Mobile Ad hoc Networks (MANETs), sending emergency messages in Vehicular Ad hoc Networks (VANETs) or sharing local measurements in Wireless Sensor Networks (WSNs). Many studies of these networks tackled the broadcasting issues. They tried to handle the adaptation to density, the reduction of useless redundant packets, the guarantee of confidentiality and authenticity of broadcast data. Currently, one of the research topics is the design of a flexible method to broadcast information in variable dense environments. These environments consist of hundred or even thousands of clients in the same geographical area, where they can be connected to different networks. Therefore, one of the main challenges is to find a way to send broadcast packets to all nodes,

A. Mellouk et al. (Eds.): WWIC 2014, LNCS 8458, pp. 283–296, 2014.
© Springer International Publishing Switzerland 2014

no matter the network they are connected to, or even if they are not connected to any network.

Adapting the ad hoc broadcasting algorithms proposed in the literature to work in variable dense environments brings out some considerations that must be taken into account, especially the ongoing services or communications of the nodes and the wideness of the area. For instance almost all these algorithms rely on the assumption that the nodes are connected to one network. This implies that if a node N_i wants to send a packet to another node N_j connected to a different network, at least one of them should disconnect from its original network. Indeed, normal Wi-Fi clients can be connected only to one network at the same time. This disconnection can be a problem to many users because they will have to stop using the service of their main network. In wide areas, it is usual to find users that are geographically close, but connected to different networks. But in case of emergency for example it will be beneficial if they cooperate and exchange/forward safety messages. Finding a method that allows this type of communication is the main target of this work.

In this paper, we present a new solution to use a multi-tier broadcast model to deliver messages to all the devices in a selected area, even if they are connected to different networks or not connected to any network. This communication mode relies on both multicast and broadcast operations. In order to realize this solution we need two components. The first one is an extension of the IEEE 802.11 in order to allow exchanging data without connection. We propose CoLDE (Connectionless Data Exchange) which extends the IEEE 802.11 to exchange non-confidential and small amounts of data between Wi-Fi devices without a connection between them and without requesting them to disconnect from their original networks. Exchanged data could be a broadcast message from the server or one of the clients or it could be a service request from one of the clients. The second component is a protocol to define the hierarchy and the data that could be transferred using the first component. For this purpose, we present the HyDEP (Hybrid Data Exchange Protocol) which organizes the hierarchy (if it exists) and the roles of entities, and defines the rules to send, receive and (re)broadcast the data using CoLDE.

The remaining of this paper is organized as follows: Section 1 presents some works on connectionless protocols. Section 2 introduces our first contribution on how to transfer packets without any association procedure. The hierarchical organization of entities is discussed in Section 3. Section 4 presents the performance evaluation of our contributions. And finally, some concluding remarks and future works are mentioned in Section 5.

2   Related Works

Some researches focus on using one Wi-Fi card to connect to multiple network at the same time, In [1], the author proposes a software based approach, called MultiNet, that facilitates simultaneous connections to multiple networks by virtualizing a single wireless card. The wireless card is virtualized by introducing an intermediate layer below IP. In our study, we are giving a solution to allow the device to exchange the data with many networks at the same time, even without being connected to any of them, and without adding any intermediate layer.

In this paper, we focus on two fields, which could be used together to give a stable and flexible solution to broadcast messages.

The first field concerns connectionless protocols. In [2] and [3], the authors prove the possibility of transferring messages between the access point (AP) and a client using beacons. Beacon-stuffing is a low bandwidth communication protocol for IEEE 802.11 networks that enables APs to communicate with clients without association. This enables clients to receive information from nearby APs even when they are disconnected, or when connected to another AP. This scheme is complementary to the IEEE 802.11 association and works by overloading IEEE 802.11 management frames while not breaking the standard. In [4], the authors prove it possible to transfer data between Wi-Fi clients using the probe request/response without being connected to any AP nor in ad hoc mode.

The Second field is broadcast in wireless network. Multi-tier Broadcasting using tree structure established in a network is a well-known and widely used technique in MANET as the TreeCast [6] method, which is based on a fully distributed, decentralized and resource-efficient algorithm that maintains a spanning tree. The big difference between all the tree-based broadcast and the broadcast in this work is the existence of the network, this work focuses on broadcasting messages regardless of network existence.

3   Connectionless Data Exchange Protocol (CoLDE)

3.1   Full Connection Data Exchange (Normal Mode)

Creating a connection or an alliance is an essential phase for data exchange between a Wi-Fi access point and a Wi-Fi client, or between clients themselves on the Wi-Fi network. Having a connection between the access point and the Wi-Fi client means that the client is a part of the network and can have access to the rest of the network. In public Wi-Fi networks that should not be a problem, usually there is no sensitive or confidential data in it, it just offers connection to the public Internet and it is available to anybody. But it is not the same situation for the private Wi-Fi, only authorized persons with the required credentials can connect to that Wi-Fi and use its services. In case two clients need to exchange some data, they should be connected either using a Wi-Fi access point or one of them is in ad hoc mode or a Wi-Fi direct mode, which leads to the same problem between a Wi-Fi client and a Wi-Fi access point.

3.2   CoLDE Concept

This is a suggestion to extend the IEEE 802.11 protocol by adding the functionality that allows exchanging data between two Wi-Fi entities without the need to have an alliance or establish a connection between them. The entities could be normal access points (infrastructure mode), ad hoc devices, Wi-Fi Direct or even normal Wi-Fi clients.

This extension allows broadcasting information to all Wi-Fi devices in certain areas, even if they are connected to different networks, or even if they are not connected to any network. CoLDE allows the Wi-Fi devices (i.e, mobile phones and laptops) to benefit from the new services with the help of the other devices that include these services. For example, some mobile phones do not include certain localization systems, so they can get the current position from the other devices (which include that localization system), if these devices exist in the same geographical area and most specifically in the Wi-Fi coverage area of the first device.

Examples and situations vary with localization functions, emergency evacuation, integration between Wi-Fi devices and VANET, exchanging data with access points in the same area without the need to be connected to them, or to use a service from another device.

Nowadays, the majority of Wi-Fi networks are private networks. Such networks exist in large enterprises, small companies, shops, houses and even mobile Wi-Fi as in the case of a mobile phone running in an ad hoc mode or in a Wi-Fi direct mode. These Wi-Fi networks are mostly connected to the Internet using broadband connection. Private Wi-Fi owners do not open it to the public to avoid many threats. These threats could be classified into three main points:

- **local network security** to protect the internal network.
- **public network security** to prevent others from using the network in illegal actions like hacking other networks, sending spam,... or any other action which could be considered a cyber crime.
- **Service level** to assure that nobody will use their Wi-Fi in a way that could degrade the whole performance of the network.

3.3 Working Method

The data will be carried into beacon frames for broadcasting the information, and into probe Request/Response Management Frames to request a service. This approach more specifically uses the Request Information Element (RIE) part of the management frame (in case of the probe Request/Response frames), which is a variable length part, which the client usually uses it to ask the access point for some extra information like the SSID, the supported rate,... .

Each request information element has a unique ID, the ID numbers between 32-255 have been reserved for future use. One of these IDs could be used to define a new information element to send a special request from a Wi-Fi entity to another Wi-Fi entity (broadcast if the SSID is unknown, directed if the SSID is already known). The request can include some parameters, for example: the list of their access points with their RSSIs, their current location, extra information about an accident, road conditions (VANET).

Actually, the proposed extension is only software and needs no special hardware. Any Wi-Fi device, whatever its role in the network, can be provided with

Frame Control	Duration	DA	SA	BSSID	Sequence Control	Frame Body	FCS
Octets:2	2	6	6	6	2	0 - 2312	4

Fig. 1. IEEE 802.11 Management Frame

Maximum Length = 2312							
Element ID	**Length**	**Service ID**	**Server Address**	**Data Field Size**	**Data1**	**......**	**Data N**
ID = [32 → 255]	X			Y			
1 Octet	**1 Octet**	**2 Octets**	**16 Octets**	**1 Octet**	**Y Octets**	**Y Octets**	**Y Octets**

Fig. 2. CoLDE Frame

an extension, which means it can be provided by any access point, mobile in an ad hoc mode, mobile in a direct Wi-Fi mode or even a normal mobile running in a pure client mode.

4   Hybrid Data Exchange Protocol (HyDEP)

The Hybrid Data Exchange Protocol is our proposal to organize hierarchy (if it exists), define the role of each entity, define the data structure to broadcast messages and request services between the Wi-Fi entities in the MANET/VANET networks. The system is a hybrid system which depends on a centralized and non-centralized hierarchy at the same time. There are two main characteristics in this design:

1. A centralized system in which there is a server control forming the broadcast tree on the first level only, sending broadcast messages and responding to the LightWeight Services requested by the nodes in the tree.
2. A Non-centralized system in the way that the nodes work without the need to know the parent-node or the children-nodes, the nodes can send broadcast messages, but the receivers can distinguish the messages according to their sources, among which the messages from the server should be more credible than the others.

4.1   Tree Structure

Two main components could exist in the environment:

Server: It is the root of the broadcasting tree which maintains the connections with the direct children-nodes; the connections between the server and its child-nodes are established on the Internet/Intranet. The server can push notifications/requests to a specific child-node(s) directly, and they will broadcast these messages in the sub-tree(s).

Node: The node is any device which has a wireless card that can be used to receive/send the data from/to its environment or directly from the server. Each node has many attributes, i.e. GPS info (position, number of satellites, number of child nodes, battery Level, node speed, bandwidth, traffic cost, neighbors,...).

4.2   Node Types

The nodes are categorized according to their location and their capabilities:

Main-Node Level-I (Type-I or MNL-I)

The main node level-I is a wireless device (a mobile or an access point) the parent of which is the root, it receives messages from the root as unicast on the IP network (3G, Broadband). It broadcasts the received messages (notifications, requests) in its Wi-Fi coverage. The main node level-I can send requests to the root directly as unicast, besides periodically sending a neighborhood list to the server. The delay between two updates can be either pre-defined by the server or even customized by the node.

Main-Node Level-N (Type-II or MNL-N)

The main node level-N is a wireless device (a mobile or an access point) the parent of which is one of the main nodes (N is the depth of the node in the tree), but it can communicate directly with the root on the IP network, it receives messages from the parent as broadcast on the Wi-Fi. It rebroadcasts the received messages (notifications, requests) in its Wi-Fi coverage. The main node level-N can send the requests to the root directly as unicast, it periodically sends a neighborhood list to the server. The delay between two updates can be either pre-defined by the server or even customized by the node.

Leaf-Node with Internet (Type-III or LN-WI)

The leaf-node with Internet is a wireless device (a mobile or an access point) the parent of which is the root, it receives the messages from the parent as unicast. It cannot rebroadcast the received messages and it cannot receive any broadcast from any other main node. So, the leaf-node with the Internet could either be main node level-I or main node level-N, but without the ability to receive/(re)broadcast the messages from/in its Wi-Fi coverage. This type can work in case a mobile does not include the protocol but it has Internet/Intranet connection with the server.

Leaf-Node – No Internet (Type-IV or LN-NI)

The leaf-node without Internet is a mobile. Its parent of which is another main node different from the root. It receives messages from the parent as broadcast on the Wi-Fi. It can not rebroadcast the received messages. Any request should be relayed by another main node. This type can work in case a mobile does not include the protocol and at the same time has no Internet/Intranet connection with the server.

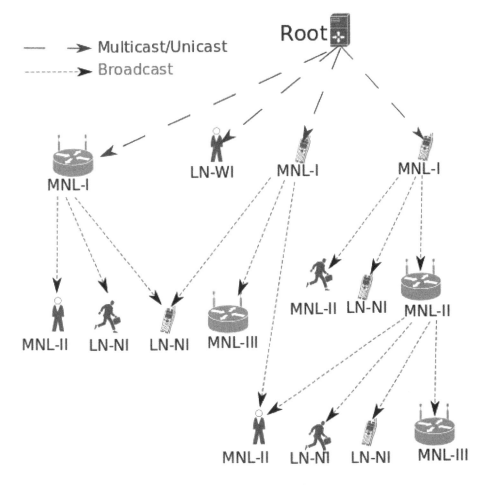

Fig. 3. HyDEP - Broadcasting Structure

4.3   Main-Nodes Selection Criteria

As soon as the node (Type-I, Type-II or Type-III) connects to the root, the parent will be the root itself, the node will be either Main-Node Level-I or Leaf-Node with the Internet (Type-III), depending on its capability to broadcast the messages in its Wi-Fi coverage. Periodically, the root evaluates the tree structure starting from its own child nodes, the evaluation process depends on the following rules:

– The node stays as a 1st level main node as long as there is no other main node in its Wi-Fi coverage area. The server can decide whether there is another node in the area either:
  • by using the geographical position of the node.
  • or because the node receives no broadcast from other main nodes.
  • or because it is moving with the highest speed than a pre-defined node speed.

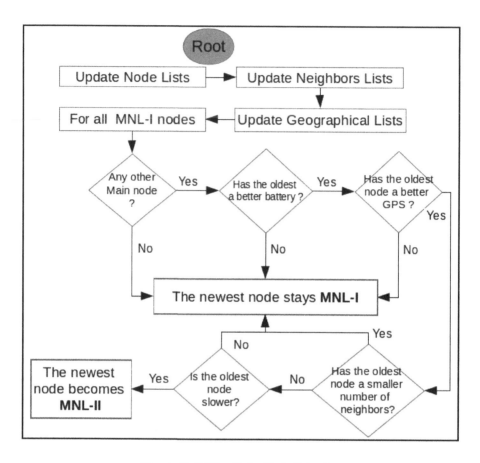

Fig. 4. HyDEP - Main Node Selection

– otherwise, the node will be moved to one of the other main nodes to be a child node in the same area according to the following priorities:
  • Age of the main node.
  • Speed of the main node.
  • The battery level of the main nodes.
  • The greatest number of satellites in view of the main nodes.
  • The lowest number of neighbors of the main nodes.

4.4   Multi-tier Broadcast

Broadcast is referred to when transmitting a message that will be received by every device on the network, while multicast is the delivery of a message or information to a group of destination computers simultaneously in a single transmission from the source[5].

If one wants to broadcast a message to all the devices in selected areas, regardless of which wireless network they are connected to, neither the multicast solution nor the broadcast solution can achieve this goal separately, but a solution consisting of both of them can.

We present a solution "Multi-Tier Broadcast" which depends on the multicast and the broadcast at the same time, and on many levels. The destined message should be sent using multicast to some devices in these areas, so they can broadcast it to the rest of the devices. Each device receiving it will rebroadcast it again till the message expires. The message expires either when the TTL is 0 or when its validity time runs out. If the devices in these areas do not include the multicast, the first phase can be done using the unicast.

But even with a Multi-Tier solution, a lot of devices will not receive the message, these devices are either not connected to any network or the devices receive no messages from the source. We can solve this problem by using Multi-Tier Broadcast with CoLDE.

In this mode, the server sends a message to its children nodes (Nodes Type-I (MNL-I) and Type-II (LN-WI)), each request has a TTL, the TTL is combined with two factors:

Number of Rebroadcasts this defines how many times the message will be rebroadcast, each node decreases this value by 1.

Expiry time this is a timestamp to define when the message will expire, this factor has priority over the first factor.

4.5   Lightweight Services Exchange System

Lightweight Services are the services that depend on a non-confidential small amount of data. This data could be transferred using only one frame, so that it will not consume the resources of the providing entity. These services could be anything, for example asking for localization information, sending an SOS signal in emergency cases, requesting evacuation instructions,...

Most of the traditional services could be used to compromise the network, but this is not the case with the suggested Lightweight Services. If we go through the list of the most dangerous threat to Wi-Fi networks (mentioned in the CoLDE concept), it will be as follows:

- **local network security** there is no need to establish a connection between the client and the access point, so the client will never be part of the network.
- **public network security** the access point can maintain a list of secure services and their servers, so the client will not be able to participate in any illegal action.
- **service level** this category of services consists of two packets only, the request and the response, so the client can never abuse the service by downloading large files, watching live broadcasts,...

The combination between the Lightweight Services and the Connectionless Data Exchange can provide the owners of the private Wi-Fi with a secure method to run their access points as a Lightweight Services Provider.

System Entities

There are three entities in the service design:

- **The LWS (LightWeight Server)** is the server that provides the lightweight service.
- **The LWSH (LightWeight Services Helper)** is the entity that provides the service, or it relays the requests to the LWS and sends back the responses.
- **The LWSB (LightWeight Service Beneficiary)** is the entity that needs a piece of data from the LWS but it is not able to get it directly without the help of a LWSH.

System Design

The main points which have been taken into consideration in the LightWeight Services design are the following:

- The LWSH and the LWSB should not need to establish a connection between them.
- The Wi-Fi access point can refuse requests to certain servers or for certain services.
- The client does not have to be connected to the Wi-Fi in order to ask for this service.
- The data could be gathered locally on the LWSH or could be relayed to a LWS.

Service Mechanism

The service consists of two or four phases, according to the type of service:

LW-Req (LightWeight Service Request) the LSWB broadcasts this request and waits for a response from a LWSH. In case it receives no response, it re-broadcasts the request after waiting for a pre-defined delay. This delay should be pre-defined in the protocol in order to prevent service abuse.

LW-Process (LightWeight Service Processing) the LWSH processes the request as follows:
- Verifies that the request is allowed according to its own list.
- If the service should be provided locally, it verifies that it is allowed to send such data.
- If the request should be relayed to a LWS, it verifies that the LWS is allowed on its own list, and then it relays the request. The UDP is used for the communication between the LWSH and the LWS.

LW-Ready (LightWeight Service Ready) as soon as the LWSH receives the response (either locally or from a LWS), it prepares the response in order to send it to the LWSB.

LW-Res (LightWeight Service Response) the LWSH sends back the result to the LWSB (Unicast).

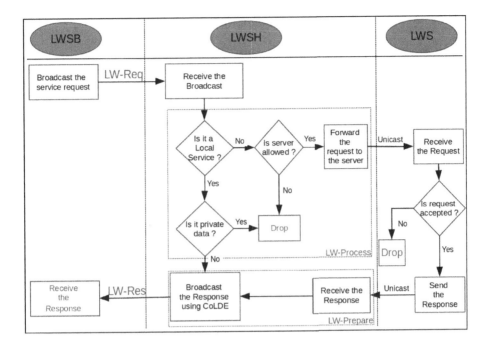

Fig. 5. LightWeight Service Mechanism

Service Categories

The service categories can be any type of public services in which no private or classified data is included. For example, localizations services, emergency request, evacuation services, warnings, evacuation directions, weather forecast,... In case of fixed Wi-Fi access points, there could be many data channels in which the Wi-Fi client can check from time to time in order to get the latest updates.

5 Simulation

For our simulations we have used the network simulator NS2 (version 2.35). We have implemented CoLDE extension using C++ language, then we modified the management frames (beacons, probe request/response) of the protocol IEEE 802.11.

The simulation environment had the following characteristics:

- **Simulation area:** a square area of dimensions X*X (different according to the different scenarios,).
- **Number of nodes:** different according to the simulation area.
- **Nodes' locations:** the nodes are distributed over the selected area in which each node is located at fixed distance from the other nodes.
- **Propagation:** Shadowing Model.
- **Mobility:** the nodes are fixed during the simulation.

We have applied the testing according to two modes:

- **Directed Mode:** in this mode we have the root (the broadcasting node) and the client nodes, all the client nodes have direct connection with the root.
- **CoLDE mode:** in this mode we have the following nodes:
  - The root: This is the broadcasting node, it is located at the center of the simulation area (1 root in each simulation).
  - MNL-I: main nodes have direct connection with the broadcasting node (4 MNL-I in all the simulations).
  - MNL-II: main nodes have no connection with the root (number of MNL-II nodes varies depending on the testing area).

  The broadcasting node sends a direct message to the main nodes MNL-I, the MNL-I nodes broadcast the message into their coverage areas using CoLDE. The message received by MNL-II, the MNL-II nodes decrease the TTL and rebroadcast the message into their coverage areas.

Both modes have been repeated using different areas and different number of nodes. In each scenario we calculated the time needed for the nodes to get the message. Table 1 shows the parameters of each scenario and its results.

The results show that CoLDE can broadcast a message to about 84 nodes in half of the time needed by the Directed mode. In the second scenario, broadcasting the message using CoLDE took 12% of the time needed by the Directed mode to broadcast the same message. In the third scenario, CoLDE needed 4% of the time needed by the Directed mode. In other words, the Directed mode needed about 24 times the time needed by CoLDE. Figure 6 shows the relation between the number of the nodes and the time needed to broadcast a message using the Directed mode and the CoLDE mode.

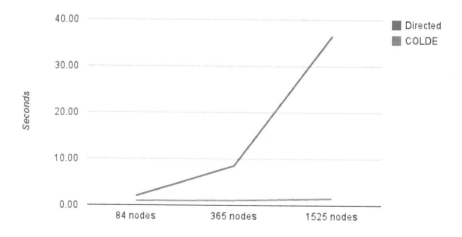

Fig. 6. Simulation - Broadcast Duration Comparison

Table 1. Simulation scenarios

Scenario			Directed		CoLDE	
Area m*m	Number of nodes	Broadcast time	Last Node	Duration	Last Node	Duration
250*250	84	2.54	4.51	1.97	3.51	0.97
500*500	365	2.54	11.02	8.48	3.61	1.07
1000*1000	1525	2.54	39.03	36.49	4.01	1.47

6   Conclusion

Exchanging data between the devices directly, without the need to have a connection and without being connected to the same network, provides a flexible method to broadcast important messages to all the devices in a selected area. Using a multi-tier broadcast model can extend the broadcast area which means that the message will reach a larger number of devices. Devices can also request some services by broadcasting the requests in their coverage area. To implement this protocol we designed a new extension to IEEE 802.11. The extension is called CoLDE, which provides a simple and efficient method to exchange non-confidential and small amounts of data (only one frame) without having an association. CoLDE loads the data in the IEEE 802.11 management frames directly which eliminate the complexity and the overhead of the network and transport layers.

Our future work consists of two main aspects:

- Porting the extension to DD-WRT and Android, so we can test it in a real environments.
- Studying the best method to prevent abusing the protocol by broadcasting fake messages. Digital signature can be added to the message, so the recipients can verify the sender's signatures and decide whether they should rebroadcast the message or not.

References

1. Chandra, R., Bahl, P., Bahl, P.: MultiNet: Connecting to Multiple IEEE 802.11 Networks Using a Single Wireless Card. In: Proceedings of IEEE INFOCOM 2004, Hong Kong (March 2004)
2. Chandra, R., Padhye, J., Ravindranath, L., Wolman, A.: Beacon-Stuffing: Wi-Fi without Associations. In: Proceeding HOTMOBILE 2007 Proceedings of the Eighth IEEE Workshop on Mobile Computing Systems and Applications, pp. 53–57 (2007)
3. Muralidharan, K., Dhanapal, K.B., Chowdhury, A.R.: BOWL: Design and implementation of a (connectionless) broadcasting system over wireless LAN. In: World of Wireless, Mobile and Multimedia Networks, WoWMoM 2008, pp. 1–6 (2008)
4. Yun, M., Kim, D., Lee, H.-S., Lee, J.: Silent Broadcast: Experience of Connectionless Messaging Using Wi-Fi P2P. In: 8th International Conference on Information Science and Digital Content Technology (ICIDT), vol. 2, pp. 239–242 (2012)

5. Tanenbaum, A.: Computer Networks, p. 368 (2003) ISBN 0-13-066102-3
6. Juttner, A., Magi, A.: Tree based broadcast in ad hoc networks. Journal Mobile Networks and Applications Archive 10(5), 753–762 (2005)
7. Wang, T., Cano, A., Giannakis, G.B., Javier Ramos, F.: Multi-Tier Cooperative Broadcasting with Hierarchical Modulations. IEEE Transactions on Wireless Communications 6(8), 3047–3057 (2007)

Persistent Behaviour in Healthcare Facilities: From Actimetric Tele-Surveillance to Therapy Education

Gilles Virone[1], Nicolas Vuillerme[1], Mounir Mokhtari[2], and Jacques Demongeot[1]

[1] AGIM (Ageing, Imaging & Modelling) Laboratory, FRE 3405 CNRS-UJF-UPMF-EPHE,
Faculty of Medicine of Grenoble, University J. Fourier, 38700 La Tronche, France
[2] IPAL (Image and Pervasive Access Laboratory), UMI 2955 CNRS-UJF-IMT-UPMC-NUS,
1 Fusionopolis Way, #21-01 Connexis (South Tower), NUS 138632 Singapore
{Gilles.Virone,Nicolas.Vuillerme,Jacques.Demongeot}@agim.eu,
Mounir.Mokhtari@int-edu.eu

Abstract. This article discusses persistent behaviors emulated on the basis of atypical and recurrent scenarios of daily life, originally developed for the domicile and now extended to health facilities. The pathologic persistence (called also perseveration) in tasks of daily life is a marker of neurodegenerative diseases such as Alzheimer's disease, and its non-invasive detection can lead to early diagnosis, if it triggers a battery of diagnostic tests based on imaging, clinical neurology and cognitive tests to confirm the suspicion of neuronal degeneration. Finally, the tele-monitoring of daily activity, called actimetric monitoring, allows the detection of abnormal repetitive tasks, and contributes also to the content of a custom folder of health data, which can provide a therapeutic education adapted to the person followed at home.

Keywords: tele-surveillance at home, persistence in daily life tasks, therapeutic education.

1 Introduction

It is known that the worldwide population is ageing, especially in developed countries. In 2050 for example, the number of elders aged 65+ in the world will have increased by 100% compared to the year 1950 [1]. The socio-economic consequences are hazardous (*e.g.*, lack of medical workload, overburdened medical institutions, increasing healthcare costs, etc.). In the market place, this societal drift leads to the development of more and more specialized commercial devices, improving the well-being and security of the elders (and disabled), while helping them at staying at home as long as possible. New community care settings equipped with pervasive technologies are also an alternative to nursing homes, medicalized institutions for dependent people or hospitals, for watching the elders in a controlled and respectable environment. Conventional research developments on smart homes [2-3] and assistive technologies [4] often utilize experimental platforms as a support for conducting experiments taking normally place in a healthcare facility. This offers numerous advantages such as the ability to pre-validate experimental prototypes before their use in the

A. Mellouk et al. (Eds.): WWIC 2014, LNCS 8458, pp. 297–311, 2014.
© Springer International Publishing Switzerland 2014

real-world. In case of infrastructure absence, computer simulations, multivariate in the healthcare area [5-11], can play a key role. They can simulate different activity trends based on heterogeneous parameters (*e.g.*, age, education, seasons, etc.) [12], replacing specific components, or whole intelligent systems with new designs (and hence avoiding tedious lab experiments or real-world deployments) [13-15]. They can also be used for testing uncommon scenarios of everyday life on demand (instead of waiting for unpredictable real-life apparitions), for managing sensor distributions, or for assessing specific algorithms invented and used in the area of activity, sound, and speech recognition, or in the behavioral sciences as well [16-20].

In what follows, we describe the simulation process for generating persistent behaviors (Methods section). This section also makes a census of the sensors that we have used for modeling data. The following section gives simulated results based on persistent calibrated parameters, which can be perceived as visible symptoms. A global scenario is also studied as a case study to emulate a more generalized cognitive decline. The discussion section deals with our methodology and the conclusion summarizes the paper.

2   Methods

To emulate persistent behaviors linked to the Alzheimer disease in residential care settings, we first start from stable behaviors deriving from basic scenarios encountered in everyday life in the home environment [13]. Based on the fact that we all possess basic needs and patterns (*e.g.*, circadian or nychthemeral activity rhythms (CARs) in the macroscopic way [2-3], [22-23]), no matter the living conditions and the geographical location, we have assumed that these scenarios would remain essentially identical in centers for Alzheimer's. In other words, we basically model the Alzheimer's conditions of life in a healthcare setting putting forward the hypothesis that clients still tend to follow a regular life rhythm based on 24 hours (circadian) [2-3], such as in their familiar environment at-home. Then, we slightly modify these scenarios to reveal persistent behaviors at the spatial-temporal level setting abnormal prolonged periods of time in a room or dedicated to perform a daily routine. To reinforce the phenomenon of persistence, we have also selected a couple of physiological parameters revealing additional consequences due to a spatial-temporal disorientation. Next sections deal with a) virtual sensors used to emulate the occupancy parameter in a room or to perform daily routine, b) the associated data models, and c) the software implementation, producing experimental data.

2.1   Virtual Sensors and Data

Our simulator emulates three distinct types of virtual sensors as follows: a) infrastructure sensors coming from home security systems, b) physiological sensors (generally associated to personal care devices), and c) environmental sensors for measuring climate parameters. Associated data are discussed below:

Activity Data
"Activity data" relate to physical activity (*e.g.*, body movements or more complex activities such as a daily routine or an activity of daily living). They can be collected using accelerometers worn on the body (producing body network) or infrastructure

sensors (coming from home security systems); among the latter ones, the operator interface Nematron® DP8111 is mimicked by the simulator for generating displacements from one room to another.

Physiological Data

They deliver information about personal health status. Our simulations reflect directly the outputs of the following personal healthcare devices:

- Body scale (Moulinex®)
- Blood pressure and Heart rate monitor (model EW 285–NAIS Matsushita®)
- Oximeter (model OEM 2367 Nonin®)

Environmental Data

They give information about ambient environment (*e.g.*, indoor temperature, acoustic noise, speech, air quality, etc.) concerning the monitored living space. In general, they are adjusted either by users or automatically with HVAC[1] systems. Simulating environmental conditions is an important task as they can relate to health decline. For instance, a drop in body temperature (hyperthermia) can be due to a high elevation of external temperature and a fall can be due to a lack of light or a poor relative humidity due to a severe drought, and might be signs of alert situations provoked by exogenous factors. Our simulation model includes the following environmental indoor sensors:

- Thermometer (temperature)
- Hygrometer (relative humidity)
- Luxmeter (luminosity).

2.2 Data Modeling

To model usual scenarios of daily living progressing toward persistent behaviors, we have used homogeneous Markov chain model, which is a sequential method quite adapted to describe resident's successive room occupancies (or activities) in a home or by extension in a healthcare facility. We have loaded the diagonal terms of the transition matrix with a geometric distribution stating that a) the states correspond either to rooms or activities (that we consider as independent), and b) the transition probability $P_{ij}(k)_T$ from room or activity i to room or activity j at time k is constant during the time period T. In other words, $P_{ii}(k)_1$ and $P_{ij}(k)_1$ represents respectively the probability either to stay in the same room (or activity) i and the probability to leave the room i and to enter in a new room (or activity) j after one minute (a minute being the time unit). To configure these probabilities, denoted in the following $P_{ij}(k)$ and $P_{ij}(k)$, if the reference period T remains equal to 1, we have used two distinct methods exploiting the properties of the geometric distribution:

   1) median $m(P_{ii}(k))$ of length of time periods during which is observed a stay in-state i from time k at which i is observed until changing, is given by equation (1),

   2) expectancy $E(K)$ of the random variable K equal to the number of time periods from time k at which state i is observed before changing of state from i to j, is given by equation (2):

---

[1] HVAC: heating, ventilation, and air conditioning.

$$m(P_{ij}(k)) = -1-\mathrm{Log}(2)/\mathrm{Log}(P_{ii}(k)) \tag{1}$$

$$E(J) = P_{ij}(k)/(1-P_{ii}(k)) \tag{2}$$

Table 1 and 2 below calibrate respectively, using (1) and (2), different persistent time periods for m and $E(J)$ depending on a range of values for the probabilities $P_{ii}(k)$.

Table 1. Calibration of the median for atypically persisting in a same room or activity i

Probability $P_{ii}(k)$ to remain in room i or continue to perform same activity (over next time period)	$m(P_{ii}(k))$ (mn)	$m(P_{ii}(k))$ (hh:mn:sec)
0.5	0	00:00:00
0.707	0.99912886019	00:01:00
0.793	1.98857858844	00:02:00
0.840	2.97553034048	00:03:00
0.870	3.97728630511	00:04:00
0.933	8.99490122005	00:09:00
0.954	13.719123361	00:13:43
0.977	28.7889163106	00:28:47
0.988	56.4149941184	00:56:25
0.994	114.17760888	01:54:11
0.997	229.702323049	03:49:42
0.998	345.226901049	05:45:14

Table 2. Calibrated expectancies $E(J)$ for leaving a room or performing a new activity

Probability $1-P_{ii}(k)=P_{ij}(k)$	$E(J)$ (mn)	$E(J)$ (hh:mn:sec)
0.001	999.0	16:39:00
0.002	499.0	08:19:00
0.003	332.333333333	05:32:20
0.004	249.0	04:09:00
0.0045	221.22222222	03:41:13
0.005	199	03:19:00
0.007	141.857142	02:21:51
0.0083	119.481927711	01:59:28
0.01	99	01:39:00
0.02	49	00:49:00
0.03	32.3333333333	00:32:20
0.04	24	00:24:00
0.05	19.0	00:19:00
0.10	9	00:09:00
0.15	5.6666666666	00:05:40
0.20	4	00:04:00
0.25	3	00:03:00
0.3	2.33333333333	00:02:20

After 70 days of observation, we get the statistics given on Figure 1 for staying in the different rooms of the observed smart flat in which different sensors record the activity of the person at home (see Figure 2). The statistics given on Figure 1 allow to calculate different temporal or histogram profiles assigning the observed person in different clusters corresponding to a normal or a pathologic behavior (see Figure 3).

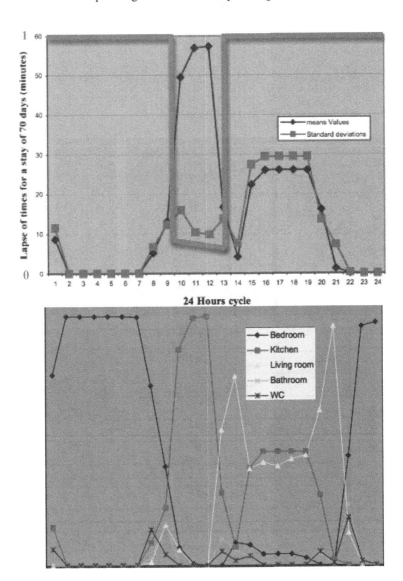

Fig. 1. Top: expectation (in blue), standard deviation (in pink) and variation coefficient (in orange) of the lapse of times passed in the kitchen at different hours of the nychthemeron, calculated after 70 days of observation. Bottom: expectation of the lapse of times passed in different rooms at different hours of the nycthemeron, calculated after 70 days of observation.

Alarms can be triggered when passing from a normal type of nychthemeral activity to a pathologic one. For example, in a degenerative neural pathology like Alzheimer's disease, we observe an abnormal repetition of activities in the same room, called perseveration, which is a pathologic repetition of actions in general already successful ("errare humanum est, perseverare diabolicum"). We model this phenomenon of persistence in a pathologic activity by setting atypical extended occupancy periods in a room, or by performing repetitively a specific daily routine (or activity), in comparison to more standard scenarios encountered in everyday life.

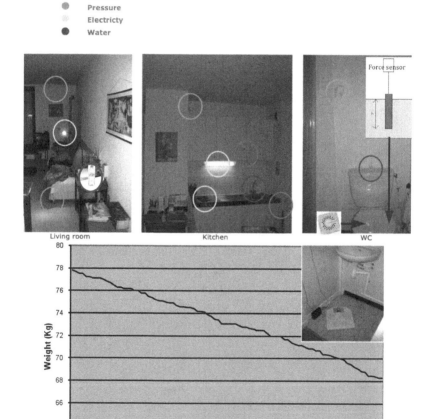

Fig. 2. Top: different types of sensors (infrared, contact, pressure, electrical and related to the water consumption and excretion, with a classical level sensor and a recent electronic nose, called Cyranose® - cf. http://www.nespal.org/machine%20olfactory.html) dispatched in the observed smart flat. Bottom: an example of the evolution of the weight recorded with an electronic body scale during the observed month.

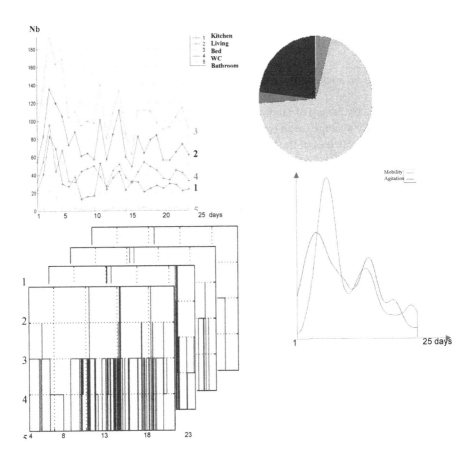

Fig. 3. Top left: evolution during the nychthemeron of the number of actimetric events of entrance in room for the different rooms and successive 25 days. Top right: actimetric summary in circular histogram form. Bottom left: collection during 4 consecutive days of times of passage between the different rooms. Bottom right: evolution during 25 days of observation of scores of mobility (number of physiologic entrance in a room for performing a precise task) and agitation (pathologic entrance in a room, *e.g.*, due to perseveration behavior).

3 Modeling Persistence: Results

We have modeled a simple example of persistence in an activity associated with a spatial-temporal disorientation of eating patterns (possibly due to a temporal shift between diurnal and nocturnal activities), through a 10 kilos weight loss modeled using equation 3.

We have required two random measurements per day:

Modulation function (linear + sinusoidal):

$$m + at_k + b\sin(\frac{2\pi t_k}{T} - \varphi) \tag{3}$$

where the parameters are defined and quantified as follows:

- f=2: daily frequency of randomly generated measurements
- m=77.8 kg: average mean (initial value)
- a=-0.22: coefficient of the linear function
- $t_k = k\Delta t$, with Δt =1 minute (sampling time)
- b=0.2: amplitude of the sinusoïdal function
- T=7200 sec: period of the sinusoïdal function (sec), T ∈ [0,86400]

We have also coupled the weight loss to a chronic state of fatigue, modeled with an acute hypotension selected among eight physiological anomalies available in the software simulator.

3.1. Simulation Process and Data Outputs

At the programming level, we have implemented a software simulator in C code using LabWindows/CVI[2], mimicking the real-time procedures of a sensor network, and gathering the different models. Each simulation consists in generating (automatically) XML events (activity, physiological or environmental data) in a unique dataset (as described in [15]). Events of displacement are produced every minutes; physiological and environmental events are produced only a certain number of times per day, depending on a pre-selected sampling period, and until the end of the simulation. Events related to medical problems are directly injected in the same XML dataset.

3.2 Localized Spatial-temporal Persistence

We have run using the simulator two series of 10 simulations out of 20 days (cf. Table 4) for testing independently the median and the expectancy with a persistent time approximately setup at two hours for both time series (cf. Table 3). Table 4 gives the results. On the whole, we obtain respectively a general median and expectancy equal respectively to 04:10:00 and 7:13:00 out of 10 simulations for both time series.

3.3 Global Persistence Simulation

We have also generated over 45 days a more comprehensive corpus of data (using the median calibrated in Table 3) including a weight loss and an acute hypotension. The template of our global simulation (generating a variety of pseudo-random scenarios), was kept exactly the same. Figure 2 shows the 10 kilos weight loss on a graph, mixed in the global simulation. The acute hypotension giving insights about chronic fatigue, was also injected (on several occasions) in the XML dataset during the generation process. Figure 4 presents, as examples, two scenarios showing chronological merged

---

[2] LabWindows/CVI: ANSI C programming environment developed by National Instruments.

events happening at night. We can notice a disrupt sleep punctuated by hypotension events, combined with a persistence time in kitchen, probably leading to the eating disorder, and consequently to the weight loss.

Table 3. Calibration of persistent parameters

Persistence time n (mn)				Location / associated activity
$P_{ii}(k)$	Median m (hh:mn)	$P_{ij}(k)$	$E(J)$ (hh:mn)	
0.994	01:54:11			kitchen/eating
		0.0083	01:59:28	

Scenario 1	`<date>13/09/2011</date><time>00:00:00</time><room>kitchen</room>`
	`<date>13/09/2011</date><time>01:24:00</time><room>bedroom</room>`
	`<date>13/09/2011</date><time>02:00:00</time><room>kitchen</room>`
	`<date>13/09/2011</date><time>02:04:00</time><PS>13</PS>`
	`<PD>9</PD><PM>10</PM><HR>80</HR>`
	`<date>13/09/2011</date><time>02:07:00</time><PS>9</PS><PD>9</PD>`
	`<PM>8</PM><HR>80</HR>`
	`<date>13/09/2011</date><time>02:10:00</time><room>bedroom</room>`
	`<date>13/09/2011</date><time>07:00:00</time><room>WC</room>`	

Scenario 2	`<date>19/09/2011</date><time>00:00:00</time><room>kitchen</room>`
	`<date>19/09/2011</date><time>02:46:00</time><room> bedroom </room>`
	`<date>19/09/2011</date><time>04:18:00</time><room>kitchen</room>`
	`<date>19/09/2011</date><time>04:07:00</time><PS>13</PS>`
	`<PD>9</PD><PM>10</PM><HR>80</HR>`
	`<date>19/09/2011</date><time>04:10:00</time><PS>9</PS>`
	`<PD>9</PD><PM>8</PM><HR>80</HR>`
	`<date>19/09/2011</date><time>06:01:00</time><room>WC</room>`	

Fig. 4. Scenarios with acute hypotension events (red) drown in a flow of displacements events (PS, PD and PM represent respectively Systolic, Diastolic and Mean Arterial Pressure)

Pathologic behaviors corresponding to simulations of Figure 4 and Table 4 can be studied using statistics of Figure 1 allowing to define different temporal or histogram profiles assigning observed person in different clusters. Then alarms can be triggered when passing from a normal type of nychthemeral activity to a pathologic one.

4 Discussion

4.1 The Choice of the Calibration Method

In this study, we have assessed the efficiency of two distinct methods based on the median $m(P_{ii}(k))$ and expectancy $E(J)$ aiming at generating multivariate corpus of heterogeneous smart home data. Both methods provide relatively sporadic results because trials are independent (they do not depend each other on previous trials).

Table 4. Simulation results for a set of persistence parameters: pathologic behavior (in red) corresponds to median and expectancy more than 4 hours

Simulations #	Median (hh:mn)	Expectancy (hh:mn)
1	02:18	03:58
2	02:44	06:40
3	07:12	08:02
4	03:56	06:58
5	04:28	07:39
6	04:25	05:10
7	02:55	09:18
8	03:34	07:09
9	02:29	09:16
10	07:32	07:59

However, for calibrating the persistent effects, the first method using the median is preferable to the second one (using $E(J)$) because the median provides less scattered results than the expectancy (cf. Table 4). In other words, there is no memory effects involved in the persistence parameters, taking into account the lapse of time spent in the ongoing state. This can be perceived as an advantage to better fit computer simulations to reality. This technique allows us for example to model a shifting insomnia appearing during a sleep wake cycle of 7 to 8 hours. In case where the random repartition of the time periods needs to be narrow down around the median (or expectancy), then we can use either non-homogeneous Markov chains or a Polya's urn model [24], which both make use of memory effects as explained in the next section.

4.2 Modeling Persistent Behaviors with Memory Parameters

Modeling persistence with memory effects consists in taking into account the time elapsed in a state before to determine the outcome of the next trial. In other words, trials are not independent. Let's consider a Polya urn model using first a geometric law of parameter $\alpha=1$. This provokes an increasing waiting time (to stay in a state) as the trials go along without any success. If W and B denote respectively a white and a black ball, and k the number of successes (*i.e.*, we have drawn consecutively k black balls before drawing a white ball), then (4) gives the probability to stay in a state (a room or an activity):

$$P(Y = k) = \left(\frac{B}{B+W}\right) \times \left(\frac{B+1}{B+1+W}\right) \cdots \left(\frac{B+k}{B+K+W}\right)\left(\frac{B}{B+K+W}\right) P(Y = k) = \left(\frac{B}{B+W}\right) \times \left(\frac{B+1}{B+1+W}\right) \cdots \left(\frac{B+k}{B+K+W}\right)\left(\frac{B}{B+K+W}\right) = \left(\frac{B^k}{(B+W)}\right) \times \frac{W}{B+W} \quad (4)$$

The reverse effect (the more we stay in the room, the more we have some chance to leave it) can be thus obtained using a negative geometric law of parameter $\alpha<0$ (5) whose expectancy $E(Y)$ is given by (6):

$$P(Y = k) = \left(\frac{B}{B+W}\right) \times \left(\frac{B+\alpha}{B+\alpha+W}\right) \cdots \left(\frac{B+k\alpha}{B+\alpha+W}\right)\left(\frac{B}{B+K\alpha+W}\right) \quad (5)$$

$$P(Y = k) = \left(\frac{B}{B + W}\right) \times \left(\frac{B + \alpha}{B + \alpha + W}\right) \cdots \left(\frac{B + k\alpha}{B + \alpha + W}\right)\left(\frac{B}{B + K\alpha + W}\right)$$

$$E(Y) = \sum_{k=0}^{\infty} k\left(\frac{B}{B+W}\right) \cdots \left(\frac{B+k\alpha}{B+\alpha+W}\right)\left(\frac{B}{B+K\alpha+W}\right) \quad (6)$$

We can approximate (6) using the Stirling's approximation for large factorials (7), which gives (8).

$$M! \approx \frac{M^M\sqrt{2\pi M}}{e^M} \quad (7)$$

$$E(Y) = \sum_{k=0}^{\infty} k\frac{(B+k)^{N+k}\sqrt{2\pi(B+k)}e^{N-1}}{e^{B+k}(B-1)^{B-1}\sqrt{2\pi(B-1)}} \quad (8)$$

$$E(Y) = \frac{(B + W - 1)^{B+W-1}\sqrt{2\pi(B + W - 1)}e^{B+k+W}W}{e^{W+W-1}(B + k + W)^{B+K+W}\sqrt{2\pi(B + k + W)(B + K + W)}}$$

$$E(Y) \approx \sum_{k=0}^{\infty} k\frac{(B + W - 1)^W}{(B + k)^W} \quad E(Y) \approx \sum_{k=0}^{\infty} k\frac{(B + W - 1)^W}{(B + k)^W}$$

$$E(Y) \approx \sum_{k=0}^{\infty} k\frac{(B + W - 1)^W}{(B + k)^W}$$

Considering B<<N, permits to simplify (8) in (9):

$$E(Y) \approx B^W \sum_{k=0}^{\infty} \frac{k}{(B+k)^W} \quad E(Y) \approx \sum_{k=0}^{\infty} \frac{k}{\left(1+\frac{k}{n}\right)^W} \quad E(Y) \approx$$

$$\sum_{k=0}^{\infty} \left(1 - \frac{Wk}{B}\right) \quad (9)$$

4.3 Persistence and Perseveration

In the present study, we have focused on persistent behaviors setting excessive occupancy periods in a state (*i.e.*, a room or possibly a well identified daily routine or activity). However, due to the inherent daily periodicity of the scenarios involved in the computer simulations, we could also have simulated perseveration behaviors more oriented around non functional routines or rituals such as often checking doors unnecessarily or watching specific shows on TV. This would have however jeopardized the activities defined in the computer simulations.

We have used Table 1 and Table 2 above to emulate such repetitive behaviors. Table 3 emphasizes our parameter selection with $m=114$ mn and $E(J)=119$ mn. This configuration enables us to emulate a fitful sleep (lasting normally around 7 to 8 hours), interrupted by pre-defined scenarios of persistence (*e.g.*, staying, at night, in the kitchen eating or wandering).

5 Conclusion and Perspectives

We have used an existing simulator embedding scenarios of daily living to emulate a persistent behavior using non-memory parameters in the context of healthcare settings. The notion of persistence is modeled using spatial-temporal events. Two series of ten computer simulations each out of twenty days were run to assess the feasibility of two different methods, based on one hand side on the median and on the other one on the expectancy, to setup persistent periods. As expected, both methods result in a scattering of persistence times because trials are independent. These simulations offer however a good start for representing context reality. The paper also proposes an improvement to reduce sparse data using memory parameters. A weight loss and a chronic acute hypotension, part of the whole simulation process, are combined with the persistent behavior to show how individuals with a spatial-temporal disorientation are vulnerable to a quicker degradation of their health status.

The perspectives of the work outlined in this article consider two complementary aspects of the actimetric supervision of a person at home [25-27]:

i) the ability to record noninvasively different physiological parameters should allow, in the future, documenting automatically after a suitable filtering (because the data volume is very large) the personalized medical record of this person (whose prototype is currently elaborated in France after about 10 years without much progress), which would greatly facilitate its updating, so enhance its pertinence

2) the ability to customize the therapeutic education, for example by visualizing didactically the weight curve and the metabolic evolution showing changes in blood glucose level in a type II diabetic, or to choose appropriate activities for the rehabilitation of a diabetic foot with ulcer complications (see Figure 5), or eventually to accompany dietary advices by showing the water balance (especially in case of renal complications) from the assessment made by water sensors shown in Figure 3 (recording both consumption and excretion).

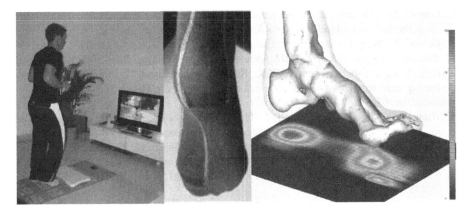

Fig. 5. Left: pressure sensor by the company Texisense® showing the consequence of a patho-logic running in a virtual environment. Middle: smart sock by Texisense® made of a pressure sensitive textile giving the same information during the real walk, for detecting some progresses during the reeducation process. Right: combination of the pressure information with an osteodensitometric study showing the consequences of a pathologic running on the bone reconstruction.

Acknowledgements. This work has been supported by a PEPS CNRS - UJF - INSIS grant and by the Project VHP of the French Program "Investissements d'Avenir".

References

1. World Population Ageing 2009. Department of Economical and Social Affairs Report. United Nations publication, New York (2010)
2. Demongeot, J., Virone, G., Duchêne, F., Benchetrit, G., Hervé, T., Noury, N., Rialle, V.: Multi-sensors acquisition, data fusion, knowledge mining and triggering in health smart homes for elderly people. C. R. Biologies 325, 673–682 (2002)
3. Virone, G., Noury, N., Demongeot, J.: A system for automatic measurement of circadian activity deviation in telemedicine. IEEE Transactions on Biomedical Engineering 49, 1463–1469 (2002)
4. Abdulrazak, B., Mokhtari, M., Feki, M.A., Ghorbel, M.: Integration of home networking in a smart environment dedicated to people with disabilities. In: ICTTA 2004 International Conference on Information & Communication Technologies: From Theory to Applica-tions, pp. 125–126. IEEE Press, Piscataway (2004)
5. Benneyan, J.C.: An introduction to using computer simulation in healthcare: patient wait case study. Journal of the Society for Health Systems 5, 1–15 (1997)
6. Lowery, J.C.: Introduction to simulation in healthcare. In: WSC 1996 28th Conference on Winter Simulation, pp. 78–84. IEEE Press, Piscataway (1996)
7. O'Connor, C.M., Smith, R., Nott, M.T., Lorang, C., Mathews, R.M.: Using video simu-lated presence to reduce resistance to care and increase participation of adults with demen-tia. American Journal of Alzeimer's Disease and Other Dementias 26, 317–325 (2011)

8. Lowery, J.C., Martin, J.B.: Design and validation of a critical care simulation model. Journal of the Society for Health Systems 3, 15–36 (1992)

9. Gibson, B., Weir, C.: Development and preliminary evaluation of a simulation-based diabetes education module. In: AMIA Annu. Symp. Proc. 2010, pp. 246–250 (2010)

10. Berg, D.R., Carlson, A., Durfee, W.K., Sweet, R.M., Reihsen, T.: Low-cost, take-home, beating heart simulator for health-care education. Studies in Health Technologies and Informatics 163, 57–59 (2011)

11. Wong, P., Graves, M.J., Lomas, D.J.: Integrated physiological flow simulator and pulse sequence monitoring system for MRI. Med. Biol. Eng. Comput. 46, 399–406 (2008)

12. Mahmoud, S.M., Akhlaghinia, M.J., Lotfi, A., Langensiepen, C.: Trend Modelling of Elderly Lifestyle within an Occupancy Simulator. In: UKSim 2011 International Conference on Computer Modelling and Simulation, Cambridge, pp. 156–161. IEEE Press, Piscataway (2011)

13. Virone, G., Lefebvre, B., Noury, N., Demongeot, J.: Modeling and Computer Simulation of Physiological Rhythms and Behaviors at Home for Data Fusion Programs in a Telecare System. In: HealthCom 2003 International Workshop on Enterprise Networking and Computing in Healthcare Industry, Santa Monica, pp. 118–127. IEEE Press, Piscataway (2003)

14. Nabih, K., Gomaa, M.M., Osman, H.S., Aly, G.M.: Modeling, Simulation, and Control of Smart Homes Using Petri Nets. International Journal of Smart Home 5, 1 (2011)

15. Cardinaux, F., Brownsell, S., Hawley, M.S., Bradley, D.: A home daily activity simulation model for the evaluation of lifestyle monitoring systems. Computers in Biology and Medicine 43, 1428–1436 (2013)

16. Lazovik, A., Kaldeli, E., Lazovik, E., Aiello, M.: Planning in a Smart Home: Visualization and Simulation. In: Int. Conf. on Automated Planning and Scheduling (ICAPS), pp. 13–16. AAAI Press, Menlo Park (2009)

17. Poland, M.P., Nugent, C.D., Wang, H., Chen, L.: Development of a smart home simulator for use as a heuristic tool for management of sensor distribution. Technol. Health Care 17, 171–182 (2009)

18. Virone, G., Istrate, D.: Integration of an Environmental Sound Module to an Existing In-Home Activity Simulator. In: 29th IEEE-EMBS Engineering in Medicine and Biology Society) Microtechnologies in Medicine & Biology, pp. 3810–3813. IEEE Press, Piscataway (2007)

19. Istrate, D., Castelli, E.: Information Extraction from Sound for Medical Telemonitoring. IEEE Transactions on Information Technology in Biomedicine 10, 264–274 (2006)

20. Alwan, M., Dalal, S., Kell, S., Felder, R.: Derivation of basic human gait characteristics from floor vibrations. In: Summer Bioengineering Conference Key Biscayne, Florida, pp. 231–232. ASME, New York (2003)

21. Young, K.W.H., Greenwood, C.E.: Shift in diurnal feeding patterns in nursing home residents with Alzheimer's disease. The Journals of Gerontology. Series A, Biological Sciences and Medical Sciences 56, 700–706 (2001)

22. Virone, G., Alwan, M., Dalal, S., Kell, S., Stankovic, J.A., Felder, R.: Behavioral Patterns of Older Adults in Assisted Living. IEEE Transactions on Information Technology in Biomedicine 12, 387–398 (2008)

23. Virone, G.: Assessing Behavioral Rhythms in Everyday Life for the Older Generation. IEEE Pervasive and Mobile Computing 5, 606–622 (2009)

24. Fouquet, Y., Franco, C., Diot, B., Demongeot, J., Vuillerme, N.: Estimation of Task Persistence Parameter from Pervasive Medical Systems with Censored Data. IEEE Transactions On Mobile Computing 12, 633–646 (2013)

25. Chenu, O., Payan, Y., Hlavackova, P., Demongeot, J., Cannard, F., Diot, B., Vuillerme, N.: Pressure sores prevention for paraplegic people: effects of visual, auditive and tactile supplementations on overpressures distribution in seated posture. Applied Bionics and Biomechanics 9, 61–67 (2012)

26. Teymoori, F., Mousavi, D., Demongeot, J., Biglarian, A., Sarmadi, M., Shirazikhah, M.F.-C.: Score of old people by community based Information system. Healthmed. 6, 2018–2022 (2012)

27. Franco, C., Fleury, A., Guméry, P.Y., Diot, B.J., Demongeot, J., Vuillerme, N.: iBalance-ABF: a Smartphone-Based Audio-Biofeedback Balance System. IEEE Transactions on Biomedical Engineering 60, 211–215 (2013)

Author Index